Scientific Studies In Special Creation

WALTER E. LAMMERTS, *Editor*

Selected Articles from the
CREATION RESEARCH SOCIETY QUARTERLY
Volumes I through V (1964–1968)

PRESBYTERIAN AND REFORMED PUBLISHING CO.
1971

CREATION RESEARCH SOCIETY BOOKS
1990

Copyright 1971
Presbyterian and Reformed Publishing Company

Copyright 1990
Creation Research Society

Library of Congress Catalog Card No. 70-150955
Printed in the United States of America

ISBN 0-940384-08-6

Contents

I. The Premises of Evolutionary Thought 1
   ROUSAS JOHN RUSHDOONY

II. Does Genesis 1:1-3 Teach a Creation
    Out of Nothing? 9
    ROBERT L. REYMOND

III. The Creation of the Heavens and the Earth 22
     JOHN C. WHITCOMB, JR.

IV. The Ruin Reconstruction Theory of Genesis 1:2 32
    JOHN C. WHITCOMB, JR.

V. There Was Evening—And There Was Morning 41
   RICHARD G. KORTHALS

VI. The Power of Energy 60
    HENRY M. MORRIS

VII. Problems in Absolute Age Determination 72
     D. O. ACREY

VIII. Radiological Dating and Some Pertinent
      Applications of Historical Interest—
      Do Radiological "Clocks" Need Repair? 79
      MELVIN A. COOK

IX. An Attempt to Correct for the Effects of
    of the Flood in Determining Dates
    by Radioactive Carbon 98
    HAROLD L. ARMSTRONG

X. Science Versus Scientism in Historical Geology 103
   HENRY M. MORRIS

XI.	Streamlining Stratigraphy .... CLIFFORD BURDICK	125
XII.	The Genesis Kinds in the Modern World .... FRANK LEWIS MARSH	136
XIII.	The Mystery of the Red Beds .... HAROLD W. CLARK	156
XIV.	A Paleoecological Misinterpretation .... HAROLD G. COFFIN	165
XV.	A Summary of the *Monera* Fallacy .... N. A. RUPKE	169
XVI.	A Study of English Micraster Research .... RITA RHODES WARD	184
XVII.	World Population and Bible Chronology .... HENRY M. MORRIS	198
XVIII.	Evolution and the Problem of Man .... GEORGE F. HOWE	206
XIX.	Immorality in Natural Selection .... WILLIAM J. TINKLE	229
XX.	Land-Dwelling Vertebrates and the Origin of the Tetrapod Limb .... P. W. DAVIS, JR.	234
XXI.	Homology, Analogy, and Creative Components in Plants .... GEORGE F. HOWE	243
XXII.	Remarkable Adaptations .... E. V. SHUTE	258
XXIII.	Planned Inductions of Commercially Desirable Variation of Roses by Neutron Radiation .... WALTER E. LAMMERTS	269

Table of Contents

XXIV.	Seed Germination, Sea Water, and Plant Survival in the Great Flood	285
	GEORGE F. HOWE	
XXV.	Wild Flowers: A Problem for Evolution	299
	WILLIAM J. TINKLE	
XXVI.	"The Plants Will Teach You"	303
	HAROLD W. CLARK	
XXVII.	DNA: Its History and Potential	308
	DUANE T. GISH	
XXVIII.	The Spontaneous Generation of Life	317
	PAUL A. ZIMMERMAN	
XXIX.	The Possibility of the Artificial Creation of Life	328
	HAROLD L. ARMSTRONG	
XXX.	A Scientific Alternative to Evolution	330
	THOMAS G. BARNES	
XXXI.	Social Darwinism	338
	BOLTON DAVIDHEISER	

INTRODUCTION

This second volume of selected papers published while I was editor of the *Creation Research Society Quarterly* needs only a short introduction. The first group of selections was published in 1970 under the title of *Why Not Creation?* and the reader is referred to the introduction of that book for a complete history of the origin of the Creation Research Society. Only lack of space made it impossible to publish all of the pertinent articles in one volume, and those held over were in no way any less compelling in their rejection of the evolution theory than the ones already published. Many of them, in fact, discuss facets of the evidence for a young earth and its destruction by a universal flood in a more detailed and positive way.

In my introduction to *Why Not Creation?* I made the prediction that not even a small percentage of the ten trillion tons of meteors anticipated as having fallen on the moon in its *presumed* 4.5 billion years of existence would be found. Also one of astronomer Robert Jastrow's hopes was that some clue to the evolution of life during the time from the beginning of the moon's existence until the first terrestrial rock of assumed 3.3 billion years age might be found. As he said, "What happened during the missing 1.2 billion years?" (Robert Jastrow, then director of NASA's Goddard Institute for Space Studies in New York, quoted in *Time* Magazine, July 18, 1969, p. 23).

I also predicted, on the basis of creation concepts, that not a trace of life either now or in the past would be found on the moon. Both of the predictions came true, for only a very slight number of meteors have been found on the moon and absolutely no evidence of life. As astronaut Edgar Mitchell said while Apollo 14 circled the moon: "That's the most stark, desolate looking piece of country I've ever seen!" (*Time* Magazine, February 15, 1971, p. 12).

Surely as we spend more and more billions of dollars in space exploration it is becoming increasingly clear that God created only this world to be inhabited, and that all of the other planets He created in our solar system are utterly devoid of life. Though some astronomers still have a slight hope that some lowly form of plant life such as lichens or mosses may be found on Mars, it is my prediction that none will be found.

Meanwhile our society continues to grow in its scientific membership as more and more open-minded investigators come to the conclusion that the remarkable features of life and the various living creatures could result only from the creative design of a supreme being whom we Christians know as our Lord and Savior Jesus Christ. For as St. John says: "All things were made by him: and without him was not anything made that was made" (John 1:3).

WALTER E. LAMMERTS, *Editor*
P.O. Box 496
Freedom, California 95019
February 24, 1971

THE CONTRIBUTORS

Donald O. Acrey, B.Sc., is a geophysicist. At present he is assistant to the president at Graham Plow, Inc., Amarillo, Texas.

Harold Armstrong holds a master of science degree from Queens University (Canada), where he is a member of the Physics Department.

Thomas G. Barnes, M.S., Brown University, D.Sc., Hardin Simmons University, is professor of physics at the University of Texas (El Paso). He is also consulting physicist at Globe Universal Sciences in El Paso.

Clifford Burdick is a consulting geologist. A geology major at the University of Wisconsin, he has an honorary Ph.D. from the University of Physical Sciences (Phoenix).

Harold W. Clark is associated with the Life Origins Foundation at Angwin, California.

Harold G. Coffin is the author of *Creation: Accident or Design*. Dr. Coffin is research professor of paleontology at the Geo-Science Research Institute, which is affiliated with Andrews University at Berrien Springs, Michigan.

Melvin A. Cook, Ph.D. (physical chemistry), Yale, is professor of metallurgy at the University of Utah and the president of I.R.E.C. Chemicals in West Jordan, Utah. The author of *Prehistory and Earth Models* and other books, he was the recipient in 1968 of the Nitro Nobel Medal Award.

Bolton Davidheiser, B.A., Swarthmore College, Ph.D., Johns Hopkins University, is the author of *Evolution and the Christian Faith*. Formerly a professor of biology at Westmont College and Biola College, he is currently devoting his time to writing and lecturing.

P. W. Davis, Jr., is an associate professor of biology at Tampa Junior College. He is the co-author of *The Case for Creation*.

Duane T. Gish, Ph.D., University of California (Berkeley), is currently a research biochemist at the Upjohn Company, Kalamazoo, Michigan.

George F. Howe, M.Sc., Ph.D., Ohio State, is chairman of the Division of Natural Sciences at Los Angeles Baptist College, Newhall, California. He is currently the editor of the *Creation Research Society Journal* and *Creation Research Society Quarterly*, and the co-author of *The Bible, Science and Creation.*

Richard G. Korthals is a lieutenant colonel (retired) in the U. S. Air Force. Formerly professor and acting head of astronautics at the U. S. Air Force Academy, his specialty is space engineering. He is at present assistant professor of physics at the Concordia Lutheran Junior College, Ann Arbor, Michigan.

Walter E. Lammerts, noted rose breeder and the former director of research at Germain's Horticulturist in Livermore, California. The past president of the Creation Research Society and formerly editor of their publications, he holds a Ph.D. in genetics from the University of California (Los Angeles).

Frank Lewis Marsh, Ph.D., University of Nebraska, is professor of biology at Andews University, Berrien Springs, Michigan. His published works include *Life, Man, and Time.*

Henry M. Morris, B.S., Rice University, Ph.D., University of Minnesota. For 13 years he was professor of hydraulic engineering and chairman of the Civil Engineering Department at Virginia Polytechnic Institute. At present he is director of the Creation Science Research Center. The co-author of *The Genesis Flood*, his other publications include *The Twilight of Evolution, Studies in the Bible and Science,* and *Evolution and the Modern Christian.*

Robert L. Reymond, Ph.D., Bob Jones University, is professor of Old Testament at the Covenant Theological Seminary. He is editor of the "Biblical and Theological Studies Series" in the *International Library of Philosophy and Theology.*

N. A. Rupke, B.S. in geology, State University of Groningen (Netherlands), is currently doing graduate work in the Geology Department at Princeton University.

Rousas J. Rushdoony, M.A., University of California, is currently engaged in research, and lectures extensively. The editor of "Philosophical and Historical Studies" in the *International Library of Philosophy and Theology* and of "Philosophical Studies" in the *University Series,* he is the president of Chalcedon, Inc. His published

The Contributors

works include *The Messianic Character of American Education*, *The Mythology of Science*, *This Independent Republic*, and *The Biblical Philosophy of History*.

Evan Shute, a fellow of the Royal College of Surgeons of Canada, received both his undergraduate and medical degrees from the University of Toronto. A lecturer of international renown, he is the author of *Flaws in the Theory of Evolution* and numerous other works.

William J. Tinkle, Ph.D., Ohio State, is Professor Emeritus of Biology at Anderson College ((Indiana). He is the secretary of the Creation Research Society. He is the author of *Heredity, A Study in Science and the Bible* and other books.

Rita Rhodes Ward is on the faculty at Austin High School, El Paso, Texas. She teaches biology and physiology. She is the author of *In the Beginning*.

John C. Whitcomb, Jr., B.A., Princeton University, Th.D., Grace Theological Seminary. The co-author of *The Genesis Flood*, his other publications include *The Origin of the Solar System* and *Darius the Mede*. He is currently professor of Old Testament at Grace Theological Seminary and chairman of graduate studies there.

Paul A. Zimmerman, Ph.D., University of Illinois, is president of Concordia Lutheran Junior College, Ann Arbor, Michigan. Dr. Zimmerman was formerly president of Concordia Teachers College in Seward, Nebraska. He edited *Darwin, Evolution and Creation*.

I

THE PREMISES OF EVOLUTIONARY THOUGHT

Rousas John Rushdoony

Sigmund Freud, as an evolutionary scientist, has been a source of embarrassment to his many dedicated followers at one critical point: Freud grounded his evolutionary thinking firmly on the theories of Lamarck. The inheritance of acquired characteristics is basic to Freud's anthropology, biology, and psychology. In the face of extensive criticism, Freud "adhered throughout his life" to "the Lamarckian belief."[1] At this point, even his devoted disciple and biographer, Dr. Ernest Jones, criticized Freud as "What one must call an obstinate adherent of this discredited Lamarckism."[2] Freud, however, was resolute. Because of his hostility to religion, the doctrine of evolution was intensely important to Freud, and evolutionary theory provided for no effective mechanism for evolution apart from Lamarck. To deny Lamarck and the inheritance of acquired characteristics was to posit a god-like power somewhere in or behind evolution and to introduce illegitimately an element resembling the supernatural. It pointed to an entelechy of being, a potentiality or power far exceeding the original elements of the universe. If *nothing is acquired*, then *everything is involved*, and what has evolved was originally involved in the original spark of energy or matter out of which all the universe has developed. Such an assumption would be ridiculous; it would place in that original atom powers commensurate with God. Freud saw only one consistent theory on which to ground his evolutionary faith: Lamarck's concept of acquired characteristics. Freud stated his thesis succinctly: "If nothing is acquired nothing can be inherited."[3] All of Freud's psychology rests on this concept of acquired characteristics. It is not our purpose here to analyze the implications of this position for Freud's psychoanalytic theory: this has been done in another context.[4] What does concern us is Freud's thesis: "If nothing is acquired nothing can be inherited." To introduce any other mechanism is to introduce the miraculous in disguise.

Freud's shrewd observation deserves renewed attention. The miraculous is indeed commonplace in evolutionary theory, although in disguised manner. An important aspect of the standard evolutionary geological time tables is the urgent necessity for countless millions of years to dilute the miracles of evolution and make them "natural." It is assumed that changes which are impossilble or else miraculous when pinpointed in time can be rendered possible and natural when blanketed with millions of years. Given millions of years, spontaneous generation is also "naturalized" as well as other necessary steps in the evolution of species. *Philosophically*, the basic assumption of these positions is the inherent power of all being; the entire spectrum of nature has within itself a *being in process* of almost unlimited potentialities. This being in process has manifested already a measure of potentiality in the universe we know; there is no reason to suppose that its potentiality is exhausted or that somewhere continuous creation is not in process. This being, which is the whole of the natural world, possesses, therefore, whether consciously or not, probably unconsciously, all the vast reservoir of power which orthodox Christianity has associated with God. In a sense, of course, the greater faith rests with the evolutionist in assuming that the order, structure, and design of creation is the product of a blind and unconscious potentiality rather than the totally self-conscious and ontological Trinity.

The implications of this position are especially of interest when we analyze the philosophical position of those who hold to creative evolution or progressive creationism. This compromising position represents an attempt by neo-evangelical Christians to retain the respectability of science and of Christianity as well. Basic to their position is the denial of the *creative act* in favor of a *creative process*. The six days of creation give way to the geological time table, a substitute god of like creative power. But the moment creativity is transferred or to any degree ascribed to the process of being, to the inner powers of nature, to that extent sovereignty and power are transferred from God to nature. Nature having developed as a result of its creative process has within itself inherently the laws of its being. God is an outsider to nature, able to give inspiration to men within nature but unable to govern them because He is not their Creator and hence not their source of law. Of course, the creative evolutionist denies that he is surrendering God; he is trying to retain all the values of two systems of thought. But, in attempting to serve two masters, he is clearly being disloyal to one, since both have mutually exclusive claims. Where does creativity rest, within God or within nature? If it rests in God, then the universe is, as Genesis One declares it to be, the result of a series of creative acts without process in the short span of six days, and all perfect and good. If creativity rests in nature, then the universe is the result of a creative process, and the laws of its being and of its creatures are to be derived, not from an alien God who is an outsider, but from nature itself. The creative evolutionist attempts to hold to either an outright dualism, and in every dualism one god becomes the evil god, or he attempts to maintain the two in dialectical tension. It is not without significance that virtually all progressive creationists, while professing degrees of criticism of dialectical theology, do nevertheless maintain a relatively appreciative and even friendly attitude towards this radical departure from orthodox Christianity. Indeed, progressive creationism or creative evolution must be described as at least incipient dialectical theology.

This was clearly apparent in the American Scientific Affiliation symposium, edited by Russell L. Mixter, *Evolution and Christian Thought Today* (1959). The Thomistic (or dialectic) nature of this symposium was cited by this writer in a review article.[5] Such progressive creationist writers hold commonly to a double-revelation theory, a revelation of spiritual truths through the Bible by God, and the revelation of God in nature. It is held that these two truths cannot be in contradiction.[6] Basic to this double-revelation theory is the Thomistic and Greek concept that the reason of autonomous man is capable of impartially and objectively investigating the truths of creation and of establishing them into a valid revelation of nature. The source of "revelation," then, concerning the universe is man's reason and science. The source of revelation concerning God and the supernatural is the Bible. Reason and science can establish firmly truth in their realm, the knowable, whereas the province of the Bible lies beyond the natural world. To use the Bible as a source-book for facts concerning nature and history is thus regarded as illegitimate. Jan Lever has gone so far as to say "that we may not consider the language of the Bible as scientifically conceptual language; hence, we may never demand from Scripture exact physical, astronomical, biological and thus also not exact historical knowledge."[7] This position rules out of history not only the prosaic account of Genesis One, but also the accounts of the resurrection and the poetical narratives of the virgin birth. Such a view of the Bible is not Christian: it is dialectical, and the difference between these scholars and Karl Barth is only one of degree, not of kind.

Moreover, this dialectical position, by holding to two realms of truth, gives us two sets of infallible truth which cannot be attacked. Since the Bible is limited to revealing only spiritual truths, most of it is open, of course, to attack because it is within the domain of science and history. What about evolution? Wherein lies its immunity? James O. Buswell III has given clear expression of this area of infallible truth:

> One of the chief drawbacks to the anti-evolutionists, from Darwin's early critics to the present day (familiar as some of their leaders are with the data), is that their activities and literature have been almost completely wrapped up in arguments over petty fragments of the record, assuming that to attack evolution as a total philosophy one must show the data upon which the assumptions are based to be untrue.[8]

This is an amazing statement. The data and facts of evolution can be untrue, but the "total philosophy" of evolution cannot be disproved, and it is wrong to assume that "to attack evolution as a total philosophy one must show the data upon which the assumptions are based to be untrue." What other recourse does a scientist have? If fallacious and "untrue" data as the foundation of a theory fail to disprove that hypothesis, what can be done? Buswell does not give an answer, but it is apparent that the double-revelation theory is implicit in this perspective. We have an area of immunity from disproof because it is an area of revelation.

The appearance of Darwin's thesis was the appearance of an alternative revelation to the Bible. According to George Bernard Shaw, "If you can realize how insufferably the world was oppressed by the notion that everything that happened was an arbitrary personal act of an arbitrary personal God of dangerous, jealous and cruel personal character, you will understand how the world jumped at Darwin."[9] Although Shaw's conception of God is a gross caricature, his basic analysis is correct. On the one hand, man faced an account of origins as the creative act of the ontological trinity, a totally self-conscious Person, omnipotent, omniscient, and sovereign, and to whom man is totally responsible. On the other hand, Darwinism offered an account of origins which performed also all the miracles of creation and yet was totally impersonal, materialistic, and held no man to account. An unregenerate world jumped to it as "liberation." It provided, to cite the title of a modern book, a "god without thunder." In this evolutionary perspective, potentiality resides *within* the universe, not beyond it in God. This position is an article of faith. A prominent philosopher, in discussing the question of origins, stated candidly that the philosophically astute naturalist will refuse to ask the question of origins: just as the Christian will take God and the Bible as his "given," so the pragmatic naturalist should insist on taking the world as it exists today and the concept of evolution as his "given," his basic assumption about reality.

The creative evolutionist holds, therefore, a position which lacks the philosophical consistency of either the naturalist or the orthodox Christian: he attempts to operate in terms of two "givens" and to maintain them in dialectical tension. But every dialectical position, because it is an attempt to maintain and reconcile two mutually exclusive concepts or "givens," is doomed ultimately to resolve the tension in favor of one. A dialectical position is precisely the insistence on maintaining this hold on two warring concepts, and, while it is doomed to collapse, it finds nothing more difficult to accept than this inevitable collapse.

We have thus two rival faiths, each with its belief in miracles, one by God, the other by the potentiality inherent in the universe. We have a third position, the attempt to unite these two. But Freud's resort to Lamarck had as it motive the resolution to avoid this dilemma of rival miracles. *Granted* the validity of acquiring characteristics, then evolution is a thoroughly natural and explicable phenomenon. But here Freud introduced as much faith as he had rejected: the faith in acquired characteristics is a faith, and an amazing one. Systematically, according to this theory, from the beginning of time, important new characteristics have been acquired by various forms of being and have been transmitted to successive forms of matter and then of life. These modifications are "induced by the action of environment." [10] Lamarckism is environmentalism, and while Lamarck is disowned, environmentalism is basic to many areas of study other than Freudian psychology, and the implicit Lamarckism in much evolutionary thought is considerable. The point which concerns us is the inescapable miracles built into this position as into every form of evolutionary thought.

God, clearly, is an inescapable premise of human thought. Man either faces a world of total chance and brute factuality, a world in which no fact has meaning and no fact has any relationship to any other fact, or else he accepts the world of God's creation and sovereign law. But men often refuse this choice. They deny the world of brute factuality, but they also deny God openly while trying to reintroduce all the attributes of God's creative power in naturalized form. They cannot escape God as a premise of their thinking, but they refuse to accept Him as God. Their science operates on borrowed premises, and their hypothesis conceals a hidden and utterly irrational miraculous power. If evolutionary scientists eliminated this faith and confined themselves to the facts, they would have no knowledge at all, only a vast ocean of meaningless and unrelated facts which could not be related to one another except by positing a world of meaning whose hidden premise is God. With Cornelius Van Til, we must assert that, where it is consistently and rigorously applied, "science is absolutely impossible on the non-Christian principle." [11]

> An illustration may indicate more clearly what is meant. Suppose we think of a man made of water in an infinitely extended and bottomless ocean of water. Desiring to get out of water, he makes a ladder of water. He sets this ladder upon the water and against the water and then attempts to climb out of the water. So hopeless and senseless a picture must be drawn of the natural man's methodology based as it is upon the assumption that time or chance is ultimate. On his assumption his own rationality is a product of chance. On his assumption even the laws of logic which he employs are products of chance. The rationality and purpose that he may be searching for are still bound to be products of chance....
>
> It will then appear that Christian theism, which was first rejected because of its supposed authoritarian character, is the only position which gives human reason a field for successful operation and a method of true progress in knowledge.[12]

Only on the presupposition of Christian theism is a valid science possible. The orthodox Christian holds that God as Creator has created both the facts and the laws of physical existence, so that the facts exist in the context of law. God stands behind all creation as Creator and sustainer. He has, Van Til points out, adapted "the laws of our minds" to the "laws of the facts," so that "the knowledge that we have of the simplest objects of the physical universe is still based upon the revelational activity of God." Science is possible because the biblical revelation is true.

The Premises of Evolutionary Thought

Thus the truth of Christianity appears to be the immediately indispensable presupposition of the fruitful study of nature. In the first place without it the physical scientist could have no assurance that his hypothesis would have any relevance to any of the facts in his field of study. For then Chance would be supreme. There would be no facts distinguishable from other facts. Unless the plan and therewith the interpretation or thought of God be back of all facts in their relations to all other facts, no idea, no hypothesis that the human mind could make with respect to them, would have any application to them.

Secondly, except for the truth of Christianity, it would be impossible to *exclude* one hypothesis rather than another. It would be impossible to exclude such ideas as would enter "into the minds of the insane." This second point is involved in the first.

In the third place, without the truth of Christianity there would be no possibility of testing one hypothesis as over against another. The idea of testing hypotheses by means of "brute facts" . . . is meaningless. Brute facts, i.e., facts not created and controlled by God, are mute facts. They have no discernible character. They cannot, together, operate in regularity, thus forming a uniformity of nature. Thus they cannot constitute the reality which Christians and non-Christians know in common in order by it to test the "hypotheses" of the existence or the non-existence of God. It is the truth of Christianity alone that permits us to attach any significance to the idea of testing of an hypothesis.[13]

The non-Christian scientist therefore is able to formulate and discover only because he operates on secretly Christian premises while denying that faith. "The natural man has valid knowledge only as a thief possesses goods."[14] Factuality apart from God is totally meaningless factuality. "No fact, then, is truly known unless its createdness in the biblical sense is owned by the scientist,"[15] although this acceptance is generally an unacknowledged one.

But God remains as the inescapable premise of human thought. Because God is the Creator, every aspect of the universe and of man is structured by God's creative act and eternal decree, and therefore reflects His law and order. Men cannot escape Him nor can they shut Him out. If they attempt to think without Him as their premise, they simply re-introduce His attributes in the form of miraculous potentialities and processes which reduce science to irrationalism and self-contradiction.

NOTES AND REFERENCES

1. Ernest Jones, M.D.: *The Life and Work of Sigmund Freud*, vol. I, p. 347 New York: Basic Books, 1953, 1961.
2. Jones, II, p. 311, 1957, 1960.
3. Jones, II, p. 222, 1955, 1962.
4. See R. J. Rushdoony: *Freud*. Nutley, N. J.: Presbyterian and Reformed Publishing Company, 1965.
5. *Westminster Theological Journal*, pp. 59-68, November, 1960, vol. XXIII, no. 1.
6. See John C. Whitcomb, Jr.: *The Origin of the Solar System: Biblical Inerrancy and the Double-Revelation Theory*, Philadelphia: Presbyterian and Reformed Publishing Company, 1964. Adherents of the double-revelation theory are cited on p. 31f.
7. Jan Lever: *Creation and Evolution*, p. 171. Translated by Peter G. Berkhout, M.D., Grand Rapids: International Publications, 1958.
8. James O. Buswell III in Russel L. Mixter, editor: *Evolution and Christian Thought Today*, p. 169. Grand Rapids: Eerdmans, 1959.
9. Cited by Arnold Lunn, in Introduction to *Is Evolution Proved?* A Debate between Douglas Dewar and H. S. Shelton, p. 4. London: Hollis and Carter, 1947.
10. Sir William Cecil Dampier: *A History of Science and Its Relations With Philosophy and Religion*, p. 294. Cambridge: University Press, 1944. Third edition.
11. Cornelius Van Til: *The Defense of the Faith*, p. 285. Philadelphia: The Presbyterian and Reformed Publishing Company, 1955.
12. *Ibid.*, p. 119.
13. *Ibid.*, p. 283f.
14. R. J. Rushdoony: *By What Standard?* p. 24. Philadelphia: Presbyterian and Reformed Publishing Company, 1959.
15. Robert L. Reymond: *A Christian View of Modern Science*, p. 10. Philadelphia: Presbyterian and Reformed Publishing Company, 1964.

II

DOES GENESIS 1:1-3 TEACH A CREATION OUT OF NOTHING?

Robert L. Reymond

The first three verses of Genesis have fallen upon hard times in recent years. Two widely acclaimed modern translations of the first book of the Bible, representing the consensus of many internationally known Old Testament scholars (Harry M. Orlinsky, H. L. Ginsberg, the late Ephraim A. Speiser, William F. Albright, and David Noel Freedman, to name only a few) have rejected the traditional translation found in the older English versions. The traditional translation in the King James Version, the Revised Version, and the American Standard Version has been replaced by another translation that does away, by the proverbial stroke of the pen, with the doctrine of *creation ex nihilo* in the first and second chapters of Genesis.

One Modern Translation

The first of these two translations is a distinctly Jewish publication. In 1955 the Jewish Publication Society of America appointed a committee of seven scholars to prepare a new English translation of the Hebrew Scriptures, the first English translation of the Hebrew Scriptures to be sponsored by the Society since 1917. Late in 1962 the first part appeared under the title, *The Torah, The Five Books of Moses: A new Translation of the Holy Scriptures according to the Masoretic Text*. This New Jewish Version (NJV) translates the first three verses of Genesis as follows:

> 1 When God began to create[a] the heaven and the earth—2 the earth being unformed and void, with darkness over the surface of the deep and a wind from[b] God sweeping over the water— 3 God said, "Let there be light"; and there was light.
>
> a Or "In the beginning God created"
> b Others "the spirit of"

A careful examination of the two footnotes will reveal that footnote (a) does acknowledge the traditional translation as a possibility by the little introductory word "Or." By the word "Others" in footnote (b) the editor-in-chief, Harry M. Orlinsky, explains that the traditional reading was "excluded altogether as an alternate rendering."[1] It is not my purpose at this time to defend the traditional translation of *ruach elohim*, although two reasons for the traditional translation may be noted:

(1) Whenever the phrase *ruach elohim* occurs in the Old Testament, it refers to the Spirit of God and never to a mighty wind (cf., for example, Ex. 31:3; Num. 24:2; I Sam. 10:10; II Chron. 24:20; and Ezek. 11:24).

(2) The participle *merachepeth*, traditionally translated "moved" and describing the action of *ruach elohim*, does not describe the action of wind. In Deuteronomy 32:11 the verb from the same root describes the action of an eagle hovering over her young. The idea in Genesis 1:2 is that of the Holy Spirit, as an active agent in the creation, hovering over the uninhabited earth, ready to carry out the divine fiat. It is a most revealing fact that in his defense of the NJV translation[2] Professor Orlinsky says not one word about the participle used with *ruach elohim*, an amazing (and, no doubt, an embarrassing) omission, but rather collects ancient testimony to the correctness of his translation. In every case, this testimony may be discounted as either weak and unconvincing or simply indicating that "wind" rather than "Spirit" enjoyed some acceptance among Jewish scholars.

Let us then concentrate on the particular problem raised in footnote (a) and the variant reading found in the body of the text of NJV. Orlinsky's explanation points up the fact that the traditional translation—recognized in footnote (a) by the word "Or"—is at least grammatically possible in the opinion of these translators. Or at least they thought so in 1962, for since then a 1965 revision of the NJV has appeared in which footnote (a) is introduced by the word "Others." This change indicates, according to Orlinsky, "a traditional rendering no longer considered tenable, but worth mentioning because of its familiar and sometimes significant character."[3]

Such a revision points up, if nothing else, the rapidity of change which modern scholarly opinion constantly undergoes. But be that as it may, the body of the text suffered no essential change. It still regards verse 1 as a temporal clause, verse 2 as containing three circumstantial clauses, and verse 3 as the main clause of the opening

Genesis 1:1–3—A Creation Out of Nothing Taught?

statement of Genesis. This means that the first two verses are subordinated grammatically and connotatively to verse 3. The implications of this rendering are, of course, quite clear. The Hebrew text thus states absolutely nothing about a creation out of nothing or about the beginning of time. To the contrary, these verses now teach the preëxistence, if not the eternality, of matter. The influence of such a teaching on Christian theology hardly need be stated. Ultimately, it would alter all Christian thought in every area of dogmatics, the religious and spiritual no less than the biological and scientific.

Second Modern Translation

The second modern translation of Genesis which affords a change in the traditional rendering fo Genesis 1:1-3 is in *The Anchor Bible* series, published by Doubleday and Company, which purports to be "a project of international and interfaith scope: Protestant, Catholic, and Jewish scholars from many countries [will] contribute individual volumes," all under the general editorship of William F. Albright and his former student, David Noel Freedman. The volume on Genesis was contributed by the late Ephraim A. Speiser of the University of Pennsylvania and was published in 1964. That translation opens with the following words:

> 1 When God set about to create heaven and earth—2 the world being then a formless waste, with darkness over the seas and only an awesome wind sweeping over the water—3 God said, "Let there be light." And there was light.

Again note that verse 1 is rendered as a temporal clause, verse 2 as circumstantial thoughts, and verse 3 as the independent thought of the sentence.

Now these quite similar translations are by no means new. With minor variations this "subordination [of the first two verses to verse 3] view" was suggested by the Jewish expositor Rashi, later by Heinrich Ewald, and then by other scholars in our time. Theophile J. Meek, in his translation of Genesis for *The Bible, An American Translation*,[4] adopted this construction. *The Westminster Study Edition of the Holy Bible*[5] states in a footnote a preference for this construction over the traditional one. James Moffatt's translation also follows this view. The Revised Standard Version, though following the traditional construction in the body of its text, inserts the footnote, "Or *When*

God began to create." Even Dr. Merrill F. Unger of Dallas Theological Seminary suggests that the first three verses of Genesis says nothing about the original creation *ex nihilo*, escaping, however, the odious implications of the suggestion by affirming that a period of time should very likely be postulated *before* Genesis 1:1 wherein the the Bible student should insert the original creation and the fall of the angels.

Reasons for such a sweeping alteration of the meaning of these verses by these scholars away from the traditional meaning attached to them certainly must be compelling. What are they? They are basically two: the *cultural* and the *grammatical*.

The Cultural Reason

The Genesis account of creation, so this reason asserts, being an ancient Near Eastern cosmogony, must be placed within its cultural *milieu*. When this is done, a remarkable similarity is seen to exist between the biblical account of creation and other ancient Near Eastern cosmogonies, particularly in that they all agree on the preëxistence of matter at the time of the first creative act. Specifically, (1) the Babylonian account, popularly titled *Enuma Elish,* and (2) the "second" account of creation allegedly found in Genesis 2:4b-25 are cited as proofs of this fact. (Unger, of course, does not affirm this cultural reason.)

It is true that *Enuma Elish* does begin with a temporal clause— "When above the heavens had not [yet] been named, [and] below the earth had not [yet] existed as such," and it is also true that lines 3-8 may be construed either as another temporal clause (or possibly two) or as circumstantial thoughts, with the main clause introduced at line 9: "Then were the gods created. . . ." Too, the Bible student must frankly recognize that similarities between Genesis 1 and *Enuma Elish* do exist. But are mere similarities sufficient reason to insist that the Genesis account recognizes, as does *Enuma Elish,* the preëxistence of matter? May not these similarities be traced back to a common source of fact, which originated in an actual occurrence?

There is very good reason to believe that Moses was enabled by the inspiration of the Holy Spirit of God to record the true account of creation accurately, purged of all the crude mythological and polytheistic incrustations replete in the other accounts. Certainly one cannot find a primitive polytheism in the Mosaic record. Why then insist that the Mosaic record must teach the preëxistence of matter?

Genesis 1:1-3—A Creation Out of Nothing Taught?

Perhaps those who do so insist ought to recognize that they do so, not on an empirically established, objective basis founded on unimpeachable exegesis, but rather on an *a priori* assumption received by faith—the assumption that the Genesis account of creation is *not* unique among ancient cosmogonies, the assumption that Genesis One is *not* an inspired account of what actually took place at the beginning of earth history, but rather the combined efforts of the so-called Priestly School of late Israelite history.

Regarding the use of Genesis 2:4b-25 as another illustration of a creation account which begins with a temporal clause followed by circumstantial thoughts, the main clause being introduced at verse 7, I unhesitatingly affirm that this passage may *not* in good faith be employed as a parallel to Genesis 1:1-3 for three reasons:

(1) Such usage assumes at the outset that Genesis 2:4b-25 is a *second* account of creation, an assumption far from being proved or universally accepted; rather, Genesis 2 is a more detailed treatment of the sixth creative day of Genesis One.

(2) The division of Genesis 2:4 into two parts is both arbitrary and unbiblical. The first part (2:4a) is regarded as a subscription to the creation account of Genesis 1:2 - 2:3, and the second part (2:4b) is construed as the opening temporal clause of the second creation account (a division, by the way, which is absolutely essential to the view that Genesis 2:4b ff. is a precise parallel to Genesis 1:1-3).

It is arbitrary in that the division is made only in the interest of the theory of two parallel accounts of creation. It is unbiblical in that, if the phrase in Genesis 2:4a—"These are the generations of . . ."—be construed as a postscript to the preceding passage, it is the *only* time out of eleven different times that the phrase is used in Genesis where it is appended to a preceding passage rather than serving as a superscription to a following passage.

(3) The syntax in the two accounts actually differs, Genesis 2:4b containing a Hebrew infinitive construct in a very crucial place, whereas Genesis 1:1 contains the finite verb in the same place, a fact which can easily make all the difference in the world in the way the two verses are translated. In any translation Genesis 2:4b would have to be regarded as subordinate, while Genesis 1:1 may be rendered as an independent statement, a fact which footnote (a) of the NJV (1962) of Genesis 1:1 readily recognized.

Thus we conclude that the cultural reason for the "subordination view" of Genesis 1:1-3 is not compelling. But what about the grammatical reason? Actually, the major reason for accepting or rejecting a particular rendering of any passage of Scripture must be based on sound grammatical and exegetical considerations found in the passage itself. Consequently, we need to look now at the grammatical reason for the proffered change in translation.

The Grammatical Reason

Briefly stated, the grammatical reason is as follows: the particular form of the first word of Genesis 1:1 (*bereshith*, taken to be in the construct state) demands that verse 1 be translated as a temporal clause—literally, "In the beginning of God's creating . . . ," which normally is smoothed out to "When God began to create"; and the clauses of verse 2, interpreted as noun or circumstantial clauses, require a rendering which shows the circumstances which they speak of as existing at the time of the divine fiat of verse 3. Let us now draw nearer to the actual text of Genesis 1:1-3 for a critical examination of the Hebrew. I find, needless to say, no fault in either of the two modern translations with the rendering of verse 3; verse 3 is not really germane to the problem before us. But the first two verses do need examining, which we shall now do in reverse order.

The Meaning of Verse 2

If the reader is to understand what we are about to say regarding the meaning of verse 2, a short lesson in Hebrew syntax is in order regarding the significance of noun and verbal clauses, and the relation of noun clauses to adjoining clauses. Note the following rules:

> (1) *Noun clause*: "Every sentence, the subject and predicate of which are nouns or their equivalents (esp. participles), is called a *noun-clause*," [7] and the fundamental meaning of the noun clause is to "represent something *fixed, a state* or in short, *a being* so and so." [8]
>
> (2) *Verbal clause*s "Every sentence, the subject of which is a noun (or pronoun included in a verbal-form) and its predicate a finite verb, is called a *verbal-clause*," [9] and its fundamental meaning is to represent "something *moveable* and in *progress*, an *event* or *action*." [10]
>
> (3) *Syntactical relation of the noun clause to the verbal clause*: "The noun-clause connected . . . to a verbal clause, or its equivalent, always describes a state *contemporaneous* with the principal action. . . ." [11]

Genesis 1:1–3—A Creation Out of Nothing Taught?

With these three rules we are ready to proceed; we shall hereafter refer to these rules as "rule 1," "rule 2," and "rule 3."

Verse 2 is comprised of three clauses, namely (1) "and the earth was empty and formless"; (2) "and darkness was upon the face of the deep"; and (3) "and the Spirit of God hovered upon the face of the waters." In the English translation each of these three clauses might appear to be a verbal clause, possessing a subject and a finite verb, but the Hebrew text discloses that the situation is actually quite different.

Beginning with the last clause and working forward to the front of the verse, an analysis reveals that the third clause is actually comprised of a noun subject—"Spirit"—and a participial predicate—"hovered," thereby establishing this third clause as a Hebrew noun clause denoting a state (cf. rule 1).

The middle clause is actually nothing more than a noun subject—"darkness"—and a prepositional phrase—"upon the face of the deep"—with the verb "was" understood. The King James Version, wherein words not in the original are indicated by italics, will verify this fact. Thus this clause is also a noun clause denoting a state (cf. rule 1).

The first clause is somewhat more problematical, in that it is composed of a noun subject—"earth," a finite verbal form—"was" (specifically the Qal perfect third person feminine singular), and the adjectives "empty and formless." Does not the presence of the finite verb form necessitate at least the first clause of verse 2 be construed as a verbal clause representing an action (cf. rule 2)? In my opinion it does not and cannot, and for the following reasons:

(1) This clause is so written in the Hebrew that the subject—"earth" precedes the verbal "was," contrary to the normal word order of the verbal clause in which the verb normally precedes the subject. *Gesenius' Hebrew Grammar* states:

> ... the subject does sometimes precede ... in the verbal clause proper, ... especially so if there is special emphasis upon it. ... In the great majority of instances, however, the position of the subject at the beginning of a verbal clause is to be explained from the fact that the clause is not intended to introduce a new fact carrying on the narrative, but rather to describe a *state*. Verbal-clauses of this kind approximate closely in character to noun-clauses, and not infrequently ... it is doubtful whether the writer did not in fact intend a noun-clause.[12]

Thus the word order is greatly in favor of this clause being construed as a noun clause describing a state of being—"the earth was in a state of emptiness and formlessness." In fact, *Gesenius' Hebrew Grammar* actually lists this particular clause as a noun clause.[13]

(2) If the verb *hayethah* (translated "was" in KJV) had been intended to be more than a mere copula, that is, if it had been intended to convey the idea of "becoming so and so," it would most likely have been inflected as an imperfect verb form followed by the *lamedh* preposition as in Genesis 2:7. The verb *hayah*, while it may at times be translated with a transitive sense, that is, "come to be," is here in the perfect aspect of the verb, which denotes actions, events, or states, not in progress, but from the point of view of completion. I agree with J. Wash Watts, when he writes: "A translation [of *hayethah* in Genesis 1:2] like 'came to be' would be contrary to the nature of the perfect." [14] Thus its correct translation is "was," denoting a state.

(3) Even if the verb could possibly be translated "became," thereby construing this clause as a verbal clause, this is usually done in the interest of teaching the intrusion of a divine judgment upon something, usually said to be the fallen angel horde, with a gap of indeterminate duration inserted between verse 1 and verse 2. But such a gap in turn would separate verse 1 in time from the first creative day, which is clearly at variance with Exodus 20:11, which affirms in no uncertain terms that "in six days the Lord made heaven and earth, the sea, and all that in them is." Here is clear biblical proof that verse 1 must be viewed as standing within and encompassed by the time limits of the creation week itself and that the creation week was not preceded by a divine judgment.

The first clause of verse 2 should be taken, then, as a noun clause, and is so regarded by a vast majority of Hebrew grammarians; i.e., *hayethah* is used in Genesis 1:2 "only for the purpose of referring to past time a statement which, as the description of a state, might also appear in the form of a pure noun-clause." [15]

In the light of this discussion, then, we may conclude that verse 2 does, in fact, contain three noun or circumstantial clauses, all describing states of being existing at a particular time. But the particular time when this threefold condition existed will be determined by the principal action with which it is construed by the interpreter (cf. rule 3).

The existing state of things described in verse 2 may quite conceivably be construed as existing contemporaneously with the action expressed in verse 1 (if verse 1 is an independent clause) or with the action of God expressed in verse 3. But before this decision can be made, verse 1 must be examined to determine if its grammar and syntax demand that it be regarded as a temporal (and thus a subordinate) clause or as an independent clause.

The Meaning of Verse 1

The entire problem of whether to translate verse 1 as it has been traditionally rendered, that is, "In the beginning God created the heaven and the earth," or to render it as a temporal clause, that is, "When God began to create the heaven and the earth," revolves around the first Hebrew word in Genesis—*bereshith*, traditionally translated "In the beginning."

This word is composed of the Hebrew preposition *beth* meaning "in," and the noun *reshith* meaning "beginning." It has no article. In Hebrew the noun may be placed in either of two states which the grammarian, for lack of better terminology, calls the absolute state and the construct state. As far as its form is concerned, *bereshith* could be either.

Admittedly, however, when a definite noun is in the construct state, it is anarthrous and derives it definiteness from the following definite noun or verbal idea. Hence it is argued by many modern scholars that since *bereshith* is anarthrous, (1) it is standing in a related sense to what follows, (2) it is thus made definite by the following verbal idea, and (3) it is thus to be translated (literally): "In the beginning of God's creating," which resolves itself quite naturally into the temporal thought: "When God began to create." (N.B. The noun in the construct state is normally followed by another noun, while here it is followed by the finite verb *bara*; but that this is a genuine Semetic usage is evident from constructions in Exodus 4:13; 6:28; Leviticus 14:46; Deuteronomy 4:15; I Samuel 5:9; 25:15; Psalms 16:3; 58:9; 81:6; Isaiah 29:1; and Hosea 1:2.)

But does the mere omission of the article in *bereshith* demand that *reshith* be regarded as standing in a construct relation to the following verbal idea? Not necessarily, for in Isaiah 46:10 this very word is anarthrous, and yet is clearly in the absolute state: "the one declaring from [the] beginning the end." Thus the mere absence of the article is not enough evidence, standing alone, for determining the state of this noun in Genesis 1:1. The decision must be based upon other considerations, and here I follow Edward J. Young's thought:

(1) In the Hebrew text *bereshith* is accented with the disjunctive *tiphcha*, indicating that the word has its own independent accent and is thus construed by the Masoretes as an absolute.

(2) Though this comes *ab extra*, it is significant that without exception the ancient versions regarded *bereshith* as an absolute.

(3) In the Old Testament when a construct noun precedes a finite verb, the fact of constructness is apparent, either from the form of the noun in construct, or from the demand of the context that the noun be so taken. But in Genesis 1:1 neither of these conditions is present. In fact, the context, specifically the finite verb *bara* ("create"), favors the absolute state, because *bara* in the Qal stem, as it is here, is employed exclusively of the divine activity.[16]

Further, while the word is frequently employed with the accusative of the *product produced*, it is *never* used in a context where the accusative of the *material employed* in the creative act is mentioned, which would be the case if *bereshith* were construed as a construct noun, thereby rendering verse 1 as a temporal clause. Even Gerhard von Rad, the form-critical Old Testament scholar, feels obliged to write: "Since pre-existent matter is never mentioned in connexion with this activity [denoted by *bara*], the idea of *creatio ex nihilo* is connected with it."[17]

I conclude, therefore, that *bereshith* is an absolute noun (as *en arche* in John 1:1) and view verse 1 as a simple declaration of the fact of absolute creation—as it has been traditionally translated.

Syntactical Relation of Verse 2

We may now decide whether verse 2 is to be construed as describing a state existing contemporaneously with the action of verse 1 or with the action of verse 3. If the former alternative is followed, the meaning would be that the threefold condition described in verse 2 was present as God began the activity expressed in *bara* of verse 1, but this would not make for good sense and is unsuitable to the significance of *bara*. The presence of *bara* makes it clear that the chapter is not concerned merely with the transformation of already existing material; the concern of the chapter is far grander than that.

The only meaningful interpretation is to regard verse 2 as describing the state of the created earth as it stood at the time of the divine fiat of verse 3, with verse 1 serving as a grand summary statement of all that follows in the chapter.

But why regard verse 1 as a grand summary statement of all that follows? First, because "the heaven and the earth" is a peculiar Hebrew idiom, known as an antonymic pair, standing for the universe, but more than that, for the well-ordered universe. Second, because in the verses that follow verse 1, the reader actually sees, there described, God's consecutive acts whereby He created the heaven and the earth of verse 1. Admittedly, this view of the matter, in the words of Young, sees regarding verse 2, "no explicit statement of the creation of the primeval material from which the universe we know was formed," [18] but we may assume that this great event is included in the broad statement of verse 1.

We are now ready to offer the following paraphrase of Genesis 1:1-3, in which we will gather together the several points and nuances which we have made throughout this discussion:

> 1 In the beginning God created the well-ordered universe. 2 Now the earth, being empty and formless with darkness upon the face of the deep, and the Spirit of God hovering over the face of the waters [a condition, the result of the first creative act, existing in the past but not in existence at the time of the recording of the event],[3] God said, "Let there be light." And there was light.

Immediately, the gap theorist will object that if the creative activity of God should be so conceived, then God's first creative act produced a "chaotic, desolate waste," an act unbecoming to the perfections of the divine nature. And too, does not Isaiah 45:18 distinctly state that God created the earth "not in vain"?

As for Isaiah's statement, such an interpretation as the gap theorist places on his words overlooks the true significance of the final phrase of this verse: "he formed it to be inhabited." The real point of the passage is that God did not ultimately intend the world to be devoid of life, but rather that it should be filled with living things. In John C. Whitcomb's words,

> Thus, He did not allow it to *remain* in the empty and formless condition in which He first created it, but in six creative days filled it with living things and fashioned it as a beautiful home for man. The verse thus speaks of God's *ultimate purpose* in creation, and the contrast in this verse between *"tohu"* ["in vain"] and "inhabited" shows clearly that *"tohu"* means empty or *uninhabited*, rather than judged, destroyed, or chaotic."[19]

As for the objection that this view of things would make God create a chaos, an act insulting to the divine nature, two things may be said. First, such an objection is based on a finite *a priori* assumption of what God should or should not do in keeping with the perfection of His nature. Second, I suggest that expositors should exercise caution before they designate the condition of Genesis 1:2 for which the Spirit of God is obviously tenderly caring and which is under His complete control as a chaos or in a topsy-turvy condition. This charge really is insulting to the God of order.

The presence of the Holy Spirit in verse 2, I feel to the contrary, is beautifully explained by Keil and Delitzsch when they perceive the Holy Spirit as standing, so to speak, in a state of readiness to carry out the divine fiats of the Logos of God and to bring the creation to a habitable state for man.[20] Such a view of the matter has the advantage, too, of giving more prominence than has been done in in the past to the role which the Holy Spirit played in creation and which is borne out in other parts of Scripture (Psa. 104:30; Job 26:13).

In answer, then, to the question posed in the title of this essay, I am prepared to answer unhesitatingly in the affirmative: yes, the opening verses of Genesis do teach a creation out of nothing. Furthermore, the emphasis of Genesis 1 appears to be, not so much on God's *power* to create—that is assumed, but on His *ability* as an architect to "build" from originally created material, supplemented with subsequently created material, a beautiful world for mankind. The two modern translations, herein discussed, have thus grievously erred.

NOTES AND REFERENCES

1. Harry M. Orlinsky, "The New Jewish Version of the Torah," *Journal of Biblical Literature*, LXXXII, 1963, pp. 252-253.
2. *Ibid.*
3. Orlinsky, "The Rage to Translate: The New Age of Bible Translations," *Genesis* (New York: Harper & Row, 1966), p. xiv.
4. Theophile J. Meek, in his translation of Genesis for *The Bible, An American Translation* (Chicago: University of Chicago Press, 1931).
5. Published by the Westminster Press, Philadelphia, 1948.
6. Merrill F. Unger, "Rethinking the Genesis Account of Creation," *Bibliotheca*, Vol. 115, No. 457, p. 28; see also, *Unger's Bible Handbook* (Chicago: Moody Press, 1966).
7. *Gesenius' Hebrew Grammar*, 140a.

8. *Ibid.*, 140e.
9. *Ibid.*, 140b.
10. *Ibid.*, 140e.
11. *Ibid.*, 141e; cf. *ibid.*, 156c.
12. *Ibid.*, 142a.
13. *Ibid.*, 141i, 142c.
14. J. Wash Watts, *A Survey of Syntax in the Hebrew Old Testament*, pp. 25-36.
15. *Gesenius' Hebrew Grammar*, 141i.
16. Edward J. Young, *Studies in Genesis One*, pp. 5-7.
17. Gerhard von Rad, *Old Testament Theology*, I, 142.
18. Young, *op. cit.*, p. 11.
19. John C. Whitcomb, "The Ruin-Reconstruction Theory of Genesis 1:2," *Creation Research Society Annual*, 1965, p. 3; Chapter IV of this book.
20. Keil and Delitzsch, *Pentateuch*, I, 49.

III

THE CREATION OF THE HEAVENS AND THE EARTH

John C. Whitcomb, Jr.

Ex Nihilo Creation

The Word of God teaches that all non-living things were created supernaturally, instantaneously, and without the use of pre-existent materials. In the strictest sense, this is the meaning of Hebrews 11:3 —"By faith we understand that the worlds (*aionas,* the time-space universe) were framed by the Word of God, so that what is seen hath not been made out of things which appear" (cf. Rom. 4:17). This certainly cannot mean that visible material substances are composed of "invisible" atomic particles! Spiritual faith is certainly not required to accept the atomic theory in its current form! The point of the verse is that the physical substances that compose our visible universe did not exist in any form whatsoever, other than in the mind of an omniscient God, until He spoke the creative Word.

Not only was creation *ex nihilo,* but it also involved the instantaneous appearance of complex physical entities. The evolutionary concept of a gradual development of heavier and heavier elements throughout cosmic history, for example, is excluded by Scripture. Note the emphasis on the immediate effect of God's creative word in Psalm 33:6, 9—"By the word of the Lord were the heavens made; and all the host of them by the breath of His mouth . . . for He spake, and it was done; he commanded, and it stood fast." There is certainly no thought here of delay, or resistance, or a gradual, step-by-step build-up to fulfillment.

Some scholars, in the name of evangelical Christianity, have denounced this view as philosophically "unhealthy" because it does not line up satisfactorily with empirical evidence (e.g., Thomas H. Leith, "Some Logical Problems with the Thesis of Apparent Age," *Journal of the American Scientific Affiliation,* December, 1965, pp. 121, 122). Not only so, but it is claimed that this position makes God a deceiver (J. Laurence Kulp, "The Christian Concept of Uniformity in the Universe," *His* Magazine, May, 1952, p. 23; Leith, *op. cit.*, p. 122). An appropriate answer to such assertions has been expressed by Lloyd G. Multhauf, Department of Physics, Pennsylvania State University:

> If the Bible tells us of a non-uniformity in our fundamental laws and/or that it does not allow for millions or billions of years as the age of the earth, then God is not fooling man, rather man is going on a vain search in spite of what God has said. . . . Biblical revelation as well as science is a means of gaining knowledge for the Christian.[1]

Christians who truly desire to honor God's Word should not come to it with preconceived ideas of what could or could not have happened, or what can or cannot be true. To be sure, many of the great doctrines and events set forth in Scripture are foolish to the natural mind, because they are spiritually discerned (I Cor. 2:14). And supernatural creation is one of those doctrines.

No amount of philosophical reasoning or scientific empiricism can modify the pure supernaturalism of such passages as Genesis 1:3—"And God said, Let there be light: and there was light." Analogous to this is the absolute supernaturalism, perfection, and suddenness of God's work of regeneration in the sinful heart of man: "For God, who commanded the light to shine out of darkness, hath shined in our hearts to give the light of the knowledge of the glory of God in the face of Jesus Christ" (II Cor. 4:6).

The Creation of the Heavens

For convenience of human thought and expression, the Bible refers to three different heavens. The *third* heaven is that glorious place surrounding the immediate presence of God, to which Paul was carried in a transcendent vision early in his Christian experience (II Cor. 12:1-4). The *second* heaven seems to be equivalent to what we call "outer space"; while the *first* heaven consists of the atmospheric blanket surrounding the earth, in which clouds move and birds fly.

In the first chapter of Genesis, a distinction may be seen between the first heaven, above which the waters were lifted (vss. 8, 20) and the second heaven in which the luminaries were placed (vss. 14-17). There is certainly nothing crude or "pre-scientific," in the bad sense of that expression, about the cosmology of Genesis, as many able expositors have successfully and repeatedly demonstrated.[2]

What were the "heavens" like at the moment they came from the

Creator's hand "in the beginning"? The *third* heaven was populated with hundreds of millions of angelic beings (Dan. 7:10), each one a "son of God" in the sense of a direct creation by God (cf. Job 1:6) and therefore perfect in all their ways (Ezek. 28:15). They must have been created at the very beginning of the first day of creation, for Job 38:6-7 tells of their singing and of their shout of joy at the creation of the earth.

That they did not exist *before* the first day is indicated by Colossians 1:16 (which tells us that Christ created all *invisible* as well as visible thrones, dominions, principalities, and powers *in the heavens* as well as upon the earth) in the light of Exodus 20:11 (*"in six days* Jehovah made heaven and earth, the sea, and *all that in them is"*). (Compare also Psa. 33:6 and Ezek. 28:13, 15.)

The *second* heaven, the realm of "outer space," was presumably empty and dark, for the sun, moon, and stars were not created until the fourth day, and the special light source which divided the light from the darkness had not yet been spoken into existence.

The *first* heaven, or atmospheric blanket, had neither vapor canopy nor clouds, for the waters were not yet lifted above the expanse ("firmament") in the form of a vast, invisible thermal vapor blanket, as must have existed until the Flood, and there were no clouds or rain as in our present post-Flood world. Neither Genesis nor geology gives any support to the idea that earth's primitive atmosphere consisted of ammonia, methane, hydrogen, and water, as the evolutionary theory of spontaneous generation of life requires. Philip Abelson, Director of the Geophysical Laboratory, Carnegie Institution of Washington, has shown that such an atmosphere could not have existed[3]

Some Bible students believe that the heavenly bodies were created in the beginning, but not be seen from the earth because of a cloud blanket so dense that darkness covered the face of the deep. However, the waters were not lifted up until the second day, and the light that was created on the first day was clearly visible from the earth. Also, if God's work on the fourth day involved merely the unveiling of previously created heavenly bodies, this idea could have been more clearly expressed by the use of the verb "appeared" as in verse 9—"and let the dry land *appear*" Instead of this, we are told that God "made" two great lights on the fourth day, and that He "made" the stars also.

Although in its general biblical usage this verb *asah* ("made") is not as strong as *bara* ("created") for conveying the idea of *ex nihilo* creation, it is used as a synonym for *bara* in the creation narrative of Genesis. This can be demonstrated by comparing 1:21, where God is said to have "created" (*bara*) great whales, with 1:25, where He "made" (*asah*) the beasts of the earth. Surely we are not to understand any significant difference between the creation of sea monsters and land animals! Compare also 1:26 ("And God said, let us *make* man in our own image") with 1:27 ("So God *created* man in his own image"). Thus, the two verbs are used synonymously in this chapter, and the statement that the sun, moon, and stars were "made" on the fourth day means that they were "created" on the fourth day.

The Creation of the Earth

The earth, like the heavens, was created without the use of preexistent materials (Heb. 11:3), which clearly implies that it was created instantaneously as a dynamic, highly complex entity. It was spinning on its axis, for in reference to the light source created on the first day, it passed through a night-day cycle. It had a cool crust, for it was covered with water.

The crust, however, had no significant features, such as continents, mountains, and ocean basins, for these were formed on the third day. Nor did it have sedimentary and fossil strata, for these were basically the effects of the great Deluge. But it did contain all of the basic elements and the foundational rocks of our present earth. As a planet, it was perfect in every way, but at this stage of creation week it was not yet an appropriate home for man. It was "without form and void" (*tohu wabohu*).

Did the Earth Come from a Proto-Sun?

If Genesis teaches that the earth was created *before* the sun, moon, and stars, then Christians who believe the Book of Genesis are obviously in serious conflict with evolutionary theory at this point. For this reason, many Christians feel that Genesis must be interpreted in such a way as to avoid this conflict. After all, is it not perfectly clear from astronomical studies that the earth and the other planets came from the sun or from a proto-sun? It shall be our purpose in the following paragraphs to show that this is not true.

By 1940, all the various encounter or planetesimal theories, which postulated the near approach of another star to our sun, resulting in the drawing off of embryonic planets, had been discarded as hopelessly inadequate explanations of the origin of the solar system.[5] In more recent years, Von Weizsäcker, Whipple, Spitzer, Urey, Gamow, Hoyle, Kuiper, and others have attempted to avoid the difficulties of the planetesimal theories by returning to a form of nebular hypothesis, whereby the sun and its planets supposedly condensed out of swirling eddies of cold, dark, interstellar clouds of gas and dust. How well this currently popular theory succeeds in explaining the solar system in terms of physical, chemical, and mathematical principles alone may be judged by the Christian for himself after considering some of the *basic problems* which remain to be solved by evolutionary cosmogonists:

First, before any condensation of gas and dust could occur, the nebula would have diffused into outer space. Dr. Gerald P. Kuiper, a leading proponent of the evolutionary concept, admits that before gravitational attraction would become significant, the particles would have to be as big as the moon.[6]

Second, the theory demands a complex system of roller-bearing eddies of gas and dust, but this is impossible because such vortices must remain perfectly intact during essentially the entire period of planetary accretion. But Dr. Kuiper confesses that "it is difficult to conceive that the beautiful system of vortices would actually have been in existence long enough—even for 10 or 100 years—to get the condensation of the building material for the planets under way." Yet the theory demands many *millions* of years.

Third, what stopped the process from continuing so that the entire mass of material did not form one large body? The sun makes up 99 and 6/7 percent of the mass of the solar system, so what would have kept the remaining 1/7 of one percent from falling into the main body?

Fourth, other suns do not seem to be condensing or developing planetary systems. There is much interstellar material in the vicinity of our sun, but it is not condensing. Greenstein of the Mount Wilson Observatory is of the opinion that the known stars rotate so fast that one must conclude that they could never have been formed by a condensation process. David Layzer, professor of astronomy at Harvard University, says that there is no known solution to the problem of the small angular momentum (the property that keeps the sun rotating and keeps the planets revolving around it) of the sun. If it had been part of a gaseous protogalaxy, its angular momentum would have to have been a billion times as much as it now possesses. How it could have lost all but 1/10,000,000 of 1 percent of its original angular momentum has never been explained.[7]

Fifth, the planets contain less than one percent of the mass of the solar system but a staggering 98 percent of its angular momentum. David Bergamini observes, "A theory of evolution that fails to account for this peculiar fact is ruled out before it starts." [8]

Sixth, evolutionary theory cannot explain why seven of the nine planets have direct rotation in reference to their revolution around the sun, but Venus rotates slowly backwards, and Uranus rotates at a 98-degree angle from its orbital plane, even though its orbit inclines less than that of any other planet. Professor Layzer states: "It is an open question whether this state of affairs is consistent" with current theories of the origin of the solar system.

Seventh, evolution has no answer to the problem of retrograde satellites. Of the thirty-two moons in our solar system, eleven orbit in directions opposite that of the rotational direction of their mother planets. Of special interest is Triton, the inner of Neptune's two satellites, which has nearly twice the mass of our moon (its diameter being 3,000 miles) and which revolves every six days in a nearly circluar orbit only 220,000 miles from Neptune (closer than our moon to the earth).

Isaac Asimov, as well as most evolutionary cosmogonists, believes that Triton "was thrown away from that planet by some cosmic collision or other accident," and that later on Neptune recaptured its lost moon into a retrograde orbit by "a similar accident." [9] But how many such "accidents" may one be permitted to invoke to prop up a theory already tottering under the weight of its own unproved assumptions? Asimov further states that retrograde satellites are "minor exceptions" to the general rule of satellite orbits. However, eleven out of thirty-two moons having retrograde orbits can hardly be brushed aside as "minor exceptions."

Eighth, what can evolution really offer as an explanation of the angular momentum in these satellite systems? We will permit Professor Layzer of Harvard to state the problem: "Except in the Earth-Moon system (which is exceptional in other respects as well), the primary carries the bulk of angular momentum, instead of the satellites. . . . This circumstance aggravates the theoretical difficulty presented by the slow rotation of the Sun, for if the Sun has somehow managed to get rid of the angular momentum it would be expected to have, according to the nebular hypothesis, why have the planets not done likewise?"

Ninth, in spite of some ingenious and very complicated theories, it has never satisfactorily been shown why the earth is composed of such heavy elements. In the words of Professor Fred Hoyle of Cambridge University:

> Apart from hydrogen and helium, all other elements are extremely rare, all over the universe. In the sun they amount to only about 1% of the total mass. . . . The contrast [with the heavy elements which predominate in the earth] brings out two important points. First, we see that material torn from the sun would not be at all suitable for the formation of the planets as we know them. Its composition would be hopelessly wrong. And our second point in this contrast is that it is the sun that is normal and the earth that is the freak. The interstellar gas and most of the stars are composed of material like the sun, not like the earth. You must understand that, cosmically speaking, the room you are now sitting in is made of the wrong stuff. You yourself are a rarity. You are a cosmic collector's piece.

In the light of all these facts of astronomy, it seems to me that evangelical scientists have no right to lend their support to evolutionary cosmogonies. It brought me a sense of keen disappointment, therefore, when I read an article in the evangelical periodical, the *Journal of the American Scientific Affiliation,* which praises Kuiper's gas-dust nebular theory as "truly simple." The author concludes this article with these words: "It is almost gratifying that this process of planetary formation is but a special case of the universal process of binary-star formation, which seems to be one of God's universal Laws. . . . Truly God is in his Universe, and all will be right with the world." [10]

In contrast to this attitude, which presumably is quite widespread among evangelical scientists, I have become convinced that the most rational way to explain the origin of our vastly complex solar system is in terms of a direct creation by God. And if this be a reasonable position within the revealed frame of reference of biblical theism and in view of the conspicuous failures of evolutionary alternatives, may not the supernatural origin of the astronomic system we know the best serve as a model for the supernatural origin of the stellar systems that lie beyond our own?

In other words, if God created *ex nihilo* the two great lights that rule the day and night, He could also have created *ex nihilo* "the stars also." In the words of Dr. Paul A Zimmerman: "The Biblical account of creation by Almighty God has not been disproved by science. It remains today, even from the viewpoint of reason, I believe, the most logical, believable account of the beginning of the earth and the rest of the universe." [11]

The Purpose of the Stellar Creation

Why did God create the sun, moon, and stars on the fourth day rather than the first day? One possible explanation is that in this way God has emphasized the supreme importance of the earth among all astronomical bodies in the universe. In spite of its comparative smallness of size, even among the nine planets, to say nothing of the stars themselves, it is nonetheless absolutely unique in God's eternal purposes.

It was on this planet that God placed man, created in His image, to exercise dominion and to worship Him. It was to this planet that God came in the person of His Son 1900 years ago to become a permanent member of the human race and to die for human sins upon a rugged cross. And it will be to this same planet that this great God and Saviour will return again to establish His kingdom. Because of its positional superiority in the spiritual order of things, therefore, the earth was formed first, and then the stellar systems; just as Adam was first formed, then Eve (I Tim. 2:13).

Another possible reason for this order of events is that God, by this means, made it clear that the earth and life upon it do not owe their existence to the greater light that rules the day, but rather to God himself. In other words, God was perfectly able to create and take care of the earth and even living things upon it without the help of the sun. Apart from the Scriptures, of course, this would hardly be an obvious fact to mankind.

In ancient times (and even in some parts of the world today) great nations actually worshiped the sun as a god. In Egypt he was call *Re*, and in Babylon he was known as *Shamash*. After all, such worship seemed quite reasonable in view of the fact that the sun provided light, warmth, and, apparently, life itself.

Even the Jews were greatly tempted to enter into such worship, as may be judged by such passages as Deuteronomy 4:19 and 17:3. Job himself confessed: "If I beheld the sun when it shined, or the moon walking in brightness; and my heart hath been secretly enticed, or my mouth hath kissed my hand: this also were an iniquity to be punished by the judge: for I should have denied the God that is above" (Job 31:26-28).

Perhaps it is not inappropriate to suggest that the evolutionary theory provides a modern and subtle counterpart to the ancient sun-worship cult, for if we must trace our origin to the sun or to a protosun, and if we live, move, and have our being exclusively through its boundless blessings and provisions, *then it is our God!*

The creation account in Genesis completely undermines all such blasphemies by putting the sun in a secondary position with reference to the earth. It is not only a mere creature of God, but also a servant to man, the crown of God's creation.

But if the sun, moon, and stars are not ultimately essential to the earth's existence, then why did God create them? Three basic reasons are listed in Genesis 1:14. They are for lights, for seasons (a calendar), and for signs.

As *lights*, they replaced the special and temporary light of the early days.

As a *calendar*, dividing the seasons, days, and years, they enable men to plan their work accurately into the distant future, thus reflecting the purposive mind of God.

As *signs*, they teach and ever remind men of the vastly important spiritual truths concerning the Creator.

David learned from them the transcendence of God and his own comparative nothingness: "When I consider thy heavens, the work of thy fingers, the moon and the stars which thou hast ordained, what is man that thou art mindful of him?" (Psa. 8:3). The Apostle Paul insisted that men are utterly without excuse for their idolatries, for "the things that are made" give clear testimony to the "everlasting power and divinity" of the Creator (Rom. 1:20).

Apparently, the sun, moon, and stars more effectively accomplish these purposes than one great light source could have. There need be no other reason for their existence than this threefold ministry to man.

But would this have been an unnecessary waste of God's creative energies? Isaiah gives the effective answer: "Hast thou not known? hast thou not heard? The everlasting God, Jehovah, the Creator of the ends of the earth, fainteth not, neither is weary; there is no searching of his understanding" (Isa. 40:28).

The heavens are the work of God's "fingers" (Psa. 8:3), and when they have fulfilled their God-intended purpose, they will flee away from His face and no place will be found for them (Rev. 20:11).

The eternal city will have "no need of the sun, neither of the moon, to shine in it," for the glory of God will lighten it, and the Lord Jesus Christ will be the lamp thereof (Rev. 21:23; cf. 22:5).

Christ and His Word, therefore, must be our final guide as we seek to understand the origin, meaning, and destiny of the heavens and the earth.

NOTES AND REFERENCES

1. Lloyd G. Multhauf, *Journal of the American Scientific Affiliation*, June 3, 1966, p. 63.
2. Cf. R. Laird Harris, "The Bible and Cosmology," *Bulletin of the Evangelical Theological Society*, March, 1962, pp 11-17.
3. Philip Abelson, Abstracts 133rd National Meeting, Am. Chem. Soc., April, 1958, p. 53, cited by Duane T. Gish, "Critique of Biochemical Evolution," *Creation Research Society Quarterly*, October, 1964, p. 10.
4. See the *Journal of the Transactions of the Victoria Institute*, 1946, p. 21.
5. Cf. W. M. Smart, *The Origin of the Earth*, 1959, pp. 179-207.
6. Cf. Whitcomb, *The Origin of the Solar System*, Presbyterian and Reformed Publishing Company, 1964, for full documentation.
7. "Cosmogony," *McGraw-Hill Encyclopedia of Science and Technology*, 1960, III, p. 506.
8. David Bergamini, *Life* Nature Library volume on *The Universe*, p. 93.
9. Isaac Asimov, *The Intelligent Man's Guide to Science*, 1960, vol. I, p. 78.
10. Jack T. Kent, "The Origin of the Solar System, Galaxy, and the Universe," *Journal of the American Scientific Affiliation*, December, 1965, p. 117.
11. Paul A. Zimmerman, "Some Observations on Current Cosmological Theories," *Concordia Theological* Monthly, July, 1953, p. 513.

IV

THE RUIN RECONSTRUCTION THEORY OF GENESIS 1:2

JOHN C. WHITCOMB, JR.

Students of the Bible have long debated the question of whether the original creation of the heavens and the earth is to be understood as an event within the first "day" of creation, or whether a vast period of time could have elapsed between the original creation of Genesis 1:1 and the "waste and void" condition described in Genesis 1:2. Most theologians who favor a time gap between these two verses believe that the original earth was populated with plants and animals (and perhaps even men), and because of the fall of Satan it was destroyed by God. The vast ages of the geologic timetable are thought to have occurred during this interval, so that the fossil plants and animals which are found in the crust of the earth today are relics of the original world which was destroyed before the six literal days of creation (or, rather, re-creation) recorded in Genesis 1:3-31.

The "ruin-reconstruction theory," or "gap theory," has been widely accepted among Christians who interpret the Book of Genesis in the traditional historical-grammatical method, especially since the early 19th century, when Thomas Chalmers of England advocated this interpretation as a means of harmonizing the Genesis account of creation with the vast time periods of earth history demanded by uniformitarian geologists.[1] The differences between the "gap theory" and the traditional view of a recent creation of the earth within six literal days are quite profound, and may be outlined as follows: (1) The gap theory permits Christians to accept without question the complete validity of the time-table of uniformitarian geologists. (2) The gap theory leaves us with no clear word from God as to the original world—the time involved in its creation, the arrangement of its features, or its pre-judgment history—; for instead of having the entire first chapter on this important subject, we have only the first verse. (3) Because all the animals of the first world were destroyed and fossilized, they have no relation to the animals

The Ruin Reconstruction Theory of Genesis 1:2

of the present world, in spite of the fact that many of them appear to be identical in form to modern types. Likewise, those who would place human fossils into the "gap" are forced to the conclusion that such pre-Adamic "men" did not possess an eternal soul.[2] (4) The gap theory redefines the "very good" of Genesis 1:31 ("God saw every thing that he had made, and, behold, it was very good"), for Adam would have been placed as a very late arrival into a world that had just been destroyed, so that he was literally walking upon a graveyard of billions of creatures over which he would never exercise dominion (1:26). Furthermore, the earth would already have become the domain of a fallen and wicked angel who is described elsewhere in Scripture as "the god of this world" (II Cor. 4:4).

Obviously, then, the gap theory is not a minor deviation from the traditional interpretation of the Genesis creation account. For this reason, the biblical evidences that have been set forth in its defense need to be carefully examined. The four most frequently used evidences are these: (1) The verb translated "was" in Genesis 1:2 (Heb. *hayetha*) can just as well be translated "became," and thus the idea of a profound change in the earth's condition is permitted. (2) The phrase "waste and void" (Heb. *tohu wa-bohu*) appears elsewhere only in Isaiah 34:11 and Jeremiah 4:23, and the context of those passages speaks clearly of judgment and destruction. Furthermore, the word *tohu* by itself frequently has an evil connotation. (3) It is highly improbable that God, the author of light, would have originally created the world in darkness, which is generally used in Scripture as a symbol of evil. (4) There seems to be a definite distinction in the first chapter of Genesis between "created" and "made," thus permitting us to assume that many of the things mentioned in this chapter were simply re-created.

"Was" or "Became"?

The first supporting argument for the gap theory is that the Hebrew verb *hayetha* in Genesis 1:2 may be translated "became," thus implying a tremendous transition from perfection to judgment and destruction. It is true that there are six instances in the Pentateuch where this verb is translated "became" (Gen. 3:22; 19:26; 21:20; Ex. 7:19; 8:17; 9:10). In each of these cases, however, the context clearly shows that a change of state has occurred. The same verb appears 258 other times in the Pentateuch and in each case is to be translated "was." Because Genesis 1:2 lacks contextual support for translating this verb "became," no English version of Genesis has ever been translated in this way. One graduate student questioned twenty of the leading Hebrew scholars of America concerning the exegetical evidence for a gap in Genesis 1:2. They unanimously replied that there was no such evidence.[3] The clearest way to have conveyed the idea of a change of state would be to follow the verb *hayetha* with the preposition "to" (*lamedh*), as was done in Genesis 2:7 ("and man *became* a living soul") and in twenty-five other verses in the Pentateuch. But this preposition does not appear after the verb in Genesis 1:2.

Furthermore, the sentence structure suggests that the earth's condition in verse 2 is just as God created it in verse 1, for we have an exact grammatical parallel in Jonah 3:3 ("Jonah arose, and went into Nineveh. . . . Now Nineveh *was* an exceeding great city"). Obviously, Nineveh did not *become* a great city after Jonah entered it. Dr. F. F. Bruce points out that if verse 2 indicated an event subsequent to the creation of verse 1, we might have expected in verse 2 a *"waw* consecutive" with the imperfect tense instead of a *"waw* copulative" with the perfect (i.e., *wattehi ha-arets* instead of *we-ha-arets haye-thah*).[4] In the light of this evidence, it appears that the passage is not speaking of a change in the earth's condition due to a catastrophe, but is simply describing the earth as it came into existence through God's creative word.

"Empty" or "Chaotic"?

This brings us to the second important argument in support of the gap theory. If Genesis 1:2 describes the earth's condition at the time of creation, how do we explain the phrase "waste and void" (*tohu wa-bohu*)? Would an infinitely wise and powerful God have created the earth in such a chaotic condition? The only other places in the Bible where the two words *tohu* and *bohu* appear together (Isa. 34:11 and Jer. 4:23) are passages that speak of divine judgment upon Gentile nations and upon Israel. Does not this indicate that these words must refer to judgment and destruction in Genesis 1:2? Even the word *tohu* (translated "without form" in the K.J.V. and "waste" in the A.S.V.), in the twenty verses where it appears without *bohu* in the Old Testament, is sometimes used in an evil sense.

This is admittedly an impressive argument, for one of the most dependable ways to ascertain the meaning of Hebrew words and phrases is to compare their usage in other passages. Thus, if *tohu* always refers to something evil when used elsewhere in the Old Testament, it would probably have this connotation in Genesis 1:2. But a careful examination of the usage of this word does not support such a meaning. For example, in Job 26:7 we read that God "stretcheth out the north over *empty space* (tohu), and hangeth the earth upon nothing" (ASV). Certainly we are not to find in this verse any suggestion that outer space is basically evil. In some passages the word refers to the wilderness or desert, which is conspicuous for its absence of life (Deut. 32:10; Job 6:18; 12:24; 107:40). In most of the places where the word appears in Isaiah, it is paralleled with such words as "nothing" and "nought."

Of particular interest in this connection is Isaiah 45:18, which has been used as an important proof text for the gap theory. The verse tells us of "the God that formed the earth and made it, that established it and created it not a waste *(tohu)*, that formed it to be inhabited." It has been claimed that the "tohu" condition of the earth in Genesis 1:2 could not have been its original condition, because Isaiah 45:18 says it was *not* created a "tohu." Consequently, God must have originally created an earth replete with living things, and later destroyed it, causing it to *become* "tohu." However, such an interpretation overlooks the true significance of the final phrase in this verse: "formed it to be inhabited." The real point of the passage seems to be that God did not ultimately intend that the world should be devoid of life, but rather that it should be filled with living things. Thus, He did not allow it to *remain* in the empty and formless condition in which He first created it, but in six creative days filled it with living things and fashioned it as a beautiful home for man. The verse thus speaks of God's ultimate purpose in creation, and the contrast in this verse between "tohu" and "inhabited" shows clearly that "tohu" means empty or *uninhabited*, rather than judged, destroyed, or chaotic.

To be sure, the only passages besides Genesis 1:2 where *tohu* and *bohu* appear together—Isaiah 34:11 and Jeremiah 4:23—are placed in contexts which emphasize divine judgment. But even here the basic meaning of *empty* or *uninhabited* fits well. Since God's ultimate purpose for the earth, and particularly the Holy Land, was that it might be *filled with people* (Isa. 45:18; 49:19-20; Zech. 8:5), it would be a clear evidence of His wrath and displeasure for the promised land to become *empty* and *uninhabited* again. The concept of emptiness, therefore, implies divine judgment only when it speaks of the removal of something that is good. On the other hand, when emptiness follows something that is evil, it can be a comparative blessing! An example of this may be found in Christ's work of casting demons out of people (Luke 8:35; cf. Matt. 12:44—"*empty, swept, and garnished*").

In spite of the fact that the phrase *tohu wa-bohu* appears elsewhere in judgment contexts and thus takes on an evil connotation in those passages, the same phrase may have a very different connotation when it appears in a different context. Even advocates of the gap theory admit that a context of divine judgment seems to be missing in the opening verses of Genesis.[5] It is true that the earth was *empty* as far as living things are concerned, and it was devoid of many of the interesting features it later possessed, such as continents, mountains, rivers, and seas; but it was certainly not chaotic, ruined, or judged. Edward J. Young feels that "it would probably be wise to abandon the term 'chaos' as a designation of the conditions set forth in verse two. The threefold statement of circumstances in itself seems to imply order. The material of which this earth consists was at that time covered with water, and darkness was all about. Over the water, however, brooded God's Spirit." [6]

Was the Darkness Evil?

The third major argument used in support of the gap theory concerns the darkness of Genesis 1:2. Since darkness is almost always used as a symbol of sin and judgment in the Scriptures (John 3:19; Jude 13, etc.), and since God did not say that the darkness was "good" (as He did concerning the light—Gen. 1:4), we must assume that God originally created the world in light (Ps. 104:2; I Tim. 6:16) and only later plunged it into darkness because of the sin of angels and Satan.

This, again, is an impressive argument. But all of the biblical evidences need to be taken into consideration. Psalm 104:19-24, for example, makes it quite clear that *physical* darkness (absence of visible light) is not to be considered as inherently evil or as the effect of divine judgment. Speaking of the wonders of the day-night cycle, the Psalmist states: "The sun knowst his going down. *Thou makest* darkness, and it is night, wherein all the beasts of the forest creep forth. The young lions roar after their prey, and seek their food from God. . . . O Jehovah, how manifold are thy works!

The Ruin Reconstruction Theory of Genesis 1:2

In wisdom hast thou made them all: the earth is full of thy riches." If the making of darkness is a revelation of God's wisdom and riches, how can it be inherently evil?

In discussing the opening verses of Genesis, Dr. Young points out the true significance of the term "darkness."

> God gives a name to the darkness, just as he does to the light. Both are therefore good and well-pleasing to him; both are created, although the express creation of the darkness, as of other objects in verse two, is not stated, and both serve his purpose of forming the day. . . . Darkness is recognized in this chapter as a positive good for man. Whatever the precise connotation of the "evening" of each day, it certainly included darkness, and that darkness was for man's good. At times, therefore, darkness may typify evil and death; at other times it is to be looked upon as a positive blessing.[7]

It would seem reasonable to assume that the reason why God did not see that the darkness was good is that darkness is not a specific entity, or a thing, but it is rather an absence of something, namely, light. Perhaps it is for this same reason that God did not see that the "firmament" (expanse) of the second creative day was good. It, too, was a rather negative entity, being the empty space between the upper and lower waters. The fact that physical darkness is not incompatible with the presence and blessing of God is evidenced by the statement that "the Spirit of God moved upon the face of the waters" in the midst of this primeval darkness. In the words of the Psalmist, "Even the darkness hideth not from thee, but the night shineth as the day: the darkness and the light are both alike to thee" (Ps. 139:12).

How Many Creative Acts in Genesis One?

The fourth major supporting argument for the gap theory is built upon a supposed distinction between the verbs "created" (*bara*) and "made" (*asah*). For example, the second footnote in the Scofield Reference Bible states: "But three *creative* acts of God are recorded in this chapter: (1) the heavens and the earth, v. 1; (2) animal life, v. 21; and (3) human life, vs. 26, 27. The first creative act refers to the dateless past, and gives scope for all the geologic ages." Thus, the vegetation of Genesis 1:11 was not *created* on the third day, but was simply "brought forth" from the earth again following the catastrophic judgment of Genesis 1:2. Likewise, the sun, moon, and stars of Genesis 1:16 were not actually *created* on the fourth day, but were simply "made to appear" through the thick, dark clouds that covered the earth following its devastation.

It is true that the verb "made (*asah*) in Genesis 1:16 ("God made the two great lights") is not the same as the verb "created" in Genesis 1:1. Nevertheless, it seems rather obvious that these two verbs are used synonymously throughout the chapter, for God "created" (*bara*) the great sea-monsters (vs. 21), and He "made" (*asah*) the beasts of the field (vs. 25). Surely we are not to find any significant difference here. The sea-monsters were created supernaturally by God, and so were the beasts of the earth. Likewise, in 1:26 God said, "Let us *make* man in our image." But in the next verse we read that God "*created* man in his own image." Once again the verb seems to be used synonymously. Therefore, 1:16 must refer to the *original* creation of the sun, moon, and stars. If God had intended to convey to us the idea that these heavenly bodies were created on the first day, or earlier, but only "appeared" on the fourth day (presumably by a removal of clouds), the verb "to appear" could easily have been used (see vs. 9). Similarly, when we read that God commanded the earth to "put forth" grass, herbs, and fruit trees, we are to understand this as referring to their supernatural creation; even as God's command to the waters to "swarm with swarms of living creatures" (vs. 20) is explained in the following verse to mean that "God created (bara) . . . every living creature that moved, wherewith the waters swarmed." For the sake of variety and fullness of expression, then, different verbs are used to convey the concept of supernatural creation. The context makes it clear that these verbs are used synonomously throughout the chapter, so that not only animal life and human life, but also plant life and the heavenly bodies were created by God in their appropriate days.

Other Arguments

In addition to the four major arguments for the gap theory discussed above, one frequently hears the claim that the phrase "replenish the earth" in Genesis 1:28 implies that the earth was once filled but now had to be filled *again* (re-plenished, or re-filled). But the verb in the Hebrew text (*maleh*) simply means "to fill," with no suggestion of repetition.

It is also frequently claimed that Ezekiel 28:13-14 demands an originally glorious world before the "waste and void" of Genesis 1:2, for it speaks of Satan as dwelling in "Eden, the garden of God . . .

the holy mountain of God" and walking "up and down in the midst of the stones of fire" before his rebellion against God. But it seems clear from a comparison with Daniel 2:45 and Isaiah 14:13 that "the holy mountain of God" must refer to the third heaven of God's immediate presence and not to an earthly domain. It should be noted that Satan was "cast . . . out of the mountain of God *to the ground*" (Ezek. 28:16-17; cf. Isa. 14:12). Apparently the Lord Jesus Christ spoke of this event when He said: "I beheld Satan *fallen* as lightning *from heaven*" (Luke 10:18). It should also be noted that "Eden, the garden of God" was not a garden with trees, flowers, and streams. It was composed of precious stones and "stones of fire" (Ezek. 28:13, 14, 16). When we compare this with the description of the Holy City of Revelation 21:10-21, with its various precious stones, we must conclude that Ezekiel's "garden of God" refers not to an earthly Eden back in Genesis 1:1, but to a heavenly one, from which Satan was cast down to the earth. When God created the "heavens" at the beginning of the first day of creation week, He apparently created all the angelic beings (including the unfallen Satan), who were thus on hand to sing together and shout for joy at the creation of the earth (Job 38:7). Some time after creation week and before the temptation of Eve, Satan rebelled against his Creator. The visible earthly effect of his fall would thus not have been a catastrophe in Genesis 1:2, but the Edenic curse of Genesis 3, which he inflicted upon the entire earth because Adam and Eve chose to believe and obey Satan rather than God (Rom. 8:20-23).

Six Days of Creation

One clear biblical proof that creation week was *not* preceded by a divine judgment is found in Exodus 20:11. In this fourth commandment, God said to Israel: "Six days shalt thou labor, and do all thy work . . . for in six days Jehovah made heaven and earth, the sea, and all that in them is." The gap theory holds that the heavens, the earth, and the sea were created *before* the six days of Genesis One. But this passage asserts that *everything* was made by God *in six days*. The fact that the verb "made" (*asah*) is used here does not mean that the earth was "refashioned" in six days, for we have already seen that this verb is synonymous with *bara* when used in a creation context.

We would agree with advocates of the gap theory that "the earth has undergone a cataclysmic change as a result of a divine judgment.

The face of the earth bears everywhere the marks of such a catastrophe."[8] But we would identify this catastrophe with the great universal flood of Noah's day, which not only occupies three entire chapters of Genesis, but also is referred to by David (Ps. 29:10), Isaiah (Is. 54:9), Christ (Matt. 25:39), and Peter (I Peter 3:20; II Peter 2:5; 3:6). It was through the vast and complex current patterns of this year-long deluge that the living creatures of the entire world were buried forever in the great fossil strata that encircle the globe.[9] It is *this* catastrophe that provides for us the God-given answer to the false uniformitarianism of these last days (II Peter 3:4) and thus effectively foreshadows the final universal destruction of all things by fire at the climax of the day of the Lord.

NOTES AND REFERENCES

1. As early as 1814, Dr. Thomas Chalmers of Edinburgh University was promoting the views of George Cuvier, and became the first great popularizer of the "gap theory." See *The Works of Thomas Chalmers on Natural Theology*, Glasgow: Wm. Collins & Co., n.d. See also Francis C. Haber, *The Age of the World: Moses to Darwin* (Baltimore: The Johns Hopkins Press, 1959), pp. 201-204.
2. For a recent defense of the pre-Adamic race view, see Gleason L. Archer, *A Survey of Old Testament Introduction* (Chicago: Moody Press, 1964), pp. 188-189.
3. Milford Henkel, "Fundamental Christianity and Evolution" (Th.M. thesis for the Winona Lake School of Theology, 1948), cited by Edwin K. Gedney, "Geology and the Bible," Chapter III in *Modern Science and Christian Faith* (Wheaton, Ill.: Van Kampen Press, 2nd ed. rev., 1950), p. 49.
4. F. F. Bruce, "And the Earth Was Without Form and Void," *Journal of the Transactions of the Victoria Institute*, Vol. 78, 1946), pp. 21-23.
5. J. H. Kurtz, *Manual of Sacred History*, 1888, p. xxvi. Cited by Curtis C. Mitchell, "A Biblical and Theological Study of the Gap Theory" (B.D. thesis for Talbot Theological Seminary, 1962), p. 45.
6. Edward J. Young, *Studies in Genesis One* (Nutley, N. J.: Presbyterian and Reformed Publishing Company, 1964), p. 13.
7. *Ibid.*, pp. 21, 35.
8. *Scofield Reference Bible* (New York: Oxford University Press, 1917), Footnote No. 3 on Genesis 1:2.
9. For a recent discussion of the implications of the biblical doctrine of the Flood, see Whitcomb and Morris, *The Genesis Flood* (Nutley, N. J.: Presbyterian and Reformed Publishing Company, 1961). See also John W. Klotz, *Genes, Genesis, and Evolution* (St. Louis: Concordia Publishing House, 1955); Paul A. Zimmerman, ed., *Darwin, Evolution, and Creation* (St. Louis: Concordia Publishing House, 1959); and Henry M. Morris, *The Twilight of Evolution* (Grand Rapids: Baker Book House, 1963).

V

THERE WAS EVENING—AND THERE WAS MORNING

RICHARD G. KORTHALS

"In the beginning, God created the heavens and the earth. And the earth was without form and void and darkness was upon the face of the deep; and the Spirit of God moved upon the face of the waters, and God said, 'Let there be light.' And there was light, and God saw that the light was good, and God separated the light from the darkness. God called the light day, and the darkness he called night. And there was evening and there was morning, one day" (Gen. 1:1-5).

> Away out there alone, above,
> Without a thing to make it of,
> The world was made without a flaw,
> Without a hammer or a saw.
> Without a bit of wood or stone
> Without a bit of flesh or bone,
> Without a board or nail or screw,
> Or anything to nail it to.
> Without a foothold or a trace
> Of anything at all but space.
> The only thing the Lord could do
> Was simply speak a word or two
> And if the story told is true,
> The world came boldly into view.

And if the story told is true.... Two centuries ago the mere hint that this story could possibly be false would have been sufficient to brand the speaker a heretic. Today the acceptance of this story of the creation as true can result in the word "fool" being attached to your name. Why has this almost violent change in attitude taken place—and who, if anybody, is correct?

The why can probably best be answered by quoting a recent Life Nature Library publication entitled *Evolution*. The following is written on page 10 concerning evolution:

> Darwin did not invent the concept. But when he started his

career, the doctrine of special creation could be doubted only by heretics. When he finished, the fact of evolution could be denied only by the abandonment of reason. He demolished the old theory with two books. One, published in 1859, he titled *On the Origin of Species by Means of Natural Selection, or the Preservation of Favored Races in the Struggle for Life.* The second, published in 1871, he called *The Descent of Man, and Selection in Relation to Sex.*

The books did not so much undermine the old, comfortable order of things as simply overwhelm it; nobody had ever bothered to try documenting the other side—instantaneous creation—with such a painstaking built structure of evidence. At two strokes Darwin gave modern science a rationale, a philosophy, an evolutionary, and thereby revolutionary, way of thinking about the universe and everything in it, and incidentally established himself as the Newton of biology. But at the same time he dealt mankind's preening self-esteem a body blow from which it may never recover, and for which Darwin may never be quite forgiven. For it is one thing for man to be told (and want to believe) that he was created in the literal image of God. It is quite another for him to be told (and have to accept) that he is, while unique, merely the culmination of a billion years of ever-evolving life, and that he must trace his godhood down a gnarled and twisted family tree through mammals and amphibians to the lowly fish and thence to some anonymous, if miraculous, Adam molecule.[1]

Was Darwin right? Is the world, and its inhabitants, the result of a cosmic accident? Are we the descendants of some lower order of mammal, and as such then constantly evolving into a more perfect form of mankind? If we realize that Darwin was a scientist, committed to the method of science, *and if we accept this method*, then we must answer yes to the question regarding evolution. It is very evident in studying history that Darwin was a product of his time, a time when science came into its own. Had Darwin not developed the concept of evolution, then somebody else would have. Therefore, if I must think as a pure scientist, committed to using only the methods of science, then I must agree with him—I really have little choice.

Should we then re-examine our position on creation? Are we justified in having people research biblical documents line by line, word by word, letter by letter, looking for hidden and obscure meanings which would enable us to re-interpret the first chapters of Genesis? Is a well-known Bible Study course correct when it spends an entire lesson on discussion of the various forms of biblical writing, namely historical, poetical, personification, fable, allegory, imagery, and symbolism, a discussion which is carried out in order that this question can then be asked concerning Genesis two and three: "What literary medium do we find here, historical event in poetic form, imagery/personification? Whatever our findings, barring a wooden literalism, our conclusions on the overarching message of this portion of scripture will be the same."

Must we continue in our attempt to modify scriptural interpretation so as to bring about agreement with scientific theories, changing days to eons, miracles to modified natural events? Perhaps theologians— or you as Christian Day School teachers—may disagree, but my answer to all of these questions, my answer as a layman with a strong belief in religion, is a resounding no. I feel a conservative position— a literal interpretation—on creation and miracles is as justified today as it was centuries ago. I can see no reason for a change.

I imagine that if I could examine each of your minds right now I would find this thought present: "Well—here is a real two-faced individual—a true middle-of-the-roader, fence-riding type. First he says it is, and then it ain't—first that evolution is true, and then that the literal interpretation of Genesis is true. Come now, it must be one or the other."

I agree with you, it must be one or the other. If you are puzzled, then it is because you missed the fact that I prefaced my statements of agreement with the method of analysis being used. In the one case, it was scientific, in the other religious. This question of methodology, and the implications it carries, is, in my estimation, the crux of the entire problem. To explain why, I would like to review something which you are already familiar with, but which is so important to our understanding that we should have a common ground from which to start. This is the definition of what many outstanding philosophers feel are the three main kinds, spheres, or domains of knowledge. These are philosophy, science, and religion. Let us begin by defining science, and describing its limitations.

If we were looking for one word which would best describe the methods of science it would be "investigate." All sciences look into things and discover data which are not a part of the common experience of mankind. Now what do I mean by this "common experience of mankind"? By this I mean the experiences that you and I, our ancestors, our children—men of all times and ages—have in common—experiences we have simply by being awake, not looking for anything, not observing any method. If I clap my hands, snap my fingers, drop a book, you know subconsciously what has happened, even if you didn't witness the event. We have all seen and heard a storm, seen things grow and die, observed changes in nature, watched things move. These are simple experiences which everyone has had—they are the common experiences of mankind.

If you stay with the common experiences of mankind you will never develop sciences. Science deals with that which is on the periphery—outside the common experiences of mankind. It investigates, using telescope, microscope, photographic emulsion, or nuclear reaction. A scientist forms a hypothetical theory as to why something happens, and then sets out to prove it is correct by conducting experiments, using special equipment such as mentioned previously. The experiences which he has are generally limited to a small number of people, they are uncommon—or unique—experiences.

If we were then to define the tools, or the methods, of science, we would say they are observations which affect the senses of the observer—senses such as sight, smell, touch or hearing—causing sensations which he must then analyze and formulate using his power of reason. Because this is the method of science, then it is limited to describing—not *explaining why*, but *describing how*. Science by its method stays on the surface of reality, dealing with the apparent or phenomenal, and as a result there are a host of questions which it cannot answer.

Take a very simple question in which you many be interested as teachers, one concerning knowledge. What are the different kinds of knowledge—what does it mean to know? How do you know? What is knowing in itself? We could investigate from now till the end of time and not answer these questions. You can answer them by thinking, but not by looking.

Neither can science answer questions which require placing a value on something. It cannot tell you whether your occupation is good or bad, whether a society is exemplary or corrupt. And science will never develop to the extent where it can answer these questions. These are questions which are beyond the competence of scientific inquiry—the method used is inadequate, it is not appropriate.

This is not to say that science is bad, for this would be far from the truth. Science is extremely useful, but its utility lies in its ability to produce—the production of goods and services which contribute the mastery of the physical world. Because of this ability science powerful, but it is a tremendous power that by itself cannot and does not tell us where to go, or what to do.

Philosophy, on the other hand, produces nothing physical, and but it also serves a high purpose—a good—in that it can answer many of the questions which science cannot touch. The philosopher makes use of the common experiences of mankind in attempting to describe the reason behind all events. Philosophy and philosophical inquiries are not investigative. The philosopher needs no data, no special instruments. He is an armchair thinker who can sit in a dark room and contemplate the common experiences of mankind. His question is not how things operate, but rather what they are—and why they are as we find them. At first it would appear that he has little value, since nothing physical comes out of this room—he doesn't make anything. However, if we use this line of reasoning, then there are many things which have no value. As an example, consider a road map. It contains knowledge, yet it never makes anything. Yet that map can become our most precious possession when we are in strange territory—for it directs us where to go (if we can read it).

Science is concerned with phenomena—philosophy delves into the what, the why of things—the underlying existence. In science reason serves sense. In philosophy sense serves reason—the main work is done by reason, not sense. Because of this the very questions science cannot answer, philosophy can. As a example, suppose you all ask yourselves this question: "What is the difference between science and philosophy?" You can agree with what I have said, or you can say that all this is wrong and instead give some other answer. But if you give any answer to that question at all, then you do it as a philosopher, not a scientist. There is no method whereby you can scientifically answer that question. Just pause and think for a moment. Could you possibly—by any means of investigation, experiment, or laboratory research—discover the difference between science and philosophy? Obviously not!

Philosophy can solve the questions which require the establishment of values. The philosopher can answer questions concerning human happiness, whether a form of government is good or bad—a war just or unjust—your job beneficial or harmful to mankind. He can demonstrate that democracy is, in terms of justice, the only perfectly just form of government. These are questions that are philosophical, but totally untouchable by the methods of science.

So much for science and philosophy, their methods and equipment, usefulness, and limitations. Now where does the third realm of knowledge—namely religion—fit into this picture? What is its method—its usefulness? If there is religion, distinct as a body of knowledge, practically and speculatively, then what would it be like? There is no distinction possible between religion on one hand and science and philosophy on the other, unless that distinction is made in the separate realms of faith as opposed to reason. Allow me to explain to you what I mean. Over here, science and philosophy are both knowledge, obtainable by the exercise of man's faculties, his mind, his senses, and his reason. Whatever man obtains is gotten through his own efforts. He observes, analyzes, invents techniques, and performs experiments—acquiring knowledge through his own hard work—using his natural faculties.

If religion is nothing but some other form of inquiry using natural means, then it can be reduced to these two. For religion to be distinct it must consist of knowledge which man receives—but does not acquire by his own efforts—and is this not the definition of revelation? A true religion claims to say something which could not possibly be said if it had not been revealed by God. They do not claim to know it by investigation, historical analysis, or historical research. They claim to know it as a gift from God. The knowledge is literally handed down to them.

Religion, having this revelation, this gift from God, is enabled through this means to answer questions which the scientist and the philosopher cannot begin to solve. I could, as examples of these questions, take the Christian doctrines of the Trinity or the Incarnation—but I don't want to. Instead I would like to take a doctrine which you may feel does not belong in this class, the doctrine of creation. Neither philosopher nor scientist can tell you with the slightest degree of certainty whether or not the world had a beginning. As a Christian, however, you have an answer. You know the world began—it had a beginning—for God has chosen to reveal to you the answer. That answer is found in the first verse of the first chapter of Genesis: "In the beginning God created the heavens and the earth." It is an answer which is impossible to prove by reason or investigation. If you have an answer to that question, then you have it on the basis of your religion—and your religious faith.

This means that a body of knowledge can be properly classified as a religion only if this faith is present. If you do not admit to faith, then forget religion. Following Christ as a great moral leader and teacher, even imitating His exemplary character, is not religion. You might as well follow the moral teachings of Socrates, for all you have is a moral philosophy.

Three bodies of knowledge, each separate and distinct, each with a method, each with a purpose, each with limitations. On the basis of this common understanding let us now go back and re-examine the questions asked earlier—and the answers given.

What about the statement made to the effect that if we realize that Darwin was a scientist, and if we accept his method, then we must agree with him? Did we not just agree that only religion could answer questions concerning the beginning of the world? Yes, this is true, for Darwin was stepping out of his field of competence in attempting to answer this question—science was overstepping its boundaries. Then doesn't agreement with Darwin and those following him indirectly acknowledge acceptance of the unbiblical theory of evolution? Yes it does—if, and please notice this key phrase—*if we accept the application of his method to this question.* Let me explain why.

I would like to have your full cooperation during the next several minutes. This may prove extremely difficult—but please make the attempt—try to the greatest extent possible. Try to cleanse your mind of all previous ideas and concepts, and for a moment imagine that you are a pure scientist, committed to using only the methods of science. This will mean using only observable data—and your senses to reason and interpret it. You have never heard of the Bible—and even if you did, your method forbids the use of this knowledge. As you are sitting in your seat you let your thoughts stray, and you begin to think and wonder about the origin of the world and its inhabitants. You know you must depend upon data and reason, but this doesn't trouble you, for you are well trained, highly intelligent, and have a wealth of data at your disposal. And so you start correlating facts—forming hypotheses—making assumptions. You look at the world's inhabitants around you, noting differences and similarities—seeing the effects of mutations, the results of hybrids. You see dairy cattle producing twice as much milk as their ancestors—blocky beef cattle as opposed to the rangy Texas Longhorn—all changes which have been brought about because of selective breeding. You see horses of sturdier stock, chickens which lay only large white eggs, children who are larger than their parents. Suddenly the thought comes to you that everything is improving, is evolving from some lower and less perfect form—suddenly you have the key, a hypothetical answer to the question of the origin of life. You see with clarity that everything seen on earth today has evolved from some lower form of life. But where do you start? You, as a scientist, can use only the laws of nature around you, and using these you extrapolate back through time to the only place where you can stop—a single cell—formed by pure chance. You—restricted to using only the methods of science—have no choice.

You have formed your hypothesis—your theory or idea—now you must substantiate it. First you realize that the process you are visualizing and proposing is extremely slow, therefore the world must be billions of years old. How can you show this? Well, if you say that the earth was formed as a smooth, homogeneous ball, then you can look at the Grand Canyon, and calculate the millions of years it took the Colorado River to carve this chasm from the smooth surface. Your estimate is made using the present measurable erosion rates as your yardstick.

You also realize that you must show that a common tie exists between various forms of animal life. You notice that there is a similarity between some bone structures—for instance the two bones present in the forearms of many animals. Backbones are similar, as are the fetal forms in some instances. You propose that this is evidence demonstrating that the animals—including man—must have a common ancestor. Ancient fossil remains are found in rocks. In some cases you use the rocks to establish the age of fossil remains —in other cases, where there is an apparent discontinuity in the rock structure, the fossil establishes the age of the rocks. You use these fossils as evidence that at one time this was the only form of life which existed—and therefore everything must have evolved from it.

So you—in your own mind—using only your reason to evaluate data—gradually develop your theory. True, there are many gaps in your observations, ideas which you cannot substantiate with actual evidence—but as you go along you make what you feel are reasonable assumptions—and complete the picture using to a certain extent your imagination. With the pattern developing, you decide to consolidate your thoughts by putting them in writing. Then, at your friend's persuasion, you write a book—which is eagerly read by all who have been looking for a solution for this particularly difficult problem dealing with origins. Soon other books are written—some by pseudo scientists who popularize your complex theory in a paperback version—and who in the process somehow have forgotten to put in the "if's" which you so carefuly included. So suddenly the assumptions you made—the guesses and the musings, the dreams and the imaginations—become fact, and anyone who doesn't believe them is either obstinate or biased. You find yourself a celebrity, acclaimed by all for having found the answer to the mystery surrounding the question of man's origin.

"But," you say, "I don't want to go back that far. I will base part of my theory on biblical knowledge, and will assume that at least man was created." How can you—for remember our initial agreement? You are a pure scientist, utilizing only the methods which that body of knowledge can use. Therefore you cannot stop at that point in time—you have no justification for such an assumption—no valid reason. You must go back to a single cell, because your reason tells you—after evaluating available evidence—that man could not instantaneously be created out of nothing. There are no scientific data to substantiate this—nor is there an experiment which you can perform which will duplicate it. It is against every law of nature in existence today—and these laws are the tools of your trade, immutable laws which you use to project present day findings into the past. The very idea is unreasonable and incomprehensible.

This is true not only with respect to the question of the origin of life; you must also assume that the earth started out as a homogeneous sphere, smooth and untarnished, with all elements in their basic form. You really have no choice, for where else can you start? Could you say that the Grand Canyon was 1000 feet deep when the world was formed—or 1627 feet deep—or that it had a depth of 2369 feet? You must start somewhere—and that somewhere must be a smooth surface if you are to substantiate your arguments.

So now do you see why the methods of science dictate an evolutionary theory? Reason, senses, and observable data all tell us there can be no other way. If you were all scientists I would stop right here, for though you may have different ideas concerning the details, yet the basic concept is one you would accept and uphold.

But you are not scientists, you are people with religious beliefs—people who not only use reason, but also have faith in God's revelation to us. As such you are told in the revealed Word that the earth was created by God—and that He created us in His image—

breathed into our nostrils the breath of life. As a result of this knowledge a struggle exists in your mind, a mental conflict which says you should accept one or the other idea, but not both. Which will it be?

Much hinges on the validity of scientific claims—the amount of truth which can be attached to the theories presently being advanced. Let me state now that the theory of evolution will never—in my estimation—be completely disproved. In fact, "evolution" or variation does take place—we can see it in nature around us. God did not necessarily create all the varieties of dogs, cats, and even humans which are present in the world today. Most of these "evolved." But I firmly believe that He did create the various kinds—biologically speaking. The theory that things evolved from a single source, and that the rattlesnake, butterfly, eagle, whale, and man all have the same common ancestor is far from proved. This is evidenced by the fact that scientists themselves have trouble finding a theory which is agreeable to all.

I have neither the time today—nor the ability—to present all the arguments against single source evolution. I am neither a biologist, a geologist, nor a paleontologist. If you want specific facts, then I would like to refer you to two excellent books on this subject. One is entitled *Darwin, Evolution, and Creation*, edited by Dr. Paul A. Zimmerman and published by Concordia Publishing House, St. Louis, Mo. The other is *The Genesis Flood* by Henry Morris and John Whitcomb, and published by Presbyterian and Reformed Publishing Company, Nutley, N. J. However, as an engineer familiar with scientific methods, I would like to explain to you several general weaknesses.

First let us examine the question of assumptions. How can these lead us astray? Let me give you a very simple example. Suppose we are going down an interstate highway in the middle of the desert, miles from nowhere, at 11 o'clock in the morning, and come upon a car which has just run out of gas and is standing deserted. The question arises as to how many hours the man had been driving since his last gas stop, since it is considered a violation to impede traffic. You are a scientist, so you look at the gas tank and determine it has a 20-gallon capacity. The car is exactly like yours, and you know you have been getting 15 miles per gallon. The speed limit is 60 miles per hour, and almost everyone drives at this rate, so your car has been consuming 4 gallons per hour. Using this data you estimate then that he must have driven 5 hours since his last stop. You get into your car, and pretty soon encounter the driver trudging down the road. Anxious to demonstrate to your partner the validity of your assumptions and the wisdom of your scientific analysis, you stop, roll down your window, and ask the disgruntled and footsore hiker how long he had been driving before running out of gas. "Thirty minutes," he angrily shouts back. "Next time I'm going to fill up the gas tank when I stop, and not put in only 3 gallons—and I will check the gas lines for leaks." You turn your embarrassed countenance toward your partner, who is chuckling over your error—and admit you made a mistake—not in calculations—but in assumptions. Yes, your assumptions, which seemed so valid and factual when you made them, were wrong.

The theory of evolution is based upon many assumptions. The first and foremost is that there was no special creation. It is also based in part upon the assumption of uniformitarianism, unchanging rates. But allow me to make another assumption—the assumption that God created the world and all its inhabitants in 6 days. And now let us imagine that Adam was a scientist interested in determining the age of the earth. He starts his research on the 8th day after creation, in and around the garden of Eden. He looks at himself and Eve, and, realizing that they are both mature individuals, states that they and the earth are at least 20 years old. He cuts down a tree in order to build a fire, and counts the growth rings. According to this, the earth is at least 139 years old. He and Eve stroll down to the river banks, where he notices the deep channel cut by the stream. By carefully measuring the erosion rate, he estimates and concludes that 5,000 years have gone by since the stream started as a tiny trickle. They pause and marvel at the magnificent mountains in the distance, watching the sun as it slowly sinks beneath the peaks. He knows that internal pressures within the earth are slowly pushing these mountains higher—and, using the present established rate, he calculates that the mountain range is at least 1.5 billion years old. The next day they explore a canyon started 750,000 years ago by a river and marvel at the layers of rock, some formed almost 3 billion years in the past, according to his geologic time scale, which is based upon rock formation phenomena. He sees fossils imbedded in some of the rock—and wonders what conditions on this earth were like 1 billion years ago when this was the only form of life which was present. They stumble upon a cave and find bones which a carbon check shows are 10,000 years old. He taps a rock with his hammer until it breaks, and finds therein a mixture of uranium and lead. A quick radiological test and he knows that at least 1 billion years have elapsed since this rock was formed . . . And so Adam, the scientist, determines the age of the world upon which he is living—a world which according to his reasoning, observations, calculations, and assumptions, is at least 3 billion years old—yet it is a world which was created just 8 days earlier.

"Absurd," you say, "you are prejudiced and biased. Why should God create a world in that condition?" Is it? Not everything I said may be true, and much of it such as the fossils in the rocks, and bones in the cave, we have reason to believe were deposited during the cataclysm known as Noah's Flood and later on in major upheavals of nature. Indeed many of the layers of stratified or sedimentary rock were deposited during this period, thus giving the appearance of great age. But the idea is the same, and God indeed might have created a world exactly as it looks now with every appearance of great age. Only by His revelation do we know that many of the earth's features are not part of His original creation. This assumption of a built-in apparent age may not be reasonable according to our senses—but it certainly can be true. It is just as valid to make this assumption as it is to assume that the earth was formed in a "big bang" and that all life evolved from a chance encounter between the right atoms.

The only way that this assumption can be disproved is for science to prove their theory without a shadow of a doubt, and this will never be done. It would take an eye witness account to prove that the creation theory is wrong—and yet, strange as it may seem, all written history indicates otherwise. The material evidence which we do have to work with can be shaped and interpreted to prove almost any theory you would care to advance. This fact is quite evident when we see the number of theories which do exist.

As an example, consider current theories concerning the origin of the universe. One group vigorously upholds Lemaitre's Big Bang idea, while the other group vehemently claims this is wrong, and adheres to the Steady State Universe of Hoyle and his colleagues. Allan Broms, a scientist, in his book, *Our Emerging Universe*, comments on the latter and says: "He does not tell us how new matter comes into being, but asks us (at least for the time being) to take its continuous creation on faith (scientific faith, that is), which of course means that we will take it all back the instant any positive fact gives us the slightest excuse. Furthermore, he does not explain why this accumulation of new matter should push the older matter more and more apart to give us the expanding Universe, but again asks for another bit of scientific faith, subject to the same proviso. And when we look dubious over taking so much on faith, he properly reminds us that we ourselves have no way of explaining how matter otherwise came to be (even originally, suddenly, and in a lump), and that we are taking the Big Bang itself very nearly on faith." . . . And we say it takes too much faith to accept Genesis One literally?

The same can be said about the origin of life. Here you must accept the philosophy of uniformitarianism. Physical processes both on earth and in the earth are thought to be subject to unchanging natural laws, and therefore more or less continuous and uniform over the past—hence the word "uniformitarianism." Once the assumption is accepted, one can study actual processes and extrapolate these into the geological past to interpret our factual findings, forming them into a genetical, historical picture. The implications of uniformitarianism in the search for the origin of life on earth are clear. You look for natural causes of the same character as are in operation at the present time. You do not—and cannot—envision some sudden event which caused life to appear all at once as a full fledged phenomenon in every corner of the earth. Rather, the origin of life will have covered an enormous time span if measured against human standards. During this period development will have been slow, almost beyond imagination.

How firm is this theory—this assumption? Allow me to quote from a book written by M. G. Rutten, a professor of Geology, entitled *The Geological Aspects of the Origin of Life on Earth*, a book published in 1962:

> So on the one hand we geologists have the possibility of studying the evolution of life on earth, of paleontological research, with a wealth of factual data. Although the gaps in the paleontological records are so large that anyone with a bias can still make a case against natural evolution, the development of paleontological research clearly points towards its general acceptance. Many gaps in the records have been lately filled by lucky finds, and we feel sure what this research is leading up to.
>
> On the other hand, there is the problem of the origin of life on earth. Here the data are extremely poor. The time lapsed is so enormous that it is difficult to prove anything at all, because

the records are not only incomplete in the extreme, but also often changed beyond recognition by younger events. Moreover, such research implies a doubt toward popular views on creation and thereby provokes criticism on immaterial grounds from the side of church people: criticism which cannot be effectively answered owing to lack of data. . . .

And we are at times ashamed and apologetic of our faith in Genesis One?

Neither are historical dates firmly established. C. W. Ceram, in his book *Gods, Graves, and Scholars*, writes this:

How far the scholars of the West have departed from Manetho's chronology is shown by the following array of dates assigned, through the years, by different authorities to the unification of Egypt by King Menes, an event that marked the real beginning of Egyptian history and may be taken as the earliest happenings of dynastic significance: Champollian, 5867 B.C.; Lesueur, 5770; Bokh, 5702; Unger, 5613; Mariette, 5004; Brugsch, 4455; Lauth, 4157; Chabas, 4000; Lepsius, 3892; Bunsen, 3623; Eduard Meyer, 3180; Wilkinson, 2320; Palmer, 2224. Recently the date has been pushed back again, Breasted dates Menes at 3400, George Steindorff at 3200, and the newest research at 2900. It is significant that all dates become more difficult to determine the farther back one goes into history.

And we struggle to find a means whereby we can logically change the meaning of the word "day" in Genesis One?

I could go on for hours citing similar examples—how Hooton in his book *Up From the Ape* devotes an entire section to explaining the tremendous significance of the Piltdown Man—a fossil we now know to have been a fraud—how White in *The Warfare of Science with Religion* flagrantly misinterprets the significance of the Chaldean cuneiforms, using them to prove the Bible is a myth, when actually they substantiate the Bible. But I feel I have shown you enough to make you realize that the scientific theory of the origin of the universe and the life it holds has not been proven—and furthermore will never be proven on this earth. It is a theory which must be accepted on faith—faith in science and its method.

But why, you ask, is this theory so readily accepted, while religious faith is scoffed at? The answer lies in the dominant role played by science in our lives today, and in the philosophy which is accepted and adhered to by most people. The philosophy is that originated by David Hume, and is called positivism. This doctrine claims that the only knowledge that has any accessible validity is the knowledge obtained by the positive—or empirical and experimental—sciences. It asserts that science gives us this positive knowledge—and denies that we can have any other knowledge but this. Reason, not faith, is the key word. Therefore religious beliefs are automatically false, since we cannot conduct a controlled experiment to prove them. To many, science is the only knowledge, serving in addition as a philosophy and religion. It can provide the answer to the common question of our times—namely "Show me."

So today to question science is almost tantamount to being labeled a heretic. Question their theories—and your beliefs are ridiculed—your faith in other forms of knowledge made to appear groundless and foolish. In some circles to be unscientific is to be automatically wrong. The Church, subjected to an almost overwhelming intellectual pressure, starts to look for methods of obtaining relief. The first avenue explored is that of modifying doctrine and interpretation to make it more reasonable—to appeal to reason—to agree with science and its theories. You, as teachers, are subjected to this temptation probably more than anyone else—since you, of necessity, teach both religion and science.

Where do we start to modify? At what appears to be our most vulnerable point, of course, the doctrine of creation. After all, what difference does it make if I believe the earth is 4 billion years old? Isn't evolution also a form of creation, evidence of the power and wisdom of Almighty God? Since evolved man is constantly improving, he could never have been perfect and sinless, therefore Genesis three becomes a poetical way of explaining why things aren't perfect today . . . The flood? Well, you know how events magnify when told and retold. After all, Moses had to rely on stories handed down from generation to generation. In the process a small local inundation becomes a world-wide flood. Reason tells us there just isn't enough water to cover the entire earth . . . God leading the children of Israel in a pillar of cloud and fire? What reasonable explanation can be found for this? Well, the Israelites, in their fear, wanted to believe God was near, so they imagined this, and the writings of Moses reflect the people's imagination and impression. Actually, the smoke and fire came from a distant volcano—they just thought it was leading them, and God was using a natural phenomenon to help them . . . The waters of the River Jordan parted? Now this could have happened if, for instance, a large rock slide upstream had temporarily held back the waters. True, God caused the avalanche, but Joshua got carried away in his description. He omitted the real facts.

And so we make the Bible reasonable—changing our interpretation to what we feel is acceptable to the public—using as our excuse the fact that none of these changes are affecting beliefs necessary to salvation. We never give to God the almighty power so rightly His—the power to act in ways different from His usual ones, that is, miraculously—because we feel our people will never accept this. *But where do we stop?* Are the doctrines of the Trinity—the Immaculate Conception—the Virgin Birth—the dual nature of Christ—the Resurrection—the Ascension—salvation by grace through faith—are these doctrines reasonable? How do you tell someone to have faith in these doctrines, when you have trained him to use his reason throughout the rest of the Bible? How do you explain to him that in one case we accept the literal translation, and in the next we modify? Would it not appear to the outsider that the church itself is unsure of what to believe?

The argument is often advanced that we must "stay with the times"—we must revise our teachings if we are to appeal to the modern man. There is a tendency to react to this philosophy in a manner symptomatic of our times, we try to make it easy for a potential member to join—or our members to believe—asking little of them by way of mental effort. We try to make everything reasonable—instead of appealing to their faith—instead of taking the time and effort to go through a logical explanation. We are afraid we might turn away a prospect by unreasonable demands—so every effort is made to make the instructions "easy to swallow."

In the process we try to bring God down to man, rather than taking man up to God—we try to give him a God whose action and power can be understood. We feel we are helping—and yet are we not actually depriving? For I want a God whose wisdom, power, attributes, and might are so great that my frail human mind cannot begin to understand Him. I want a God who fills me with such wonder and awe that I feel compelled to fall on my face and worship Him. I want a God so all-knowing and powerful that He can reverse the forces of nature, if necessary, to protect me. I want a God so loving that He will forgive me again—and again—and again.

To have this kind of God I must have faith—a faith which He gives me—using as His instruments the pastors, teachers, and mem-

There Was Evening—And There Was Morning 57

bers of His Church. Are we doing all we can to aid in instilling this faith in our people today? Faith, not works—was the battle cry of the Reformation. Faith, not reason—should be the watchword of tomorrow. Thank God our church has adhered to a sound, fundamental, and conservative doctrine in the past, a doctrine based on faith. Pray God that she may continue to do so in the future.

A question you may rightly ask concerns how this applies to you. Does this all mean that you should ignore reason in your instructions? Should we, for instance, forbid the teaching of the evolution theory in our parochial school system? No—for reason is the tool of science and philosophy, one they will certainly be called upon to use as they continue their education. Evolution, for instance, should not only be mentioned, it should be taught as a required subject, in my way of thinking. Unless we do this, the student will feel we are trying to suppress the truth, and will be all the more prone to accept the theory for fact in advanced education courses. But when it is taught include all the "if's" and the "but's"—and the "why's" and "therefore's." If the textbook you use makes theory sound like fact—and almost all elementary texts will—then supplement your reading with others more truthful. In fact, I think there is a crying need today for a small handbook which briefly explains the weaknesses in the evolutionary theory in layman's language—and I hope that the Creation Research Society, in which I proudly claim membership, will soon publish one.

Reason or Faith—which will you emphasize when you return to your school? Reason—which tells us that there must be a Supreme Being who established the order in nature, who wound the clock which runs the universe, and who now sits back and watches it run without interference—or faith, which tells us we have an all powerful God who not only created the world and its inhabitants, but who still today guides, controls, and directs it . . . Reason, which tells us that man evolved from lower mammals, and is better in all respects today than he ever was in the past—or faith, which tells us that man was created by God in His image, righteous, in perfect communion with God. Man, who chose to sin, and who today pays the penalty. Man, who from the moment of conception is in need of a Savior . . . Reason, which gives to God a human form, and which then tells us that He could not possibly be at all places in the same instant—or faith, which tells us that He is omnipresent, always close to us, always guarding, guiding, and protecting . . . Reason, which tells us that God sits back and watches the world, indifferent to our individual problems—or faith, which tells us our God is omniscient, He knows our thoughts, our troubles, our joys, He stands by ever to help us, no matter how deserted we may feel . . . Reason, which tells us that God must be a stern judge constantly condemning us for breaking impossible laws—or faith, which leads us to know God as a kind and loving Father, who cherishes us as His children, who sacrificed His Son that we might live, who forgives us when we sin, who loves us with a love incomprehensible to human understanding.

What will be the predominant theme in your classroom in days to come—faith in man's ability, in his reason—or faith in the almighty power of a God who has revealed himself to us. Choose reason if you want to take the easy—the popular—route. Choose reason if you want to impress the scientific community, if you want to have popular appeal. But choose faith if you are concerned about the eternal welfare of the children in your charge. Choose faith if you want to give them that peace which we cannot understand. Choose faith if you want them some day to say: "I shall be forever grateful to that parochial school teacher I once had."

I have, during the past hour, attempted to show you that science depends on reason, religion on faith—that science is forced, by its method, to adopt a theory such as evolution, and that this theory has many serious weaknesses. My examples of these have been few—I ask you to accept my word that there are others. I would like to share with you, however, my beliefs after a lengthy study of scientific and religious books. I believe that God created this world and its inhabitants in a period of six days. I believe that God created man in His image, and that my desire to sin is a result of the fall of one man, a man named Adam. I believe that the miracles of the Bible occurred as described, that God used His power to suspend the forces of nature which He once set into being. I believe that I am a child of God—not because of my works, but because Christ has atoned for my sins—an atonement which the Holy Spirit has led me to accept. I believe that I can go through life confident in the knowledge that God is in control, allowing only those things to happen which will ultimately be for my good. I believe that this faith will be challenged severely in the years to come, years in which science and reason will become more prominent, years in which apparent proofs will arise to support existing theories. But I believe that God will keep that faith ever present in me—and that some day that faith

There Was Evening—And There Was Morning

will be justified—the day when the cloudy lid shall be removed from my eyes and I shall know all things—the day when I stand before my Father, my God, my King, in heaven.

Prejudiced? Perhaps. Biased? Yes, I guess I am. A fool? If this means believing that very apparent physical evidence can be misinterpreted, then the accusation may be just. You, too, may be the recipient of such titles. If such should happen, and if as a result you feel insecure, then why not turn to St. Paul's first letter to the Corinthians, in the first chapter, where his inspired words tell us: "For the word of the cross is folly to those who are perishing, but to us who are being saved it is the power of God. For it is written, 'I will destroy the wisdom of the wise, and the cleverness of the clever I will thwart.' Where is the wise man? Where is the scribe? Has not God made foolish the wisdom of the world? . . . For the foolishness of God is wiser than men, and the weakness of God is stronger than men."

There was evening, and there was morning. . . . And if the story told is true, the world came boldly into view. . . . Faith—or reason? Which will it be? As you go to your respective congregations I would like to have you take seven words with you—words I have repeated so often in the past—words which I hope you will learn to use in the future. The words, in the form of a prayer, are these— *Lord, I believe, help thou my unbelief.*

VI

THE POWER OF ENERGY

Henry M. Morris

This title may at first disturb the disciplined scientific mind because of its apparent dimensional inconsistency. As a matter of fact, for our present purposes, it might just as well be titled "The Energy of Power." The point to be made, in either case, is that *energy,* as a concept, is tremendously powerful, both in the solution of technical problems and in its implications with reference to the true understanding of nature and the universe. And this is true whether we are speaking technically of energy or its time-derivative, power. Neither is an actual physical substance, of course, but each is an extremely useful and significant concept, without which the great contributions of modern science could hardly have been possible. Dr. R. B. Lindsay, Director of the Ultrasonics Laboratory at Brown University and Dean of its Graduate School, says:

> Of all unifying concepts in the whole field of physical science, that of energy has proved to be the most significant and useful. Not only has it played a major role in the logical development of the structure of science, but, by common consent, it is the physical concept which has had and still has the widest influence on human life in all its aspects. Under the prevailing misnomer "power," it is the stock-in-trade of the engineer and that which makes the wheels of the world go round.... the interpretation of phenomena in terms of the transfer of energy between natural systems is the most powerful single tool in the understanding of the external world.[1]

The power of the energy concept is implicit in the two great laws of thermodynamics, which are without question the two most basic and securely founded of all the laws of physical science. All real processes in the physical or biologic realms necessarily involve transformations of energy from one form into another. The first law of thermodynamics, that of energy conservation, expresses the quantitative equivalence of total energy before and after the transformations. The second law, that of energy deterioration, states that in the process some of the energy must be transformed into non-recoverable heat energy—not destroyed, but rendered unavailable for use. In terms of "entropy," which is merely a measure of the non-availability of the energy of a system, any natural process or transformation of energy in a closed mechanical system, necessarily involves an increase in the entropy of the system. According to the great Harvard physicist, P. W. Bridgman:

> The two laws of thermodynamics are, I suppose, accepted by physicists as perhaps the most secure generalizations from experience that we have. The physicist does not hesitate to apply the two laws to any concrete physical situation in the confidence that nature will not let him down.[2]

The universal validity of the first law, that of energy conservation, is also indicated by Gerald Feinberg and Maurice Goldhaber:

> The physicist's confidence in the conservation principles rests on long and thoroughgoing experience. The conservation of energy, of momentum, and of electric charge have been found to hold, within the limits of accuracy of measurement, in every case that has been studied. An elaborate structure of physical theory has been built on these fundamental concepts, and its predictions have been confirmed without fail.[3]

With respect to the second law, the following evaluation by A. R. Ubbelohde is typical:

> In its most modern forms, the Second Law is considered to have an extremely wide range of validity. It is a remarkable illustration of the ranging power of the human intellect that a principle first detected in connection with the clumsy puffing of a steam engine should be found to apply to the whole world, and possibly even to the whole cosmic universe.[4]

It would be difficult to point to any of our basic methods or formulas in any branch of mechanics or engineering which are not intimately related to these energy requirements. Though the working scientist or engineer may be inclined to overlook them, being engrossed in a tangle of technical details and specific procedures, he will find that both his techniques and basic insights will be greatly strengthened if he maintains a continual awareness of the fundamental energy relationships to which his designs and decisions must conform.

It is not too surprising, then, to find that these relationships and the very concept of energy itself lead to tremendous inferences far beyond the realm of mechanics and thermodynamics to which they were first applied. The basic nature of "energy" or "power" is still enveloped in mystery. Energy can appear in many quantitatively interchangeable forms—electrical energy, chemical energy, sound, heat, light, pressure, magnetic energy, mechanical energy, etc. And one of man's greatest scientific discoveries has been that of the identification of matter itself as merely one form of energy, so that the law of mass conservation becomes only a special case of the law of conservation of energy, and matter becomes under the proper conditions interconvertible with other energy forms.

Since all the physical universe, including matter, is ultimately energy, and since energy can be neither created nor destroyed, according to the conservation principle, the inference is that the totality of energy in the universe has never changed since its origination. Either the universe has always existed in its present state (and this is contradicted by the second law of thermodynamics), or it was at some time in the past brought into its present state, necessarily by means of laws or principles not now operative in the universe. Once these latter laws were superseded by the present conservation-deterioration laws, there could have been no additional creation or destruction of the physical stuff of the universe.

This fact is not obvious from a superficial examination of nature, which exhibits numerous cases of *apparent* causeless origins and *apparent* increases of order, reflected in the many crude notions of spontaneous generation and evolution held by ancient philosophers. The conservation law has only been accepted within the past 120 years, after much scientific labor and against much opposition. It is remarkable, therefore, that in the first chapter of Genesis, following the familiar biblical account of creation, appears the following:

> Thus the heavens and the earth *were finished*, and all the host of them. And on the seventh day God *ended his work which he had made*; and he *rested* on the seventh day *from all his work which he had made* (Gen. 2:1, 2).

With reference to the energy balance of the earth, which of course depends almost wholly upon the influx of solar radiant energy, the further significant statement is made that the function of the sun, relative to the earth, was: ". . . to give light unto the earth" (Gen. 1:17).

Whether or not the writer understood the significance of this assertion, the fact remains that the sun's "light," or radiant energy, provides

The Power of Energy

all the earth's usable energy except that of its own rotation and the nuclear energy of its atomic structure. The sun's light maintains the physical and biologic life of the earth. It has been calculated[5] that all of the stored-up energy sources of the earth—its coal, oil and gas reserves, its peat and timber, even its fissionable uranium, would only suffice to keep the earth going for about three days if the sun's energy were to be cut off.

The energy of light, in fact, may be considered as the most basic of all the forms of energy. It includes all radiant energy, from the X-rays and cosmic rays and other short-wave-length radiation at one extreme, through visible light, heat, and the electro-magnetic rays at the opposite end of the spectrum. The energy of matter is basically light energy, with matter and energy related by the Einstein equation through the fundamental and universal constant of the velocity of light. The first creative command of God, according to the Genesis record, is thus very significantly said to have been: "... Let there be light: and there was light" (Gen. 1:3).

The energy conservation law is occasionally said not to have proved universally successful when applied to phenomena on the sub-atomic scale. Quite possibly this is because of the still very incompletely understood nature of these phenomena, and in fact the somewhat still mysterious relation between matter and energy. Of course, this area of investigation is so complex and specialized and so rapidly changing that no one but a very up-to-date nuclear physicist should hazard any definite statement about the basic significance of nuclear phenomena.

However, within the accuracy of all pertinent experimental evidence, it is true that the energy conservation principle has been demonstrated true on the sub-nuclear scale no less than on the scale of ordinary experience. As Feinberg and Goldhaber have recently pointed out:

> Thousands of laboratory experiments, performed in different ways and measuring all the quantities involved, have confirmed that the laws of conservation of energy and momentum do hold true in the domain of elementary particles. . . . It is clear that the laws of conservation of energy and momentum, introduced . . . to describe collisions between macroscopic bodies, also apply with remarkable accuracy to the collisions and interactions of sub-atomic particles.[6]

One thing is certain, and that is that the energies associated with the various nuclear particles are tremendous and, when partially converted into other forms of energy through nuclear fission or thermonuclear fusion processes, the physical effects can be cataclysmic. The source and nature of the binding energy that normally maintain the integrity of the atomic structure against the powerful electrical forces tending to disintegrate it are yet quite uncertain, although many of its characteristics have been determined.

As the physicist R. E. Peierls says:

> The next fundamental problem that arises is that of the nature of the forces which hold the neutrons and protons in a nucleus together . . . the attractive energy that holds any one particle in the nucleus is, in general, of the order of 6 to 8 million volts . . . to obtain the precise laws of the nuclear forces is one of the central problems of nuclear physics, which is not, as yet, completely solved.[7]

And the problem today seems as far from solution as ever. As modern research has thrown more and more light on the nature of the nucleus, with its various sub-nuclear particles, the more complex does its nature seem to be. Even if its physical character is eventually completely understood, its basic origin and source would still be at best a matter of pure speculation. Peierls admits:

> Even if one day we find our knowledge of the basic laws concerning inanimate nature to be complete, this would not mean that we had "explained" all of inanimate nature. All we should have done is to show that all the complex phenomena of our experience are derived from some simple basic laws. But how to explain the laws themselves?[8]

Another quite remarkable assertion of the Scriptures is pertinent here. The writer of the Epistle to the Hebrews mentions that, having first made the worlds, God (through His Son) now is continually "upholding all things by the word of his power" (Heb. 1:3). A legitimate paraphrase of the Greek original here would be that He is "maintaining the physical integrity of the matter of the universe by means of the continual efficacious outflow and outworking of His innate infinite reservoir of basic energy."

The same intimation of the maintenance of the integrity of matter by a certain basic and primal form of energy (and therefore of the essential equivalence of matter and energy) is suggested also by St. Paul, when he says: "In him [Christ] all things hold together" (Col. 1:17), and by St. Peter, who says that ". . . the heavens and the earth which are now, by the same word are kept in store" (II Peter 3:7).

But the full import of the energy concept cannot be grasped until we consider also the second law of thermodynamics. In any closed system, in which energy transactions take place, the availability of the energy for the performance of useful work must always decrease. The total energy remains unchanged, but its usefulness has decreased.

This physical phenomenon is not at all obvious on the surface of things and had to overcome much opposition before it became generally accepted as scientific truth. It seemed to contradict the philosophy of progress and developmental evolution. Nevertheless, the brilliant theoretical and experimental researches of Carnot, Clausius, and Lord Kelvin, followed by numerous others in more recent decades, have definitely proved this second law to be of essentially equal validity with the first. In recent times, it has been possible to analyze and predict in some cases actual rates of energy dissipation (or entropy increase). This sort of study, of course, becomes of great practical importance in engineering design and analysis. Energy dissipation is often of paramount importance in the mechanics of the conversion process and its efficiency, and therefore in its cost of operation. The second law of thermodynamics precludes the design of any process or machine one hundred percent efficient, as well as any sort of perpetual motion device.

Because of the historical background, it has been customary to think of these two laws of thermodynamics as more or less interdependent. However, there does not seem to be any necessary connection between them. The fact that the totality of energy remains constant does not in itself imply at all that its availability should continually decrease. In fact, there now exists a considerable body of evidence that this so-called second law of thermodynamics is only a particular application of a much more general law which deals not only with the phenomena of physical energy but also with many other categories of phenomena in the physical, biological, and perhaps even in the psychological and sociological realms. This broader law has been called, by the British physicist, Dr. R. E. D. Clarke, the "law of morpholysis," [9] a term derived from two Greek words, and meaning simply "loosing" of structure.

This term seems admirably adapted to describe a very important and apparently universal phenomenon, namely that there always exists a tendency in nature towards disorder or disorganization. The law of morpholysis merely formalizes the everyday observation that any evidence of order or organization requires some sort of explanation to account for it, whereas anything exhibiting randomness or disorder or heterogeneity is *per se* "natural" and does not call for any explanation as to how it was thus arranged. The natural tendency is always from the state of maximum improbability to that of maximum probability, from the organized to the disorganized. Any sort of ordered arrangement requires some sort of external agency to bring it about. Harold F. Blum, Professor of Biology at Princeton, says:

> All real processes go with an increase in entropy. The entropy also measures the randomness or lack of orderliness of the system, the greater the randomness the greater the entropy;—the idea of a continual tendency toward greater randomness provides the most fundamental way of viewing the second law....[10]

Even from an engineering viewpoint, this is now recognized as the real significance of the second law of thermodynamics. This concept of entropy explains energy deterioration in terms of decreased order of molecular or atomic structure. In discussing the entropy concept and some of its newer applications, Dr. W. L. Everitt, Dean of Engineering at the University of Illinois and past president of the American Society for Engineering Education, points out that:

> ... it may be inferred that entropy is a measure of randomness, confusion, or lack of organization. Such a term can be applied not only in a thermodynamic sense, but also to information problems.[11]

This tendency toward disorder is of course apparent in many realms besides that of energy dissipation. There is the phenomenon of aging and death in living creatures, for example, still very incompletely understood but apparently related to the breakdown of complex and unstable protein molecules into simpler and more stable ones, less able to transmit free energy for biologic processes.

Similarly, the primary mechanism of biologic evolution of species, that of mutation of genes in the germ cells, operates when some disorganizing medium such as short-wave-length radiation, certain powerful chemicals, etc., penetrate the germ cell and disturb its previously highly organized chemical structure. The reshuffling of genetic factors thus induced would nearly always decrease its degree of order and organization and therefore result in a less viable and efficient organism. This is why almost all, perhaps all, mutations are either lethal or harmful to the creatures experiencing them, in their struggle for existence. This is supported by no less an authority than Dr. H. J. Muller, perhaps the world's outstanding living geneticist and authority on mutational mechanics:

> It is entirely in line with the accidental nature of natural mutations that extensive tests have agreed in showing the vast majority of them to be detrimental to the organism in its job of surviving and reproducing, just as changes accidentally introduced into any artificial mechanism are predominantly harmful to its useful operation. According to the conception of evolution based on the studies of modern genetics, the whole organism has its basis in its genes. Of these there are thousands of different kinds, interacting with great nicety in the production and maintenance of the complicated mechanism of the given type of organism. Accordingly, by the mutation of one of these genes or another, any component structure or function, and in many cases combinations of these components, may become diversely altered. Yet in all except very rare cases the change will be disadvantageous, involving an impairment of function.[12]

It is probable that such mutational deteriorations account for many phenomena of paleontology and morphology, such as vestigial organs and the fact that most modern creatures are represented in the fossil record by larger and more highly developed individuals than their modern counterparts. Mutation, isolation, inbreeding, etc., also may account for the historical deterioration of once virile sociological units of peoples and cultures, encountered so frequently in the study of history.

But it is the cosmological implication of morpholysis that is of greater significance. If the entropy or disorder of any closed system must continually increase, and since the universe may be regarded as a very large, but finite, closed system, it follows that the universe as a whole is becoming progressively more disordered. Its reservoir of physical energy is continually degrading, tending ultimately to a state where all energy will have deteriorated to unavailable heat energy. The universe, in other words, is "running down"; it is growing old, wearing out.

It cannot, therefore, be infinitely old; if it were, it would already have attained this state of maximum entropy. It must have had a beginning. If it is growing old, it must once have been young; if it is wearing out, it must have once been new. A universe now running down must first have been "wound up."

This is the inexorable conclusion of the second law, unless one is disposed to assert a continual evolution of fresh matter or energy out of nothing somewhere in space (according to the theory of Fred Hoyle and others) or to insist that the universe is pulsating, with the entropy as periodically reversed to permit its rewinding. Neither of these alternatives, of course, is supported by a shred of *direct physical evidence*, but only by assumptions as to what, in the judgment of their proponents, the nature of things *ought* to be.[13] On the other hand, there is literally a tremendous mass of direct physical evidence supporting the entropy law.

However, these alternate hypotheses do point up one fact, namely that the morpholysis principle is not inherent in the basic nature of things. The very fact that men of intellect can conceive and support alternative theories proves this. This tendency toward disorder seems somehow, intuitively, to be an unwelcome intruder into the ideal nature of things, something that *ought not to be*, but which nevertheless *is*. Just *why* this deteriorative principle is an apparently universal law is seemingly beyond the reach of scientific discovery.

But here it is possible that the Scriptures, already seen to contain remarkable intimations about the fundamental nature of things, may again have something significant to say. The basically spiritual nature of energy has already been inferred, so that the principle of deterioration of energy may likewise involve spiritual overtones.

Thus the Christian doctrine of the Fall of man and the resultant curse of God on His creation, as taught in Genesis,[14] although often rejected as mythological by modern intellectuals, is able to provide at least a causal explanation for the universal phenomenon of morpholysis. At the same time, it refutes the hopelessly pessimistic future of the universe implied by the second law of thermodynamics by reminding us that He who established the creation and who later imposed upon it the curse of corruptibility and decay, is yet himself outside the creation and therefore not subject to its laws. For example, quoting again the author of Hebrews, who in turn is quoting Psalm 102:

> And, Thou, Lord, in the beginning hast laid the foundation of the earth; and the heavens are the works of thine hands: They shall perish; but thou remainest; and they all shall wax old as doth a garment; And as a vesture shalt thou fold them up, and they

The Power of Energy

shall be changed: but thou art the same, and thy years shall not fail.[15]

A future time when the curse shall be removed from the earth and when, therefore, the law of morpholysis will presumably be "repealed" is often promised in Scripture. In the classic eighth chapter of Romans, said by Martin Luther to be the greatest chapter in the Bible, St. Paul says:

> For the creation was made subject to vanity, not willingly, but by reason of him who hath subjected the same in hope, Because the creation also shall be delivered from the bondage of corruption [decay] into the glorious liberty of the children of God. For we know that the whole creation groaneth and travaileth in pain together until now.[16]

But for the present we must continue to live with the entropy principle. The engineer must continue to design his machine or process with full allowance for the effects of energy dissipation. Great strides are being made in the broader application of these concepts of energy conservation and deterioration, in atomic energy, computers and automation, rocketry, inertial guidance, and even in such fields as information theory. A more incisive and inclusive understanding of the real character of the second law, especially, will undoubtedly result in still more remarkable technological advances, in probably every area of science.

But one cannot help but sense a danger, even perhaps a probability, that new scientific and technological break-throughs may, as has often been true in the past, only accelerate the sociological and moral morpholysis. Energy and entropy are, we repeat, basically nonmaterial, even spiritual in essence.

As to sources of strictly physical power, it appears that the so-called Christian West is rapidly being overwhelmed by the anti-Christian forces of the world. In manpower, it has long been obvious that the West is immensely inferior. In potential energy sources, considering the vast and largely untapped resources of Russia, Asia, and probably Africa, the reservoir of the East is again far larger than that of the West. Even in the non-material resources of intellectual and moral power, there is no little evidence today that the Eastern peoples are at least the equals of those in the free world.

In a day and age in which the balance of power in a technological sense has been superimposed upon the old concept of the balance of power in a military sense as determinative of the world's future, we have suddenly come to realize that our Western delusion of perpetual superiority may be tragically unrealistic. Evidences are multiplying that the true balance of power in the world henceforth may favor those forces that are being arrayed in opposition to us.

But there does remain one largely unused source of power, access to which is more to be valued than all others combined. The One who inhabits eternity, who has created and who "upholds all things by the word of his power," is himself the source of all physical, intellectual, moral, and spiritual energy. Access to this spiritual power (and often even to physical and intellectual strength) is obtained through prayer and a Christ-centered faith, according to the testimony both of biblical revelation and of millions of individual Christians across the centuries, including the writer of this paragraph. In the words of St. Paul, "For I am not ashamed of the gospel of Christ, for it is the *power* of God unto salvation, to everyone that believeth . . ." (Rom. 1:16).

Therefore, for instruction in the matter of power sources for those who deal in science and technology, for insight into the universal significance of the concepts of energy and power, for encouragement to all who are disturbed over world conditions, and for personal exhortation to those individuals who would seek for roots in eternity, we close with the words of Him who, after dying in atonement for the sins of fallen man and then after winning the ultimate triumph over the universal rule of decay and death by his bodily resurrection from the tomb, could say with all assurance: "*All power* is given unto me in heaven and in earth. . . . And, lo, I am with you alway, even unto the end of the world. Amen" (Matt. 28:18, 20).

NOTES AND REFERENCES

1. R. B. Lindsay, "Concept of Energy in Mechanisms," *Scientific Monthly*, October 1957, p. 188.
2. P. W. Bridgman, "Reflections on Thermodynamics," *American Scientist*, October 1953, p. 549.
3. Gerald Feinberg and Maurice Goldhaber, "The Conservation Laws of Physics," *Scientific American*, October 1963, p. 36.
4. A. R. Ubbelohde, *Man and Energy* (New York: George Brazillier, Inc., 1955), p. 146. Ubbelohde is Professor of Thermodynamics at the Imperial College of Science and Technology of the University of London.
5. Eugene Ayres and Charles A. Scarlott, *Energy Sources* (New York: McGraw-Hill Book Company, 1955), p. 186.
6. Feinberg, *op. cit.*, pp. 39, 42. Dr. Feinberg is Associate Professor of

Physics at Columbia University, and Dr. Goldhaber is Director of the Brookhaven National Laboratory.
7. R. E. Peierls, *The Laws of Nature* (New York: Charles Scribner's Sons, 1956), p. 240.
8. *Ibid.*, p. 275. Peierls is Professor of Mathematical Physics at the University of Birmingham in England, and a past president of the Atomic Scientists Association.
9. R. E. D. Clarke, *Darwin: Before and After* (London: Paeternoster Press, 1948), p. 150.
10. Harold F. Blum, *Time's Arrow and Evolution* (New York: Harper and Brothers, 1962), p. 15.
11. W. L. Everitt, "Empathy and Entropy," *Journal of Engineering Education*, April 1957, p. 658.
12. H. J. Muller, "How Radiation Changes the Genetic Constitution," *Bulletin of the Atomic Scientists*, paper prepared for the U. N. Conference on Peacetime Uses of Atomic Energy, at Geneva, 1955.
13. See, for example, the cogent criticism of theories of this kind in an article by Dr. Herbert Dingle, Professor of the History and Philosophy of Sciences at the University of London, "Cosmology and Science," *Scientific American*, September 1956, pp. 224-236.
14. Genesis 3:17-19. See also Romans 5:12, I Corinthians 15:21, 22.
15. Hebrews 1:10-12. See also I Peter 1:24, 25; Matthew 24:35; Isaiah 51:6, etc.
16. Romans 8:20-22. See also Revelation 21:1, 4,; 22:3; Isaiah 66:22; II Peter 3:13.

VII

PROBLEMS IN ABSOLUTE AGE DETERMINATION

D. O. Acrey

The use of radioactive decay as a basis for absolute age determinations involves the premise that a parent element decays at a known rate, which remains constant, into a daughter element. The decaying mechanism is assumed in all cases to occur directly or in a radioactive chain with nothing added or removed during the process of decay. The original rock or mineral must be free of the ultimate daughter isotope or contain this isotope in a known proportion to other isotopes so that the original content of the decay material can be ascertained.

The Lead : Uranium Method (or Lead : Thorium Method)

In an isolated chemical system, the determination of the quantity of parent and daughter material and the knowledge of the rate of decay of the parent leads to the solution of the age of the system. When considering a uranium mineral and *assuming* that nothing is added, or removed, and that *no lead* was present when the system was formed, an age can be found by determining the quantities of lead and uranium (or thorium) and solving the equation

$$(\text{Daughter})_{\text{now}} = (\text{Parent})_{\text{now}} \times (e^{at} - 1)$$

where 'a' is the rate of decay and 't' is the age determination. Alpha emission is indicated by 'e' and involves the following nuclear processes:

$$U^{238} \text{—emission of 8 alphas—} Pb^{206}$$
$$U^{235} \text{—emission of 7 alphas—} Pb^{207}$$
$$Th^{232} \text{—emission of 6 alphas—} Pb^{208}$$

A great many determinations have been made by this method; however, it has been found that the premises on which the method is based are not valid for most uranium minerals. There is definite evidence of selective uranium leaching by acid waters (Phair and Levine, 1953), and it is now known that *most radioactive minerals contained some lead when they were formed.* As a result, the early lead:uranium age determinations can be considered highly questionable.

The Lead : Alpha Method

An attempt has been made in recent years to revive the lead : uranium method. Larsen and his co-workers found that a few common minerals such as zircon and monazite are sufficiently resistant to chemical change and were sufficiently low in lead content at the time that they were formed to satisfy what they considered to be the basic requirements of the method so that age determinations can be made with small enough error to be useful (Larsen, Keevil, and Harrison, 1952).

The minerals to be studied are separated from the rock by standard mineralogic techniques (heavy liquids, magnetic separator, flotation, etc.) and their total thick-source alpha activity is determined. The lead content is established spectrochemically (Waring and Worthing, 1953) and the approximate age is determined from the relation

$$t = \frac{c\ Pb}{a}$$

where 't' is the age in millions of years, 'Pb' is the lead content in parts per million, and 'a' is the radioactivity in alphas per milligram-hour. The constant 'c' is 2600 for uranium alone and 1990 for thorium alone.

One of the major problems arising from this method is the fact that so many of the earth's minerals have unknown proportions of thorium and uranium.

The Isotopic Lead : Uranium Method

Analyses of whole rocks and a large number of lead minerals, associated with little or no radioactive material, show that their lead is composed of four isotopes: Lead[204], Lead[206], Lead[207], and Lead[208]. The variation in the composition of this so-called "common" lead has been explained as a gradual addition of small amounts of *Radiogenic* Lead (lead derived from radioactive decay) throughout geologic time. Proponents of this method point out that the error introduced by the variability of the common lead will not be serious *IF* most of the lead present is radiogenic. Presupposition that no great quantity of common lead was present in the rocks or minerals at the instant of creation is without foundation. Two disadvantages of the method are (1) that hexavalent uranium is readily leached and (2) that radon ^{222}, which forms in the decay of uranium^{238}, is gaseous and might escape from the system (Wickman, 1942).

The Lead : Lead Method

Using the corrected values for radiogenic lead isotopes, which were obtained by the subtraction of original lead and uranium, age determination is attempted from the equation

$$\frac{Pb^{207}}{Pb^{206}} = \frac{U^{235} (e^{at} -1)}{U^{238} (e^{at} -1)}$$

At first glance, this method seems to be the best in that it deals only in isotopic ratios, and some physicists consider it to be the superior of all lead methods. Actually, the method is subject to several errors. Loss of radon^{222} raises the lead : lead ratio and the calculated age. A rather large error may be introduced by the uncertainty in the composition of the original lead. Presence of old radiogenic lead (formed in a prior site of the parent uranium) may cause great error. Instrumental errors in mass spectrometry may yield consistently high apparent proportions of Lead^{204} and Lead^{207}. Redistribution of elements by renewed hydrothermal activity may be a serious source of error in all lead methods.

The Isotopic Lead : Thorium Method

This method is analogous to the isotopic lead : uranium method except for the fact that only one parent isotope is involved. Most of the ages obtained by this method disagree with the ages of the same minerals computed by other lead methods. The reasons for this disagreement are largely unknown.

The Lead 210 Method

This method is essentially a refinement of the old lead : uranium method. This newer procedure is based on the principle that the age of a uranium or thorium mineral can be determined by the ratio of any one of the members of the decay series to the stable end product, *as long as the series is in equilibrium.* Unfortunately, the Lead 210 Method is subject to the same errors as the lead : uranium and lead : lead methods, owing to loss of constituents of the radioactive series by *leaching* or *emanation.* The radon loss could be ignored if it were constant throughout the existence of the mineral; such conditions, however, are believed to be rare or non-existent in nature.

The Helium Method

Helium has a geological occurence and distribution that are unique among the elements. On the average, it is continuously increasing in amount in the earth's crust, being formed at the expense of the elements of the uranium and thorium series. On the other hand, the crust is continuously losing helium at a rate that is less than the amount being formed by radioactive decay, and there has been an increasing flow of helium to the surface throughout geologic time in stable crustal areas. It has been felt that the understanding of the magnitude and distribution of this helium flux in continental areas could best be obtained by a study of the ratios of helium to uranium and thorium in rocks and minerals. Many complex and intricate techniques have been tried in this method of analysis, with varying results. The helium ratios in most cases showed ages corresponding roughly with ages inferred from the lead method studies. In addition to the weaknesses of the lead method, there are notable exceptions to the accuracy of the Helium Method. Magnetite obtained from rocks of a granitic type seem very unreliable. The unreliability of this type of rock seems to lie at least in part in the presence of acid-soluble radioactive contaminants.

A principal problem of this method is the low or variable helium ratio. It has commonly been assumed that helium ratios are low because helium atoms diffuse through the crystalline structures of rock minerals, accumulate in the boundary regions of the crystals, and gradually find ways to escape to the surface through the openings in the rock. If this were known to be true for all minerals, work on the method would have stopped long ago. It is known that the diffusion coefficient for helium in undisturbed crystals of magnetite, zircon, and sphene are so small as to permit no measurable loss of helium in periods of the order of 10^9 years. It is not known that the coefficients for common minerals such as quartz and feldspar are significantly higher. One difference between these two groups of minerals unrelated to the permeability of their structures to the diffusion of helium, is the tolerance of the structures to substitutions of uranium and thorium for their essential constituents. Although the helium content of quartz and feldspar can be measured easily, *it is impossible to know how much of the radioactivity is contamination.* Since quartz and feldspar crystals probably always grow with less radioactive element content than their surroundings, they are no doubt subject to radioactive contamination from their surroundings. Another factor which is known to be causing helium loss and which may account for discrepancies not explained by contamination is the damage to crystalline structure caused by concentration of the radioactive elements into localized centers that become intensely irradiated.

The Strontium Method

A wide variety of analytical procedures have been used to determine rubidium and strontium and their isotopes for the purpose of making geological age determinations. Three most common procedures are (1) the determination of rubidium, (2) a short-cut spectro-chemical procedure for determining strontium : rubidium ratios, and (3) the determination of the strontium and rubidium by isotope dilution. Differences in the distillation rates of strontium and rubidium as well as the variation of the degree of ionization of strontium, create problems for accurate age determinations by this method. Another source of error is the incompleteness of precipitation at low concentrations of strontium, as in comparatively young lepidolites. There are definite inconsistencies now apparent in the results of spectrochemical and mass spectrometric strontium : rubidium methods.

Argon^{40} : Potassium^{40} Dating

The discovery of a long-lived radioactive isotope of potassium was thought to have opened up many possibilities in the field of geological dating. It is known that potassium^{40} decays by K-electron capture to argon^{40} with the emission of a gamma and by beta emission to calcium^{40}. More exact determinations of the decay constants are necessary before this method can really be developed. Another problem is the loss of argon by diffusion. The amount lost would be critically dependent on the grain size and structure of the potassium minerals. The high argon content of the atmosphere is another source of error by contamination.

The Carbon[14] Method

Carbon[14] emits a beta with an energy of 0.155 Mev and has a half-life of approximately 5600 years. It can be made in the neutron pile by the reaction

$$N^{14}(n,p)C^{14}$$

Since the cross sections of oxygen, argon, carbon, and hydrogen are much lower than that of nitrogen, the reaction will consume nearly all of the neutrons formed. Thus the rate of production of neutrons is substantially the same as the rate of production of Carbon[14]. One of the assumptions of this technique is that cosmic radiation has been constant in intensity over the last 30,000 years or more. A steady state is predicted, exactly analogous to the secular equilibrium among the decay products of radioactive chains. It is assumed that the rate of decay of Carbon[14] will then equal its rate of formation.

The Carbon[14] thus formed can be expected to follow a definite geochemical path. In the oxidizing conditions of the upper atmosphere it will be converted rapidly to carbon dioxide, and once in this form will enter the carbon cycle. In time it will be mixed throughout the atmosphere, living and other organic matter, and the carbonate dissolved in the sea.

Another problem involving this technique is a further assumption when using this method in dating studies. There must be materials in which, after a definite period, no exchange reactions or gross replacement of materials can take place. This critical time can occur at the death of the organism, or at the time of laying down of wood or shell; however, there is no supporting scientific fact to back up this assumption. The difficulty of reconciling some of the dates obtained from this method with other evidence has led some geologists to question the applicability of the method to samples stored under moist conditions.

Conclusion

The old argument still holds that stratigraphic time boundaries stem from the study of sediments, but nuclear determinations of absolute time can be made only on igneous rocks, with very few exceptions. The geologic time relationship between sediments and igneous rocks is rough and frequently obscure, even in areas that have been studied geologically in great detail. Most of the geologic time scales that have been published are based on uncritical compilation of a wide variety of data, so that the overall figures are necessarily very rough. The basic assumptions should always be remembered.

LITERATURE

Ahrens, L. H., "Determination of the Age of Minerals by Means of the Radioactivity of Rb," *Nature* (1946), 157:269.

Ahrens, L. H., "Measuring Geologic Time by the Strontium Method," *Bull. Geol. Soc. Amer.* (1948), 60:217-266.

Aldrich, L. T., J. B. Doak, and G. L. Davis, "The Use of Ion Exchange Column in Mineral Analysis for Age Determination," *Am. J. Sci.* (1953), 251: 377-387.

Allan, D. W., R. M. Farquhar, and R. D. Russell, "A Note on the Lead Isotope Method of Age Determination," *Science* (1953), 118:486-488.

Carnegie Institution, Washington, "Age of Rocks," *Year Book* (1954), 53: 78-84.

Collins, C. B., R. M. Farquhar, and R. D. Russell, "Isotopic Constitution of Radiogenic Leads and the Measurement of Geologic Time," *Bull. Geol. Soc. Amer.* (1954), 65:1-22.

Flint, R. F., and E. S. Deevy, Jr., "Radiocarbon Dating of Late Pleistocene Events," *Amer. J. Sci.* (1951), 239:257-300.

Fritze, K., and F. Strassmann, "Determination of Geologic Age by the Potassium-Argon Method," *Naturwissenschaften* (1952), 39:522-523.

Gerling, E. K., G. M. Ermoline, N. V. Baranovskaia, and N. E. Titov, "First Results in the Application of the Argon Method to Determination of the Age of Minerals," *Doklady Akad. S.S.S.R.* (1952), 86:593-596.

Holland, H. D., and J. L. Kulp, "Geologic Age from Metamict Minerals," *Science* (1950), 111:312.

Holmes, Arthur, "The Oldest Dated Minerals of the Rhodesian Shield," *Nature* (1954), 173:612-614.

Johnsin, F., "Radiocarbon Dating," *Mem. Soc. Am. Archaeology* (1951), No. 8.

Kulp, J. L., G. L. Bate, and W. S. Broecker, "Present Status of the Lead Method of Age Determination," *Am. J. Sci.* (1954), 252:346-365.

Zeuner, F. E., *Dating the Past* (London: Methuen, 1952, 495 pp.).

VIII

RADIOLOGICAL DATING AND SOME PERTINENT APPLICATIONS OF HISTORICAL INTEREST
DO RADIOLOGICAL "CLOCKS" NEED REPAIR?

MELVIN A. COOK

In a recent book, *Prehistory and Earth Models*[1] (abbreviated in this article: PEM), the prominent radioactive "time clocks" were examined, including radiocarbon, the six uranium-thorium-lead methods, and the potassium-argon and rubidium-thorium rock dating methods.

The conclusions are summarized below, along with more recent findings and interesting applications of radiocarbon dating. They may be further summarized by the simple statement that there are really *no reliable* long-time radiological "clocks," and even the short-time radiocarbon "clock" is in serious need of repair.

The Foundations of Radiocarbon Dating

The radiocarbon (or C-14) method of dating biospheric (dead) specimens, and other carbon-containing substances that have lost contact with the carbon cycle at some point in time is based on the *incorrect* assumption that C-14 is in steady state (or in equilibrium) in the earth as a whole—in the sense that its overall rate of formation is equal to its rate of decay. Direct, reconfirmed observations show that the rate of decay is only about two thirds as great as the rate of formation, and therefore that C-14 must still be building up in the carbon cycle of the earth.

In analyzing this equilibrium postulate, Libby, the author of the radiocarbon method, himself found evidence for this unbalance. However, he *discounted* the evidence in favor of what he took to be more compelling, albeit hearsay, evidence that the earth is too old for C-14 to be out of balance, because it would, in all practical considerations, come into balance from any conceivable unbalance within about 30,000 years.[2] Libby found the rate of decay R_d to be 15.3

counts per gram per minute for carbon from the living biosphere, and the rate of formation R_f (normalized to the same units) to be 18.8 giving for the ratio $R = R_d/R_f$ the value 0.81.

More recent studies of Hess et al[3] on the neutron source strength raised R_f to 21.2. Lingenfelter[4] then recalculated R_f and lowered it to 18.4 ± 4.3. Suess[5] later lowered R_d to 13.3 on the basis of much more extensive data on the decay rate, and gave a more careful analysis of the carbon inventory in the carbon cycle, taking into account the ocean circulation lag.

Thus, basing our claim for an unbalance of radiocarbon in this cycle on the most recent findings of Lingenfelter and Suess, the value now assigned to R is $13.3/18.4 = 0.72$. Recognizing this evidence for an unbalance, Lingenfelter himself attempted an explanation based on fluctuations, thus carefully avoiding the short age-of-the-atmosphere implication of this nonequilibrium condition— no doubt realizing the difficulties the present writer encountered in attempting to point out this nonequilibrium condition, and its dating implication six years earlier.[6]

It is, of course, natural that creationists would adopt the seemingly obvious nonequilibrium model, and use it to date the atmosphere itself, whereas conventional science would seek to hide this drastic implication of the unbalance of C-14 in the earth's atmosphere.

Unbalance of Radiocarbon

The suggestion that radiocarbon is still increasing in the earth and that it is appreciably below an equilibrium value, where $R = 1.0$, was given additional support in a recent symposium participated in by Libby and Suess and reported by Switzer.[7] The latter remarked that "these results (referring to calibrations via tree rings and sedimentation rates) confirm a *change* in carbon-14 concentration (in the atmosphere) that occurred 2500 years ago and *indicate* that the *concentration increases* at least during the past 10,000 years" (parentheses and emphasis added).

With such reappearing support for an unbalance of radiocarbon in the atmosphere it would appear the only scientific thing to do is to discard the equilibrium model in which $R = 1.0$ and go, instead, with the evidence that R is only about two thirds this great, either to a nonequilibrium model based on the actual value of R observed, or else discard the radiocarbon model of a short time clock altogether.

Do Radiological "Clocks" Need Repair?

In the nonequilibrium model one has no more difficulty in dating a sample than in the equilibrium model as far as tractability is concerned. Moreover, it would seem to be the only model that can really avoid the necessity of having to discard the radiocarbon method of dating in the face of the compelling and recurrent evidence for an unbalance in C-14 in the carbon cycle—the atmosphere, hydrosphere, and biosphere.

Particularly interesting is the fact that the nonequilibrium model brings the results of radiocarbon dating much closer to Bible chronology in "historical" comparisons, which is why scientists avoid it so tenaciously. Indeed, the value $R = 0.72$ *telescopes* all results by this method to about 10,000 years or less! This may be seen only by going through the mathematics of the radiocarbon theory, and it is, therefore, presented below in its most elemental form for the benefit of non-mathematicians. Figure 1 illustrates quantitatively the application of the nonequilibrium model by showing (1) buildup of radiocarbon in the earth as a whole, and (2) the nature of the discrepancy between the equilibrium and the nonequilibrium model as regards radiocarbon dating of biosphere specimens.

When radiocarbon is out of balance in the earth, as it is at present, its concentration C builds up in accord with the equation $R = R_f - R_d$ given by the differential equation of rudimentary calculus: $dC/dt = k_f - k_d C$, in which k_f expresses the constant rate of formation and $k_d C$ expresses the (first-order) rate of decay which, like any radioactive substance, is proportional to the C-14 concentration C.

If the C-14 were in equilibrium, dC/dt would be zero, so that $k_f = k_d C_m$, where C_m is the maximum or steady state concentration, a value $1/0.72$ greater than the present value according to the above evidence. The constant k_d is related to the half-life T by the equation $k_d = 0.693/T$. The observed half-life of C-14 is 5,760 years, giving for k_d the value $1.2 \cdot 10^{-4}$ years^{-1}. Thus, introducing the ratio $x = C/C_m$ in place of C by dividing through the differential equation of the C-14 balance by C_m, we obtain the equation in the simple form

$$dx/dt = 1.2 \cdot 10^{-4} (1 - x)$$

(Editor's note: Half-life of carbon is an estimate, and 5,568 years has been preferred. A more precise value from the mass spectrometer gas counting method is 5,760 years.)

We wish to obtain from this differential equation the time interval t_p from the beginning of the carbon cycle to the present. This cannot actually be done without knowing the ratio C/C_m or x at the "beginning" which, of course, we do not know. However, we can compute an *upper limit* for this time by assuming that $x = x_b = 0$ at the beginning. The above equation may then be integrated between the limits ($x_b = 0$, $t_b = 0$), and ($x_p = 0.72$, t_p) with the result:

$$-\log_e (1 - x_p)/(1 - x_b) = 1.2 \cdot 10^{-4} t_p \text{, or,}$$

$$t_p = -\log_e (1 - 0.72)/1.2 \cdot 10^{-4} = 10^4 \text{ years}$$

Note also that if x_b were any finite value less, of course, than x_p, the time t_p computed by this equation would be less than 10,000 years. However, if we take the extremes of uncertainty given by Lingenfelter for R_f, we would have x_b between 0.59 and 0.94. Then the upper limit for t_p (taking again $x_b = 0$) would be somewhere in the range between 7,500 and 23,000 years.

The Foundations of Dating by Radiological "Long-time" Clocks

Uranium-Thorium Lead (U-Th-Pb) "time clocks" are six in number: the "Lead-Alpha" method, the U-238/Pb-206, U-235/Pb-207, Th-232/Pb-208 methods, the "common lead" method, and the "Lead-Ratio" method. Difficulties in these methods are summarized below with particular emphasis placed on the (circumstantial) evidence for artificial aging by the so-called "neutron-gamma" or (n, γ) reactions.

1. "Time clock" readings from which the oft-quoted 4.51 billion years for the age of the earth have been obtained are inconsistent with observed atom and isotope abundance data understood (at least for atoms without radioactivity or radioactive sources) by the familiar "even-odd" and "magic number" rules. That is, an isotope with mass number A, atomic number Z, and neutron number N, all even, is expected to occur in greater natural abundance than one with one or more of these numbers odd. Lead-206 is an even-even-even isotope, whereas Pb-207 is odd-even-odd.

The observed "modern" relative abundance Pb-206/Pb-207 is is about 1.2, which is normal, considering the proximity of these isotopes to the magic number 126 (Pb-208, an even-even-even isotope, has 126 nucleons, all alike, other magic numbers being 2, 8,

Do Radiological "Clocks" Need Repair? 83

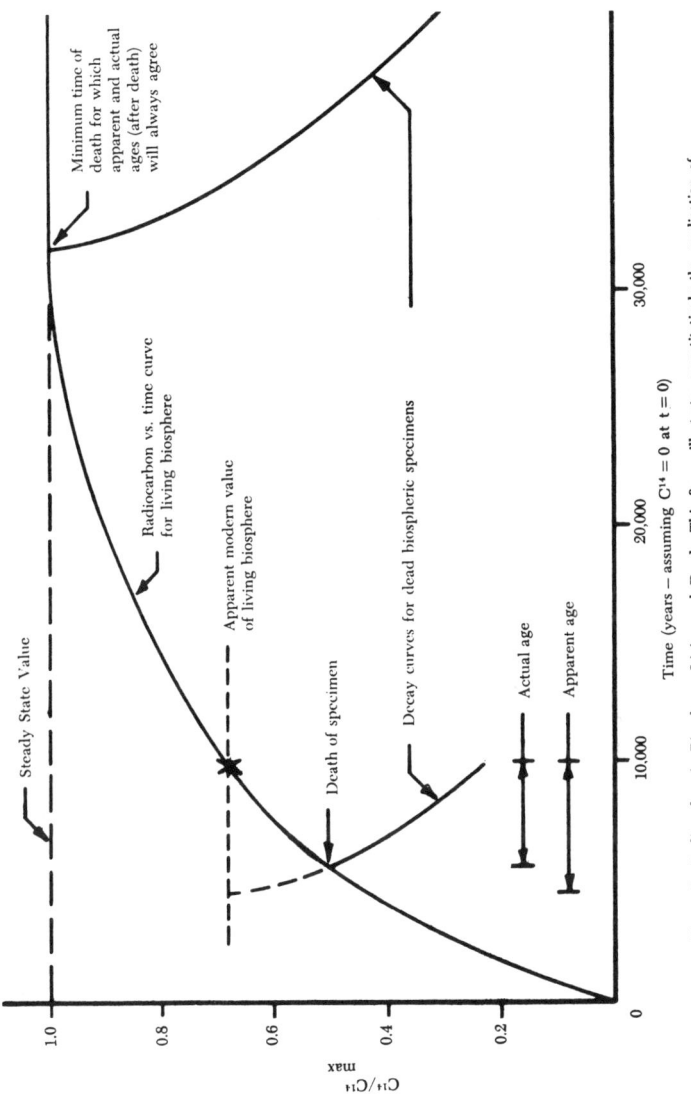

Figure 1. Radiocarbon in Biosphere—Living and Dead. This figure illustrates quantitatively the application of the non-equilibrium model by showing (1) buildup of radiocarbon in the earth as a whole, and (2) the nature of the discrepancy between the equilibrium and the non-equilibrium model as regards radiocarbon dating of biospheric specimens.

20, 50, and 82). However, if the earth were really 4.5 billion years old, the ratio Pb-206/Pb-207 at the beginning would have been *only* 0.45, a value which would seemingly violate these natural abundance rules. While interesting, this is, of course, not a crucial argument against the conventional claim for great antiquity.

2. Differences in isotope concentrations applied in reading these time clocks are often much less than isotope variations from one mineral to another in the nonradioactive elements with no radioactive sources—of which twelve having atomic weights less than that of zinc were found to show average variations of 6.6 percent. This is a value which would mean a billion years or so discrepancy in the long time clocks of geochronometry, i.e., those of the U-Th-Pb, potassium-40/argon-40, and rubidium-87/strontium-87 systems.

3. A statistical analysis of the extensive available data for common leads[8] from identical geological formations made by applying the conventional theory of radiological dating revealed that common leads really have in them *no time index* that can be sorted out and differentiated from observed random variations like those needed to account for variations from one sample to another in nonradioactive and nonradiogenic elements. This was very surprising to one led to think that the common leads could be accurately dated by the lead ratio method.

Lead-204, incidently, is used as the index in dating common leads because it has no radioactive source. The assumption is made that the ratios Pb-204/Pb-206/Pb-207/Pb-208 are 1.0/18.5/15.7/38.0 or thereabouts, in common leads that have never been contaminated with radiogenic lead from U-Th decay. Any difference from this or some other set of lead-isotope assumed to represent uncontaminated lead is supposed to represent the radioactive decay contribution to the common lead before mineralization in the present occurrence. From this one computes the time before mineralization by the lead ratios.

4. The most serious difficulty is the impossibility of defining initial conditions and isotope concentrations needed in all calculations of time with the radioactive time clocks. One can really never know these necessary concentrations so that the science of radiological dating has become merely a *science of guessing*. The best guess is supposed to be that based on lead isotope ratios, all other methods such as the helium and the lead-alpha methods having thus fallen into disrepute.

5. There are interesting and revealing systematic differences in

the four most important clocks of the U-Th-Pb system employing these ratios. Let ust take t_1, t_2, t_3 and t_4 as the times found from the lead ratio method Pb-206/Pb-207, the U-235/Pb-207, the U-238/Pb-206 and the Th/Pb-208 methods respectively.

The interesting situation is that the ratios $t_1/t_2/t_3/t_4$ average 1.35/1.18/1.12/1.0! Why this systematic difference between these closely related time clocks? The answer, when completely appreciated, may well prove to be fatal to the U-Th-Pb time clocks. It is definitely not due to diffusion, radon leakage or any of the usual explanations. Chemical and physical analyses are not at fault either; analytical methods are next to perfect in the U-Th-Pb system.

While it cannot affect $t_1/t_2/t_3$, uranium accretion via micrometeorites could easily upset dating by this method, because accretion products are concentrated at the surface, where scientists take their samples, rather than uniformly throughout the rocks of the crust. A slight surface contaminant of this nature could well be serious when differentiation is considered.

Leaching of uranium from rocks and runoff in river waters into the oceans, actually at rates comparable to the overall decay in the entire crust, can also cause serious discrepancies. While almost as much uranium is disappearing in this way from the surface sediments as is decaying in the entire crust of the earth, particularly revealing is the dilemma that the oceans have in them only a few thousand years of such uranium accumulation. How old are the oceans, after all?

6. As mentioned, the *most significant* consideration in explaining the systematic discrepancies in the U-Th-Pb time clocks, which if correct, would obviously all tell the same time, pertains to the neutron-gamma or (n, γ) reactions. That they are very important seems (circumstantially) obvious when one considers the fact discussed at length elsewhere[9] that the nitrogen-14/nitrogen-15 ratio is only about 65 percent as great in nitrogen found in compounds like nitrates occuring in radioactive minerals as in the atmosphere.

The N^{14} (n, γ) N^{15} reaction is seemingly the obvious answer, and one that has been given by others for this observation. But if radiation in a radioactive deposit can knock down the N-14/N-15 ratio this much, surely the (n, γ) reactions must also be important in the U-Th-Pb system!

Reasons have been given,[10] furthermore, that fast neutron "pile" factors should be involved in large U-Th ore bodies. While fast neutron concentrations are no doubt small compared with those pos-

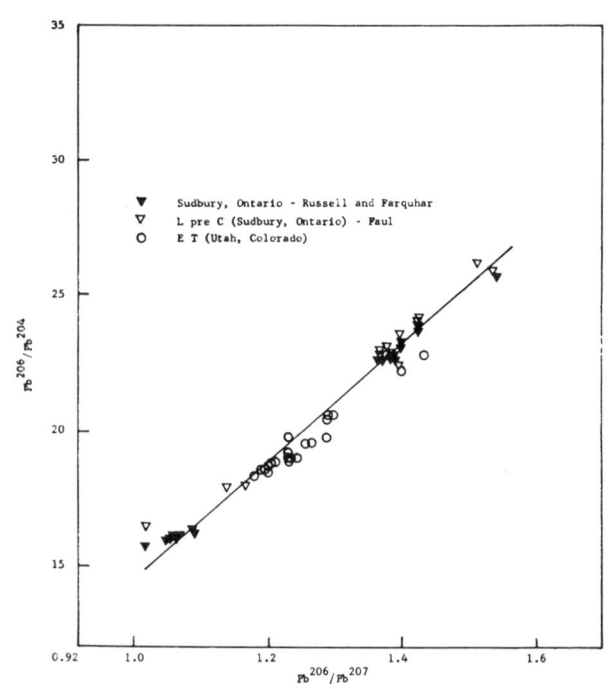

Figure 2. Does the Lead-Ratio method really work? This figure illustrates that common leads may not provide a reliable time clock. Note, for example, that the "preferred" lead ratio method fails to distinquish between Pre-Cambrian (assigned ages of greater than 500 million years) and Early Tertiary (assigned an age of less than 60 million years). (L pre C = Pre-Cambrian, E.T. = Early Tertiary

sible in man-made fast neutron piles, they need to be only around a millionth as great to upset completely the U-Th-Pb time clocks! Not only would fast neutrons (and slow neutrons also) tend to speed up the apparent decay rates of the radioactive species, but would also convert some Pb-206 to Pb-207 and some Pb-207 to Pb-208. Both of these types of reactions would tend to "age" unrealistically the U-Th-Pb minerals, depending on the relative importance of radioactive decay and the (n, γ) reactions.

There are a number of apparently crucial examples where it would appear that the (n, γ) reactions far outweigh the conventional U-decay and Th-decay reactions. Furthermore, the situation appears to be very general! These include cases where both Pb-204 and Th

Do Radiological "Clocks" Need Repair?

are absent or negligible, but where Pb-208 is present. By approximately quantitative age corrections based on the observed Pb-208 concentrations, and the assumption that they came from the (n, γ) reactions, it *appears* that one *effectively wipes out all of geologic time.* The following are two striking examples:

(a) The uranium ore at Shinkolobwe, Katanga, contains no Pb-204 (thus no common lead) and no Th-232, but it contains 0.08 percent Pb-208. The observed ratio Pb-206/Pb-207 is 94.2/5.72 = 16.5, from which the ore has been assigned the age 640 million years. The questions are: where did the Pb-208 come from, and what does it mean concerning age?

If we assume that it came from the Pb^{207} (n, γ) Pb^{208} reaction and that Pb-207 was also reinforced by the Pb^{206} (n, γ) Pb^{207} reaction (the correction,† based also on the assumption that the neutron cross-sections of the leads are all about the same), we arrive at the striking result that this ore is really "modern"! That is, the ratio x = Pb-206/Pb-207 is 21.7 for the leads currently being generated by U-decay. But the correction in x in this case is given by x = (94.2 + 1.3)/(5.72 − 1.3 + 0.08) based on the actual composition of the leads and the assumption that the 0.08 percent Pb-208 came from Pb-207. Thus, instead of the value 16.5, the ratio x would have been 21.2 without the (n, γ) reactions.

(b) The uranium ore at Martin Lake, Canada, also contains no Pb-204 and only 0.02 percent as much Th as U. But it has in it an average of 0.53 percent Pb-208. The x-ratio in this case is 90.4/9.1 = 9.93 and the ore has accoringly been assigned an age of 1,640 million years. But what about the lead-208?

The (n, γ) correction† in this example is given by the ratio x = (90.4 + 5.2)/(9.1 + 0.52 − 5.2) = 21.7. Strange, is it not, that this would *agree precisely* with the ratio of leads being generated

---

†To correct the x = (Pb-206/Pb-207) ratio for the influence of (n, γ) reactions so it will be useful in the lead-ratio radioactive time clock in cases where Th and Pb-204 are both negligible as in the Shinkolobwe and Martin Lake examples, the Pb-208 must be accounted as Pb-207, since it came from the reaction Pb-207 (n, γ) Pb-208. Likewise, at equal cross sections for Pb-206 and Pb-207 an amount of Pb-207 equal to x • Pb-208 must be accounted as Pb-206 since it came from the Pb-206 (n, γ) Pb-207 reaction. Therefore, the corrected x-ratio is:

$$x \text{ (corrected)} = \frac{Pb\text{-}206 + x \cdot Pb\text{-}208}{Pb\text{-}207 - x \cdot Pb\text{-}208 + Pb\text{-}208}$$

This is the basis for the data given in these two examples.

today by U? This is, of course, somewhat fortuitous, because the leads do not have precisely the same neutron cross-section, and there are some varations in the dozens or so samples of the ore from which the average values here used were obtained.

The *important point* is that the (n, γ) mechanism of the systematic discrepancies not only explains these discrepancies but, at the same time, erases all readable ages read from the "long time clocks." Figure 2 illustrates that common leads may not provide a reliable time clock. Note, for example, that the "preferred" lead ratio method fails to distinguish between pre-Cambrian (assigned ages of greater than 500 million years) and Early Tertiary (assigned an age of less than 60 million years)! (Pre-Cambrian = L pre C, Early Tertiary = E.T.)

The Potassium/Argon or K-40/A-40 method of radioactive dating may likewise be seriously questioned at least for the following significant reasons:

(1) There is altogether too much argon-40 in the earth for an appreciable part of it to have been generated by potassium-40 decay even if one grants for the sake of argument that the earth is several billion years old.

(2) The K-40/A-40 method is based on uncertain half-life and branching ratio data (Ca-40 about 88 percent to 92 percent and A-40 about 8 to 12 percent of K-40 decay). Even by tacitly assuming the minimum branching ratio of 0.08 this method gives "ages" averaging greater than those of the lead ratio method which in turn yields the oldest ages read from the U-Th-Pb "time clocks."

(3) Like the situation in the U-Th-Pb system, physical chemical analyses of (present) concentrations of the necessary elements and isotopes of the K-40 "clock" are excellent, but sampling is irreproducible and initial concentrations (also quite necessary in applying dating formulae) can be known only by guesswork, however scientific. For instance, what is the justification for applying highly precise analytical methods in an environment where contamination (by precisely the same isotope being analyzed) is greater by a factor of more than a hundred than the radioactivity-generated product one wants to determine?

The Rubidium-Strontium, or Rb-87/Sr-87 "time clock" is another one where pure guesswork is required to *establish* the actual concentrations of the isotopes of this "time clock" at the beginning of a particular mineral.

Do Radiological "Clocks" Need Repair?

Sr-87 occurs in the crust at an abundance at least ten times greater than could be generated from the available rubidium-87 in five billion years.

On the other hand, Rb-87 occurs in the same rocks at 50 ppm and with a half-life of 60 billion years. Therefore, even if one were to agree for the sake of argument that the earth is five billion years old, radiogenic Sr-87 would be only about 5 percent of all Sr-87 present in the rocks.

Again, how can one possibly use this method under such an overall contamination? An indirect answer in this case may have been found already in the empiricism that has developed out of extended efforts to apply the method, i.e., in trying to devise scientific guesses for the necessary initial concentrations of Rb-87 and Sr-87.

The ratio Sr-87/Sr-86 ranges between 0.7 and 0.9 in all samples, "old" or "young," but the value needed for internal consistency with other dating methods turns out to be 0.708 ± 0.001. This was the guess decided upon by some authorities to arrive at how much Sr-87 was present in a particular mineral at its beginning.

This guess eventually became popular in dating rocks by this method; it circumvented more difficult procedures designed to answer the really unanswerable question regarding the isotope concentrations at the beginning of a mineral that one needs to know in order to apply any radioactive time clocks. On the other hand, it was shown that unless all rocks are really the same age within about 45 million years, this guess would be inconsistent with observed total abundance data, i.e., it would require exceptions to the rule to be as prominent as the rule.

Radiocarbon Dating of a Global Sea Level Cycle

Uplifts in Canada and Fennoscandia following (the sudden) loss (from the continent into the sea) of the Wisconsin ice caps were correlated, and evidence for this catastrophic disappearance of the ice caps has been presented in the ice cap model of continental drift as outlined in PEM. Eardley[11] noticed in 1964 the global sea level changes predicted three years earlier[12] by the ice cap model; however, he considered them to be caused not by ice caps, but by a slowing of the rate of rotation of the earth over the past 100 million years.

It was pointed out in PEM (pp. 138-139) and by Flatte[13] that this would be impossible simply because the relaxation of an unbalance in the crust of the earth is much too rapid (only about 4,000 years for a 60 percent adjustment). In other words, the oceans and continents would adjust at precisely the same rate to a uniform slowing of only about two percent in 100 million years. Hence no differential shoreline changes would occur by this mechanism.

Eardley regarded the shoreline data described in the U. S. Navy Hydrographic Charts studied by him to be independent of the ice cap effects on the basis that the maps used by Gutenberg[14] and others (from which they concluded that "sea level has risen around the world in amounts ranging from 10 to 20 cm in the past century") showed no latitude effects. However, ice sheet build up and decay occurring over a period of only a few thousand years would simply have to produce latitude effects in land mass adjustments of the character described by him.

There is little doubt that polar land masses were depressed (roughly the amounts noticed by Eardley) by the Wisconsin ice caps. These depressions were under a total load corresponding to about 20 million square miles of ice several miles deep on the two poles. This not only depressed the original continent in polar regions, but also elevated the crust in equatorial and low latitude regions as required by mass (or volume) conservation. Following sudden loss of this ice into the seas, the land mass adjustments reversed themselves, causing a rise at the poles and submergence at low latitudes.

Shoreline regressions in Canada were studied by Farrand and Gajda.[15] Two recent "back to back" publications by Emery and Garrison[16] and Redfield[17] describe the corresponding (reverse) situation for the seashores in low latitudes along the Atlantic, Gulf, and Pacific Coasts. In addition, an article by Emery et al.[18] described the nature of samples used in radiocarbon dating of these conditions. Taken together these studies of (radiocarbon-dated) uplifts and submergences confirm the type of global shoreline reactions predicted in the ice cap model.

Shoreline Predictions Confirmed

They show first (by their coincidence in time) that the high and low latitude shoreline adjustments are really part of the same global adjustment to an isostatic unbalance over the whole crust.

Second, they show that the adjustment cycle changed from equator to pole as predicted by a model in which the crust was suddenly thrown out of balance by unloading at previously heavily loaded poles.

Third, they show the required exponential decay in time of this unbalance and the fact that there remains even yet an appreciable unbalance. The latter point is especially significant when one also realizes that any such unbalance would be more than 75 percent adjusted in 20,000 years and only about two thirds of it has adjusted so far.

As for Canada, a remarkable plot of "isobases of the marine limit" by Farrand and Gajda[19] shows that the shorelines once extended to the very apex of the North American continent. This means that the farthest advance of the shorelines corresponded to an arc with a center in the islands off northwest Greenland, passing through the southwest edges of the Great Lakes, i.e., the region which divides the flow of water from south and southwestward (into the Mississippi, Ohio, Missouri Rivers), and northeastward into Hudson Bay and the St. Lawrence River.

These shorelines have since receded in high (northern) latitudes quite regularly and over thousands of miles to their present positions. The greatest advance of the shorelines over the continent was described by a semi-circle called by Farrand and Gajda the "limit of warping-Whittlesey zero" which not only passes through the southwest Great Lakes region but also the Northwest Territories and part of New England. The high latitude shoreline regression is associated with uplifting land masses amounting to more than 1,500 feet in some places.

While these uplifts were going on in northeastern Canada, data presented by Emery and Garrison,[20] and by Redfield[21] (also based on conventional-equilibrium-radiocarbon dating) reveal just the reverse situation at low latitudes. Emery and Garrison, in fact, recognized the connection between the high latitude and low latitude vertical landmass adjustments.

Like the uplifts in Canada, those at low latitudes are still in progress at ever-decreasing rates. For example, the down-warping is now at a rate of about 0.025 inches per year in Long Island. They both began at much faster rates, but are slowing in the rate of adjustment as the unbalance gradually disappears, showing again the effects of the catastrophic, sudden denudation at the beginning of the adjustment cycle.

Global Extent of Adjustments

The global extent of these land mass adjustments is shown by the fact that the same conditions were found in Argentina, Nigeria, Mexico, and California as those found along the Atlantic Coast of the U.S.A. Also significant are the facts that the rates and total depths of adjustment were smallest at lowest latitudes, increased northward to a maximum, decreased still northward, and changed sign at the "Whittlesey zero," growing to large opposite magnitudes on northward.

A discrepancy of a few thousand years seems to exist for the time of beginning of the adjustment. That is, the data of Emery and Garrison seem to show evidence for an artificial aging associated with the fact that their curves extrapolate (without the help of very young specimens taken from near present shorelines) to finite ages at zero depth. This may be the result of (C-12 and C-14) ion exchange which may have unrealistically aged specimens used in the analysis associated with exposure to initial highly saline conditions (see p. 4 of PEM).

A striking fact noted in the data is that the dates of samples taken at the very edge of the Atlantic shelf are not greatly different, if at all, from those at the beginning of the uplifts in Canada. This correlation also supports the theory that these dates are also those to be assigned to the Atlantic rift itself and to continental drift. Appropriate allowances, of course, should be made for the unbalance of radiocarbon and the possible unrealistic aging by ion exchange.

When the ice sheets of the Wisconsin were building up (according to the ice cap model of continental drift) the primordial continent ("Pangaea") at high latitudes (both north and south) was subsiding regularly under the ever-increasing polar ice loads. The total load eventually exceeded the strength of the continent and suddenly ruptured it from pole to pole. Immediately after this catastrophic continental rupture, the shorelines were in the positions, approximately, described by Eardley, corresponding to maximum unbalance.

Since then they have readjusted at a maximum rate at first, but at ever-decreasing rates as the global isostatic anomaly lessened exponentially. This situation may be observed in all (radiocarbon-calibrated) depth vs. time results for these readjustments. The proximity in time of continental drift thus seems to be shown by the time scale placed on the related shoreline adjustments accompanying this catastrophic event.

Radiocarbon and Biblical Dates

But, in fact, all of this occurred only about 4,500 years ago (after the Flood in the "days of Peleg"), not even 10,000 to 15,000 years ago, much less the 100 million years ago suggested by the slowing

Do Radiological "Clocks" Need Repair?

rotational model. After all, it is a matter of Bible history, is it not? (See Gen. 10:25, understanding "earth" as used there to refer to the usage in Gen. 1:10. Gen. 10:25 surely cannot refer to Gen. 10:32, as many have supposed.)

While radiocarbon may (when the facts become thoroughly appreciated) be forcing scientists ever closer to the biblical account, one may still be disturbed by the fact that even the nonequilibrium model of radiocarbon does not bring the scientific and biblical "records" into coincidence. Instead, there remains even in the nonequilibrium model a discrepancy of 50 percent or more. This may be due to ion exchange, according to the following explanation:

(a) The Noachin Deluge should have raised the pH of the oceans appreciably when the hot, ultrabasic, emulsified materials of the upper mantle were churned into the waters flowing into the great rift.

(b) The dolomites found abundantly at and toward the bottom of the sediments seem to require basic, high temperature deposition based on what has been learned about conditions for their deposition.

(c) In this regard, an increase of pH of only two units (from 7.0 to 9.0) would be all that would be needed to account for the solution of all the "precipitates" at once in the waters of the Flood.

(d) In this connection Libby gave for the solubility of carbon (in the form of HCO_3^- and CO_3^{-2}) in contact with the limestones, dolomites, etc., the value $S = A(1 - 0.74)$ showing that carbon would become soluble in proportion to $(OH-)$. Subsequent neutralization of the basic solution by cooling and settling of the basic emulsion would then reprecipitate the carbonates rapidly and in a manner that would have trapped debris rich in fossils in the frozen carbonate rocks.

(e) Particularly interesting in this regard were the observations[22] that mollusks living in warm, basic waters high in carbonates had sufficiently reduced radiocarbon content to make them appear as though they had been dead 1,000 to 2,300 years! A similar condition may be noted for "Danger Cave" on the west banks of Great Salt Lake. This cave could not have been occupied as long as the 10,000 to 15,000 years ago indicated by the radiocarbon dating of artifacts found in it, because it was most likely under the waters of Lake Bonneville until only 1,500 to no more than 2,000 years ago!

(f) Other radiocarbon dates of samples taken from the highly saline environment around the Great Salt Lake likewise show unrealistic radiocarbon aging caused by C-12 and C-14 exchange.

Radiocarbon Dating of Ancient Civilizations

Two quotations typify the situation quite well.

> Between five and six thousand years ago, in a few favored areas of the world, man firmly mastered the formulas that released him from an immeasurably long past of savagery, barbarism, and nomadism. . . . For the first time in his history on earth he became aware of his humanity. He became civilized.[23]

> Perhaps the most important turning point in human history occurred thousands of years before anyone could record it. This was the point in time when, after two million years of vagabond hunting, man settled in villages and began domesticating animals and cultivating crops. Within a short one thousand years or so, the seed of civilization was planted, setting off a vastly accelerated pace of cultural and technological development that enabled man to progress from mud huts to moon shots.[24]

These quotations illustrate that not only archaeologists, but earth scientists generally seem bent on (1) establishing evidence for a supposed evolution of man not merely from savagery to civilization but from "earlier forms" of life, and (2) dating anything they find at maximum possible ages. Both of these ideas must eventually prove futile because man and beast really began their existence on the earth as civilized man and "after their kind," respectively only about six millennia ago.

On the other hand, man has degenerated enough times, and in enough places of the world, to permit archaeologists to find real evidence for the savagery to civilization (or its reverse) transition. Real discoveries of this sort do not substantiate "evolution." (Editors Note: Readers will find extensive support for the idea of degeneration of man in articles in the *Creation Research Society Annual*, 1968.)

The equilibrium radiocarbon model is popular among archaeologists, not only because it is a sophisticated modern scientific tool and practically all they have to work with, but also because it gives results often far enough removed from biblical chronology to make them feel comfortable.

Bylinsky,[25] for instance, claimed that radiocarbon has established a date of 6750 B.C. for the deepest layers of "Jarmo," an ancient village considered to represent an early stage in the transition from savagery to civilization, and that a cave called Shanidar close to

Do Radiological "Clocks" Need Repair? 95

Jarmo where "sheep bones (were found) near charcoal . . . in an ideal state for dating with carbon-14" was dated at 9000 B.C.

Bylinsky quoted others to the effect that a cave found in Iran was "occupied about 35,000 B.C. until recent times" and "a farming village . . . founded about 8500 B.C."

Absurd Claim of Accuracy

Also illustrative of a passion for overdating is a further statement by Bylinsky, "A variety of new scientific techniques is helping to expand the scope and meaning of the remote history of man. *First and foremost is radiocarbon* . . . which reaches about seventy thousand years into the past . . ." [26] (emphasis added). While expressing a majority viewpoint, it is distressing that anyone would claim such accuracy for radiocarbon dating. The claim that radiocarbon is useful in dating specimens as old as 70,000 years is absurd.

Such accuracy is not even possible under the most precise laboratory conditions, to say nothing of the uncontrollable and contaminated environment of nature. It would mean, for example, the ability to measure C-14 concentrations (against background radiation) to a precision of one part in 10,000 of the radiocarbon found in the living biosphere.

The usual, still greatly exaggerated, claim is that the upper limit of radiocarbon dating is about 40,000 years. Since the half-life of C-14 is 5,760 years, this corresponds to about seven half-life periods ($0.5^7 < 0.01$). Furthermore, the C-14 concentration would be only three percent as great at 70,000 years as at 40,000 years after death. Even 40,000 years for the resolution in radiocarbon dating would require extremely careful laboratory control quite unrealistic in the natural environment.

Moreover, such claims of accuracy ignore the possibility of even the slightest unbalance of C-14 in the earth as a whole, to say nothing of the 30 percent observed unbalance.

In spite of feverish tendencies to expand antiquity and provide evidence of "evolution" by unrealistic claims of transitions from savagery to civilization, the assigned dates of well-authenticated civilizations (Sumerian, Babylonian, and Egyptian) unearthed and described by archaeologists can, with ever growing factual information, be stretched only a millennium or so.

But the Ark landed roughly 4,500 years ago on Mt. Ararat in the mountains northeast of Mesopotamia, where the Sumerian and Babylonian civilizations flourished. Both these civilizations must have developed *after* Noah's Flood, sometime between the second and third millenia B.C., although archaeologists assign ages for them between three and four millennia B.C.

The difference of a little more than a thousand years is close incidentally to the correction increment obtained by applying the nonequilibrium model in recalculating radiocarbon-dated specimens about 4,000 years old. Considering the magnitude and nature of Noah's Flood (in which the "earth was clean dissolved")—a mechanical, not chemical, dissolution (per John Woodward), one realizes that the Flood probably completely erased evidence of all antediluvian civilizations such as to leave practically nothing readable in the "history written in the rocks."

NOTES AND REFERENCES

1. M. A. Cook, *Prehistory and Earth Models* (London: Max Parish and Co., Ltd., 1966).
2. W. F. Libby, *Radiocarbon Dating*, second edition (Chicago: University of Chicago Press, 1955).
3. W. N. Hess, E. H. Canfield, and R. E. Lingenfelter, *Journal of Geophysical Research*, 66:665 (1961).
4. R. E. Lingenfelter, *Review of Geology*, 1, No. 1:35 (1963).
5. H. E. Suess, *Journal of Geophysical Research*, 70:5937 (1965).
6. M. A. Cook, Geological chronometry. Utah Engineering Experiment Station *Bulletin*, 83, No. 18:47 (1956).
7. V. R. Switzer, *Science*, 157:726 (1967).
8. M. A. Cook, 1966, p. 44.
9. *Ibid.*, p. 53.
10. *Ibid.*, p. 59.
11. A. J. Eardley, *Journal of Geological Education*, 12:1 (1964).
12. M. A. Cook, Continental dynamics. *Bulletin* of the Institute of Metals and Explosive Research, University of Utah (1961).
13. S. M. Flatte, *Journal of Geophysical Research*, 10:5189-5191 (1965).
14. B. Gutenberg, Geological Society of American *Bulletin*, 52:721 (1941).
15. W. R. Farrand and R. T. Gajda, *Geological Bulletin*, Canadian Department of Mines and Technical Survey, Ottawa, Canada (1962).
16. K. O. Emery and L. E. Garrison, *Science*, 157:684 (1967).
17. A. C. Redfield, *Science*, 157:684 (1967).
18. K. O. Emery, R. L. Wigley, A. S. Bartlett, M. Rubin, and E. S. Barghoorn, *Science*, 158:1301 (1967).
19. M. A. Cook, 1966, p. 123.

20. K. O. Emery and L. E. Garrison, *op. cit.*, p. 686.
21. Redfield, *op. cit.*, p. 691.
22. M. A. Cook, 1966, p. 4.
23. L. Cottrell, *The Horizon Book of Lost Worlds* (New York: American Heritage Publishing Co., 1966), p. 1.
24. G. Bylinsky, *Fortune*, October, 1966, p. 159.
25. *Ibid.*, p. 162.
26. *Ibid.*, p. 159.

IX

AN ATTEMPT TO CORRECT FOR THE EFFECTS OF THE FLOOD IN DETERMINING DATES BY RADIOACTIVE CARBON

HAROLD L. ARMSTRONG

This work grew out of some thought about the suggestion in *The Genesis Flood* that, at the time of the flood, the action of cosmic rays, or similar penetrating radiation, may have caused the great reduction in lifetimes which came then, and also the building up of the amount of radioactive carbon in the air.[1] Such increase of radioactive carbon would affect, in turn, attempts to determine dates of organic remains by measuring the amount of radioactive carbon in them.

Now we have no record of the way in which the amount of radioactive carbon built up, but we have in Genesis 11 a record of the way in which the lifetimes decreased. So perhaps from the one set of information we can deduce something about the other matter.

First of all, there appears to be practically no radioactive carbon in coal. So, if we accept that much of the coal comes from vegetation which was buried at the time of the flood, and that the time back to the flood is not much more than the half-life of radioactive carbon (for which, for the present purposes, the round figure of 5,500 years will do), it must follow that there was practically no radioactive carbon in the atmosphere before the flood. I have suggested elsewhere (see legend to Figure 2) a chronology to show that the date of the flood was approximately 2444 B.C.

During the flood, then, and after, radioactive carbon accumulated in the atmosphere, and defects of some kind accumulated in the human race. The result of the latter accumulation was a decrease in lifetime. If both these things were caused by cosmic rays, which first got through to the earth at the time of the flood, we might expect some relation between these two things, such as has just been proposed.

It seems likely that most of the decrease in lifetime would come from what happened in a man's earlier years. On the other hand, Shem was already one hundred at the time of the flood, yet his lifetime was reduced to six hundred years, from the approximately nine hundred and fifty common before the flood. As a reasonable working assumption, let us take it that a man's vulnerability, so to speak, extended up to the age at which he is first recorded as having begotten a son.

In Table 1 are listed the patriarchs, and some other men, with the dates (the flood being taken at 2444 B.C.), at which they first begat, and the lengths of their lives. In Figure 1 are plotted the lifetime vs. the date of maturity B.C. (i.e., of first begetting) and a smooth curve has been drawn through the points. Naturally, the points will scatter around the curve, for "time and chance happeneth to them all" (Eccl. 9:11). The curve might be called that of average lifetime vs. the date of maturity.

Now let us assume as already suggested that the rate of change or increase of the concentration of radioactive carbon is proportional to the rate of change or decrease of average lifetime. This seems plausible if both changes are the results of the same cause. Then, when the lifetime has settled down to its steady magnitude of seventy years, about 1000 B.C., the concentration of radioactive carbon will have settled down to its present "steady" magnitude.

Moreover, at any date the amount of radioactive carbon will be to the present amount as the amount by which the average lifetime had decreased from nine hundred and fifty years is to the total decrease, i.e., from nine hundred and fifty to seventy or eight hundred and eighty years. For instance, at a date when the average lifetime was five hundred and ten years, the amount of radioactive carbon was just half what it is now.

Actually, there should be some averaging of the amount of radioactive carbon over all the time in which the sample concerned was growing. But then, there ought to be some averaging over the time in which the man concerned was growing. Since these two effects should be somewhat parallel, relating lifetime to concentration of radioactive carbon at the time of maturity should be reasonable.

The amount of radioactive carbon in a sample at any subsequent time is given by $\exp(-T/8000)$ times the amount with which it started, T being the time in years. (The number 8000 is given by $5500/\log_e 2$.) If the sample started out with only $1/x$ the supposed concentration, one assuming that it started with the supposed (i.e., present) concentration, would take the age as the true age plus the time for the concentration to decay to $1/x$, i.e., plus $8000 \log_e x$ years.

The concentrations as various dates, from 1000 B.C. back to 2440 B.C. have been taken from the graph in Figure 1, as suggested, the fraction 1/x of the present concentration calculated, and 8000 $\log_e x$ years added to the (true) date to give the indicated date, i.e., indicated by the method of radioactive carbon. In Figure 2 are plotted the true date vs. indicated date. The graph goes back from 1000 B.C.; for more recent dates the indicated age will be very nearly correct.

It can be seen that a sample from about 2100 B.C. would be dated as fully one thousand years too old, and for older samples the error would increase rapidly. It is interesting to notice that samples seem to keep on being found which give by radioactive carbon dates around 2500 B.C. to 3000 B.C. but which are dated by other evidence as nearly 1,000 years later.[2]

For samples from between about 2400 B.C. and the flood, the dating by radioactive carbon would be very unreliable, and for antediluvian samples it would, of course, be quite impossible. However, let us consider a little more closely what antediluvian samples might show.

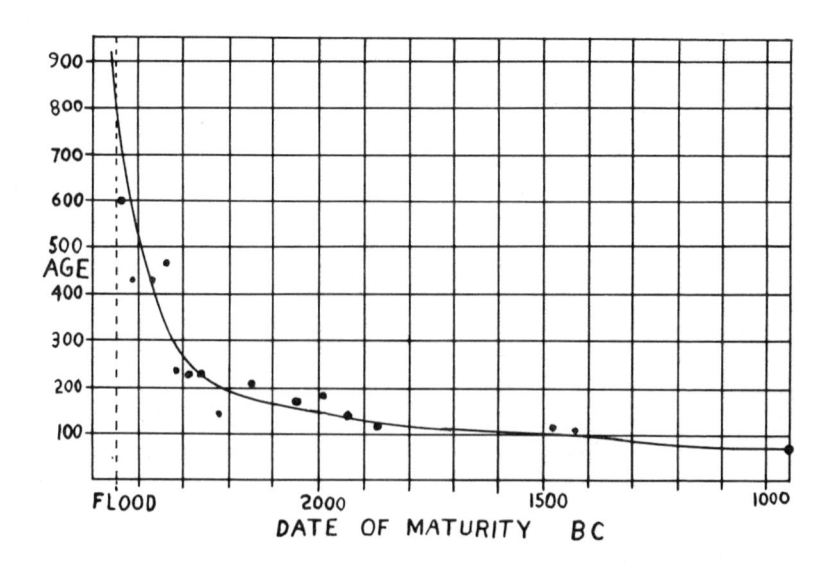

Figure 1. Here the age to which patriarchs and others lived has been plotted vs. their date of maturity, i.e., of first recorded beget-

Correcting Flood Effects on Carbon Dating 101

ting, and a smooth curve drawn through the points. The chronology is one which has been worked out for this purpose, but the substitution of a similar one, e.g., Ussher's, would not affect things appreciably.

TABLE 1

	Date of First Begetting	Lived to Age
Shem	2442	600
Arphaxed	2407	438
Salah	2377	433
Eber	2343	464
Peleg	2313	239
Reu	2281	239
Serug	2251	230
Nahor	2222	148
Terah	2152	205
Abraham	2052	175
Isaac	1992	180
Jacob	1932(?)	147
Joseph	1869(?)	110
Moses	1470(?)	120
Joshua	1420(?)	110
Solomon	950(?)	70(?)

Table 1. Here the date of maturity, i.e., of the first recorded begetting, and the age to which they lived, are collected for patriarchs and some others. The dates are from a chronology which has been worked out for this purpose; the substitution, however, of another one such as Ussher's would not change things seriously.

Thus these would indicate some quite large age, and the indicated age, like the history of the remains, would be exceedingly varied. It may well be such antediluvian remains which are found from time to time and indicate ages of some tens of thousands of years.

It must be granted that the assumption that average lifetimes and concentration of radioactive carbon are related in the way proposed is indeed an assumption. Moreover, the curve of average lifetime cannot be fitted with very great precision because the points scatter so. Nevertheless, this method seems to offer some hope of estimating the amount of error involved in trying to date samples by radioactive carbon.

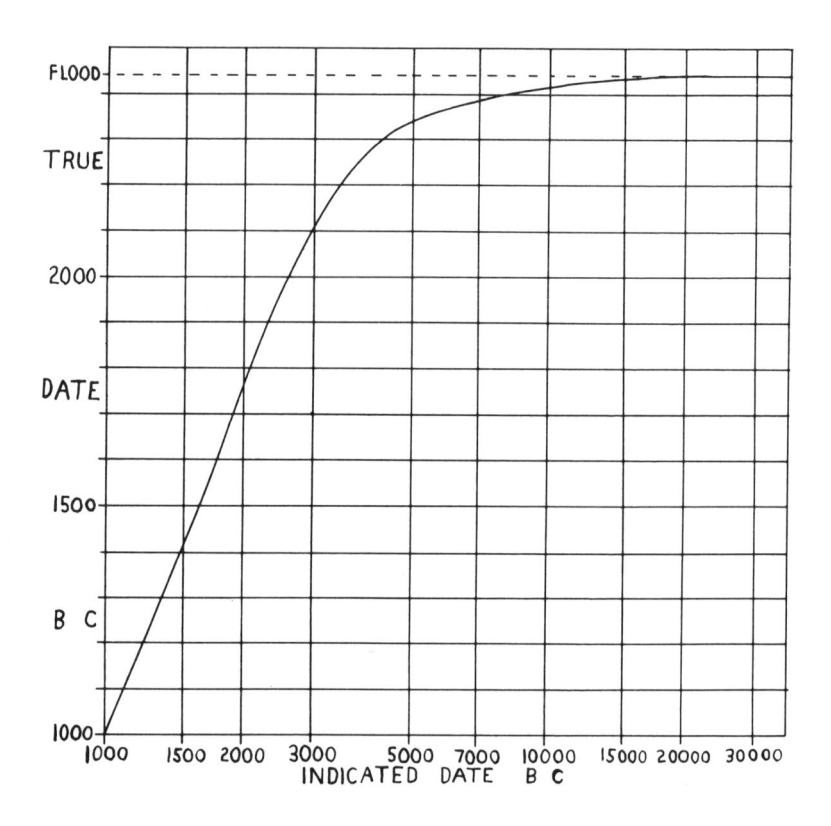

Figure 2. This shows the true date vs. date indicated by dating with radioactive carbon on the usual assumption that the sample started off with the same concentration of radioactive carbon that it would have if it started now. The chronology used puts the flood at 2444 B.C., but another date near that, such as Ussher's 2349 B.C., would merely shift the curve bodily up or down a bit. Note that the scale of indicated dates is logarithmic.

NOTES AND REFERENCES

1. J. C. Whitcomb and H. M. Morris, *The Genesis Flood* (Philadelphia: Presbyterian and Reformed Publishing Company, 1961), pp. 23ff, 374ff, 404ff.
2. *Op. cit.*, p. 43, for comments and further references.

X

SCIENCE VERSUS SCIENTISM IN HISTORICAL GEOLOGY

Henry M. Morris

The study of historical geology holds great fascination for many people who are neither historians nor geologists. This discipline occupies a uniquely interesting and important position in human thought. Among the humanities, the study of history surely is of singular significance and, among the sciences, geology, dealing as it does with the very earth itself, is similarly of unique interest. When the two are combined in historical geology, which professes to be able to decipher the mystery of the origin and history of the earth and its processes, the resulting panorama is of marvelous interest and significance. Such a picture, in fact, is of far more than historical and geological pertinence. Anything which elucidates origins is necessarily of philosophical and theological interest, with strong implications regarding meanings and purposes and destinies as well.

It is little wonder, then, that historical geology has attracted the intense interest and concern of a great variety of people. As a matter of fact, the basic structure of modern historical geology was worked out over a hundred years ago by such men as James Hutton (an agriculturalist with medical training), John Playfair (a mathematician), William Smith (a surveyor), Charles Lyell (a lawyer), Georges Cuvier (a comparative anatomist), Charles Darwin (an apostate divinity student and naturalist), Robert Chambers (a journalist), William Buckland (a theologian), Roderick Murchison (a soldier and gentleman of leisure), Adam Sedgwick (who, when seeking election to the chair of geology at Cambridge, boasted that he knew nothing of geology), Hugh Miller (a stonemason), John Fleming (a zoologist), and others of like assortment.

Although the basic framework of historical geology, as worked out by these men, has not changed to the present day, there has arisen a group of specialists in historical geology who have come to regard this field as their own particular field of *science*, and who now regard with some disdain any who venture to write or speak in this field without giving full allegiance to the accepted system. By its very nature, however, historical geology is not, and can never be, a genuine *science*, and therefore the dogmatic insistence that one follow the interpretations of its founders and present-day leaders, with all the implications of origins and meanings that are involved, is nothing less than *scientism*.

This is in no way meant to be a reflection upon the science of geology, which is a true science in every sense of the word, and which has made a tremendous contribution to our understanding and application of the laws of nature. When, however, a geologist (or lawyer or surveyor or naturalist or anything else) seeks to become a *historical* geologist, he must leave the realm of science and enter that of philosophy or religion. The presently accepted system of historical geology is basically nothing else than a philosophy or a religion of evolutionary uniformitarianism. If this fact were only recognized and acknowledged by its adherents, no one would be greatly disturbed, but, when this system is widely promulgated and insisted upon in the name of *science*, it has degenerated into mere scientism instead. This will become more evident as we consider the true meaning of science and the true nature of those physical processes studied by science.

What Is Science?

The word "science" itself of course, is derived from the Latin *scientia* ("knowledge"), and this is essentially what it means. A more formal definition as given in the Oxford dictionary, is as follows: "A branch of study which is concerned either with a connected body of demonstrated truths or with observed facts systematically classified and more or less colligated by being brought under general laws, and which includes trustworthy methods for the discovery of new truth within its own domain."

Science thus involves facts which are observed and laws which have been demonstrated. The scientific method involves experimental reproducibility, with like causes producing like effects. It is *knowledge*, not inference or speculation or extrapolation.

True science thus is necessarily limited to the measurement and study of *present* phenomena and processes. Data which have been actually observed in the present, or which have been recorded by human observers in the historic past, are properly called scientific data. Laws which have been deduced from these data, which satisfactorily correlate the pertinent data and which have predictive value for the correlation of similar data obtained from like experiments in the future, are properly regarded as scientific laws.

But there is obviously no way of knowing that these processes and the laws which describe them have always been the same in the past or that they will always be the same in the future. It is possible to make an assumption of this kind, of course, and this is the well-known principle of *uniformitarianism*. The assumption is reasonable, in the light of our experience with present processes, and it is no doubt safe to extrapolate on this basis for a certain time into the future and back into the past. But to insist that uniformitarianism is the only scientific approach to the understanding of *all* past and future time is clearly nothing but a dogmatic tenet of a particular form of religion.

That uniformitarianism has been the foundational and guiding principle of historical geology is widely recognized. A standard textbook on the subject says, for example:

> The uprooting of such fantastic beliefs [of the catastrophist] began with the Scottish geologist, James Hutton, whose *Theory of the Earth*, published in 1785, maintained that the *present is the key to the past* and that, given sufficient time, processes now at work could account for all the geologic features of the globe. This philosophy, which came to be known as the *doctrine of uniformitarianism*, demands an immensity of time; it has now gained universal acceptance among intelligent and informed people.[1]

Thus, science deals with the data and processes of the present, which can be experimentally measured and observationally verified. The principle of uniformity is a philosophy, or faith, by which it is hoped that these processes of the past can be extrapolated into the distant past and the distant future to explain all that has ever happened and to predict all that will ever happen.

But, when viewed in these terms, it is obvious that uniformity is not proved, and therefore is not properly included in the definition of science. There may be any number of other assumptions which might serve as the basis of such extrapolation, and all would similarly be mere acts of faith.

It is perfectly possible and reasonable, as we shall see, to assume that the processes studied by science were themselves created at some time in the past and will be terminated at some time in the future. The processes themselves, then, could tell us nothing about their creation or termination—this would be outside the domain of scientific investigation. Such information could come, if at all, only by revelation from their Creator.

As a matter of fact, a full and complete understanding of any process, even in its present character, could in that case be obtained only in the context and framework of the fact of its prior creation. This is because *meaning* is inextricably inter-related with *origin* and *destiny*.

Apart from this stricture, however, it is possible and proper to study science, in the sense of present processes, without reference to the past or future. Thus, the science of physics deals with the present processes of the physical world; the science of chemistry deals with the present chemical properties and behavior of matters; the science of geology deals with present geological processes and earth features; the science of biology deals with the processes of life in plants, animals, and man. So long as the question of *origins* or *ends* is not considered, there will be no conflct between the Bible and science. The Bible has numerous references to present phenomena of science, and all will be found in strict accord with the actual observed data. It is only when questions of origins or destinies (or fundamental meanings) are considered that conflicts appear.

To a considerable degree, therefore, a *Christian* study of physics or chemistry or other science can proceed along the same lines as a treatment by non-Christians. The same textbooks can be used, the same experimental apparatus, the same methods, provided only that the study is limited to an elucidation of the actual present properties and processes of the data of that science. But as soon as intrinsic meanings or origins or destinies are brought into the treatment, there will inevitably be conflict between the uniformitarian and Christian world-views.

The Processes of Science

Assuming that our study of science will be, as is proper, limited to the study of present processes, we soon encounter a most remarkable and significant fact. Regardless of the particular discipline of science we study—physics, chemistry, biology, geology, etc.—these processes all are built upon two basic concepts and follow two basic laws. The two basic concepts are *energy* and *entropy*, and the two laws are the *first and second laws of thermodynamics*.

Since the implications of these laws are highly important to the

Christian cosmology, it will be well to allow a non-theist, thoroughly evolutionary and uniformitarian in his philosophy, to define them. Dr. Harold F. Blum, the Princeton biologist, states them as follows:

> Energy appears in various forms: heat, light, kinetic energy, mechanical work, chemical energy, and so forth. Energy can change its form but not its quantity—this is a statement of the *first law of thermodynamics*, which until quite recently could be accepted without qualification. We know, now, that matter is another form of energy, but that does not alter this fundamental principle which is also called the law of conservation of energy.[2]

Energy is the concept which measures the capacity of doing work. Thus, everything in the physical universe, including matter and all the phenomena associated with matter, is essentially one or another form of energy. This first law of thermodynamics, which was proved empirically about a century ago, is really the most basic of all scientific laws. It has been verified in countless thousands of experiments, ranging from those on the scale of the sub-nuclear particles to measurements of the stars and galaxies, and there is no known exception. Thus, according to this most basic and best-proved of all scientific laws, there is *nothing which is now being created or destroyed*. Present processes, with which alone true science is able to deal, are *not* processes of creation.

With respect to the second law, Blum continues:

> The *second law of thermodynamics* cannot be put in such concise form as the first; it is stated in numerous ways, according to the kind of problem under study.... It is one of this law's consequences that all real processes go irreversibly. Let us consider a universe in which the total amount of energy remains, supposedly, constant. Any given process in this universe is accompanied by a change in magnitude of a quantity called the *entropy*.... All real processes go with an increase of entropy. The entropy also measures the randomness or lack of orderliness of the system, the greater the randomness the greater the entropy....[3]

Thus, the second law of thermodynamics states that there is a universal tendency toward disorder and decay. In any finite open system, of course, there may be temporarily and locally an increase of order, due to the influx of ordering energy from outside the system, but the tendency is always ultimately downward toward disintegration and death. This law also is proved beyond question, with no known exceptions. As Blum says in the preface to the third edition of his book:

> Wishful thinking to the contrary, the second law of thermodynamics remains with us; . . . no wise scientist will, I think, deny its existence or import.[4]

Since we are here specially concerned with geological processes, the testimony of a prominent geologist will also be cited. Dr. Brian Mason, who is Curator of Physical Geology and Mineralogy at the American Museum of Natural History, says:

> In redistribution and recombination of the chemical elements in minerals and rocks the atoms or ions lose part of their energy and yield more stable systems. Every rock exemplifies the laws conditioning the stability of crystal lattices, laws which follow the general principles of the structure of matter and of thermodynamics . . . the study of equilibria in laboratory experiments and by thermodynamic methods has thrown a flood of light on geochemical reactions, such as the origin of rocks and minerals, the processes of weathering and decomposition, and other kinds of transformations going on within the earth. . . . The major value of thermodynamics in geochemistry is that it provides a general approach to problems of stability, equilibrium, and chemical change.[5]

Thus, the two laws of thermodynamics are not simply laws of physics and engineering, as they are too often considered to be, but are universal laws governing the behavior of all matter and processes on the earth, including those of biology, as Blum has shown, and of geology, as Mason has shown. The first law teaches that energy (which includes everything in the physical universe) is quantitatively constant. The second law teaches that energy is qualitatively deteriorating. Thus *the present processes of nature are not processes of creation and integration, but rather of conservation and disintegration.*

All real processes in the universe, of course, therefore involve change, which means essentially exchanges of of energy, or transformations of energy from one kind into another. But these changes are basically processes of decay. Locally and temporarily there may be processes which seem to be processes of growth and integration (such as the growth of a child or the growth of a crystal or the manufacture of an automobile). But these are due to a temporary excess influx of ordering energy into the system. Eventually, though, the child will grow old and die, the crystal will disintegrate, and the automobile will end up in the auto graveyard. Most processes fail even to exhibit this tentative growth character. In geology, for example, typical processes are erosion, heat flow, and radioactive decay. In fact, it is such processes as these whose measured rates have served as the basis for geochronological calculations. But here a very important caution is in order. Although the second law of thermodynamics indicates that any system must decay, it says nothing about the rate of decay. As Mason says:

> It is important to realize, however, that thermodynamics cannot predict the *rate* at which a reaction will proceed and does not tell us anything of the mechanism of the reaction.[6]

And, similarly, Blum says:

> The second law of thermodynamics points the direction of events in time, but does not tell when or how fast they will go.[7]

These rates of decay will depend upon many variables, and in nearly all cases must be determined empirically, by actual measurements. There is never any assurance that the decay rates will be constant, as they may well change if the factors which influence them change. All geochronometers are suspect from this cause alone.

The True Uniformitarianism

We can now see that the concept of uniformitarianism, while perfectly valid and proper in its legitimate framework, has been applied quite illegitimately in historical geology. True uniformity has to do with the inviolability of natural *law* (e.g., the laws of thermodynamics), and not to the uniformity of process *rates*. The laws of thermodynamics indicate what the character of all natural processes must be, but they do not indicate how fast or how slow such processes will proceed. And there is certainly never any assurance that the rate of any given process will always be constant.

But it is this assumed uniformity of process rates which is at the very hub of the principle of uniformity as it has been applied in historical geology. This is evident from the following rather typical description of the principle:

> Opposed to this line of thinking was Sir Charles Lyell (1797-1875), a contemporary of Cuvier, who held that earth changes were gradual, taking place at the same uniform slowness that

they are today. Lyell is thus credited with the propagation of the premise that more or less has guided geological thought ever since, namely, that *the present is the key to the past.* In essence, Lyell's *doctrine of uniformitarianism* stated that past geological processes operated in the same manner and at the same rate they do today.[8]

Now it is quite obvious that if geological processes have always been going on at the same slow rates they exhibit today, the earth must be immensely old. Age calculations by certain of these processes—such as radioactive decay, continental erosion, canyon-cutting, deltaic deposition, oceanic sodium increments, etc.—when based on present rates, are of course bound to give extremely high values, far greater than can possibly be accommodated within the framework of biblical chronology.

But there is clearly no scientific basis for assuming such uniformity of process rates. It is quite valid to assume that running water will erode soil and rock, that radioactive minerals will decay, and that all other such processes will proceed irreversibly in accord with the second law of thermodynamics, but neither this nor any other scientific law provides any guarantee that such rates will always be slow and uniform. In fact, it is certain that all such real decay processes are so intricately complex and are affected by such a great number of factors (a change in any one of which may drastically affect the process rate) that it will forever be quite impossible to say exactly what the rate will be except under very precisely known and experimentally confirmed conditions.

It is encouraging that many geologists in recent years are beginning to recognize and acknowledge this distinction. For example, Zumberge, in a widely used introductory text, after defining uniformitarianism as above, cautions:

> From a purely scientific point of view, it is unwise to accept uniformitarianism as unalterable dogma. As pointed out in chapter one, man's experience with geological processes is restricted to only a minute fraction of the total span of earth history. He should never close his mind to the possibility that conditions in past geological time were different than today, and that the doctrine of uniformitarianism may not apply in every case where the reconstruction of some segment of earth history is involved.[9]

A very strong statement of the pitfalls of uniformitarianism in attempting to explain the sedimentary rocks is given by a member of the geology faculty at Pennsylvania State University:

Conventional uniformitarianism, or "gradualism," i.e., the doctrine of unchanging change, is verily contradicted by all post-Cambrian sedimentary data and the geotectonic histories of which these sediments are the record. Thus, quantitative interpretations of the Ordovician from the Recent are meaningless.[10]

More recently, a Columbia University geologist has clearly tried to distinguish between the true and the fallacious uniformitarianism (calling them methodological and substantive uniformitarianism, respectively):

> Uniformitarianism is a dual concept. Substantive uniformitarianism (a testable theory of geologic change postulating uniformity of rates or material conditions) is false and stifling to hypothesis formation. Methodological uniformitarianism (a procedural principle asserting spatial and temporal invariance of natural laws) belongs to the definition of science and is not unique to geology.[11]

With this we would heartily agree. Uniformity of natural laws is basic in science, and is quite in accord with Scripture (always allowing, of course, for the possible miraculous interruption of those laws by the Creator when He so wills). But the type of geological uniformitarianism which has held sway for a hundred years, and which has indeed served as the very foundation of the theory of evolution, is not only contrary to the biblical record, but is completely inadequate to explain the actual data of geology.

> Substantive uniformitarianism as a descriptive theory has not withstood the test of new data and can no longer be maintained in any strict manner.[12]

Since geological uniformitarianism in the traditional sense can no longer be maintained, and since uniformitarianism in the true sense is in no way a peculiar possession of the science of geology, it is thus completely wrong to refer to uniformitarianism as being in some way particularly the possession of geological theory. An illuminating admission giving the reason why this identification continues to be made is revealed in the following:

> As a special term, methodological uniformitarianism was useful only when science was debating the status of the supernatural in its realm for if God intervenes, then laws are not invariant and induction becomes invalid. . . . The term today is an anachronism for we need no longer take special pains to affirm the scientific nature of our discipline.[13]

If one looks beneath the surface of these reasonings, he begins to see that the real problem is not one of science at all, but of scientism! That is, historical geologists have attempted to defend substantive uniformitarianism(i.e., uniformity of process rates) by citing the undisputed evidence of methodological uniformitarianism (i.e., uniformity of natural law). Whether this fallacy in reasoning has been conscious or subconscious is really immaterial; the basic reason for it in either case has been the innate desire to relegate the position of the Creator and His possible intervention in history as far back in time as possible, and perhaps even to eliminate Him altogether. A full-orbed philosophy—nay a religion—of origins and development has thus been erected upon a fallacious uniformitarianism. And this is scientism, not science.

The Evolutionary Framework

The vast ages of earth history which supposedly are implied by the principle of uniformity have been subdivided into a more or less standard series of geological eras and periods, each with a generally accepted name and approximate duration. The whole sequence is known as the "geological column," and the corresponding chronology is known as the "geological time scale." This, of course, is the very backbone of the so-called historical geology. Any given rock formation must occupy a certain position in the column, and presumably it can be dated as to time of formation in terms of the time scale.

A highly pertinent question needs asking at this point. On what basis are the various rock types and formations identified and classified? How is one system assigned to, say, the Devonian Period and another to the Ordovician? How do we know which is older and which is younger? How are the divisions between successive periods recognized?

As a matter of fact, this problem of stratigraphic classification is involved in no little uncertainty and controversy at the present time, even though the geologic time scale has been generally accepted in its present form for about a hundred years.

The layman is inclined to assume that the principle of superposition is the main factor in determining relative age, and that equivalent strata in different areas can be recognized by their chemical or physical composition. However, this is not so. The factor which is by all odds the most important in assigning an age to a given stratum is its biological content—that is, the *fossils* it contains.

Science versus Scientism in Historical Geology   113

That it appears that the only presently available rational geochronological indices are biostratigraphically based—i.e., *biochronologic*.[14]

This means plainly that *only* the fossils can be relied upon as a criterion for determining the time in earth history when a particular formation was deposited. Other data—vertical position, physico-chemical characteristics, and other factors—are essentially insignificant.

> Physico-geometrical data (apart from radiometric) can do no more than provide a crude local relative chronology or circumstantial evidence in support of a biochronologic framework.[15]

Now the only way in which the fossil contents of a rock could possibly indicate how old the rock might be is if the animals found as fossils were living only at that specific time in earth history. This means that there have been different kinds of life at different periods in history, and that therefore the living forms provide an unambiguous index to the chronology.

But how do we know which forms were living when? There must be some systematic way of viewing and classifying the changes of life forms with the passage of geologic time. The key, of course, is evolution! If we are to explain everything in terms of uniform laws and uniform processes, this must include the development of the biological world as well as the physical world. All kinds of animals must therefore have gradually developed from earlier and simpler forms. There must have been a slow increase of organization and complexity of living forms during geologic history. And this is the clue we need! Simple fossils mean a formation is ancient; complex fossils are recent.

The fossil record thus is of absolutely paramount importance in geologic dating. The fossil forms are classified according to the underlying evolutionary assumptions, and then they in turn become "index fossils" for future dating purposes.

> In each sedimentary stratum certain fossils seem to be characteristically abundant: these fossils are known as *index fossils*. If in a strange formation an index fossil is found, it is easy to date that particular layer of rock and to correlate it with other exposures in distant regions containing the same species.[16]

The evolutionary significance of this methodology is clearly indicated by the following:

> Once it was understood that each fossil represents a biologic entity, instead of a special divinely created life form, it became quite obvious that the plants and animals of each stratigraphic division had simply evolved from those of the preceding epoch through gradual adaptation. They were, in turn, ancestral to those that followed.[17]

This technique might have merit if it were actually known, from historical records or from divine revelation or from some other source, that in fact all living forms had actually evolved from prior forms. But the actual evidence for evolution on such a scale as this is, as implied by the above quotation, limited to the fossil record itself. In a presidential address before the Geological Society of America, Dr. Hollis Hedberg also stressed the evolutionary significance of the fossil record, as follows:

> That our present-day knowledge of the sequence of strata in the earth's crust is in major part due to the evidence supplied by fossils is a truism. Merely in their role as distinctive rock constituents, fossils have furnished one of the best and most widely used means of tracing beds and correlating them. However, going far beyond this, fossils have furnished, through their record of the evolution of life on this planet, an amazingly effective key to the relative positioning of strata in widely separated regions and from continent to continent.[18]

Thus, the primary means of dating rock formations relative to each other, in the Geologic Column, is the evolutionary sequence of life on the earth through geologic time, and the preservation of distinctive life forms as fossils deposited in the rocks laid down during each successive period. But, then, in turn, the history of evolution on the earth has been built up on the basis of the record revealed in the rocks representing the successive geologic ages. In fact, the only genuine historical evidence for the truth of evolution is found in this fossil record. As Dunbar says:

> Although the comparative study of living plants and animals may give very convincing circumstantial evidence, fossils provide the only historical, documentary evidence that life has evolved from simpler to more and more complex forms.[19]

The evidence for evolution afforded by living plants and animals is, indeed, hardly convincing at all. The most universally accepted biologic mechanism for producing evolutionary change is supposed to be genetic mutation (a sudden, random change in the biochemical structure of the germ cell) preserved, if favorable, by natural selection. This is confirmed by the very prominent Edinburgh geneticist, C. H. Waddington:

> It remains true to say that we know of no way other than random mutation by which new hereditary variation comes into being, nor any process other than natural selection by which the hereditary constitution of a population changes from one generation to the next.[20]

Since our focus of attention in this paper is geology, we do not wish to digress into a discussion of genetic theory at this point, except to call attention to the fact that *present* processes of biologic change are associated almost exclusively with mutations, as far as permanent, hereditary, truly novel changes are concerned. Presumably if evolution is actually a fact of nature, it is to be explained in terms of mutation and natural selection. This, in fact, is undoubtedly the consensus of thinking of most leading evolutionists today, not only those working in the field of genetics, but also those in the field of paleontology.

Furthermore, it is admitted by all geneticists that the great majority—in fact, almost *all*—mutations are basically harmful. This is only to be expected, since they represent random changes in very highly ordered systems:

> Mutations occur at random, not because it would be convenient to have one. Any chance alteration in the composition and properties of a highly complex operating system is not likely to improve its manner of operation and most mutations are disadvantageous for this reason. There is a delicate balance between an organism and its environment which a mutation can easily upset. One could as well expect that altering the position of the foot brake or the gas pedal at random would improve the operation of an automobile.[21]

As a matter of fact, mutations provide a very fine illustration of the second law of thermodynamics—the universal tendency toward disorder and decay. In any case, truly beneficial mutations are obviously such very rare events, if they occur at all, that it is quite impossible to see real evolution occurring among present plants and animals. There is, of course, a great deal of variation within basic kinds of creatures—in fact, no two individuals are exactly alike—but there are also quite clear-cut gaps between such basic kinds of creatures.

Since evolution cannot be demonstrated as occurring in the present, and since, indeed, such evidence as does exist of biologic change in the present seems to be evidence of decay and death, rather than growth and increasing organization, it is obvious that, in the last analysis, the only real evidence for evolution in the broad sense is that contained in the fossil record.

But the fossil record is based on the geologic ages, and the geologic ages have been built up as an interpretive framework for earth history on the very basis of the assumption of evolution! This is obviously circular reasoning, but that in itself does not condemn it since, in the final analysis, all philosophies are based on circular reasoning. One always brings certain innate presuppositions with him when he tries to philosophize on origins and meanings, and these necessarily determine his conclusions. It is only when such circular reasoning is called *science* that it really becomes scientism. As a religious faith, it may be a live option, but not as science!

Basic Inconsistencies in Evolutionary Uniformitarianism

The fallacious application of uniformitarian reasoning to geological process rates thus has led to the system of the evolutionary geologic ages. This in turn forms the evidential basis of the theory of evolution, which presumably accounts for the origin and development of all things, including life and including man. All of this, as we have just seen, involves a powerful system of circular reasoning, somewhat disguised but nonetheless real.

But there is another, perhaps even more significant, fallacy in this system, which will now be discussed. True uniformitarianism involves the constancy and reliability of natural laws. These laws are formulated to describe the processes of nature, and by their very nature, as concepts developed by scientific measurements and methods, these processes are known only in their *present* form. As noted earlier, these laws deal basically with the concepts of energy and entropy, and are ultimately structured around the two laws of thermodynamics.

The most basic and universal of all scientific laws is that of conservation. There are, of course, a number of different conservation laws (energy, mass, momentum, electric charge, etc.), but the most important is that of energy (including mass, as a form of energy).

> The physicist's confidence in the conservation principles rests on long and thoroughgoing experience. The conservation of energy,

of momentum and of electrical charge have been found to hold, within the limits of accuracy of measurement, in every case that has been studied. An elaborate structure of physical theory has been built on these fundamental concepts, and its predictions have been confirmed without fail.[22]

Thus, the basic structure of the universe, in so far as *science* knows it, is conservative. That is, nothing is now being created or destroyed. The present processes of nature, *including all geologic processes and all biologic processes*, are not creative in nature.

Consequently, it is fundamentally impossible for science to learn anything about origins. Science deals with present processes, and present processes are conservative, not creative. Thus, historical geology, professing to discover the history of the origin and evolution of the earth and its inhabitants through a scientific study and extrapolation of present processes, is a self-contradiction.

And the situation becomes even more contradictory when the second law of thermodynamics is considered. Not only is the universe basically conservative in quantity, but it is also basically degradational in quality.

> Man has long been aware that his world has a tendency to fall apart. Tools wear out, fishing nets need repair, roofs leak, iron rusts, wood decays, loved ones sicken and die, relatives quarrel, and nations make war. . . . We instinctively resent the decay of orderly systems such as the living organism and work to restore such systems to their former or even higher level of organization.[23]

Thus, all systems, no matter how large or how small, living or nonliving, tend to become disordered and disorganized, to decay and die. Application of an excess of ordering energy from outside the system is continually needed to offset this decadent tendency, and even more is needed if, for a while, the system is to manifest a period of growth and integration.

There could hardly be imagined a philosophy more in fundamental contradiction with this actual and unquestioned law of nature than the philosophy of evolution. According to evolution, there is an innate principle of development and progress in the universe, leading always to higher and higher levels of complexity and integration.

> Most enlightened persons now accept as a fact that everything in the cosmos—from heavenly bodies to human beings—has developed and continues to develop through evolutionary proc-

esses. The great religions of the West have come to accept a historical view of creation. Evolutionary concepts are applied also to social institutions and to the arts. Indeed, most political parties, as well as schools of theology, sociology, history, or arts, teach these concepts and make them the basis of their doctrines. Thus, theoretical biology now pervades all of Western culture indirectly through the concept of progressive historical change.[24]

We would agree completely that modern science reveals a concept of universal change—but this change is one of decay and dissipation. The supposed universal process of evolution, on the other hand, postulates a universal law of progress and increased organization. Thus, the theory of evolution and the second law of thermodynamics squarely confront and contradict each other. Each is precisely the converse of the other. One is a universal law of change upward, the other is a universal law of change downward! It should be plain and obvious that only one of these principles can possibly be valid.

Herein is another, and climactic, contradiction in evolutionary historical geology. Historical geology purports to tell us of the evolutionary development of life on the earth, and to do so in terms of *present* processes. But present processes are processes of decay, and therefore contradict the very concept of evolution.

If historical geology would be truly scientific, as it claims to be, then it must recognize that it must be organized within the framework of *true* uniformitarianism, which is the uniformity of natural law. It must realize that the story of earth history which it seeks to decipher has been one enacted within the framework of laws of conservation and decay, not of creation and development.

Therefore, to assume that the origin and history of the earth can be interpreted within the framework of an assumed uniformity of process rates and an assumed innate principle of evolutionary development is to reject the very basic laws of science which it professes to follow. But this would still be a permissible point of view to take, since not even uniformity of natural law can be *proved* in the prehistoric period. It is legitimate to assume, if one wishes to do so, that the two laws of thermodynamics were not in operation during the geological ages, and therefore that evolution and progress were possible on a world-wide scale. The paleontologic data can then be interpreted to fit into that framework if one wishes so to do. All the contradiction and anomalies which abound in such a system can be explained away by piling hypothesis upon hypothesis (e.g., explaining great areas where "young" fossils are buried beneath "old" fossils by means of the theory of the overthrust fault). Since all of this can never be subjected to laboratory verification, and is thus out of reach of the "scientific method," this framework of evolutionary uniformitarianism cannot be disproved scientifically.

But to say that a system erected upon such assumptions, which contradict the basic laws of science, is itself "scientific" is entirely unwarranted. And when the theory of evolution, based as it is upon this system, and the paleontologic data interpreted in accordance with it, is then made the foundation for all modern studies in theology, sociology, history, politics, and the arts—indeed into an all-embracing evolutionary world-view—and when all of this monstrous system is taught and indoctrinated as *scientific fact* almost everywhere, as it is today—the charge of *scientism* is a gross understatement of the true situation!

Implications of Evolution

The system of evolutionary uniformitarianism is, therefore, not a science but a system. It is a form of religion, a faith in innate progress, in materialistic development, in pantheistic humanism. It is the essence of modern man-centered culture. The evolutionary philosophy, as noted by Rene Dubos,[25] has profoundly affected every field of human thought and activity. Man has been led to see himself as organically linked to all other forms of life:

> Comparative biology has revealed, furthermore, that man is linked to all living organism through a common line of descent, and share with them many characteristics of physiochemical constitution and of biological organization; the philosophical concept of the "great chain of being" can thus be restated now in the form of a scientific generalization.[26]

Not only so, but since all things can be explained in terms of this supposed universal process of evolution, effectuated by the cybernetic processes of mutation and natural selection, there is no need any longer to postulate a divine Creator originating or guiding the development of the universe. God becomes an unnecessary hypothesis. Man, as the highest stage of the evolutionary process, now having come to understand and even to guide it, is himself the creator.

What is almost certain, however, is that the various components of human culture are now required not only for the survival of man, but also for his existential realization. Man created himself even as he created his culture and thereby he became dependent upon it.[27]

In the last analysis, then, evolution is a religion that permits man to divest himself of concern for or responsibility to a divine Creator. It is not a science in any proper sense of the word at all. And the same must therefore be true for the system of evolutionary geology which both supports it and is supported by it.

We hasten to say again that this is no criticism of the sciences of geology or biology, or of the scientists who practice them. The genuine sciences of geology and biology, dealing as they do with the *present* processes of the earth and of life, are of highest merit and importance. It is believed that the great majority of geologists and biologists, who may nominally subscribe to the concept of evolution and the geological ages, have never fully considered its implications and that many of them would refute it if they did, professionally costly though such a stand might become.

It is not surprising, in view of the foregoing, that the system of evolution has been appropriated as the pseudo-scientific basis of every political or philosophical system of the past hundred years which has been opposed to Christianity, or even to theism in general. In particular has this been true of the various forms of modern "liberalism," including socialism, fascism, and communism.

The influence of Darwinism upon Marxism has been especially significant:

> Orthodox Marxian socialists in the early years of the twentieth century felt quite at home in Darwinian surroundings. Karl Marx himself, with his belief in universal "dialectical" principles, had been as much a monist as Comte or Spencer. Reading *The Origin of Species* in 1860, he reported to Friedrich Engles, and later declared to Ferdinand LaSalle, that "Darwin's book is very important, and served me as a basis in natural science for the class struggle in history." On the shelves of the socialist bookstores in Germany the works of Darwin and Marx stood side by side.[28]

The views of a prominent contemporary historian, Dean of the Graduate Faculties at Columbia University, are significant:

> It is a commonplace fact that Marx felt his own work to be the exact parallel of Darwin's. He even wished to dedicate a portion of *Das Kapital* to the author of *The Origin of Species*.[29]

Some of the reasons for this feeling of debt on the part of Marx are discussed as follows:

> It is that, like Darwin, Marx thought he had discovered the law of development. He saw history in stages, as the Darwinists saw geological strata and successive forms of life. . . . But there are even finer points of comparison. In keeping with the feelings of the age, both Marx and Darwin made struggle the means of development. Again, the measure of value in Darwin is survival with reproduction—an absolute fact occurring in time and which wholly disregards the moral or esthetic quality of the product. In Marx the measure of value is expended labor—an absolute fact occurring in time, which also disregards the utility of the product.[30]

To similar effect is the definitive historical evaluation by Dr. Gertrude Himmelfarb:

> There was truth in Engels' eulogy on Marx: "Just as Darwin discovered the law of evolution in organic nature, so Marx discovered the law of evolution in human history." What they both celebrated was the internal rhythm and course of life, the one the life of nature, the other of society, that proceeded by fixed laws, undistracted by the will of God or men. There were no catastrophes in history as there were none in nature. There were no inexplicable acts, no violations of the natural order. God was as powerless as individual men to interfere with the internal, self-adjusting dialectic of change and development.[31]

It is possible to trace similar direct connections between evolutionism and fascism, as well as other philosophical and political symptoms of the basic antipathy to God which seems to afflict a substantial segment of mankind. Perhaps of more immediate concern is the fact that evolutionism is of predominate influence in the system of John Dewey, the chief architect of modern educational theory in this country.

But that is another story and would carry us too far afield from the context of this study. Our point is simply that the presently accepted system of evolutionary uniformitarianism in the so-called historical geology has projected its influence deeply into almost every sphere of human thought and that, in general, this influence has been highly inimical to the cause of biblical Christianity. It is thus of immense concern to people in every walk of life and cannot be left simply to the self-assumed authority of those who claim jurisdiction over this field.

The Biblical Framework

The study of origins, destinies, and meanings is thus properly to be considered as outside the domain of science. Science deals with present processes, and present processes are conservative and degradational, not creative and organizational. Understanding of the creation and organization of the universe into its present form is therefore to be obtained from other sources than science. Religion necessarily enters the picture.

As noted, evolution is one such possible religous explanation for the universe. But as such, it explicitly contradicts what we know about the present world, which operates in accordance with the first and second laws of thermodynamics.

It is far more reasonable to recognize that neither the data nor the processes nor the methods of most modern science can lead to an understanding of origins. And certainly, then, the unaided speculations of human reasonings cannot do it. Therefore, divine revelation is required if we are ever really to know anything about the creation—its date, its duration, its methods, its order, or anything else about it.

It is eminently reasonable, therefore, to reorganize the data which we have obtained in our studies of the universe and its inhabitants in terms of the biblical framework given us by divine revelation. The biblical framework does give a perfectly satisfying system for harmonizing all the data of biology, geology, and paleontology, as well as other sciences.

The Bible record describes a special creation of all things, fully functioning from the very beginning, complete and finished by creative and formative processes no longer in operation, now being sustained by God in accordance with the conservation principle enunciated in the first law of thermodynamics. It also describes a Fall of man, and God's curse pronounced on the earth, introducing a universal law of decay and disorder, in accordance with the second law of thermodynamics, which for the first time brought disharmony and death into the world. It then describes a great world-destroying Flood in the days of Noah, which completely changed the first cosmos and its structure and processes. It indicates, then, that since the Flood there has been an essential uniformity of both laws and processes, which can thus now be studied and elucidated by the scientific method.

It will be found, if enough study is devoted to it, that all the real data of the fossil record, of biological mechanisms, of geologic processes, and of all natural phenomena, can be oriented and understood within this framework. Such a system will be fully consistent with both the basic laws of science and history and the data of divine revelation.

NOTES AND REFERENCES

1. Carl O. Dunbar, *Historical Geology*, 2nd Ed. (New York: John Wiley & Sons, 1960), p. 18. Emphasis is his.
2. Harold F. Blum, *Time's Arrow and Evolution*, Torchbook Edition (New York: Harper and Brothers, 1962), p. 14.
3. *Ibid.*, pp. 14, 15.
4. *Ibid.*, p. v.
5. Brian Mason, *Principles of Geochemistry*, 2nd Ed. (New York: John Wiley & Sons, Inc., 1960), pp. 64, 68.
6. *Ibid.*, p. 68.
7. Blum, *op. cit.*, p. 16.
8. James H. Zumberge, *Elements of Geology*, 2nd. Ed. (New York: John Wiley & Sons, Inc., 1963), p. 200. Emphasis is his.
9. *Ibid.*, p. 201.
10. P. D. Krynine, "Uniformitarianism Is a Dangerous Doctrine," *Journal of Paleontology*, Vol. 30, 1956, p. 1004.
11. Stephen Jay Gould, "Is Uniformitarianism Necessary?" *American Journal of Science*, Vol. 263, March 1965, p. 223.
12. *Ibid.*, p. 226.
13. *Ibid.*, p. 227.
14. T. G. Miller, "Time in Stratigraphy," *Paleontology*, Vol. 8, February 1965, p. 119. Emphasis is his. Miller is at Keele University in Staffordshire.
15. *Ibid.*, p. 128.
16. J. E. Ransom, *Fossils in America* (New York: Harper & Row, 1964), p. 43.
17. *Ibid.*
18. H. D. Hedberg, "The Stratigraphic Panorama," *Geological Society of America Bulletin*, Vol. 72, April 1961, pp. 499-518.
19. Dunbar, *op. cit.*, p. 47.
20. C. H. Waddington, *The Nature of Life* (New York: Atheneum, 1961), p. 98.
21. Frederick S. Hulse, *The Human Species* (New York: Random House, 1963), p. 53.
22. Gerald Feinberg and Maurice Goldhaber, "The Conservation Laws of Physics," *Scientific American*, Vol. 209, Oct. 1963, p. 36.
23. Van Rensselaer Potter, "Society and Science," *Science*, Vol. 146, November 20, 1964, p. 1018.

24. Rene Dubos, "Humanistic Biology," *American Scientist*, Vol. 53, March 1965, p. 6.
25. *Ibid.*
26. *Ibid.*, p. x.
27. *Ibid.*, p. 8.
28. Richard Hofstadter, *Social Darwinism in American Thought* (New York: George Braziller, Inc., 1959), p. 115.
29. Jacques Barzun, *Darwin, Marx, Wagner*, 2nd Ed. (New York: Doubleday, 1958), p. 8.
30. *Ibid.*, p. 170.
31. G. Himmelfarb, *Darwin and the Darwinian Revolution* (London: Chatto & Windus, 1959), p. 348.

XI

STREAMLINING STRATIGRAPHY

Clifford Burdick

Many problems of stratigraphy could more easily be resolved if we returned to concepts of catastrophism. Until about 1800 geologists believed that all the stratified or water-deposited rocks of the earth's surface were deposited in just one year's time during the Noachian Flood. This extreme form of catastrophism is not here championed, since obviously the earth has suffered other catastrophes since the Flood, such as widespread droughts and vulcanism. However, many of the vexing problems of stratigraphy would be solved if we simply took the evidence we see at face value instead of attempting to fit it into the concept of uniformitarianism made popular by Sir Charles Lyell. Lack of space forbids a discussion of all the simplifications resulting from a return to catastrophism. The following are illustrative.

The phenomenon of *graded bedding*, i.e., coarse conglomerate on the bottom, with finer material graded upward is pertinent. Rodgers and Dunbar have this to say: "A reasonable explanation of graded bedding in terms of the standard processes of stream or shallow-water deposition has proved difficult. The facts seem to demand that material be dumped suddenly yet fairly evenly over a large area and then allowed to settle quietly in accordance with size, coarser before finer . . . and that the dumping be endlessly repeated though separated by intervals of complete quiet." [1] This does not sound much like uniformity where a river continues its ceaseless flow, gradually building its delta farther and farther out into the sea; nor does it sound like the constant pounding of the breakers against the shore, building littoral zone deposits. We are reminded, however, of the statement in Genesis 8:1-3—how the Creator dried up the floodwaters by strong winds that drove the waters by a "going and returning," a tidal wave in one direction, then a reversal and a wave in the other direction. Thus we get the sudden dumping, followed by a period of quiet to account for the graded bedding.

Keeping this tectonic "modus operandi" in mind, let us consider briefly another common phenomenon of stratigraphy, interbedding, otherwise known as cyclic or repetitive stratification. Sometimes a rock exposure will show a white limestone band followed by a darker band of sandstone or shale, then another band of limestone until the entire exposure will resemble the American flag. Such exposures occur in Topanga Canyon, near Santa Monica, California, where layers of red conglomerate alternate with layers of white limestone. Geologists who have made observations along the new Alcan Highway from Canada to Alaska have noted as many as 150 such alternations or repetitions of similar strata. In fact, these types of formations are so common the world-over as to elicit no special wonderment, especially for those versed in Flood geology.

It would be difficult indeed to explain these features on the basis of uniformitarian geology, by river delta action, flood plain, or wave action at the seashore. But Genesis 8:1-3 mentioned above would seem to offer a far more logical explanation of the mechanics involved.

Two of the most notable examples of repetition of similar strata occur in the Highlands of Scotland and in the Alps. At least these regions have attracted more publicity on account of long-drawn-out geological controversy centering in these two regions. Not only have there been repetitions of the strata, judged from a lithological standpoint, but the fossils have also been repeated; and this violates a cardinal principle of paleontology. Five repetitions have been recorded in Scotland and six in the Alps. This presented a real challenge to orthodox geology.

Murchison and Lyell wrestled with this problem of interbedding in Scotland, where gneisses and schists were interbedded with Paleozoic sandstones and limestones. They were convinced that they were dealing with a conformable series because they failed to discover any physical evidence to the contrary. But because the fossils were repeated, it was finally decided on fossil evidence alone that some earth movement had taken place to cause the repetition of the strata.

Field[2] summed up the lesson to be learned from this experience: "Geologists all over the world began to realize that correlation by lithology alone was a dangerous procedure . . . fossils were the best and safest criteria." Field further expressed a view often held by scientists concerning Genesis: "While the Protestant Reformation helped to encourage interest in geologic research, Christianity had unfortunately included in its 'Sacred Writings' the Mosaic account of the origin of the earth as well as the Deluge." [3]

Some blame for the controversy seems to have been placed on Moses' shoulders, broad enough, incidentally, to carry the load.

Paraconformities

To many, *Disconformities* may be a more familiar term, but the meaning is the same. Some have it "Deceptive Conformities." Geike[4] perhaps gave the best definition: "Fossil evidence may be made to prove the existence of gaps which are not otherwise apparent." With *Unconformities* there is an evident hiatus or gap in time between episodes of deposition, inasmuch as the earlier beds have been tilted or folded, then eroded or truncated by a new deposition, exhibiting an angular discordance between the two formations. In a *Nonconformity* the sedimentary beds rest upon the igneous or basement complex. In a *Paraconformity* the physical evidence points to a continuous deposition, the only suggestion of a time gap being a sudden change in fossil types.

In the Grand Canyon, for example, no Pennsylvania fossils are to be found, the Permian fossils resting upon the Mississippian, and yet there is no evidence of erosion during that assumed hiatus of perhaps some 30,000,000 years. Even in our brief time since measurements have been recorded, coastlines are rising and sinking, in Scandinavia, for instance. It is then inconceivable that the crust of the earth would remain so stable and at just the right elevation that it would be unaffected by either erosion or sedimentation for millions of years. Edward Suess[5] says such things "may well be cause for astonishment." Field has this to say concerning this paraconformity in the Grand Canyon: "Without the aid of fossils, disconformities are usually very difficult to determine—the physical evidence of an hiatus between the Mississippian and the Permian periods is therefore not represented by a well defined plane of erosion." [6] But this is not the most acute stratigraphical problem in the Grand Canyon, which, incidentally, is one of the best places in the world to study stratigraphy. Below the Mississippian in most places the Devonian is not present, and nowhere does the Silurian or the Ordovician appear, which means that the Redwall formation, which is Lower Mississippian, actually rests upon the Cambrian Muav limestone, a time gap of over 50,000,000 years. Surely in this immense space of time we would expect to find effects of very extensive erosion, perhaps warping and folding with angular discordance, but what do we actually find? The appearance of a perfectly conformable series of beds, laid down in fairly quick succession. Surely there is "cause for astonishment"!

A few miles northwest of Windowrock, Arizona, in the Defiance Uplift, the Permian Supai formation rests upon the Precambrian quartzite in Bonita Canyon, near Fort Defiance. Most of the Paleozoic is missing; although in this case there is some evidence of truncation of the quartzite.

The region about Heart Mountain, Wyoming, shows the same perplexing problem of disconformities as in the Grand Canyon, where the Silurian and Devonian fossils are missing, representing a time hiatus of many millions of years, with no physical evidence to correspond. Concerning this assumed hiatus, Field has this to say: "We realize that what at first appears to be a perfectly gradational contact between the Big Horn and Madison represents a considerable stratigraphical hiatus, measured by the total absence of the Silurian and probably the Devonian sediments and fossils. This experience serves to remind us of the value of fossils in helping to determine the age of the formations, for it is extremely difficult to discover any physical evidence of even a disconformity between the sediments which were deposited in the Ordovician and those which were deposited in the Mississippian periods." [7]

The root of the difficulty here appears to be "a priori" reasoning; even reasoning in a circle. Rastall was frank enough to admit as much when he said: "It cannot be denied from a strictly philosophical standpoint that geologists are here arguing in a circle. The succession of organisms has been determined by a study of their remains embedded in the rocks, and the relative age of the rocks are determined by the remains of the organisms that they contain." [8]

Thrust Faulting

An overthrust is conceived of as a plate or block of strata in a more or less level position that is believed to have been displaced from its original position where deposited. Normal faults involve high angle dips where one block has fallen in relation to the other, involving tension or stretching of the crust at that point. Wrench faults are concerned with fractures, along which there has been differential horizontal movement. Overthrusting presupposes a previous folding of the strata due to compression in the crust of the earth at that point. If folding continues past a certain point, the top of the fold will break over like a wave or breaker on the ocean, and the continued compression will continue to move the broken and detached upper plate over the lower section until the stress is relieved. This may require considerable horizontal movement of the upper block if the rock is competent enough, or the stress may be relieved by numerous fractures in the moving block. If the block is soft enough or incompetent, we may find a series of small wrinkles. A very important factor governing the possible distance of movement is the coefficient of friction along the surface of movement.

Much new scientific data has accumulated recently and it has been found that there is a definite limit to the possible size of thrust blocks or distance that they can be moved before the crushing strength of the rock is exceeded. When that is exceeded the result will be a mass of rubble rather than apparently conformable strata. It is generally assumed that there would need to be a contact layer like shale or some material of low coefficient of friction plus an adequate gradient to permit the movement. I can still hear Professor Leith, structural geologist at the University of Wisconsin, remark: "One wonders what giant lubricator enabled the great mass to be translated forward many miles with no unconformity or brecciation?" Small overthrusts are commonplace. Thus one I examined in the southern part of the Santa Rita mountains, south of Tucson, Arizona, involved Permian blocks of limestone thrust northward for a distance of about one-half mile. At the contact line a three-foot-thick gouge layer of finely powdered rock, or mylonite, ground fine by the differential movement of the two rock plates, was exposed. Where there has been movement of many miles, as is postulated for the 40-mile Lewis thrust in Glacier National Park, Montana, one would expect a gouge layer of great thickness. Where is the evidence of such a layer?

In fact, Field was greatly puzzled over the plausibility of giant overthrusts: "If this be true, it represents one of the most astonishing and impressive features in the structures of the Alps. But what caused such a tremendous translocation as to move a portion of North Africa (Hinterland) toward and finally over Switzerland (Foreland)? The question still remains unanswered. Like any other outstanding hypothesis, even when built on careful and critical research, it must be open to discussion. What caused the western jaw to move is not known. Some geologists are skeptical of the whole interpretation of the structure of the Alps because they are unable to visualize the cause." [9]

Mention has been made of the problem of interbedding and repetition of fossils in the Highlands with which Murchison and Geikie wrestled until they sent Peach and Horne to work out the geology. They finally suggested the Moine overthrust concept involving an imbricate series of slices or thrusts. The Harmony formation is widely found in thrust sheets of various mountain ranges of Nevada. Slivers of Harmony presumably were stripped off underlying units and forced through and overrode the eugeosyniclinal rocks.[10] Hundreds of such "wrong order" formations are found.

We previously mentioned Heart Mountain in Wyoming as showing disconformities. It also has strata in the wrong order, according to fossil ages. It is capped with Paleozoic limestone, and lower down is supposedly younger Jurassic and Tertiary sediments. The same is true of nearby Sheep Mountain, and last but by no means least is the afore-mentioned Lewis thrust extending from Glacier Park in Montana at least 500 miles along the Rockies, wherein an area covering several thousand square miles is assumed to have been pushed from the west toward the east from thirty to sixty miles. The capping of the Rocky Mountain range in this section is composed of Cambrian, Precambrian, or Paleozoic strata. This mighty Rocky Mountain Cordillera rests upon a base of Cretaceous rocks, in some places showing dinosaur remains. The fossil flora of the mountain capping is mostly an alga flora.

Glacier Park in the U.S.A. and Banff and Jasper National Parks in Canada are among the most scenic sections in which to study thrusting.

There have been many phases of geology over which controversy has raged over the years, and the subject of thrusting has been an outstanding example. This appears to have been due to three factors: 1. The concept of large-scale overthrusts never has made sense from the engineering or logical viewpoint. 2. The causes and mechanics of thrusting have never been well understood. 3. It is the only explanation of the many exceptions to the fundamental assumptions of historical geology, i.e., a more or less orderly evolution of life.[11]

Small-scale thrusts have long been observed; it was therefore reasoned, why would not the same principle apply to larger ones? This type of logic may apply to many things, but in other applications there are limiting factors. For instance, in fissionable elements there is a critical size, beyond which there is danger or even certainty of an explosion. This principle applies also to thrust blocks, the larger and longer, the greater the stress of compression required to move it. Soon this stress exceeds the crushing strength of the rock, and instead of movement we get shearing or crushing. This relieves the pent up crustal stresses, and no forward translation of the block would take place.

Another illustration would be a freight train. In spite of the number of engines, there would be a theoretical limit to the number of loaded cars that could be pulled because the weakest coupling would break.

This is a vital point that should always be kept in mind when we read about how a certain thrust block was propelled a certain distance: are they talking about some thrust where physical evidences of movement can be observed, such as a gouge layer or slickensides, or are they talking about an assumed thrust where the only evidence of a thrust is not physical but theoretical, based on fossil evidence alone? By frank admission on the part of leading stratigraphers, physical evidence for thrusting is often lacking. The thrusts are assumed because "older" fossils are embedded in the upper strata and "younger" ones in the lower beds.

This point can be amply verified by statements from famous stratigraphers such as Dana, who said: "The thrust planes look like planes of bedding and were long so considered." [12] Geikie came to the same conclusion: "Had these sections been planned for the purpose of deception they could not have been more skillfully devised," and in his textbook we read, "The strata could scarcely be supposed to have been really inverted save for the evidence as to their true order of succession supplied by their included fossils." [13]

In the Alps, as well as the Scottish Highlands, there is an interlacing of relatively thin thrust slices, far too thin to have the internal stiffness to withstand such pressures as needed to push these slices so far. The same anomaly was observed in Heart Mountain, Wyoming.

Lawson sums up the subject thusly: "It seems, therefore, mechanically impossible (a priori) that a single intact prism of the earth's crust could move more than a small fraction of a mile by real overthrusting as a mobile block past a passive under-lying block, owing to the fact that strain is relieved by a succession of limited ruptures and the development of an imbricated structure." [14]

William Bowie, of the U. S. Coast Guard and Geodetic Survey, is a specialist in isostasy and the mechanics of earth movements. He has this to say: "The theory that a mountain system has been caused by lateral thrusts originating from a distance presupposes a very anomalous condition. The theory implies that the earth's crust is competent to carry thrusts that would squeeze up mountains and plateaus, and that at the same time is so weak that it can undergo the distortion incident to the movement causing the uplift—this, it seems, is an inconceivable situation because no structure that is so weak as to be distorted to this extent [folded mountains of the Appalachians] could possibly transmit the stresses necessary to hoist the mountains. From an engineering standpoint, we cannot conceive of horizontal movements originating outside of the area occupied by the mountains as the cause of a mountain uplift." [15]

The foregoing pronouncements, although sound, still do not reflect the latest information available. Such laborers as Terzaghi, Hubbert, Rubey, Moore, Birch, and others have investigated the problem of large overthrusts from laboratory investigation, as well as applied mathematics. Although Hubbert and Rubey have certainly contributed much of value to the science, it appears that their conclusions have by no means been universally accepted, as evidenced by the running debates from time to time appearing in recent issues of the bulletins of the Geological Society of America.

Their computations are far too technical and mathematical to outline here, but their conclusions may be summarized. Smoluchowski discussed the problem of sliding a rectangular block along a horizontal surface. The pressure needed would be equal to $\frac{F}{ac} = Wbc$. If (b) equals 100 miles, the length of the block, the strength of the block must be capable of supporting a column 15 miles high; but the crushing strength of granite will be reached in supporting a rock column only two miles high.[16]

One alternative proposed was gravitational gliding when a bentonite or shaly layer acts as a lubricator between the top and bottom blocks. However, Chester Longell showed that gravitational gliding down a geologically acceptable slope is incompatible with known values of the coefficent of friction.

Hubbert and Rubey[17] argued from the analogy of high fluid pressures in an oil well whether the fluid be oil or water. This pore water pressure in porous rocks is assumed to cause the rocks to partially float over the lower block, and thus reduce the shearing force needed to overcome the coefficient of friction.

Terzaghi showed the low angle landslides occur in loose soils when the water pressures in the clays became great enough to reduce the frictional force pulling the block down the given slope. However, let it be pointed out that landslides in loose soils are not analogous to solid blocks. In the landslides, the discrete particles, sand grains, or larger pebbles and rocks in a semi-viscous state are free to rotate or give way in relation to the other particles when obstructions are met. In the case of the thrust in solid blocks, if a rock knob or obstruction meets an obstruction in the other blocks, nothing gives, but the coefficient of friction rises sharply and greater force is required to grind off the salient, for it would be almost impossible to find two blocks in contact that were perfectly smooth.

I examined an exposure in the Empire Mountains of southern Arizona where the Paleozoic (Permian) limestone is mapped as having overridden a Cretaceous rock formation. However, in places the contact resembled the meshing of gears. There could have been no sliding without grinding off the intermeshing projections without the creation of a thick layer of mylonite or goupe, which was not in evidence. It is difficult to envision how pore water pressure could have solved this problem. The top layer fitted the bottom one like a glove or as melted metal fits a mold.

To help clarify the picture of pore water pressure, the authors have used a homely illustration. If a frozen beer can is taken from the refrigerator and set upon an inclined glass plate, it will just sit there. However, if the bottom cap is cut off it will sit there until the heat of the room begins to expand the beer in the can, when the can will start to creep down the inclined glass because the friction between the glass and the can has been reduced by the pressure of the beer in the can. In other words, the can of beer starts to float down the glass. This all sounds very plausible, but Francis Birch replied to Hubbert and Rubey in a subsequent issue of the G.S.A. Bulletin, contending that the beer can was not analogous to pore water pressure in rocks.

Birch also says that if the pore water pressure so weakens the underlying rock layer that less shearing force is required to start the thrust, then the upper block must also be weakened, thus lowering its innate crushing strength, resulting in fracture instead of forward movement.

However, the possible help of pore water pressure would not eliminate the grinding effect of rock against rock. If there has been thrusting one should observe gouge layers and slickenslides. If the formations appear perfectly conformable, with no physical evidences of thrusting, caution would appear to be the watchword in diagnosing a giant thrust as such based on other criteria.

In summation let us return to the original theme, Catastrophism vs. Uniformity. In the December 23, 1963, issue of *Newsweek,* the science editor had this to say: "Catastrophism is a fighting word among geologists. It is a theory based on divine intervention, and its adherents held that the history of the earth and life on it were moved by a series of disasters inspired by God, the last one—Noah's Flood. It was the major line of thought for a few decades last century but a vigorous counterattack by naturalists against the supernaturalists eventually pushed it aside.

"But now many geologists believe the counterattack may have been all too vigorous. In their haste to reject the hand of God, they have passed over some solid evidence that could help improve their understanding of both geology and evolution. As a result many geologists at the recent meeting of the American Geological Society were advising the rehabilitation of catastrophism, without recourse to the supernatural agent."

Norman Newell, paleontologist of the American Museum of Natural History in New York, admits the past mistake of the orthodox viewpoint by saying, "Geology students are taught that the 'present is the key to the past' and they too often take it to mean that nothing ever happened that isn't happening now. But since the end of World War Two, when a new generation moved in, we have gathered more data and we have begun to realize that there were many catastrophic events in the past, some of which happened just once."

How like a breath of spring to hear paleontologists finally admit that perhaps after all the Creationists and Flood geologists have produced valid evidence that demands recognition.

NOTES AND REFERENCES

1. John Rodgers and Carl Dunbar, *Principles of Stratigraphy* (New York: John Wiley & Son, Co., 1957).
2. Richard M. Field, *The Principles of Historical Geology* (Princeton University Press, 1933), p. 194.
3. *Ibid.*
4. Sir Archibald Geikie in *Encyclopedia Britannica,* 11:667.

5. Edward Suess, *The Face of the Earth*, 2:543.
6. Field, *op. cit.*
7. *Ibid.*, p. 242.
8. R. R. Rastal, in *Encyclopedia Britannica*, 10:167.
9. Field, *op. cit.*, pp. 224, 231, 234.
10. Ralph J. Roberts, Preston E. Holz, James Gilluly, and H. G. Ferguson, *Paleozoic Rocks of North Central Nevada*, American Association of Petroleum Geologists, 42:3812-3857.
11. Hollis D. Hedberg, "Stratigraphic Classification and Terminology, Bulletin of the American Association of Petroleum Geologists, 42, 8:1881-1896. Quotes rule 5: "The more or less orderly evolution of life forms throughout geologic time makes fossils particularly valuable in time correlations of strata and in fossil age dating, and in placing of rocks in a world-wide geologic time scale."
12. James W. Dana, *Manual of Geology*, 4th Edition (1894), p. 534.
13. Sir Archibald Geikie, *Textbook of Geology* (1903), p. 837.
14. A. D. Lawson, *Bulletin of the Geological Society of America*, 1928, 33:340.
15. William Bowie, "Isostatic Investigations, U. S. Coast and Geodetic Survey, Special Publication 99, 1924.
16. Where F equals force needed, a equals breadth of block, c equals thickness, b equals length, w equals weight per unit of volume.
17. King Hubbert and W. W. Rubey, "The Effect of Pore Water Pressure on Overthrusting, *Geological Society Bulletin*, 1959, 70:115, 167; May 1960, p. 611; September 1961, p. 1441; October 1961, p. 1581.

XII

THE GENESIS KINDS IN THE MODERN WORLD

Frank Lewis Marsh

In the first chapter of Genesis we read that the basic types of plants and animals appeared upon our earth through an act of special fiat creation. These basic types are described as not only being formed each after its specific morphological pattern, but in the case of the plants, also with a reproductive mechanism which caused each type to produce new individuals like itself.

The briefness of this Genesis account of origins gives opportunity for the development of at least two schools of interpretation with regard to the degree of fixity in nature indicated by this terse record. During the Middle Ages or medieval period of history, from about A.D. 400 to A.D. 1400, the opinion prevailed among scientists that the statements of Genesis declared that in reproduction the new individuals of a kind were as like as pennies from a mint. With regard to origins, the general premise was always the assertion of extreme fixity. In certain theological centers this idea resisted the changes of the Renaissance and the shift to the inductive method of reasoning, and was still taught as dogma to the students of theology at Cambridge when Charles Darwin was graduated from the department of theology in that university in 1831.

At Cambridge, Darwin was also taught that all modern forms of plants and animals had been created and set down in the very pattern of geographical distribution in which we find them today. Actually there is no scriptural ground for this latter teaching. However, these two bits of dogma were presented to the students in theology at Cambridge as the only orthodox understanding of Christians on these points. Accoutered with these extreme views of special creation, Darwin went forth on his five-year circumnavigation of the globe as a sincere creationist naturalist.

During the progress of that voyage he carefully observed the abundant evidence that species varied considerably, usually in proportion to the degree of isolation from their relatives. He became more and more troubled about the concept of fixity of the kinds which he had been told was the teaching of Genesis. We wish that Charles Darwin had studied Genesis for himself and seen the actual harmony between the Bible and nature. After pondering over the problem for years, he finally reached the tragic decision to abandon the idea of the fiat creation of basic types of organisms.

This decision was reached in the year 1844. At that time, in a letter to his lifelong friend, the botanist Joseph Dalton Hooker, he said:

> I had read heaps of agricultural and horticultural books and have never ceased collecting facts. At last gleams of light have come, and I am almost convinced (quite contrary to the opinions I started with) that species are not (it is like confessing a murder) immutable.[1]

A second school of interpretation with regard to the degree of fixity within the kinds indicated by the statement of Genesis is based upon the opinion that the book of nature and the Written Word shed light upon each other. Correctly interpreted these two sources *do* agree. They have the same Author. The Bible itself directs us to go to nature for confirmation of profound verities. In Job 12:7-11 we read:

> But ask now the beasts, and they shall teach thee; and the fowls of the air, and they shall tell thee: or speak to the earth, and it shall teach them: and the fishes of the sea shall declare unto thee. Who knoweth not in all these that the hand of the Lord hath wrought this? In whose hand is the soul of every living thing, and the breath of all mankind.

Therefore, the members of this school of interpretation go first to the Scriptures and learn that the statements of Genesis neither exclude the possibilities of variation within the kinds, nor do they assert that plants and animals were created in their present details and set down in the areas where we find them today. Then, turning to nature, these students find that Darwin was entirely correct in his observation of migration over the earth accompanied with variation. What Darwin failed to observe was that variation is not without bounds, and is definitely limited in each case to the locus of its basic type or Genesis kind. All individuals of even abundantly variable forms, such as men and dogs, are unquestionably in every instance *bona fide* members of their respective basic types.

Because of his outstanding ability and because of his great contributions to the basic science of taxonomy, believers in special creation are always glad to recall that the Swedish botanist Carolus Linnaeus, 1707-1778, was a creationist. Interestingly it is not unusual even in our day to find people who are of the opinion that he was specially endowed by heaven in his ability to point out the created units or Genesis kinds among living forms. However, an endeavor to learn just what classification groups in nature were considered by Linnaeus to be the Genesis kinds is likely to end in some confusion, because during his life he published at least two points of view on the loci of the basic created units. During the most active period of his life we find in the first eleven editions of his *Systema Naturae*, beginning in 1735, the following assertion:

> We count as many species as have been created from the beginning; the individual creatures are reproduced from eggs, and each egg produces a progeny in all respects like the parents.

Linnaeus realized the difficulty of determining natural affinities and did, in my opinion, make mistakes in his endeavor to distinguish the created kinds in nature. Illustrations here would be his assignment of different species names to the American bison and the European bison, and to spring wheat and winter wheat.

In his later life, after a great deal of observation of the bordering of some species on one another, and particularly as a result of his own experiments in hybridization, he changed his opinion of the created unit. From his twelfth and last edition of *Systema Naturae*, 1768, he omitted the statement, "No new species arise." Then in his *Systema Vegetabilium*, published in 1774, four years before his death, we read the following interesting opinion regarding the original created units:

> Let us suppose that the Divine Being in the beginning progressed from the simpler to the complex; from few to many; similarly that He in the beginning of the plant kingdom created as many plants as there were natural orders. These plant orders He Himself, therefrom producing, mixed among themselves until from them originated those plants which today exist as genera.

> Nature then mixed up these plant genera among themselves through generations of double origin (hybrids) and multiplied them into existing species, as many as possible (whereby the flower structures were not changed) excluding from the number of species the almost sterile hybrids, which are produced by the same mode of origin.[2]

Because Linnaeus used a purely artificial system of classification and recognized only the four taxonomic categories, Class, Order, Genus, and Species, it is not easy from the above statement to secure a clear picture of what *was* his mature conception of the created unit. It may be helpful, in an effort to understand his mature opinion here, to select his order *Gymnospermia* as an example. Today our taxonomists use the name *Gymnospermae* for a class of plants made up of cycads, ginkgo, and conifers. However, Linnaeus' *Gymnospermia* consisted largely of the mints and snapdragons.

Thus in Linnaeus' opinion God spoke into being parent forms of such groups as the mints and snapdragons, and then by His own controlled hybridization developed among these additional plant groups which we call biological species, groups which, to continue with our example, are illustrated by such plants as skull-cap, catnip, motherworth, sage, horsemint, mullein, toadflax, and painted cup. It is possible that not all special creationists of today would be willing to concede that plants as varied as mullein and foxglove had evolved naturally from a single created unit. However, we would stress the fact that we believe Linnaeus was certainly on the right track when he judged that *any forms which would hybridize had sprung from a common ancestor.* This would be a limited form of change, but certainly not evolution of new basic types. Possibly it would be more accurate to designate such change as mere variation within the original basic units.

The expressions "after his kind," "after their kinds," appear ten times in Genesis 1. A survey of the 32 Bible commentaries in the James White Memorial Library of Andrews University regarding the significance of these expressions in Genesis 1 showed that six made no comment on them, four were evolutionist, and the remaining 22 were agreed that these expressions indicated that in the beginning God created the basic types of plants and animals at all levels of complexity. Some commentators in this group even state that the expressions mean that on the third, fifth, and sixth days by divine command not only all the basic units appeared but also subordinate groups within the kinds.

With regard to Genesis 1:12, ". . . plants yielding seed according to their own kinds" (RSV), sixteen of the 22 definitely went on to express the opinion that reference was here made to reproductive behavior, e.g., "received power to propagate and multiply their own kind" (Keil and Delitzsch); "the race should be perpetuated from generation to generation" (Cook); "the growth will always be the same kind as the seed" (Excell); "Determinate propagation of plants" (Lange); and so on.

It is obvious from the wording in Genesis that the expression "after his kind" includes both morphological and physiological characteristics. That is to say, when the plants and animals appeared upon the earth the individuals of each basic type were distinctly different in the details of their form, structure, and internal chemistry from the individuals of all other basic types. To express it mildly, in the light of Genesis 1:12 it is difficult to understand how a basic type could transmute into a new basic type or could give rise to a new basic type if its reproductive performance was such as to bring forth additional individuals of the same kind as their parents.

Today when we see so many varieties among our domesticated plants and animals we wonder how the schoolmen could insist upon believing that the creation described in Genesis demanded *no variation* within the created kinds. This was the extreme interpretation of Genesis which the theologians at Cambridge gave to Charles Darwin before his graduation.

Because John Milton, 1608-1674, had been largely responsible for swinging the Christian in England from the Aristotelian philosophy of a derivative type of origins to acceptance of the literal account of Genesis, he is blamed by some evolutionists for the extreme view actually developed later by the university schoolmen. Thomas Huxley's statement that the new theory of evolution found itself in conflict with the Miltonic, rather than the Mosaic "cosmology" (it is actually a cosmogony) is an interesting one although inaccurate.[3] It is true that the natural facts of variation emphasized by Darwin were in conflict with the extreme "no variation" interpretation developed by the schoolmen after Milton pointed the way back to a literal Genesis, but it is not true that this new evolution was in harmony with the Mosaic cosmogony. This new evolution demanded extended periods of time for the assumed gradual development of more complex and specialized types from simpler types, while the Mosaic account clearly states that the multiplicity of basic types was spoken into existence from the raw materials within the limits of one solar week.

When a number of the self-styled "higher literary critics of the Bible" had been persuaded by scientists that living things had originated by a process of evolution, they went back to Genesis and pondered how to interpret the simple historical account of an origin by special creation of basic types, in such a way as to bring it into harmony with the doctrine of evolution. Finally, considerable agreement was reached among them that Genesis should be understood to be not prose, but *poetry,* and that this poem set forth but one basic fact only, the fact that living things had come into being through the activity of a Creator. According to this new turn, the author's use of descriptions of days and of instantaneous appearances of plants and animals from the earth was merely an employment of poetic license to give body to the poem but to add nothing in the way of actual facts. However, that the creation account is prose, *not* poetry, is authoritatively attested by the body of translators of the recent and generally more accurate version of the Bible, the Revised Standard Version, who in this translation set the creation account before us as *prose,* not poetry, a prose which at times indeed has the scope, majesty, and beauty of exalted poetry. Albeit, even if the Genesis account *were* in poetic form it still could state the literal truth, and possibly even state that truth more effectively than in prose.

What does the literal, inspired historical account of beginnings tell us about the origin of living things? Genesis 1:11-13, 20-28, 31 clearly portrays that on days three, five, and six of creation week the Creator populated the earth with all the basic kinds of plants and animals. At His spoken command these organisms came into being from the raw materials of the earth. There was no blood relationship between the basic types, merely a pattern of unity within diversity resulting from one omniscient Creator with a master plan. The fact that the Creator did have an overall plan for plants and animals is indicated in the oft repeated expression, "after his (their) kind." Plants appeared in all their forms from the most lowly to the giants of the forest. Animals swarmed in the sea, crept and walked upon dry ground, and flew through the air. The account makes it very clear that by the close of creation week the earth, at the word and voice of one Creator, had its full complement of basic kinds of plants and animals. That this creation of basic types was not to continue beyond creation week is made clear in Genesis 2:1, 2, where we read that on the seventh day "God finished his work (declared His work on which He was engaged, finished)." This declaration is repeated in Commandment IV, "For in six days the Lord made heaven and earth, the sea, and all that in them is, and rested the seventh day" (Exod. 20:11). What is written? "It is written" that all basic kinds of plants and animals miraculously appeared upon the earth within one literal, 24-hour-day week, at the command of the Creator.

The schoolmen were correct in their understanding of the origin of the living kinds. But they were incorrect in their teaching regarding the reproductive behavior of these kinds. They asserted that Genesis declared that the created kinds brought forth after their kinds, and that this increase in number was like the coinage of dimes, no variation. It is true that Genesis 1:12, RSV, describes "plants yielding seed according to their own kinds." This is a description of reproductive behavior, but no assertion in just so many words is made regarding the reproductive behavior of animals. Certainly there is no justification in Genesis for the extreme "no-variation-among-individuals-of-a-kind" interpretation of the schoolmen.

Nevertheless, Genesis, in its assertion that plants *and* animals were created in all their kinds, *does* teach a fixity in the living world. However, many scores of years of careful biological research has shown that this fixity is higher than the individual level, i.e., at the level of the basic kind, best illustrated by our own species (mankind). In all their wishful endeavors in scientific study, even evolutionists will admit that not one instance of basic type, like a cat, producing a new basic type, like a dog, is known. We have kinds of cats, but the fixity of Genesis is at a higher level of the cat kind and not at the lower level of kinds of cats. Variation does occur abundantly within kinds, but no coercive, compulsive evidence can be produced to show the production of even one new basic kind. The very most that Darwin could discover was that new varieties of tortoises had apparently developed on the various islands of the Galapagos group,[4] and apparently new varieties and even new "species" of finches,[5] but he failed to recognize the tremendously important fact that the tortoises were still tortoises and the finches still finches, field evidence which helps us to understand the true fixity that exists in the world of living things. In his demonstration of variation within well-marked limits of the kind, Darwin, instead of disproving Genesis, as he thought, actually witnessed to its veracity.

One basic kind is unlike all other basic kinds because of its own peculiar internal chemistry, the DNA of its genes. If different kinds are present we know these different chemistries are present also and effectively isolate one kind from another by bridgeless chemical abysses.

Such is the letter of the written record. The creationist of today believes that the Bible and nature are complemental, each helping to explain the other. Therefore, we turn to nature to discover the degree of fixity indicated by Genesis. In speaking of this situation in nature, Theodosius Dobzansky, Professor of Zoology, Columbia University, says:

> Organic diversity is an observational fact more or less familiar to everyone. . . .
>
> If we assemble as many individuals living at a given time as we can, we notice at once that the observed variation does not form any kind of continuous distribution. Instead, a multitude of separate, discrete distributions are found. The living world is not a single array of individuals in which any two variants are connected by unbroken series of intergrades, but an array of more or less distinctly separate arrays, intermediates between which are absent or at least rare.[6]

This discontinuity is one of the most familiar characteristics of the living world as we recognize men, horses, cows, dogs, and cats, roses, petunias, marigolds, zinnias, and water-lilies. This same discontinuity is also one of the most striking features of the fossil world.

This very real existence of gaps between the basic types of organisms is one of the great problems of the evolutionist. If all modern forms have evolved from one or a few primeval protoplasmic blobs, why should both the fossils and the living world present us with this striking discontinuity just as if the different kinds had originated as Genesis declares they did?

This problem was one of the topics in a series of letter discussions which I had with one of the old guard of neo-Darwinian evolution a few years ago. This zoologist is today one of the leading American disciples of the theory of evolution. In our discussion I pressed him to give me just one instance in our living world where evolution of a new basic type is *known* to have occurred. His reply was as follows:

> When one says that evolution is established beyond reasonable doubt one obviously does not mean that one can see evolution happen and reproduce it in a test tube, but this is the evidence which you escape by your device of saying that it is all change within a "kind." What you are after is evidently evidence for the thing which is called by this rather unfortunate term "macro-evolution." Now, this is a process taking place in geological time, hence it, as any other historical process (human or natural), can be proven or disproved only by inference from the available evidence.

This authority's admission of the impossibility to demonstrate the evolution of new basic types among living forms is typical of the testimony of all evolutionists who are really conversant with the pertinent facts. After having admitted that evolution of new basic types cannot be demonstrated among living forms, this zoologist passed the burden of demonstration over to the paleontologists who, in his opinion, could demonstrate that evolution of new basic types had occurred during geological time. He referred me to the then new work of George Gaylord Simpson, widely known paleontologist of the American Museum of Natural History, and Professor of Paleontology, Columbia University, which book had just come from the press.[7] Of this book my correspondent remarked, "To me at least this is a most lucid explanation of paleontological evidence."

I secured a copy of Simpson's book, and among much interesting material found the following assertions:

> On still higher levels, those of what is here called "mega evolution," the inferences might still apply, but caution is enjoined, because here essentially continuous sequences are not merely rare, but are virtually absent. These large discontinuities are less numerous, so that paleontological examples of their origin should also be less numerous; but their absence is so nearly universal that it cannot, offhand, be imputed entirely to chance and does require some attempt at special explanation, as has been felt by most paleontologists.[8]

> The facts are that many species and genera, indeed the majority, do appear suddenly in the record, differing sharply and in many ways from any earlier group, and that this appearance of discontinuity becomes more common the higher the level, until it is virtually universal as regards order and all higher steps in the taxonomic hierarchy.

> The face of the record thus does really suggest normal discontinuity at all levels, most particularly at high levels, and some paleontologists (e.g., Spath and Schindewolf) insist on taking the record at this face value. Others (e.g., Matthew and Osborn) discount this evidence completely and maintain that the breaks neither prove nor suggest that there is any normal mode of evolution other than that seen in continuously evolving and abundantly recorded groups. This essentially paleontological problem is also of crucial interest for all other biologists, and, since there is such a conflict of opinion, non-paleontologists may choose either to believe the authority who agrees with their prejudices or to discard the evidence as worthless.[9]

The Genesis Kinds in the Modern World 145

Naturally after reading such assertions as these by so high a paleontological authority as Simpson, I could not refrain from again writing my friend and asking him, in the face of these declarations that the same discontinuity which occurred among living forms and made a demonstration of evolution among them impossible also existed among the fossils, how could he say that Simpson had made a lucid presentation of the origin of new basic types during geological time. A number of years have gone by since I put that question, and several letters have passed between us, but for some reason reference to the topic of paleontological evidence for evolution has been omitted.

In 1953 Simpson again, in the following words, asserted that discontinuity is a fact among the fossils:

> In spite of these examples, it remains true, as every paleontologist knows, that *most* new species, genera, and families, and that nearly all new categories above the level of families, appear in the record suddenly and are not led up to by known, gradual, completely continuous transitional sequences.[10]

On this point of gaps between the various types of fossil forms, D. Dwight Davis, Curator, Division of Vertebrate Anatomy, Chicago Natural History Museum, remarks:

> The sudden emergence of major adaptive types, as seen in the abrupt appearance in the fossil record of families and orders, continued to give trouble. The phenomenon lay in the genetical no man's land beyond the limits of experimentation. A few paleontologists even today cling to the idea that these gaps will be closed by further collecting, i.e., that they are accidents of sampling; but most regard the observed discontinuity as real and have sought an explanation for them.[11]

> But the facts of paleontology conform equally well with other interpretations that have been discredited by neobiological work, e.g., divine creation, etc., and paleontology by itself can neither prove nor refute such ideas.[12]

With regard to the persistence of these gaps in the fossil record in spite of the great amount of work being done in the exploration of this record, Norman D. Newell, Curator of Historical Geology and Fossil Invertebrates, American Museum of Natural History, and Professor of Geology, Columbia University, has recently written:

> From time to time discoveries are made of connecting links that provide clues to the relationships,[13] as between fishes and am-

phibians, amphibians and reptiles, and reptiles and mammals. These isolated discoveries, of course, stimulate hope that more complete records will be found and other gaps closed. These finds are, however, rare; and experience shows that the gaps which separate the highest categories may never be bridged in the fossil record. Many of the discontinuities tend to be more and more emphasized with increased collecting.[14]

We will agree with Davis that it is correct that divine creation of basic types cannot be demonstrated by the fossil record, but we cannot refrain from saying that the distinctness of the basic types in the fossil record with absence of inter-grading forms is completely in harmony with the creation of plants and animals after their kinds as portrayed in Genesis. The fossil record constitutes the only natural record we have of what occurred before the dawn of secular history. In the light of the fossil record, the theory of evolution, which asserts that all modern types have evolved gradually from one or more simple blobs of protoplasm, requires more faith for its acceptance than does the theory of special creation, which asserts that God created the basic types instantaneously in all their characteristic morphological differences. We hear every now and then of "the missing link." Actually among both fossil and living forms great chains of links are everywhere absent between the basic types.

A study of the fossil record reveals to us that groups of organisms have maintained their individuality all the way down to our time. Austin H. Clark, who was with the United States National Museum many years, referred to this fact in the following words:

> Since all the fossils are determinable as members of their respective groups by the application of definitions of these groups drawn up from and based entirely on living types, and since none of these definitions of the phyla or major groups of animals need be in any way altered or expended to include the fossils, it naturally follows that throughout the fossil record these major groups have remained essentially unchanged. This means that the inter-relationships between them likewise have remained unchanged.

> Strange as it may seem, the animals of the very earliest fauna of which our knowledge is sufficient to enable us to speak with confidence, the fauna of the Cambrian period, were singularly similar to the animals of the present day. In the Cambrian crustaceans were crustaceans, echinoderms were echinoderms, arrow worms were arrow worms, and mollusks were mollusks just as unmistakably as they are now.[15]

The Genesis Kinds in the Modern World 147

Here is the sort of fixity referred to in Genesis, and behold, nature shows us that the fixity is that of group characters and not a fixity of all individual characters. Each individual bears the distinguishing marks of his kind but is not necessarily identical with other individuals of his kind. Clark referred to this fact in the following statement:

> In the details of their structure these fossils are not necessarily like the crustaceans, starfishes, brachiopods, annelids, or other creatures living in the present seas. Nevertheless, if they are sufficiently well-preserved we have no difficulty in recognizing at once the group to which each and every fossil animal belongs.[16]

The testimony of *living* nature with regard to the extent of fixity indicated in Genesis is all about us in most intriguing forms. The processes of variation furnish us with many interesting breeds of plants and animals. Individuals often vary considerably within some groups. We have over 500 varieties of the sweetly scented sweet pea, and over two hundred breeds of dogs. One author has divided human beings into as many as 160 breeds.[17] Evolutionists love to call our attention to all this variation that is going on, and to insist that here is evolution before our very eyes. We all observe that variation *does* occur, but evolutionists fail to perceive that when all that the processes of variation can accomplish has been accomplished, we unquestionably still have sweet peas, dogs, and men. The sort of change that the theory of evolution requires is the natural development of *new basic types*. But every additional case of variation that is studied, be it among the fossils or living forms, merely brings additional evidence that there is a law in nature which declares that every organism can produce only individuals which are unquestionably of the same basic type as the parents.

The evolutionist makes a creator out of Father Time by affirming that if we will only assume enough duration then processes of variation will produce new basic types. The plea that time will do it is no more reasonable here than it would be should we invoke it in trying to lift ourselves. If we see a lad trying to lift himself by his bootstraps, we would be incorrect if we were to say to him, "Just keep trying long enough, Sonny, and finally you will be able to do it!" Such a feat can *never* be accomplished because there is a law in nature which says that just as hard as you pull up that hard you push down. In the same way, time cannot accomplish the appearance of new basic types because there are no mechanisms in existence which can accomplish changes of sufficient magnitude to produce one new basic type. Every additional case of variation studied adds one more bit of evidence further to clarify this principle.

Interestingly, there is an international quarterly journal, now in its 18th volume, whose pages contain data which purport to demonstrate that organic evolution is a fact. I was privileged to be a charter member of the Society for the Study of Evolution, of which this journal is the official organ, and each number delights me, a creationist, because every case of change in organisms presented is further substantiation of the natural fact that all processes of change can do no more than accomplish mere variation within already established basic types.

Not infrequently the creationistic biologist is asked, "In our present system of classification of plants and animals is there any category which is an equivalent of the Genesis kind or created unit?" Depending upon one's point of view, the answer to this question can be "no." At the time of creation the kinds or basic types were each created after a distinguishing pattern in form and structure, and we are told specifically that the plants were able to produce other individuals like themselves. The descriptions of kinds in Genesis 1 give us ground for hypothesizing that the individuals of any particular Genesis kind would have chemistries sufficiently alike to make them fertile *inter se*, but sufficiently different to make them incompatible with individuals of every other kind. If this hypothesis is valid then ability to cross would demonstrate membership in the same basic type.

With this hypothesis in mind, as we look into nature today we find that man, *Homo sapiens*, can cross with no other animal. So in his case the species could be the created unit. In other instances we find that the dog, *Canis familiaris*, will cross with the gray wolf, *Canis nubilis*, and the horse, *Equus caballus*, will cross with the ass, *Equus asinus*. Here the genus could be the created unit. Again the common goat, genus *Capra*, will cross with the common sheep, genus *Ovis*, to the extent of at least producing fetuses which will live until just before time for birth. A more successful generic hybrid is the case of the Indian Gayal, genus *Biblos*, which will cross with the Brahma cow, genus *Bos*, possibly here making the family the created unit.[18] Yet again, the domestic hen, family *Phasianidae*, has been crossed with the turkey, family *Meleagrididae,* and also with the guineafowl, family *Numididate*.[19] In these cases the order would be the created unit.

In the modern classification of plants we find the same lack of harmony with the Genesis kind. Very commonly species of the same genus will cross, as the Bur Oak with the Swamp White Oak. Genera not infrequently cross, for example, rye with wheat, and field corn with Teosinte and gama grass. One of the most interesting crosses in plants probably is that of radish with cabbage, both representing genera of the Mustard family. To my knowledge, among plants, members of two different families have not been crossed.

It thus becomes obvious that if our hypothesis is correct and crossability among the members is a characteristic of any given Genesis kind, then there is no single category in modern taxonomy which is in all cases equivalent to the created kind. Because many new modern "biological species" appear through time as products of variation, neither can this presently popular category always qualify as to taxonomic equivalent of the created unit.

It is not to be expected that any harmony could exist between Genesis kinds and our present-day classification lists. The reasonableness of this opinion becomes apparent as we recall that plants and animals have been assigned to classfication categories in part by natural criteria and in other cases by purely arbitrary criteria; some are the work of lumper taxonomists and some that of splitters.

Another difficulty the creationists encounters here is the fact of the undependability of many of our lists of plant crosses and animal crosses. To illustrate, S. G. Morton, in a perfectly sober paper read before the Academy of Natural Sciences of Philadelphia in 1846 reported a cross between a bull and a sheep.[20] In modern times a less spectacular but equally unverified report is that by Annie P. Gray in England of a cross between a domestic hen and a domestic duck. However, she warns us on page x of her book that "the listing of a particular cross does not necessarily mean that it has occurred." [21] The difficulty of preparation of a list of *bona fide* hybrids can be realized only by the one who has tried to draw up such a list. Not infrequently the Muscovy Duck gets into the newspapers as a valid duck x turkey hybrid. The reporter is always sure of the parentage because the red carbuncles on the face of this duck look much like those of the turkey. Nevertheless the Muscovy Duck is pure duck, and just about 99 percent of newspaper reports of hybrids is pure imagination. In all the confused picture, of course, it must be borne in mind that sexual cohabitation is *not* hybridization.

A prominent evolutionist once said to me, "If you insist that all basic types were created in the same beginning, and that no changes have occurred since then which were sufficient to produce new kinds, then you should today point out to us these Genesis kinds, or keep still about them!" I thought his statement was entirely reasonable; in fact, I was already prepared to suggest a test which I believed would do the very thing he demanded. As early as 1941,[22] I had suggested a fertility test which might be used to trace out the modern loci of the original kinds. In 1944 (revised in 1947),[23] because of, as pointed out above, the apparent inability of any modern taxonomic category to qualify as equivalent to the Genesis kind, I suggested that the new word *baramin* (plural *baramins*), built from the Hebrew words *bara*, "created," and *min*, "kind," be used to designate the created types.[24] This name would have the advantage, in the biologist's mind, of separating the Genesis kind from all taxonomic categories now being used. In 1950 the baramin hypothesis was further elucidated.[25]

In 1957 this fertility hypothesis for discovery of the created kinds was sharpened still more by the suggestion that only in cases of *true fertilization* would membership in the same Genesis kind be indicated.[26] In true fertilization both reduced parental sets of chromosomes join and participate in the first division of the fertilized egg or zygote. This would rule out membership in the same baramin of those individuals whose sperm would enter the egg and instigate embryonic development but whose male chromosomes would later be cast out and take no part in the heredity of the new individual. Loeb once reported that all marine teleost fishes would hybridize.[27] However, it was later found that this was a situation where the sperms instigated embryonic development but were later thrown out of the embryo, thus having no part in inheritance. These foreign sperms actually acted only in an artificially parthenogenetic manner.

My reasonably demanding evolutionist friend at first was loath to accept such a hypothesis because he affirmed it was not sufficiently concrete to be practical. It was only after I showed him that the fertility test was just as concrete and practical for the baramin as it was for the biological species which he and several of his evolutionist colleagues were pushing at that time, that he grudgingly admitted that it could constitute a valid test.

Deductively, of course, the idea of the baramin springs from Genesis 1:12, where we are told that the plants not only were made after their kinds, but also brought forth after their kinds. The animals

The Genesis Kinds in the Modern World

likewise were created after their kinds (Gen. 1:21, 24-25), and the genetical physiologist knows that in animals as well as in plants the different chemistries which cause different form and structure also make crossing of kinds impossible. Because the Creator was careful enough to create all the different basic kinds, it is reasonable to suppose He furnished them with physiological mechanisms which would enable the different basic types to continue to exist through successive generations. Why form all the minutae of different type if only immediately to lose them in the confusion of hybridization?

Inductively, in every known instance in living nature where true fertilization can occur, the parents are sufficiently similar morphologically to be considered members of a single kind, such as the man kind, the dog kind, the cow kind, the oak kind, the corn kind, the apple kind, and so on.

It is sometimes objected that the baramin concept is weak in that many of the crosses obtained have occurred in captivity and probably would not take place in undisturbed nature. Actually animal psychology does not enter into the baramin concept. Rather it is physiological, that is, chemical, test, and still applies whether occurring naturally in the aisles of the forest, on the paths of the prairie, or artificially in vitro in the laboratory. The essential assumption is that the chemistry of the DNA molecules of the Genesis kind is identical enough to cause them to produce germ cells which will be compatible and capable of union in true fertilization. Artificial pollination and artificial insemination would be the best tools for the discovery of the limits of the baramin.

We realize that the processes of variation, principally mutation, recombination, and chromosomal aberration, have been working in these basic kinds since Creation, and have produced physiological incompatibilities within the Genesis kinds, so we may assume that ability to interbreed with complete fertility may not now exist among all members of the baramin. In such instances morphological characters will be used to determine membership. An illustration here would be the two groups of the fruit fly, *Drosophila pseudo-obscura,* which were formerly called Race A and Race B of this insect. Because hybrid males resulting from a cross between these races were completely sterile, Dobzhansky and Epling assigned to Race B the new species name, *D. persimilis.*[28] The individuals of *D. pseudo-obscura* and *D. persimilis* appear identical in external characters but may be completely sterile when mated. In such cases the morphological similarity of adults is sufficient to show that they belong to the same baramin.

Sometimes the question is asked, "Is the modern widely accepted biological species identical with the Genesis kind?" I would answer that such may occasionally be the case. An example would be the biological species *man,* which is also a Genesis kind. To be true members of the same biological species the individuals must be fertile *interse.* If within a biological species a group arises whose members are sterile when mated with others of the group, a new biological species would have arisen. The fruit fly mentioned above probably illustrates such a case. *D. persimilis* would be a new biological species arising within the older biological species *D. pseudoobscura.* Thus obviously all modern biological species are not originally created units. The growing popularity of the biological species concept among evolutionists is evidenced by the fact that, except for one, all eight contributors to a recent symposium on the species problem accept the biological species and are rather enthusiastic about it.[29] Mayr's new book, *Animal Species and Evolution,*[30] might be described as a testimonial to the advantages of the biological species concept. In recognizing the biological species as a natural unit, biologists are becoming less artificial in their classification, and are making progress in the discovery of the Genesis kinds in nature.

Of course there are many forms in nature where the fertility test cannot be applied to determine either the biological species or the baramin. This situation would exist where new individuals are produced by such asexual processes as simple fission, budding, formation of spores, and even by the sexual process of hermaphroditism. The fertilization of their own eggs is quite common in higher plants and in a few animals. However, in these forms it is clearly evident that each is following closely the law of Genesis which says that basic types bring forth after their kinds.

As to the practicability of the baramin concept as a classification unit, interestingly the following recent comment by Mayr on the biological species, in my opinion, very accurately describes the situation with regard to the Genesis kind if it is assumed generally to be determinable by the possibility or impossibility of true fertilization:

> Is the biological species concept invalidated by the difficulties in application that have been listed?
>
> One can confidently answer this question: "No!" Almost any concept is occasionally difficult to apply, without thereby being

invalidated. The advantages of the biological species are far greater than its shortcomings. Difficulties are rather infrequent in most groups of animals and are well circumscribed when they do occur. Such difficulties are least frequent in nondimensional situations where (except in paleontology) most species studies are done. Indeed the biological species concept, even where it has to be based on inference, nearly always permits the delimitation of sounder taxonomic species than does the morphological concepts.[31]

The scientist reads in Genesis of the fiat creation and instantaneous appearance in the beginning, of basic types of plants and animals which were made and which reproduced according to a certain fixity. The book of nature, through its fossil record and in the world of living things, reveals that an actual fixity has ever existed and still does exist among these forms. The fixity is not one which produced identical individuals, but rather is one which produces physiologically isolated groups which enjoy considerable variation within their boundaries. These original groups demonstrate that they have no power to produce any new basic types. In this complete verification in nature of the assertions of Genesis, the Christian man of science receives added assurance that the Bible is indeed a book breathed by the God of Truth.

NOTES AND REFERENCES

1. Erik Nordenskiold, *The History of Biology* (New York: Alfred A. Knopf, Inc., 1928), p. 463.
2. This translation of Linnaeus' Latin text was published by Jens Clausen, *Stages in the Evolution of Plant Species* (Ithaca, N. Y.: Cornell University Press, 1951), pp. 4-5.
3. William A. Locy, *Biology and Its Makers* (New York: Henry Holt and Co., 1935), p. 419.
4. John Van Denburgh, "The Giant Land Tortoises of the Galapagos Archipelago," *Proceedings of the California Academy of Science*, 1914 (4) 2:203-374; cf. Ruth Moore, *Evolution* (New York: Time, Inc., 1962), pp. 24-25.
5. David Lack, *Darwin's Finches* (New York: Harper and Brothers, 1939); cf. Moore, in *ibid.*, pp. 30-31.
6. Theodosius Dobzhansky, *Genetics and the Origin of Species,* 3rd ed. (New York: Columbia University Press, 1951), p. 4.
7. George Gaylord Simpson, *Tempo and Mode in Evolution* (New York: Columbia University Press, 1944).
8. *Ibid.*, pp. 105-106.

9. *Ibid.*, p. 99.
10. George Gaylord Simpson, *The Major Features of Evolution* (New York: Columbia University Press, 1953), p. 360.
11. G. L. Jepsen, G. G. Simpson, and E. Mayr, editors, *Genetics, Paleontology, and Evolution* (Princeton, N. J.: Princeton University Press, 1949), p. 74.
12. *Ibid.*, p. 77.
13. These discoveries "provide clues" only provided the student already believes in organic evolution. To the creationist they merely illustrate further the complexity of creation, and, in some instances, the degree of variation which had occurred before the organisms were buried.
14. Norman D. Newell, "The Nature of the Fossil Record," *Proceedings of the American Philosophical Society* (April 23, 1959), Vol. 103, No. 2, p. 267.
15. Austin H. Clark, *The New Evolution: Zoogenesis* (Baltimore: The Williams and Wilkins Co., 1930), pp. 100-101.
16. *Ibid.*, p. 100.
17. Griffith Taylor, *Environment and Race* (London: Oxford University Press, 1926).
18. W. S. Spector, editor, *Handbook of Biological Data* (Philadelphia: W. B. Saunders Co., 1956), p. 109; cf. Annie F. Gray, *Mammalian Hybrids* (Farnham Royal, Bucks, England: Commonwealth Agricultural Bureaux, 1954); cf. also Philip Altman and Dorothy S. Dittmer, *Growth, Including Reproduction and Morphological Development* (Washington, D. C.: Federation of American Societies for Experimental Bioliogy, 1962), pp. 127-128.
19. Cf. Altman in *ibid.*, p. 128.
20. Samuel George Morton, "Hybridity in Animals and Plants," read before the Academy of Natural Sciences of Philadelphia, November 4 and 11, 1846. Reprinted (New Haven, 1847), from the *American Journal of Science and Arts*, Vol. 3, 2nd series, p. 7.
21. Annie P. Gray, *Bird Hybrids* (Farnham Royal, Bucks, England: Commonwealth Agricultural Bureaux, 1958), p. x.
22. Frank L. Marsh, *Fundamental Biology* (Lincoln, Neb.: Published by the author, 1941), pp. 94-100 (now out of print).
23. Frank L. Marsh, *Evolution, Creation, and Science*, 2nd Edition (Washington, D. C.: Review and Herald Publishing Association, 1947), pp. 161-201.
24. *Ibid.*, p. 174.
25. Frank L. Marsh, *Studies in Creationism* (Washington, D. C.: Review and Herald Publishing Association, 1950), pp. 237-251.
26. Frank L. Marsh, *Life, Man, and Time* (Mountain View, Calif.: Pacific Publishing Association, 1957), p. 118.
27. Jacques Loeb, *The Mechanistic Conception of Life* (Chicago: University of Chicago Press, 1912), p. 24.
28. Theodosius Dobzhansky and Carl Epling, *Contributions to the Genetics, Taxonomy, and Ecology of Drosophila Pseudoobscura and Its Relatives*

(Washington, D. C.: Carnegie Institution of Washington, Publication 554, 1944), p. 6.
29. Ernst Mayr, editor, *The Species Problem* (Washington, D. C.: American Association for the Advancement of Science, 1957).
30. Ernst Mayr, *Animal Species and Evolution* (Cambridge, Mass.: The Belknap Press of Harvard University Press, 1963).
31. *Ibid.*, p. 29.

XIII

THE MYSTERY OF THE RED BEDS

Harold W. Clark

Probably nowhere else in America are to be found more interesting and puzzling displays of rocks than in the Colorado Plateau region, which covers more than 200,000 square miles in Utah and portions of surrounding states. For a number of years I have made observations here and there in the region and have covered it quite thoroughly. I have also read widely in the literature dealing with the region, and this paper is the result of these travels and studies. The points presented will, I hope, be of value in interpretation of geology from the viewpoint of the Flood.

The accompanying figures, showing the relation of the strata over this region, have been prepared from various publications, from private correspondence, and from data obtained from the office of the Pure Oil Company at Moab, Utah. Reference to these should be

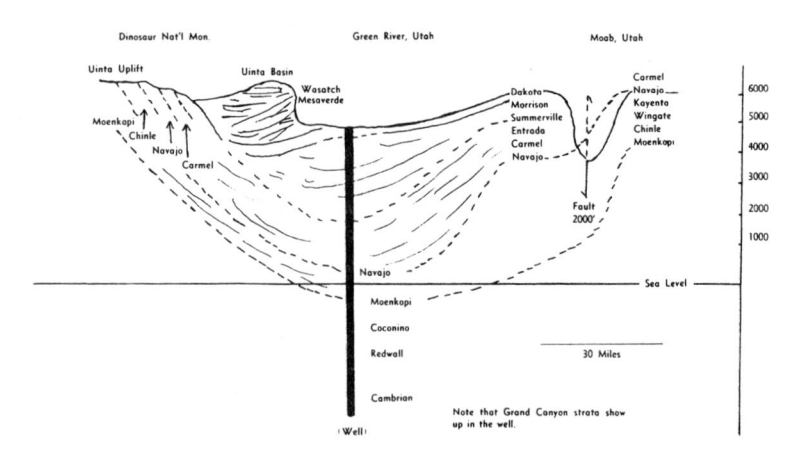

Figure 1. Section from Moab, Utah, north to the Dinosaur National Monument, showing the dip into the Uinta Basin, and the uptilted strata on the southern flank of the Uinta Mountains.

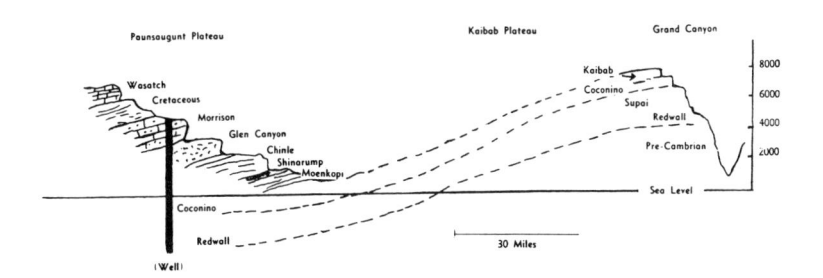

Figure 2. Section north from the Grand Canyon, showing relation of Grand Canyon strata to formations of higher stratigraphic sequence.

made as the article is read, in order to follow the data to its logical conclusion.

A visitor to the Grand Canyon stands in awe as he gazes almost a mile straight down past layer after layer of rock that has been carved by the swift-running Colorado River. At the bottom the inner gorge cuts through over a thousand feet of crystalline rocks. These rocks are classified as pre-Cambrian, and are supposed by the geologists to represent the very earliest rocks of the earth, laid down, according to popular theory, before the fossiliferous rocks were deposited.

The most striking feature of the canyon is probably the massive cliffs that are formed by the erosion of the limestones and red sandstones. Then, near the top is the spectacular white Coconino sandstone, with the grayish Kaibab limestone capping the north rim. (The left-hand column of the chart gives the classification of these strata.) We must remember that while we may not agree with the geologists as to the "age" of these rocks, we must recognize that the rocks do occur in a certain sequence.

When we go northward from the Grand Canyon, either to the east or to the north, we find more red beds spread out everywhere, with beautiful carved cliffs, monuments, and canyons. Wells in the Kanab Valley, about 75 miles north of the north rim, penetrate many of the same formations that are exposed on the walls of the canyon. It is important to note that the Moenkopi formation, which in these wells lies directly on top of the Kaibab, is exposed at some distance away, both to the east and to the west. It forms the floors of the valleys just south of Zion National Park.

Chart of Principal Formations of the Colorado Plateau

Tertiary	Wasatch
Cretaceous	Mesaverde
	Mancos
	Dakota
Jurassic	Morrison
	Summerville
	Entrada
	Carmel
Triassic	Navajo ⎫
	Kayenta ⎬ Glen Canyon Group
	Wingate ⎭
	Chinle
	Shinarump
	Moenkopi
Permian	Kaibab
	Coconino
	Hermit
	Supai
Mississippian	Redwall
Cambrian	Muav
	Bright Angel
	Tapeats
Pre-Cambrian	Grand Canyon Series
	Vishnu

(Note: Often boundary line between Triassic and Jurassic is indistinct locally.)

Rising above the Moenkopi, we find a succession of beautiful beds, which are prominently displayed over much of central Utah. Then, farther to the north and east, others appear above them, until we reach the highest members of the series in the Uinta Basin in northern Utah.

Several Questions Generated

Questions arise as we examine the lateral distribution of these

The Mystery of the Red Beds

beds. From northern Arizona to southern Wyoming, between 400 and 500 miles, and from eastern Nevada to central Colorado, 400 to 500 miles across, this great Colorado Plateau appears to be one of the greatest sedimentary basins in the world. Estimates of the amount of material deposited here before erosion washed any of it away run as high as a million cubic miles, and in some cases even more. What a movement of rock-forming sand must have taken place!

Where did it all come from? And by what means did it get there? These are simple questions, but the answers involve some of the most profound mysteries of the past. Let us examine these rocks somewhat in detail.

Perhaps the best location where we can begin our investigation is near the little city of Moab, in eastern Utah. Here, rising 2,000 feet above the Colorado River, are the beautiful red and brown cliffs classified as Triassic and Jurassic. About 50 miles north of Moab the Cretaceous Book Cliffs arise, and we note that they lie on top of the rocks that are exposed around Moab.

If we go to the Colorado National Monument near Grand Junction, Colorado, we find the same red beds we see near Moab, and across the valley to the north the gray Cretaceous cliffs rise above the Jurassic. Farther north we can catch glimpses of the Tertiary rocks. There before our eyes are spread out between 4,000 and 6,000 feet of strata in regular succession.

Coming back to Moab, let us study the formations exposed on the cliffs. Their names are as follows:

Triassic	Glen Canyon Group	Navajo / Kayenta / Wingate
	Chinle	
	Shinarump	
	Moenkopi	

The Kaibab and Coconino formations of the Grand Canyon rocks lie only a few hundred feet below these cliffs, but do not come to the surface.

The Moenkopi formation generally consists of up to 500 feet of red and brown mudstones, sandstones, or shales, and it weathers to form brilliant slopes. In some places it is much thicker. It contains very few fossils, but what are found lead to the conclusion that these beds were mostly of continental origin, not marine.

The Moenkopi underwent structural warping before the overlying sediments were laid down upon it. Yet no deep canyons appear anywhere. The next higher formation, the Shinarump, was dropped into shallow hollows of the Moenkopi. These hollows are generally not over 40 feet in depth, sometimes more, and in many places much less. We are puzzled as to how geologists can believe that millions of years could be involved in these processes without leaving deep canyons instead of shallow hollows.

The Shinarump is a very peculiar type of rock. It is a hard, resistant sandstone containing many small pebbles. This combination forms what we call a conglomerate. The pebbles are well rounded, showing that they have been washed for great distances. They are usually less than two inches in diameter, and are composed of quartzite, chalcedony, and flint, in various colors. Eighty percent of those over one fourth of an inch in diameter come from rocks not represented in the plateau.

Questions About Origin of Rocks

Where did these pebbles come from? If they had been produced by normal processes, the underlying Moenkopi rocks should have formed the landscape from which streams would wash out material to form the Shinarump deposits. The fact that the Shinarump is spread out so widely and so thinly makes it practically impossible to explain it by any normal local actions. The situation would seem to demand rapidly moving water on a tremendous scale.

The Shinarump grades into the Chinle, so that the distinction between the two is hard to make. The Chinle consists of mudstones, shales, sandstones, and conglomerates. These various rocks intergrade. They show considerable irregularity in local bedding, as if strong streams and whirling waters had dumped their loads into shallow bodies of water. This "delta" bedding is also true of the Moenkopi. Fossil wood occurs in "log jams," which is another indication of floodplain or delta conditions with rapidly running water.

The Glen Canyon group, lying above the Chinle, consists of rocks very similar to the ones just described. In some cases cuts of 15 to 20 feet have been made before the next layers were deposited, but beyond these slight irregularities no special sign of erosion can be seen. Wherever exposed, these rocks form cliffs from 700 to 1,000 feet high.

On the east side of the highway, about five miles north of Moab, another group of rocks lie exposed in the Arches National Monument. These are classified as follows:

Jurassic
- Morrison
- Summerville
- Entrada
- Carmel

Because of a fault, the Carmel, which normally lies on top of the Navajo (the top layer on the west side of the valley) is brought down to the level of the valley; and so as we go eastward into the Monument, we can follow the Jurassic series upward to the Cretaceous.

The Carmel is from 125 to 150 feet thick, and consists of pink to red or brown sandstones and mudstones, irregularly bedded. On top of it lie 250 or more feet of Entrada, a massive reddish-brown sandstone. The Summerville is less than 50 feet thick, and varies in composition. In some areas it contains great masses of agatized or opalized material.

One of the most outstanding formations in the region is the Morrison, which crops out a few miles to the north and east. This has many variations—sandstone, conglomerate, etc., similar to the Shinarump, also limestones of various colors, mudstones, and quartzites. (Note: A formation is not necessarily uniform in composition; its unitary structure is determined by its stratigraphical position and fossil content rather than by its lithographic composition.)

The Morrison has been traced for more than 100,000 square miles, and is nowhere more than 400 feet thick. It shows up as far east as Oklahoma and North Dakota. Geologists say it appears to have been laid down by rivers sweeping over extensive flood plains.

Above the Morrison lies the Dakota, a Cretaceous formation similar to the Morrison in superficial structure, but made up largely of sandstones and clays.

The Tertiary formations of the Uinta Basin are interesting, but are outside the problems we are considering in this paper. Note, however, that the lower strata crop out from beneath them on the flanks of the Uinta Mountains uplift.

Evaluation of Data

Now what conclusions can we draw from these facts? Let us try to evaluate the data and see what generalizations are possible.

Of course the first idea to propose would be that the materials forming these beds had been washed down from nearby highlands and deposited in an ancient sea. But where were these highlands? Not the Rockies nor the Wasatch nor the Uintas nor the La Sals, for all these great mountain regions were pushed up *after* most of the sediments of the Colorado Plateau were laid down. They are uplifts and intrusives that have been forced up from deep down, and have warped and twisted and inclined the overlying sediments as they arose.

Only one local area seems to have contributed much of the rocks of the basin, and that is the Uncompaghre Plateau, a mass of granite rock lying in southwestern Colorado. But what it gave could have involved only the lowest of the beds, the gray marine rocks of the strata below the red sands. Later much of this overlying material was removed, but today remnants still remain on top of the granite in some places.

Geologists are able, by examining the thickness and texture of the rocks, to tell from what direction they have been derived. In the case of the Colorado Plateau, most of the sandstones are believed to have come from the west or southwest. In some areas the formations are much thicker on the west than on the east; they thin out to the eastward. Also, as we go eastward, the materials become finer and finer. These facts show clearly that the sediments came from the west.

Of course there are local variations. One of the most recent reports on the region describes supposed ancient "seas" into which sediments were washed from the east. But this is not the general rule, although a certain amount of back and forth washing might be expected in any case, whether we interpret the situation in terms of "ages" or of Flood stages.

Studies of areas farther west fail to reveal the source of the sands. Central Nevada contains as much as 15,000 feet of the lower marine sediments, but there is nothing there that could have supplied the red sands. The conclusion seems almost inevitable that an ancient continental mass in the vicinity of California or the eastern Pacific must have been the source.

There is a possibility that some of the material may have come from the southwest, as some of the granites of Arizona contain particles of iron, which might furnish coloring material and sand. But this is only a speculation; we do not have enough information to make an effective point of it.

The Mystery of the Red Beds

A striking fact that supports the conclusion that the sands came from a long distance away is the remarkable evenness of deposition, with very little erosion such as goes on today. How beds of sandstone, mudstone, and shale could have been exposed to the atmospheric elements for millions of years and yet show no canyons or deep gorges such as recent time have produced, is a mystery.

Geologists sometimes postulate millions of years of exposure to the elements until a peneplain (a perfectly smooth plain) is formed before another layer is deposited. This explanation cannot apply here, for, as we have pointed out, the formations very commonly blend one into the other, as if their deposition had been continuous.

Had the Shinarump and Chinle deposits, for example, been derived from a landscape of Moenkopi rocks, the latter would have had to be elevated so as to furnish materials to supply these beds. There is no sign that that has happened. Everywhere the Moenkopi underlies them. How could the Shinarump and Chinle have been derived from the Moenkopi? This general principle holds good for almost any two consecutive beds. None of the layers of sandstone below the Morrison limestone, for instance, could have furnished material to build up this great formation. The material had to come from a distance.

As one studies the cliffs, even though they expose a supposed 70,000,000 years of deposit, nowhere do they show land masses, mountain ranges, badlands, river-carved canyons, or beach lines such as might be expected in the normal course of events. Look at what has happened in this region today; even if we allow the time lapse accepted by popular geological theory, not over a million years would be involved. And yet in that time (if we allow it, for the sake of argument), tremendous cutting and washing has taken place, the like of which seems to be entirely lacking in the cliffs themselves.

Furthermore, even with the great amount of cutting that has recently taken place, nothing has occurred that would spread materials such as conglomerates over a hundred thousand square miles. The action that laid those cliffs down was of a nature completely different from what was going on when they were carved into their present contours.

One more peculiar fact should be noted. Several of these successive formations are very similar, in fact, so nearly identical in composition and appearance that it is difficult to identify them unless we can follow through their sequence. In one locality the great cliffs are made of Wingate, in another Navajo, in another Entrada. There is an alternation of massive sandstone repeatedly, as also of other materials. How this could have happened over 70,000,000 years of time is very hard to understand.

Conclusions

After all the evidence has been considered, several obvious conclusions seem to be justified: (1) that the sediments have been brought in from great distances, not from local sources; (2) that they were brought in by great sweeps of water, for no ordinary river could spread them out as they are, and (3) that they were laid down one after the other in rapid succession, with no long periods of erosion between. On what other basis can we reasonably explain the evenness of the contours between formations, the irregular bedding within them, and the alternate occurrence of the massive sandstones and conglomerates?

All in all, as we study this region and try to build a picture of how the deposits have been made, we are impressed that a new approach needs to be made to geological interpretation. The current theories were proposed a century and a half ago, when very little detailed observations had been made. On the basis of these meager observations great areas have been interpreted. But the present theories are definitely inadequate to explain what we find in this vast and colorful region.

On the other hand, the facts may be fitted effectively into the Deluge interpretation. The great universal Flood, with its world-wide sweep of waters rising higher and higher and engulfing the ancient world and spreading its rocky materials far and wide, is a far more satisfactory answer to geological problems than the theory of ages of slow, normal sedimentation.

How long will it be before serious scientific consideration is given to the Flood? It is high time that we give it a place in modern thought.

XIV

A PALEOECOLOGICAL MISINTERPRETATION

HAROLD G. COFFIN

In attempting to understand the environments and relationships of ancient living organisms, a discipline called paleoecology has been developed. Interpretations, which of necessity must be tentative because of the subjective evidences on which they are based, are unavoidably influenced by the researcher's concepts of time and geological processes during the earth's past history.

A strained interpretation has been given the small marine tubeworm, *Spirorbis*. This worm, which secretes a calcareous tube for protection of its fragile body, is ubiquitous in modern oceans of the world. Because the diameter of the whole coiled tube, which has the appearance of a small snail, is not usually over 2 mm., it can be easily overlooked. It is a sessile organism which attaches on one side to any suitable substrate such as corals, mollusks, bryozoans, and other invertebrates. Floating sargassum or gulf-weed is also covered with many *Spirorbis* tubes and furnishes a planktonic environment.[1]

Description and Classification

This worm is hermaphroditic, spawns during high spring tides, and releases its larvae a certain number of days later.[2] In keeping with other organisms of this class, it produces free-swimming trochophore larvae, which move by means of bands of cilia which circle the oval-shaped body.[3] They are positively phototaxic when first released into the water, but usually become negative about three weeks later, when metamorphosis commences. A negative reaction to brackish or fresh water prevents the larvae from settling in unfavorable environments.[4]

No member of the family Surpulidae, to which *Spirorbis* belongs, is found in an aquatic (fresh-water) habitat, although the small coiled tubes of *Spirorbis* are abundant along the shores of the Black Sea, which has a salinity of approximately 18 percent at the surface, as compared to an average of 35 percent in most oceans.[5] In fact, the whole class, Polychaeta, is marine except for a few rare examples. Certain other groups of marine invertebrates in other phyla also have trochophore larvae, but *no examples of fresh-water organisms with trochophore larvae have ever been reported.*

Abundant Samples in Fossil Record

Spirorbis is abundant in the fossil record, being found in all periods from the Ordovician to the Recent. The white calcareous tubes are so similar to those now living in the oceans that there is no hesitancy about placing them in the same genus. Attempts to designate species among fossil specimens have not been very successful.[6] Marine fossils often carry attached *Spirorbis* tubes. Their arrangement on some pelecypods suggests a commensalism whereby the worm benefited from the water currents caused by the feeding of the clam.[7]

If coal deposits are not allochthonous (transported), but have originated from swamps and marshes where plant materials have ac-

Figure 1. Enlargement of white calcareous tube of *Spirorbis* in fossilized condition.

A Paleoecological Misinterpretation

cumulated to considerable depths over much time—the present popular view—then the discovery of marine organisms *within* the coal would *not* be expected. Usually coal is quite devoid of animal fossils, although there are numerous exceptions. However, *Spirorbis* is a frequent constituent of Carboniferous coal-measures. They are found attached to plant debris and mixed into coal seams. They also may be cemented to any marine organisms that are present.[8] This has been known from the time when coal and associated strata were beginning to receive detailed attention over 100 years ago.

Initial Incredible Interpretation

The swing in the early nineteenth century by geologists to concepts of uniformity and geological ages influenced the paleoecological interpretation of *Spirorbis*. Obviously the "bog theory" of coal formation cannot accommodate the abundant presence of a marine organism. Through the years this small annelid has been declared a salt-water worm throughout the geologic column except in the coal measures, where the supposed evidences for the *in situ* origin of coal made difficult the interpretation of *Spirorbis* at its face value.[9]

Consequently, seemingly without much question on the part of geologists and paleontologists through the decades, this worm when found in coal and coal-bearing rocks has been designated a *freshwater* dweller. This position has been taken despite the facts:

(a) that *Spirorbis* today is completely limited to the marine environment,

(b) that it reproduces by means of a trochophore larva, which, though characteristic of several marine phyla, is *unknown* for any fresh water invertebrates, and

(c) that it is associated with obviously marine organisms throughout the geologic column, including the Carboniferous period.

This highly questionable interpretation is a good example of the influence of a prevailing (ruling) theory.

Conclusion

Taken at face value, *Spirorbis* in coal and on plant fragments gives strong evidence for the allochthonous origin of much of the coal. Even as today the drifting Sargassum seaweed provides an attachment surface for *Spirorbis,* so flotsam of *Sigillaria, Lepidodendron, Calamites, Cordaites,* and other coal-forming plants became spotted with the coiled tubes of this small worm. When depositing conditions buried the masses of vegetable material under sand and silt, the worms also were buried.

NOTES AND REFERENCES

1. Rudolf Ruedemann, "Paleozoic Plankton of North America," *Geological Society of American Memoir* (1934), 2:18.
2. P. Korringa, "Lunar Periodicity" (in) Joel W. Hedgpeth, editor, *Treatise on Marine Ecology and Paleoecology*, Vol. 1, Ecology, Geological Society of America Memoir (1957), 67:922.
3. Robert D. Barnes, *Invertebrate Zoology* (Philadelphia: W. B. Saunders Co., 1963), p. 205.
4. Gunnar Thorson, "Bottom Communities" (in) Hedgpeth, *op. cit.*, 480.
5. Hubert Caspers, "Black Sea and Sea of Azov," (in) *ibid.*, p. 845.
6. W. H. Easton, *Invertebrate Paleontology* (New York: Harper and Row, 1960), p. 224.
7. Derek V. Ager, *Paleoecology* (New York: McGraw-Hill, 1963), p. 261.
8. G. E. Condra and M. K. Elias, "Carboniferous and Permian Ctenostomatous Bryozoa," *Geological Society of American Bulletin* (1944), 55: 517-566.
9. J. Marvin Weller, "Paleoecology of the Pennsylvanian Period in Illinois and Adjacent States," (in) Harry S. Ladd, editor, *Treatise on Marine Ecology and Paleoecology*, Vol. 2, Paleoecology, Geological Society of America (1957), 67:333.
10. Sir Arthur Trueman, *The Coalfields of Great Britain* (London: Edward Arnold, 1954), pp. 68-69.
11. John J. Sevenson, "Formation of Coal Beds, *Proceedings of American Philosophical Society*, Vols. 50-52, 1911-1913. (Published in one volume by the New Era Printing Company, Lancaster, Pa. See p. 509.)
12. J. William Dawson, *Acadian Geology* (London: Macmillan and Co., 1891).

XV

A SUMMARY OF THE *MONERA* FALLACY

N. A. Rupke

Introduction

In the year 1756 Immanuel Kant published this *Allgemeine Naturgeschichte und Theorie des Himmels*. In it he expressed an evolutionary system of cosmogony. This system was authorized when in the year 1796 Pierre-Simon, marquis de Laplace, defended it in his *Exposition du système du monde*.

Something like it occurred with regard to the hypothesis of organic evolution. It was advocated by Jean-Baptiste-Pierre-Antoine de Monet de Lamark in his *Philosophie zoologique* (1809). Later on, this hypothesis was popularized by Charles Darwin in his *The Origin of Species by means of natural selection or the preservation of favoured races in the struggle for life* (1859).

Among the consistent advocates of the idea of evolution, the need was felt of connecting the evolutionary system of cosmogony and the hypothesis of organic evolution; i.e., of bridging the gap between the inanimate matter and the living units. So evolutionists undertook to prove the origin of life from lifeless matter (*abiogenesis*, etc.) and to track some of the most simple form of life, still being, as it were, *in statu nascendi*.

However, shortly after the publication of Darwin's *The Origin of Species*, the French biochemist Louis Pasteur dealt a heavy blow to the high expectations of the evolutionary-minded naturalists. In the course of the years 1860-1866 a number of papers by Pasteur on fermentation and *abiogenesis* were presented to the *Académie des Sciences*.

The main report was published in 1861 under the title: Mémoire sur les corpuscules organisés qui existent dans l'atmosphère. Examen de la doctrine des générations spontanées." [1] Till then it was believed that microbes could originate from organic materials during fermentation, putrefaction, etc.—a belief which implied *abiogenesis*. Pasteur proved by a variety of ingenious and cogent experiments that each microbe is derived from a pre-existing microbe and that *abiogenesis* is a chimera.[2]

Evolutionists Support Abiogenesis

For all that, a number of ardent Darwinian naturalists did not lose courage in seeking after some most simple form of life, still being, as it were, *in statu nascendi*. Among them were "Darwin's Bulldogs," viz., Thomas Henry Huxley and Ernest Haeckel. In order to establish *abiogenesis* these evolutionists made a mistake practically beyond compare.

In his *Generelle Morphologie der Organismen Allgemeine Grundzüge der organischen Formen-Wissenschaft, mechanisch begründet durch die von Charles Darwin reformirte Descendenz-Theorie* (1866), Haeckel created the group of the *Monera*. This name was conferred upon some most simple *Protista*, the sarcode or protoplasm of which was conceived to be entirely homogeneous and to lack a nucleus.

Particularly, Haeckel broached the *Monera* in order to bridge the gap between the inanimate matter and the living units.[3] Shortly after, in 1868, a monograph by Haeckel on the *Monera* was published, entitled: "Monographie der Moneren."[4] In it Haeckel described in detail a number of *Monera*, among them the most simple *Moneron* which he had called before *Protamoeba primitiva*. Its minuscule body was said to be entirely homogeneous and to reproduce itself by process of fission (Figure 1).[5]

Also, in the year 1868, Huxley published a report, entitled: "On some Organisms living at Great Depths in the North Atlantic Ocean."[6] In it he dealt with a number of samples of deep-sea mud dredged up from the Atlantic. The samples were preserved in alcohol—a circumstance which later will appear essential. In the Atlantic mud, Huxley discerned some minuscule bodies, which he had called before "coccolithes" and of which he declared that they cannot be organic. He divided the *coccolithes* in "discolithes" and "cyatholithes."

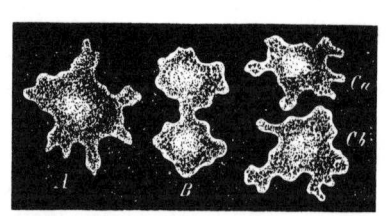

Figure 1. *Protamoeba primitiva* (Haeckel). This pretended *Moneron* turned out to be non-existent (From: Haeckel: *Natürliche Schöpfungsgeschichte*, First Edition, p. 144, Figure 1).

In addition to the *coccolithes*, other bodies, known by the name of "coccosphaeres," occurred. The minuscule bodies were imbedded between some granules in a gelatinous matter. Of this Huxley assumed that it represented a mass of protoplasm and he took this for a *Moneron*; by reason of its habitat he called the mass *Bathybius* (Figure 2). The *coccolithes* were supposed to be produced by the *Bathybius* "Urschleim." Huxley stated:

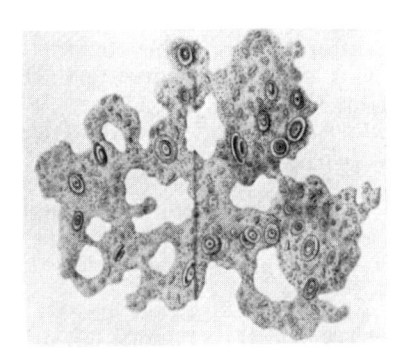

Figure 2. *Bathybius Haeckelii* (Huxley). This pretended *Moneron* appeared to be a mineral precipitate. The *coccolithes*, presumed to be produced by the glairy mass, turned out to be settled fragments of the *Coccolithophoridae*. (From: *Jenaische Zeitschrift*, 5. Band, Taf. XVII, Figure 1).

I conceive that the granule-heaps and the transparent gelatinous matter in which they are imbedded represent masses of protoplasm. Take away the cysts which characterise the *Radioloria*, and a dead *Sphaerozoum* would very nearly resemble one one of the masses of this deep-sea "Urschleim," which must, I think, be regarded as a new form of those simple animated beings which have recently been so well described by Haeckel in his "Monographie der Moneren." I proposed to confer upon this new "Moner" the generic name of *Bathybius*, and to call it after the eminent Professor of Zoology in the University of Jena, *B. Haeckelii*.

From the manner in which the youngest *Discolithi* and *Cyatholithi* are found imbedded among the granules; from the resemblance of the youngest forms of the *Discolithi* and the smallest "corpuscles" of *Cyatholithus* to the granules; and from the absence of any evident means of maintaining an independent existence in either, I am led to believe that they are not independent organisms, but that they stand in the same relation to the protoplasm of *Bathybius* as the spicula of Sponges or the *Radiolaria* do to the soft part of those animals.[7]

At that time there was a controversy in regard to the nature of supposed organic structures, discovered in the serpentine limestones of the Laurentian series in Canada. The Canadian geologist John William Dawson described these structures as those of a gigantic *Foraminifer;* on it he conferred the name *Eozoön Canadense*. Dawson's view was shared by the English naturalist William Benjamin Carpenter. Instantly, the newly discovered *Moneron B. Haecklii* was invoked to warrant the gigantic size of *Eozoön Canadense*. Carpenter stated:

the discovery of this indefinite plasmodium covering a wide area of the existing sea-bottom should afford a remarkable confirmation, to such (at least) as still think confirmation necessary, of the doctrine of organic origin of the serpentine limestone of the Laurentian formation. For if *Bathybius*, like the testaceous Rhizopods, could form for itself a shelly envelope, that envelope would closely resemble *Eozoön*. Further, as Prof. Huxley has proved the existence of *Bathybius* through a great range, not merely of depth but of temperature, I cannot but think it probable that it has existed continuously in the deep seas of all geological epochs.[8]

Later on, however, it has been recognized that the supposed organic structures are of mineral origin.

The existence of *B. Haeckelii* was affirmed by the English naturalist Sir Charles Wyville Thomson, who, later on, conducted the civilian staff of the expedition with H.M.S. Challenger. In an 1869 article, "On the Depths of the Sea," [9] Wyville Thomson contended in regard to a sample of mud from the Atlantic:

> This mud was actually alive; it stuck together in lumps, as if there were white of egg mixed with it; and the glairy mass proved, under the microscope, to be a living sarcode. Prof. Huxley regards this as a distinct creature, and calls it "Bathybius." [10]

Wyville Thomson dealt with *B. Haeckelii* more in detail in his renowned book entitled: *The Depths of the Sea, Etc.* (1873).[11]

The report on the occurrence of free albumen masses in the deep-sea was suited remarkably well to the philosophy of a universal transformism and to the implicit idea of *abiogenesis*. The report was enthusiastically received by the supporters of this philosophy; at last, nascent life was detected!

Haeckel et al. Support Huxley's Work

Above all others Haeckel contributed to the newly discovered *Moneron*, the species of which was dedicated to him. In his "Beiträge zur Plastidentheorie," [12] he confirmed in 1870 Huxley's assertions in this matter and enlarged his report in some ways ("Im Wesentlichen kann ich alle Angaben von Huxley bestätigen, doch auch nach einigen Richtungen hin dieselben vervollständigen und erweitern.").[13]

Haeckel analyzed a glass of deep-sea mud—placed in alcohol as well. The granules, imbedded in the gelatinous matrix, he conceived to be real protoplasm; for the granules colored when treated with a carmine or an iodine solution. As to the *coccolithes,* Haeckel took it for likely, though not yet altogether proved, that they were produced by *B. Haeckelii.*

In a speech in 1870 entitled, "Das Leben in den grössten Meerestiefen," [14] Haeckel assured that it was almost incontestable that *B. Haeckelii* did originate by *abiogenesis* (". . . dass die freien Urschlein-Körper des Bathybius sich an Ort und Stelle unter dem Einflusse der eigenthümlichen hier waltenden Existenz-Bedingungen aus anorganischer Substanz bilden").[15] In general, he argued—evidently *versus* Pasteur—that the question of *abiogenesis* could not be answered by experiment, but solely by philosophy.

Well then, Haeckel's evolutionary philosophy, implying a process of *abiogenesis,* turned out to be true! The discovery of the *Monera* like *Protamoebe primitiva* and *B. Haeckelii* put the matter beyond doubt. Finally, the chasm between matter and life was filled up! In his widely read *Natürliche Schöpfungsgeschichte. Etc.* (Second Edition, 1870) Haeckel wordily expressed:

> Sobald man früherhin die vorstellung der Urzeugung zu fassen suchte, scheiterte man sofort an der organischen Zusammensetzung auch der einfachsten Organismen, welche man damals kannte. Erst seitdem wir mit den höchst wichtigen Moneren bekannt geworden sind, erst seitdem wir in ihnen Organismen kennen gelernt haben, welche gar nicht aus Organen zusammengesetzt sind, welche bloss aus einer einzigen chemischen Verbindung bestehen, und dennoch wachsen, sich ernähren und fortpflazen, ist jene Hauptschwierigkeit gelöst, und die Hypothese der Urzeugung hat dadurch denjenigen Grad von Wahrscheinlichkeit gewonnen, welcher sie berechtigt, die Lücke zwischen *Kant's* Kosmogenie und *Lamarck's* Descendenztheorie auszufüllen. Es giebt sogar schon unter den bis jetzt bekannten Moneren eine Arte, die vielleicht noch heutzutage beständig durch Urzeugung entsteht. Das ist der wunderbare, von *Huxley* entdeckte und beschriebene *Bathybius Haeckelii* (English translation in note).[16]

By more or less tacit consent it had been accepted that *B. Haeckelii* covered a vast part of the sea-bottom. In a speech in 1870 before the Royal Geographical Society Huxley,[17] returning to the subject, emphatically signalized the general occurrence of his reputed discovery. In respect of *B. Haeckelii* he said:

> Evidence of its existence had been found throughout the whole North and South Atlantic, and wherever the Indian Ocean had been surveyed, so that it probably forms one continuous scum

of living matter girding the whole surface of the earth. This opinion had been confirmed in all its essential details by Prof. Haeckel, who had published an admirable account of specimens obtained by him.[18]

The discovery of the peculiar *Moneron B. Haeckelii* met with general favor. It was reported in 1871 in the *Archives des Sciences physiques et naturelles*[19] and in no time it became a public property. Several foremost scientists set themselves to a detailed study of this conclusive *Moneron*.

In an 1870 article entitled "Vorläufige Mitteilungen über Tiefseechlamm," [20] the German geologist Carl Wilhelm von Gümbel made a communication relating to deep-sea mud—preserved by him in alcohol also. Gümbel stated that he had come to the conclusion, just like Huxley and Haeckel, that the *coccolithes* and *B. Haeckelii* were a living mass (". . . dass auch mir kein Zweifel and der *organischen* Natur der *Coccolithen* und des *Bathybius übrig* blieb").[21]

Besides, he maintained the *B. Haeckelii* was not confined to a bathyal environment; he had observed it in a paralic environment as well and so he was led to conclude that *B. Haeckelii* had a universal distribution (". . . dass Coccolithen (*Bathybius*) *in allen Meeren* und *in allen Meerestiefen vorkommen*").[22] Because of the occurrence of *coccolithes* in numerous limestones Gümbel stressed the lithogenetic importance of *B. Haeckelii*.

Gümbel's compatriot Oscar Schmidt made known in an 1870 article, "Uber Coccolithen und Rhabdolithen," [23] that, during an expedition in the Adriatic, he had met with *B. Haeckelii*. Schmidt stated that in a fresh sample, *B. Haeckelii* behaved in like manner as when placed in alcohol ("Der frisch aus dem Meere gehobene Bathybius zeigt . . . genau jene Erscheinungen, welche die in Weingeist conservirten Proben wahrnehmen lassen").[24] In addition to the *coccolithes* Schmidt observed some bodies of hitherto undescribed characteristics, naming it "rhabdolithes." He, indeed, gave it as his view that the bodies were independent from *B. Haeckelii*.

A Still Lower Moneron *Reported*

At that time the existence of a still lower *Moneron* than *B. Haeckelii* was reported! It was discovered along the coast of Grinnel Land by the German naturalist Emile Bessels, both surgeon and naturalist to the U. S. Arctic expedition with the ship *Polaris*. Bessels called it *Protobathybius Robesonii*. Its existence was announced in

A Summary of the Monera Fallacy

1874 in *Nature*[25] and a description of it by the discoverer was published in 1876. The description is as follows:

> It is mainly distinguished from Bathybius by the absence of both the Discolithes and Cyatholithes. For this reason I take it to be an older form than Bathybius, whence the name given to it. It consists of nearly pure protoplasm, tinged most intensely by a solution of carmine in ammonia. It contains fine gray granules of considerable refracting power, and besides the latter a great number of oleaginous drops, soluble in ether. It manifests very marked amoeboid motions and takes up particles of carmine or other foreign substances suspended in the water in which it is kept. It hardly contained any foreign matter, except a fine sediment of limestone constituting the bottom of the sea.[26]

It is beyond the scope of this summary to bring under close scrutiny all the numerous publications and references relating to the *Monera* and particularly to *B. Haeckelii*. I will only mention that the German geologist Karl Alfred von Zittel in his *Handbuch der Paleontologie* (First part, 1876) described the *Monera,* at the head of which class he placed *B. Haeckelii*.[27]

About this time, however, the days of *B. Haeckelii* and its predecessor *Protob. Robesonii* came to an end—much though these *Monera* were a *conditio sine qua non* to any consistent hypothesis of evolution.

Criticisms Finally Published

Already the English naturalist G. C. Wallich, in an 1869 paper, "On the Vital Functions of the Deep-sea Protozoa," [28] had objected to Huxley's discovery of *B. Haeckelii*. Wallich showed that there is no connection between it and the *coccolithes* and that these peculiar bodies, whether *discolithes* or *cyatholithes,* are nothing more than the *disjecta membra* of the *coccosphaeres,* inhabiting the surface-waters of the ocean. Wallich summarized his objections in this matter in an 1875 paper, "On the true Nature of the so-called '*Bathybius*,' and its alleged Function in the Nutrition of the Protozoa." [29] He stated:

> It has been shown that, whereas Prof. Huxley, in his original report, declared that the coccoliths "*cannot be organic,*" I proved them to be organic; whereas he doubted their being the *disjecta membra of the coccospheres,* I proved them to be so; and whereas he alleged that they normally, as "coccoliths," "discoliths," or "cyatholiths," constitute part and parcel of the living thing to which he gave the name of *Bathybius,* I distinctly proved that the "coccoliths" have no physiological connexion with the viscid matter

in which they are imbedded at the bottom of the sea, but are detached and normal appendages of coccospheres which have lived in the superficial waters of the ocean, and subsided to the bottom only after death.[30]

Yet it was not until the twentieth century that the true nature of the *coccolithes* and the *rhabdolithes* was discerned. In 1902 the German biologist H. Lohmann made public an article on "Die Coccolithophoridae, ein Monographie der Coccolithen bildenden Flagellaten, etc." [31] In it he put the matter beyond doubt that the *coccolithes* and the *rhabdolithes* are nothing more than settled fragments, which at one time formed part of the calcareous envelope of floating *Coccolithophoridae*, by which name he signified a class of flagellates (Figure 3).

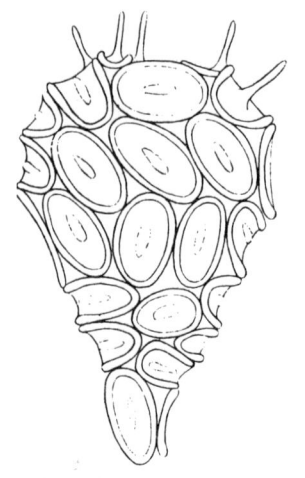

Figure 3. *Syracosphaera pulchra* (Lohmann). A representative of the *Coccolithophoridae*, a class of flagellates; the settled fragments of its calcareous envelope were claimed to be produced by the fictitious *B. Haeckelii*. (From: *Archiv der Protistenkunde*, I, Taf. IV, Figure 33).

At the end of the year 1872 an expedition was sent out with HMS *Challenger* in order to make a series of soundings and dredgings in the three great ocean basins. In the early part of the cruise, attempts were made again and again to obtain *B. Haeckelii;* however, with no definite result. J. Murray, naturalist to the expedition, observed that a sample of deep-sea mud, when placed in alcohol, assumed the aspect of *B. Haeckelii!*

Murray observed this phenomenon in such quantity that, if it was really of the supposed organic nature, the presence of organic matter should be easy to detect. However, J. Y. Buchanan, chemist to the expedition, did not find satisfactory evidence of it. What had happened to the reputed *B. Haeckelii*? Buchanan concluded:

> There remained, then, but one conclusion, namely, that the body which Mr. Murray had observed was not an organic body at all; and on examining it and its mode of preparation I determined it to be sulfate of lime, which had been eliminated from the sea-

A Summary of the Monera Fallacy

water, always present in the mud, as an amorphous precipitate on the addition of spirit of wine. The substance when analyzed consisted of sulphuric acid and lime; and when dissolved in water and the solution allowed to evaporate, it crystallized in the well-known form of gypsum, the crystals being all alike, and there being no amorphous matter amongst them.[32]

In a letter[33] to Huxley by Wyville Thomson, dated June, 1875, the tragic end of *B. Haeckelii* was made known. It was suspected that the thing which Huxley had named was nothing more than a sulphate of lime, precipitated in a flocculent state by the *strong alcohol* in which the samples had been placed. Having read this letter, Huxley was highly inclined to drop *B. Haeckelii* as reposing on a delusion.

Case for Abiogenesis Destroyed

By this time, however, the fate of *B. Haeckelii* was not yet considered to be absolutely decided. This did not happen until the "Preliminary Reports to Professor Wyville Thomson, F.R.S., Director of the Civilian Scientific Staff, on Work done on board of the Challenger" of 1876 by Murray[34] and that by Buchanan had been made public. In his reports Murray gave *B. Haeckelii* the "knock-out blow" where he informed:

> In the early part of the cruise many attempts were made by all of the naturalists to detect the presence of free protoplasm in or on the bottoms from our soundings and dredgings, but with no definite result. It was undoubted, however, that some specimens of the sea-bottom preserved in spirit assumed a very mobile or jelly-like aspect, and also that flocculent matter was often present. Mr. Buchanan determined that the flocculent matter was simply the amorphous sulphate of lime precipitated by spirit from the sea-water. Subsequently a number of experiments were made out upon the behavior of this amorphous precipitate when precipitated with different quantities of spirit and when treated with colouring-solutions. The precipitate was also examined alone and mixed up with some of the ooze. The ooze was examined at the same time and in the same manner, but without having been treated with spirit. The results were shortly these:—
>
> When sea-water is treated with twice its volume of spirit or less, nearly the whole of the amorphous precipitate assumes the crystalline form in a short time.
>
> When treated with a great excess of spirit the precipitate remains amorphous, and assumes a gelatinous aspect.

This gelatinous-like sulphate of lime colours with the carmine and iodine solutions, and when mixed with the ooze has, under the microscope, the appearances so minutely described by Haeckel.

The ooze washed with distilled water, or taken just as it comes up, and treated in the same manner with colouring-solutions, does not show these appearances. The jelly-like aspect and the matter coloured with carmine can always be removed from the spirit-preserved specimens of the ooze by treating with distilled water.

In all cases the jelly-like or mobile aspect of the ooze is found to be due to the presence of the flocculent precipitate from the sea-water associated with the ooze.

No free albuminous matter could be detected.

When it is remembered that the original describers worked with spirit-preserved specimens of the bottom, the inference seems fair that *Bathybius* and the amorphous sulphate of lime are identical, and that in placing it amongst living things, the describers have committed an error.[35]

Thus *B. Haeckelii,* the "Urschleim" from the sea-bottom, which was embraced by nearly all evolutionists of that day as bridging the gap between matter and life, turned out to be a pure mineral precipitate! In that way this most simple form of life, conceived to originate by *abiogenesis,* was wiped out of existence; and together with it the related form *Protob. Robesonii* made its exit.

Haeckel Refused to Concede

Yet Haeckel, in an 1877 paper on "Bathybius und die Moneren," [36] insisted that *B. Haeckelii* actually did exist. He only admitted that its geographical distribution was more confined than previously supposed, so that owing to this the HMS *Challenger* expedition had not met with it. However, in spite of his insistence of the actual existence of *B. Haeckelii,* Haeckel suppressed it from the publications by him ever since that time. This proves Haeckel was less than advocating the case of evolution in this matter.

By tacit agreement the "Urschleim"-fallacy, obviously discrediting the hypothesis of evolution according to which the "Urschleim" had been postulated, was generally ignored. Of that time I have read but one paper in which the "Urschleim"-fallacy was really critically discussed. The paper was written by A. de Lapparent, who made it public in 1878 under the title: "Le Bathybius. Historie d'un protoplasme."[37] Having told the story, de Lapparent drew the moral with these words:

> Devant un tel résultat, n'est-il pas permis de sourire et ne serait-on pas excusable d'évoquer ici le souvenir de cet astrologue de la légende, qui découvrait des animaux dans la lune parcequ'une souris s'était introduite dans son télescope? Voilà pourtant les surprises que la science incrédule nous réserve, toutes les fois que l'esprit de parti préside à ses investigations! Si encore de telles mésaventures la rendaient plus prudente; mais il suffit de lire les derniers écrits de MM. Huxley et Haeckel pour voir avec quel dédain, avec quelle hauteur les adversaires du transformisme sont traités par eux (English translation in note).[38]

Notwithstanding the wholesale "fade-out" of *B. Haeckelii* and *Protob. Robesonii,* the group of the *Monera* as such were sustained. Representatives of the group, like *Prota. primitiva,* were put upon the stage again and again till well into the twentieth century. Such a form, which had been defined as being entirely homogeneous and lacking a nucleus, was still considered to narrow the gap between matter and life.

The Ultimate Result

However, *Prota. primitiva,* so minutely described by Haeckel in 1868, was gradually recognized to be non-existent. Thus *Prota. primitiva,* at first conceived to be the most simple *Moneron,* turned out to be a mere hoax! The other *Monera* were gradually recognized to be non-existent as well, or, possibly, false to the definition. H. F. Copeland stated in a 1938 article on "The kingdoms of organisms"[39]:

> In his *Generelle Morphologie,* Haeckel postulated the existence of a group of organisms without nuclei; he named the group Monera (originally Moneres, but the neuter form used in later works is preferable) and included it in Protista. He is said to have postulated, rather than to have recognized or assembled, such a group, because most of the organisms which he assigned to it, *Protamoeba, Protomonas,* and *Vampurella,* are either nonexistent or false to the definition. Among Haeckel's original examples of Monera, *Vibrio* is the only one representing organisms which actually exist and are interpretable as lacking nuclei.[40]

At present, however, we know for fact, thanks mainly to relatively recent cytological, genetic and biochemical research, that the *Bacteria,* like *Vibrio,* have a DNA containing nucleus—though not surrounded by a membrane—which stores genetic information. Consequently, *Vibrio* cannot be classed properly as *Monera,* as formerly conceived by Haeckel. Presently, the group, on which that name has been conferred, must be looked upon as entirely imaginary.

Summary and Conclusions

The foregoing may be summarized as follows:

(a) In order to establish *abiogenesis*—implicit to any consistent hypothesis of transformism—the most renowned biologists of that time, viz., Huxley, Haeckel *et al.*, postulated the fictitious *Monera* and "discovered," "observed," and "analyzed" the most simple "representative," *B. Haeckelii.*

(b) Moreover, the "find" of a still lower form, namely *Protob. Robesonii,* was reported.

(c) In regard to an already "discovered" form, viz., *Prota. primitiva,* Haeckel "observed" the reproduction process of fission—though the relevant "organism" did not exist.

(d) And some naturalists "observed" *B. Haeckelii* in a fresh sample of mud—though it was a mere sulphate of lime, which formed only when placed in alcohol.

(e) Also, Gümbel, Zittel *et al.,* foremost geologists of that time, introduced the *Monera* into geological literature.

(f) Finally, to all this the majority of the contemporary biologists and geologists readily assented. As a consequence of the impact of the philosophy of evolution, these men did not observe *fact,* but a *fictitious system.* In that way the philosophy of evolution has exerted a harmful effect on the study of nature and on the progress of science.[41]

The *Monera* were "observed" with the standard microscope. In the course of the last decades, the more powerful phase and electron microscope plus such techniques as microdissection have revealed an astounding complexity in protoplasm and the cell. Thus modern techniques have widened the gap between matter and life. (Figure 4)

Now then, a hypothesis is said to be acceptable in proportion to its degree of heuristic value, i.e., in proportion as it stimulates the discovery of still unknown facts. As shown, the hypothesis of evolution did not lead to *fact* but to mere *fiction.*

On the other hand, the doctrine of creation—to which doctrine a wide gap between matter and life is implicit—proved to be in conformity with fact. In consequence, the doctrine of creation has to be accepted—at least as a working hypothesis.

Notwithstanding all that, this is not done by W. Seifriz in his book on *Protoplasm* (1936). Having wrongly ascribed the "discovery" of *B. Haeckelii* to Haeckel, Seifriz stated: "Though his find was not what he thought it to be, yet Haeckel's philosophical idea is nevertheless sound, for we cannot escape the conviction that life began in a relatively undifferentiated mass of protoplasm."[42]

This statement of *belief* is endorsed by the majority of present-day evolutionists. Consequently, these evolutionists love *system* better than *truth*; and their aversion against the doctrine of creation cannot be a matter of science, but, on the contrary, it can be only the result of an *a priori* philosophy.

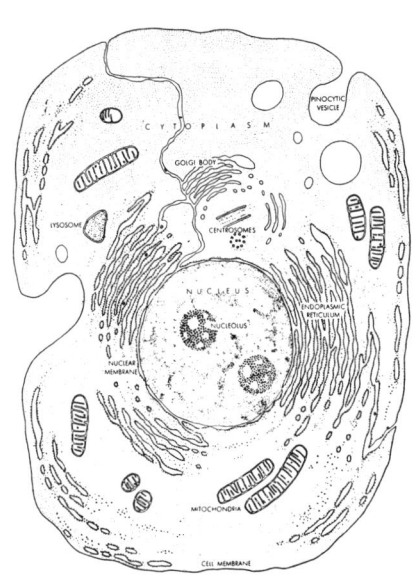

Figure 4. Diagram of a typical cell. The diagram, based on electron micrographs, gives an idea of the astounding complexity in protoplasm and the cell. (From: *The Living Cell, Readings from Scientific American*, Sept. 1961, p. 9).

NOTES AND REFERENCES

1. *Annales des sciences naturelles* (partie zoologique), 4ᵉ série, XVI, 1861, pp. 5-98, pl. I.
2. Pasteur's papers on *abiogenesis* are collected in *Oeuvres de Pasteur*, II (Paris, 1922), pp. 185-358.
3. *Generelle Morphologie der Organismen*, I, (Berlin: 1866), p. 135.
4. *Jenaische Zeitschrift für Medicin und Naturwissenschaft*, 4. Band, pp. 64-137, Taf. II, III; Leipzig, 1868.
5. *Ibid.*, pp. 104-107, Taf. III, Figures 25-30.
6. *Quarterly Journal of Microscopical Science*, new series, VIII (1868), pp. 203-212, pl. IV.
7. *Ibid.*, p. 210, pl. IV, Figure 1.
8. *Proceedings of the Royal Society of London* (1868), p. 191; quoted by G. C. Wallich: "On the true Nature of the so-called '*Bathybius*,' and its alleged Function in the Nutrition of the Protozoa" in *The Annals and Magazine of Natural History*, 4th series, XVI (1875), p. 323.
9. *The Annals and Magazine of Natural History*, 4th series, IV (1869), pp. 112-124.

10. *Ibid.*, p. 121.
11. *The Depths of the Sea* (London, 1873), pp. 410-415, Figure 63.
12. *Jenaische Zeitschrift für Medicin und Naturwissenschaft*, 5, Band, pp. 492-550, Taf. XVII; Leipzig, 1870.
13. *Ibid.*, p. 504.
14. *Sammlung gemeinverstaendlicher wissenschaftlicher Vortraege*, 5. Serie, Heft 110, pp. 1-43, 1 Titelbild; Berlin, 1870.
15. *Ibid.*, p. 38.
16. *Natürliche Schöpfungsgeschichte, Etc.*, Second Edition, (Berlin: 1870), p. 306. English translation:
    As soon as one formerly tried to visualize *abiogenesis,* one directly broke down on the organic make-up of even the most simple organisms which were known at that time. This main difficulty has not been solved until we have been acquainted with the highly important *Monera* which are not at all made up of organs, which are only composed of one single chemical compound, and still grow, feed and reproduce, and by that the hypothesis of *abiogenesis* has gained that degree of probability as to entitle it to fill up the gap between *Kant's* cosmogony and *Lamarck's* descent theory. There is already even among the till now known *Monera* one species which probably still to-day continually originates by *abiogenesis.* It is the miraculous *Bathybius Haeckelii,* discovered and described by *Huxley.*
17. *Proceedings of the Royal Geographical Society*, XV (1871), pp. 37-39.
18. *Ibid.*, p. 38.
19. *Archives des Sciences physiques et naturellas*, nouvelle période, XLI (1871), pp. 76-78.
20. *Neues Jahrbuch für Mineralogie, Geologie und Palaeontologie* (1870) pp. 753-767.
21. *Ibid.*, p. 757.
22. *Ibid.*, p. 763.
23. *Sitzungsberichte der kaiserlichen Akademie der Wissenschaften* (mathematisch-naturwissenschaftliche Classe), 62. Band, 1. Abteilung, 1870, pp. 669-682, Taf. I.
24. *Ibid.*, p. 673.
25. *Nature*, IX (1874), p. 405.
26. A. C. Packard, *Life Histories of Animals* (New York, 1876), pp. 3-4.
27. Karl A. von Zittel, *Handbuch der Palaeontologie* (First Part), München und Leipzig, 1876-1880), pp. 58-60.
28. *The Monthly Microscopical Journal*, I (1869), pp. 32-41.
29. *The Annals and Magazine of Natural History*, 4th series, XVI (1875), pp. 322-339.
30. *Ibid.*, p. 330.
31. *Archiv für Protistenkunde*, 1. Band (1902), pp. 89-165, Taf. IV-VI.
32. J. Y. Buchanan, "Preliminary Report to Professor Wyville Thomson, F.R.S., Director of the Civilian Scientific Staff, on Work (Chemical and Geological) done on board H.M.S. 'Challenger' " in *Proceedings of the Royal Society of London*, XXIV (1876), p. 605.

A Summary of the Monera Fallacy

33. *Quarterly Journal of Microscopical Science*, new series, XV (1875), pp. 390-392.
34. *Proceedings of the Royal Society of London*, XXIV (1876), pp. 471-544.
35. *Ibid.*, pp. 530-531.
36. *Kosmos. Zeitschrift für einheitliche Weltanschauung auf Grund der Entwickelungslehre*, 1. Band (1877), pp. 293-305.
37. *Revue des Questions Scieintifiques*, III (1878), 1, pp. 67-74.
38. *Ibid.*, p. 73. English translation:
    Before such a result, is it not allowed to smile, and would one not be excused for recalling to mind, that astrologer of the myth who discovered animals in the moon because a bat had entered into his telescope? These, however, are the surprises which incredulous science gives us always when bias presides at its investigations! If only such misfortunes would make incredulous scientists more cautious, but it suffices for one to read the latest writings by Huxley and Haeckel to note with what contempt and with what haughtiness the adversaries of transformism are treated by them.
39. *The Quarterly Review of Biology*, XIII (1938), pp. 383-420.
40. *Ibid.*, p. 385.
41. Already the harmful effect of the hypothesis of evolution on research has been stressed by W. E. Lammerts in a paper on "Mutations and Evolution," *The Challenge of Creation* (Caldwell, Idaho, 1965), pp. 8-9.
42. W. Seifriz, *Protoplasm* (New York and London, 1936), p. 11.

XVI

A STUDY OF ENGLISH MICRASTER RESEARCH
From a Creationist's Point of View

RITA RHODES WARD

Introduction

Because of the great importance attached by evolutionists to the English *Micraster* as an example of fossil evidence of change of species it was decided to make a study of the major research papers dealing with this genus and relate the material to creationists' concepts. Such evolutionists as K. A. Kermack,[1] D. M. S. Watson,[2] and E. R. Truman,[3] as well as other writers, consider the English Micraster to represent perhaps the best example of a gradual change from one species to the next. In this paper the basic research by A. W. Rowe[4] and that of K. A. Kermack will be given special attention. The third study, that of D. Nichols, is not available to this writer at this time. References to this work, which is of secondary importance to this paper, will be brief.

The Micrasters.—The Micrasters are sea urchins belonging to the phylum, *Echinodermata*. These spiny-skinned animals fall into two subphyla, the *Pelmatozoa* (attached forms) and the *Eleutherozoa* (free-moving forms). The latter subphylum is comprised of five classes, one of which is the *Echinoidae* or sea urchins. The *Echinoidae* are made up of two subclasses, the *Regularia* and the *Irregularia*. The *Micrasters* belong to the *Irregularia*.

The test of the sea urchins is very complex and forms fine fossils with the most minute details clearly revealed. This makes the *Echinoids* ideal material for study of presumed successional changes in structure. The size varies from some five or six mm. to as much as fourteen or more cm. in diameter. The shape may be flattened, globular, conical, or heart-shaped.

On the ventral side is found the *peristome*, a ring of plates surrounding the mouth. The peristome may be centrally placed or it may be nearer the anterior margin or *ambitus*. On the dorsal side is the *oculogenital ring,* comprised of a circle of ten plates. Five of the plates contain ocular sense organs and five alternate plates contain genital pores. In the *Micrasters,* as well as some other species, one of the genital pores does not develop. One of the genital plates is modified to form the *madreporte,* a sort of sieve which admits water. The *periproct* is a leathery structure surrounding the anus. In the *Regularia* the periproct is found within the oculogenital ring, but in the *Irregularia* the structure is outside the ring. The oculogenital ring with the structures within it are referred to as the *apical system* or *apical disk.*

Radiating from the apical system are five structures called *ambulacra,* which consist of double rows of pores. In the *Regularia* these rows extend to the peristome. In many *Irregularia,* including the *Micrasters,* the ambulacra are found on the arboral side only and resemble the petals of a flower. For this reason they are called *petals.*

This very brief and incomplete description of the morphology of the *Echinoids* will help to orient those not familiar with these structures.

The *Micrasters* are heart-shaped members of the *Irregularia,* belonging to the order *Spatangoida.* The periproct is found at the posterior end of the test while the peristome is placed anteriorly.

The Geological Formation.—The *Micrasters* which formed the basis of the studies of Rowe and Kermack were found in the White Chalk of southern England belonging to the Upper Cretaceous. These deposits of soft white limestone are several hundred feet thick. Similar deposits are found in northern England and northern continental Europe, particularly France. Rowe confined his study to five zones comprising the Turonian and most of the Senonian. The zones were the following: *Terebratulina gracilis, Holaster planus, Micraster cor-testudinarium,* and the lower third of *Micraster cor-anguinum,* which he termed low-zonal and the upper two thirds of *Micraster cor-anguinum,* which he called high-zonal. These formations cover about twenty million years in the evolutionary geological column. Kermack's study was based on one portion of Rowe's collection from the *Micraster cor-anguinum* zone.

The softness of the limestone makes removal of fossils quite easy. The tests of the *Micrasters* could be cleaned without damaging the complex ornamentation which served as the basis for much of the study.

The Major Studies of Micraster

Rowe's Research.—Rowe collected two thousand specimens from six areas in southern England. Each specimen was accurately zoned before being measured and studied. Published in 1899, this study is the only one to date which is based on a population rather than individuals. Rowe based his research on 17 characters, only part of which will be discussed here. Various factors of size and shape were measured. Particular attention was directed to the ambulacra which Rowe considered the most dependable basis of zonal determination. The position of the peristome and the characteristics of the surrounding structures were studied. Rowe disregarded the structure of the spinal system because it was obscured by deposit in so many specimens; however, he did consider its position a character of great importance.

The species used in this study and the zones in which they were found are as follows:[5]

High-zonal Series

Zone	Species
M. cor-anguinum (Upper two thirds)	M. *cor-anguinum* (Two varieties)

Low-zonal Series

Zone	Species
M. cor-anguinum (Lower third)	M. *praecursor*
M. cor-testudinarium	M. *cor-testudinarium*
	M. *cor-testudinarium*
	M. *praecursor*
Holaster planus	M. *cor-testudinarium*
	M. *praecursor*
	M. *Leskei*
	M. *cor-bovis*
Terebratulina gracilis	M. *Leskei*
	M. *cor-bovis*

Space permits only a brief discussion of the changes Rowe noted as his study proceeded from lower to higher zones. In general the test changed shape from narrow, cuneiform to broader and more oval. The dorso-ventral measurement increased proportionally. The apical disk moved from an anteriorly eccentric position to a more central position. The ambulacra or petals changed from deeply depressed, rather short structures to shallow, longer forms. The structure of the interporiferous area of the ambulacra changed from smooth to ornamented. These structures are complex and it is not possible to describe the changes in detail in this paper. Of special interest is the sub-anal fasciole which always is poorly developed in the lower zone, but is very highly developed in the higher zone. The wall of the test of *M. cor-bovis* is thin, while higher forms possess thicker tests.

The different species graded smoothly from one to another. Note what Rowe says about the species:

"True species, and even prominent varietal types, are rare, and passage forms and trivial variants are the rule. Nothing but a Group will embrace them all, and give to each series its correlative value." [6]

Accordingly, he proposed four groups of variants, namely: *M. cor-bovis, M. Leskei, M. praecursor* (*M. cor-testudinarium* is considered a variety of *M. praecursor*), and *M. cor-anguinum*.

(It should be stated at this point that this writer has in her personal collection of fossil echinoids six Micrasters, four of which belong to the species studied by Rowe. Three of them, *M. cor-bovis, M. cor-testudinarium,* and *M. Cor-anguinum* are superbly preserved. Since they form the basic phyletic line, it has been easy to follow the complex descriptions of Rowe. They exemplify not only the changes but some of the variants discussed [Figures 1-6]).

Rowe gives a very complete description of *M. cor-bovis* as the ancestral species followed by comparisons between it and *M. Leskei.* He concludes the following:

"Every possible variation between the two species may be traced in their passage forms." [7]

Following further comparisons between the two species Rowe says:

"It will therefore not be unreasonable to look upon this primitive form [*M. cor-bovis*] as the progenitor of *M. Leskei,* and through it of *M. praecursor* and *M. cor-testudinarium.*" [8]

Although he emphasizes the lack of a sharp division between species and the predominance of intermediate types, Rowe divides the *Micrasters* into two zoological divisions, the low-zonal and the high-zonal, with the break occurring at the point between the lower third and the upper two thirds of the zone of *M. cor-anguinum*. A second break in the low-zonal fossils occurs between the *M. cor-bovis* with its thin test and *M. Leskei* with its thick test.

It was the purpose of Rowe to show that:

... we can trace an unbroken continuity in the evolution of *Micraster;* so that as we mount up, zone by zone, fresh features are added to the test, simply owing to the progressive elaboration of the epistroma; and that in each zone the special features of the test are so marked that one can tell by their aid from what zone a Micraster is derived.[9]

We see here a contradiction. If there is unbroken continuity, how can there be sharp distinctions between zones? Rowe does not make clear what he means by horizontal features. He states that changes in ambulacra are horizontal, not specific, that all the species in one horizon have one type of an ambulacrum, while the species of the next horizon show other characteristics of the ambulacra. He does not explain the basis on which he determined species.

Kermack's Research

In 1954 K. A. Kermack completed a study of Micraster evolution from a different angle. He limited his work to the specimens from one area, using five hundred sixteen specimens collected by Rowe at Northfleet, Kent. It was Kermack's purpose to make a comparative study of *M. cor-anguinum and M. (Isomicraster) senonensis.* Rowe called the latter *Epiaster gibbus.* Kermack also studied allometric growth rates of certain characters in these two *Micrasters* and considered the relationships of certain characters in a supposedly single interbreeding population. A fourth purpose, that of studying methods of investigation, is not the chief concern of this paper.

After cleaning the tests and rejecting some specimens that for various reasons could not be used, Kermack made thirteen measurements on each specimen. These measurements were taken in millimeters except for one item which was measured in square millimeters and two items which consisted in counting plates. These measurements included dimensions which would reveal the shape of the test as well as its size. The measurement of the sub-anal fasciole proved challenging because of its irregularity. Details won't be included here except to say a camera was used. This measurement was particularly important, as will be discussed later.

Kermack took into consideration three classes of possible errors in determining the validity of his evidence. First, errors in measurements would be considered as in any other research. A more important error would be found in bias in the sample. Rowe's personal interests, his attitudes toward the species, his attitudes toward faulty specimens—all these factors would affect the quality of the specimens and the relative numbers of each species. Study of the specimens suggested that Rowe was biased in favor of the passage forms and of *Epiaster gibbus (M. senonensis)*. The third source of error was considered to be the age distribution of the sample. The uncertainties of preservation is believed to result in a biased representation of the living populations because some ages might be more likely to become fossilized than others.

Rowe had divided his collection into three sections: *M. coranguinum, Epiaster gibbus (M. senonensis)*, and the forms he considered transitional between the two species. Kermack approached the problem of deciding whether there were two closely related species in the population or one variable species. After measuring all the specimens as described above, Kermack came to this conclusion:

". . . none of the characters under consideration enables us to distinguish between the two species with certainty." [10]

Kermack further says:

> In all characters, except the area of the sub-anal fasciole, the two species completely intergrade. Such intergrading is due to hybridization and is not uncommon between species of recent echinoids: . . . *Micraster senonensis* and *M. coranguinum* may well have hybridized in the same way, thus producing transitional forms. By analogy with recent forms, however, there is no reason to deny to either the status of a good species, although they can certainly be distinguished on the character of the sub-anal fasciole.[11]

He explains the variations as due to differences in growth rates of characters or to inherent shape. Also, Kermack *assumes* that the differences are due to natural selection and the changes are adaptive. Also, he postulates that the two species lived in different ecological niches.

Nichols' Research

In 1959 D. Nichols published the results of a research problem in which he studied the morphology and ecology of extant Spatangoids, giving special attention to *Echinocardium cordatum*, and relating the material to the extinct *Micrasters*.[12] He formulated the hypothesis that the low-zonal forms such as *M. cor-bovis* were surface dwellers or did not burrow deeply, while the high-zonal species such as *M. coranguinum* burrowed deeply. He based this hypothesis on a comparison of the fossils with living forms. The extant forms which burrow deeply have a strong sub-anal fasciole. This circular groove containing cilia provides a sanitary tube for the removal of wastes. Surface dwelling forms do not need such a tube. Also, the smooth ambulacra of the low-zonal forms did not have as well-developed cilia as the ornamented ambulacra of the high-zonal types. The cilia facilitate the circulation of water necessary for respiration and the removal of detritus which falls on the animal. Nichols counted the number of pore pairs in the petals and by comparison with extant forms concluded that the increasing number of pairs suggested increased number of respiratory tube feet. He postulated this enabled the animal to burrow more deeply.[13] Since the lithology of the zones is similar, Nichols concluded the animals lived in different niches in a similar habitat.

Summary of the Three Studies

Rowe collected some two thousand specimens from several areas, giving particular attention to two factors, namely, the changes from zone to zone, and the many transitional forms between species. He postulated that *M. cor-bovis* was the primitive type (thin tested) from which *M. Leskei* (thick tested) evolved. Other species then followed *M. Leskei*. Rowe emphasized the difficulty of determining species because each species smoothly merges into the next with no definite place to draw a line between species. He attached particular importance to changes in the ambulacra, but he used the trait to determine zonal level, not species.

Kermack used Rowe's specimens from one locality, assuming the animals comprised one interbreeding population. Using two species, *M. cor-anguinum* and *M. senonensis,* he made a study of thirteen traits which could be measured. Kermack concluded that twelve of the characters were so overlapping that they could not be used to determine the species. The thirteenth trait, the sub-anal fasciole, is a sure way, according to Kermack, to distinguish the two species, with *M. coranguinum* having sub-anal fasciole and the other species lacking the structure. He postulated that the prevalence of transitional forms indicate hybridization, while the sub-anal fasciole suggests the animals occupied different niches, with the differences being due to adaptation to environmental pressure.

Nichols' study consisted in extensive work with living Spatangoids and use of the data to interpret the significance of the characters exhibited by the *Micrasters*. On the basis of his study he concluded that some forms were burrowers, while others lived on the surface. The structure of the ambulacra, the shape of the test, and the presence or absence of the sub-anal fasciole were the characters considered.

It is significant that the three men approached their studies from a completely evolutionary oriented viewpoint. All data were interpreted from that bias. It was not a matter of determining whether or not evolution is a fact, but of finding evidence to support an idea which was taken for granted as true.

General Problems of Fossil Species

In considering the significance of the proposed interpretation of the *Micrasters* some general problems of determining fossil species should be noted. Imbrie makes some interesting statements:

> In spite of the extended attention this problem has received, the nature of fossil species remains one of the most controversial topics in paleontology. . . . But two key questions are still being asked: What is a fossil species? How can fossil species be recognized? . . . The concept of fossil species held by most paleontologists is largely an inference, an inference based both on observed structure of living species and on a theoretical model of the evolutionary mechanism.[14]

It might be noted here that neontologists are not in agreement as to what a biological species is. It is not intended to discuss that problem in this paper. Paleontologists necessarily are more restricted in the traits they can use as a basis for specimen determination.

The concept of a *typological species* is widely used both in paleontology and in neontology. According to this plan a specimen is selected as a type specimen and the status of other specimens is determined by comparison.

Inferences as to species also are based on biogeography and ecology. The exploration of these two fields in paleontology is in its infancy, and as is the case in other phases of paleontology, is approached from a completely evolutionary point of view.

Most fossil species are termed by Imbrie[15] *transient species*. By this term is meant each species represents a brief point in the evolutionary history of the organism with gaps both preceding and succeeding the species. This is a purely evolutionary concept. Succes-

sional species are those, such as the Micraster of this study, in which there is a gradual gradation between assumed species. Examples of this are extremely rare in the fossil record.

A Consideration of Micraster Speciation

Regarding the determination of fossil species Imbrie has this to say:

> By the nature of the evolutionary process we cannot eliminate arbitrary taxonomic judgments. Species-making will remain a practical art as well as a scientific discipline.[16]

It can be seen from this quotation as well as from the discussions of Rowe and Kermack that the *Micraster* species are determined entirely within an assumed evolutionary framework. Also, that the determination of a species is arbitrary and depends on the opinion of the worker. Rowe discusses the difficulty of species determination of *Micraster* in detail and admits his judgment as to lineage is entirely a personal decision.[17]

Furthermore, those who have studied the *Micrasters* disagree. All agree on the *M. Leskei-M. cortestudinarium-M. coranguinum* sequence. But Rowe believed *M. Leskei* evolved from *M. corbovis* while Kermack postulates that *M. corbovis* branched from *M. Leskei*, which he considers only a small form of *M. cortestidunarium*. Kermack also believes that *M. senonensis* branches from *M. cortestudinarium* and followed a parallel evolution to the main line just as *M. corbovis* evolved along with the main line. Rowe considered *M. senonensis* as belonging to the genus *Epiaster* and divided *M. coranguinum* into two varieties which Kermack ignored as well as the species *praecursor*, which Rowe postulated. Kermack believed the two species he studied had evolved from stock at lower levels and both belonged to the stratum in which they were found. His basis for rejecting migration is based on comparisons with *Micraster* sequences in other deposits both in northern England and on the continent. However, Nichols believes that *M. senonensis* migrated from some other locality.

These investigators believe that the genus evolved from a burrowing type to a surface dweller but none of the scientists attempt to explain what caused the change. James R. Beerbower[18] simply states the question can't be answered at present.

Kermack states that hybridization prevented full adaptation to environment and would result in "poorly adapted transitional forms."[19] He further states that the formation of a barrier between the two species would permit more perfect adaptation. He does not explain in what way the hybrids might be faulty. If numbers in the population are indication of their success, they were more successful than the true species.

Rowe based his postulates on the assumption that the vertical stratification of the fossil beds represent a succession of evolutionary forms. R. G. Johnson[20] states that the vertical stratification of modern benthic communities suggests fossil strata will not be pure or that there will be mixing of successive populations, and life spans will overlap. That will have a bearing on the validity of Rowe's assumptions. Johnson further states that the vanishing of a species such as *M. corbovis* does not necessarily imply a change of immediate environment but that the change may be elsewhere and indirectly affect the local fauna.[21] This puts a question on the assumption of Kermack that the niche of *M. corbovis* suddenly vanished.[22]

As this writer studies her specimens she finds the differences described by Rowe, but the variations do not exceed in magnitude those observed in human species or in domesticated animals. Some of the changes in the ambulacra were so small a magnifier is required to see them well. When one considers that these changes, according to uniformitarian estimates of time, took place over a period of perhaps some twenty million years, it can be seen the presumed evolution was indeed slight. Then here is another problem. The Echinoids supposedly arose during the Ordovician about four hundred million years ago. If twenty million years were required to produce the slight differences observed in *Micraster,* how can one account for the many kinds of *Echinoids* even over the three hundred million years postulated for their evolution? There is a discrepancy in the proposed evolutionary rates with Micraster evolving much more slowly than the class *Echinoidae* as a whole.

In this brief discussion can be seen the purely subjective nature of the evidence for change of species in the *Micrasters*. Also, it is quite evident that all the investigators are interpreting the evidence from an evolutionary bias. Are the *Micrasters* one highly variable species? Do they exemplify a true change of species? If so, where are the breaks between species? Or did the forms grade so that *M. Leskei* was fertile with *M. cortestudinarium,* and *M. cortestudinarium* could cross with *M. coranguinum,* but *M. Leskei* and *M.*

coranguinum were not inter-fertile? No one can answer these questions.

Some Unexplored Problems

This entire study does not touch on the geology of the problem. Uniformitarianism is implied by the investigators. The relation of the chalk formations and their paleobiota to flood geology or catastrophism is a subject too involved for exploration in this paper. Other species of the *Micrasters,* the relation of the *Micrasters* to other *Spatangoids,* and the presumed evolution of the *Echinoidae* as a class could form the basis of extended study.

From the Creationist's Point of View

The point of view of a creationist on this problem is simply stated: It doesn't make any difference whether changes of species did or did not take place. If there were no changes, then there is no reason for concern. If there was an actual genetic as well as morphological change, then it was no different from some changes which have been observed in other organisms today. The organisms still were *Micrasters* and easily could be one of the "kinds" of Genesis. In no sense does changes of species in the *Micrasters,* if such changes did occur, prove the overall hypothesis of evolution. Such changes would not close any of the gaps in the phylogenetic tree of life. But the variations demonstrate the capacity for change the Creator placed in the original "kinds."

"Dr. R. A. Stirton, in his book *Time, Life and Man,* says that the greatest value in the study of paleontology is the satisfaction it affords the individual who enjoys it." [23]

This writer has derived much pleasure from her study of the *Micrasters*. The marvelous beauty and the intricate detail of the fossils produce feelings of awe and wonder—awe toward the Creator who put them here and wonder as to how they were formed. Faith is strengthened rather than weakened by studies such as this—a source of deep satisfaction.

Figures 1 to 7 show dorsal and ventral sides of Micraster forms given species names as they are found in the various chalk formations. The figures are in the order in which they are found in the series, from M. *leskei* in the low zonal to M. *coranguinum* from the upper horizon. The total time period according to evolutionary geological assumption is about twenty million years. The relatively slight changes, particularly from M. *corbovis* to M. *coranguinum* should be noted. These are scarcely comparable to the known variability shown by races of mankind. Yet this is one of the classic examples of evolution always referred to in courses in invertebrate paleontology.

NOTES AND REFERENCES

1. K. A. Kermack, "A Biometrical Study of *Micraster coranguinum* and *M. (Isomicraster) senonensis*," *Phil. Trans., Roy. Soc., London* (B), (1954), 237:428.
2. D. M. S. Watson, "The Evidence Afforded by Fossil Invertebrates on the Nature of Evolution," *Genetics, Paleontology, and Evolution*, edited by G. L. Jepsen, G. G. Simpson, and E. Mayr (Princeton, N. J.: Princeton University Press, 1949).
3. E. R. Trueman, "Adaptive Morphology in Paleoecological Interpretation," *Approaches to Paleoecology*, edited by John Imbrie and Norman D. Newell (New York: John Wiley and Sons, Inc., 1964).
4. A. W. Rowe, "An Analysis of the Genus *Micraster*, as Determined by Rigid Zonal Collecting from the Zone of *Rhynchonella Cuvieri* to that of *Micraster cor-anguinum*," *Quart. Jour. Geological Society of London*, Vol. 55 (London: Longmans, Green and Co., 1899).
5. *Ibid.*, p. 542.
6. *Ibid.*, p. 517.
7. *Ibid.*, p. 523.
8. *Ibid.*, p. 524.
9. *Ibid.*, p. 540.
10. Kermack, *op. cit.*, p. 393.
11. *Ibid.*, p. 406.
12. Trueman, *op. cit.*, pp. 70-72.
13. Derek V. Ager, *Principles of Paleoecology* (New York: McGraw-Hill Book Company, Inc., 1963), pp. 47-48.
14. John Imbrie, "The Species Problem with Fossil Animals," *The Species Problem*, edited by Ernst Mayr (Washington, D. C.: American Association for the Advancement of Science, 1957 [Publication No. 50]), p. 125.
15. *Ibid.*, p. 131.
16. *Ibid.*, p. 127.
17. Rowe, *op. cit.*, p. 543.
18. James R. Beerbower, *Search for the Past* (Englewood Cliffs, N. J.: Prentice-Hall, Inc. 1960), p. 133.
19. Kermack, *op. cit.*, p. 422.
20. R. G. Johnson, "The Community Approach to Paleoecology," *Approaches to Paleoecology*, edited by John Imbrie and Norman D. Newell (New York: John Wiley and Sons, Inc., 1964), p. 123.
21. *Ibid.*, p. 115.
22. Kermack, *op. cit.*, p. 422.
23. Fred C. Amos, GeoTopics," *Ward's Geology Newsletter*, No. 32 (Rochester, N. Y.: Ward's Natural Science Establishment, Dec., 1963), p. 11.

Figure 1. Micraster *leskei* Desm. Upper Cretaceous chalk Turonian, Rouen, France. Dorsal side.

Figure 2. M. *corbovis*. Upper Cretaceous: Danien chalk cliffs, Sussex, England. Dorsal side.

Figure 3. M. *corbovis*. Ventral side of Figure 2.

Figure 4. M. *cortestudinarium* Agassiz. Upper Cretaceous chalk cliffs, Norwich, England. Dorsal.

Figure 5. M. *cortestudinarium* Agassiz. Ventral side of Figure 4.

Figure 6. M. *coranguinum*. Upper chalk Cretaceous, Dorchester, Dorset, England. Dorsal side.

Figure 7. M. *coranguinum*. Ventral side of Figure 6.

XVII

WORLD POPULATION AND BIBLE CHRONOLOGY

Henry M. Morris

A remarkable commentary on human history is the fact that man as a whole has broken all of God's commandments except the very first. Immediately after the creation of man, God said to him: "Be fruitful and multiply and fill the earth" (Gen. 1:28). The population explosion of these latter days is eloquent testimony that this particular purpose of God in creation is being accomplished, though obedience to God is hardly man's intention in the fulfillment.

As a matter of fact, there has also been an earlier time when man filled the earth. In the antediluvian period, the Scriptures say that "men began to multiply on the face of the earth" (Gen. 6:1), and soon "the earth was filled"—but, also, it was "filled with violence" (Gen. 6:11, 13).

Some have been skeptical about the possibility that the early population may have grown so rapidly in the 1,656 years recorded (Gen. 5) from Adam to the Flood. Therefore, it is instructive to make calculations on the probable growth of population.

World Growth of Population

Assume that the earth had an initial population of two people, ready to assume their responsibilities as husband and wife, and then as parents. Assume also that the average number of children per family (growing to maturity and marriage) was $2c$, with c boys and c girls. In the first succeeding generation then, there would have been c families (and $2c$ individuals, plus the first two still living). The second generation, on the same basis, would contain $c \times 2c$, or $2c^2$, individuals. In the third generation, there would be $2c^3$ individuals, and so on. The total number of individuals in the world at the end of n generations, assuming no deaths, could be calculated as:

$$S_n = 2 + 2c + 2c^2 + 2c^3 + \ldots + 2c^n \qquad (1)$$

World Population and Bible Chronology

The sum, S_n, can be calculated directly:
Multiply both sides of equation (1) by c:

$$S_n(c) = 2c + 2c^2 + 2c^3 + 2c^4 \ldots + 2c^n + 2c^{n+1}$$

And subtracting the first equation from the above:

$$S_n(c) - S_n = 2c^{n+1} - 2,$$
$$\text{or } S_n(c-1) = 2c^{n+1} - 2.$$

Dividing through by $(c-1)$ yields the sum S_n as:

$$S_n = \frac{(2c^{n+1} - 2)}{(c-1)}$$

Thus, $S_n = \frac{2(c^{n+1} - 1)}{(c-1)}$ (2)

However, the number of people represented by S_n would have to be reduced by the number who had died since the first generation in order to get the actual population. Now, let the average life-span be represented by x generations. The people who had already died by the time of the *nth* generation, therefore, would be those who were were in the "$(n-x)th$" generation, or earlier. This number is:

$$S_{(n-x)} = \frac{2(c^{n-x+1} - 1)}{(c-1)} \quad (3)$$

The total population at the *nth* generation, then, combining equations (2) and (3), becomes:

$$P_n = S_n - S_{n-x} = \frac{2}{c-1}(c^{n+1} - c^{n-x+1})$$

Thus, $P_n = \frac{2}{c-1}(c^{n-x+1})(c^x - 1)$ (4)

Equation (4), in summary, will give the world population n generations after the first family, for an average life-span of x generations and an average number of children growing to maturity and marriage of $2c$ per family. The equation clearly demonstrates how rapidly populations can grow under favorable conditions.

For example, assume that $c = 2$, and $x = 2$, which is equivalent to saying that the average family has four children who later have families of their own, and that each set of parents lives to see all their own grandchildren. For these conditions, which are not at all unreasonable to assume, the following tabulation indicates the population at the end of the indicated numbers of generations:

    5 generations, population = 96 people.
    10 generations, population = 3,070 people.
    15 generations, population = 98,300 people.
    20 generations, population = 3,150,000 people.
    30 generations, population = 3,220,000,000 people.

This last number is essentially equal to the present world population, so that only 30 generations under these conditions would suffice to produce a population greater than now exists in the world!

The next obvious question is: how long is a generation? Again, a reasonable assumption is that the average marriage occurs at age 25 and that the four children have been born by age 35. Then the grandchildren will have been born by the time the parents have lived their allotted span of 70 years. A generation is thus about 35 years.

This would mean that the entire present world population could have been produced in approximately 30 x 35, or 1,050 years!

The fact that it has actually taken considerably longer than this to bring the world population to its present size indicates that the average family size is less than four children, or that the average life span is less than two generations, or both. For comparison, let us assume then that the average family has only three children and the life-span is one generation (i.e., that $c = 1.5$ and $x = 1$). Then, equation (4) yields the following figures:

    10 generations, population = 106
    20 generations, population = 6,680
    30 generations, population = 386,000
    52 generations, population = 4,340,000,000

It would thus take not quite 52 generations under these conditions to cause the present world population. At 35 years per generation, this would still be only 1,820 years. Evidently even three children per family is too much to assume for human history as a whole.

However, the average would have to be more than *two* children per family; otherwise, the population would have remained static. *It begins to be glaringly evident that the human race cannot be very old!* The traditional biblical chronology is infinitely more realistic than is the million-year history of mankind assumed by the evolutionist. If the above very conservative assumptions were made ($x = 1$, $c = 1.5$) for the over 28,600 generations assumed in a supposed million years of man's life on earth, the world population should now be over 10^{5000} people! This number, which could be written as "one" followed by 5,000 zeros, is inconceivably large. A maximum of no more than 10^{100} people could be crammed into the known universe!

The Ussher chronology, on the other hand, based on a literal acceptance of the biblical histories, gives the date of the Flood as about 4,300 years ago. The present population of the world has come originally from Noah's three sons (Gen. 9:19). To be ultra-conservative, assume that one generation is 43 years and thus that there have been only 100 generations since Noah. To produce a world population of 3 billion persons (still assuming $x = 1$), equation (4) is solved for c as follows:

$3,000,000,000 = 2(c)^{100}$ from which:

$c = (1,500,000,000)^{.01} = 1.24$, or approximately 1¼.

Thus, the average family must have had 2.5 children in order to bring the population to its present magnitude in 100 generations. This is eminently reasonable, though conservative, and is strong confirmation of at least the order-of-magnitude accuracy of the Ussher chronology. However, a period of human history much greater than indicated by the post-Deluge chronology of the Bible is evidently rendered improbable in a very high degree by the facts of population. A million years even at this rate would produce a population of 10^{2700} people.

Effects of Disease and Wars

But what about the possibility that the great plagues and wars of the past may have served to keep the population from growing at the indicated rates? Could the population have remained static for long ages and only in modern times have started to expand?

We are unable to answer these questions dogmatically, of course, since population data are not available for earlier times. We can only say that all that we *know* about population growth is based on data from the past two centuries. There are no reliable census figures, of course, except in modern times.

If the earth's population started with two people just 4,300 years ago, it would only have to have increased at the rate of 0.5 percent each year in order to reach the present population. This is significantly less than the present known rate of population growth of almost 2.0 percent per year. Thus there is ample provision for long periods when the growth rate may have been less than the average of 0.5 percent.

Furthermore, there is really no evidence that the growth of population has been retarded by wars or disease epidemics. The past century, which has experienced the greatest mushrooming of populations, has also witnessed the most destructive wars in all history, as well as the worst plagues and famines.

It is interesting to note that the best secular estimates of the world population at the time of the birth of Christ yield a probable figure of about 200 million. If we apply our formula, using the very conservative figures of 2.75 children per family, an average life-span of only one 40-year generation, and the beginning of population growth with two people in 2340 B.C., the calculations yield a probable population of 210 million at that time.

Or, to take another example, consider the nation Israel, which began with the patriarch Jacob about 3,700 years ago. Despite tremendous persecutions and pogroms over the centuries, and despite the lack of a national homeland for much of its history, the nation of Israel has maintained its national identity and now numbers probably about 14 million people.

This population could have been produced in 3,700 years if we assume the average family size was only 2.4 children (instead of 2.5, to allow for the losses due to the above-mentioned factors), but still assuming a life-span of one 43-year generation. Using these figures, the formula yields a present world population of 13,900,000 Jews.

Thus, we conclude that all that is actually *known* about present or past populations can be explained very reasonably and logically on the basis of a beginning only about 4,300 years ago, making ample allowance for the effects of wars and natural catastrophes. Therefore, the assumption of the evolutionists that man first appeared a million or more years ago becomes completely absurd when examined in the light of population statistics.

Antediluvian Populations

According to the genealogical records of Genesis 5, there were 1,656 years from Adam to the Flood. However, the population constants were significantly different then from what they now are.

Men lived to great ages and evidently had large families. Excepting Enoch, who was taken into Heaven without dying at age 365 (Gen. 5:23, 24), the average of the recorded ages of the nine antediluvian patriarchs was 912 years. Recorded ages at the births of their children ranged from 65 years (Mahalaleel—Gen. 5:15, and Enoch—Gen. 5:21) to 500 years (Noah—Gen. 5:32). Every one of them is said to have had "sons and daughters," so that each family had at least four children, and probably more.

As an ultra-conservative assumption, let $c = 3$, $x = 5$, and $n = 16.56$. These constants correspond to an average family of six children, an average generation of 100 years, and an average life-span of 500 years. On this basis the world population at the time of the Flood would have been 235 million people. This probably represents a gross under-estimate of the numbers who actually perished in the Flood.

Multiplication was probably more rapid than assumed in this calculation, especially in the earliest centuries of the antediluvian epoch. For example, if the average family size were eight, instead of six, and the length of a generation 93 years, instead of 100, the population at the time of Adam's death, 930 years after his creation, would already have been 2,800,000. At these rates, the population at the time of the Deluge would have been 137 billion!

Two obvious conclusions appear from these calculations. First, there is no problem whatever in the reference to Cain, Adam's son, as taking a wife, building a city, or fearing avengers (Gen. 4:14-17). Second, the Flood would certainly have to be a global catastrophe if its purpose of destroying all mankind were to be accomplished.

The fact that many hundreds of millions of people may have perished in the Flood does not mean, of course, that we could now expect to find any of their remains. There is no doubt that as the Flood waters rose, men would flee to the highest hills and would be the last of all living creatures on the dry land to be overtaken by the waters and drowned. They would thus not be buried in the sediments of the Deluge. It is possible, of course, that occasional individuals would be trapped and buried, and their bones thus eventually fossilized, but most even of these would never be discovered later. Some few fossils of antediluvian men have possibly been found and others may be unearthed in the future, but these are bound to be very rare.

The absence of antediluvian human fossils is, of course, not nearly as serious a problem for the creationist as is the absence of human fossils for the evolutionist. If man has actually been living on the earth for a million or more years, there have been uncounted millions upon millions of people who have lived and died. But only a scant handful of the remains of prehistoric men have ever been found!

Population Growth from Noah to Abraham

After the Flood, antediluvian conditions of longevity continued to prevail for a while, with life-spans only gradually being reduced. Noah lived 950 years (350 of them after the Flood—Gen. 9:28, 29). Noah's three sons had a recorded total of 16 sons and, presumably, about the same number of daughters, with each family thus averaging about 10 children. From the Flood to the birth of Abraham a total of 292 years and eight generations are recorded.

By the time Abraham journeyed into Canaan, about 400 years had elapsed since the Flood. There were then apparently a number of well-populated cities and countries in the world, as mentioned in Genesis 12 through 25 (Egypt, Chaldea, Philistia, etc.). Abraham died at age 175, leaving eight sons (Gen. 25:1-8).

It seems reasonable to assume, for this 400-year period of history, say, ten generations and an average family of eight, with an average life-span of five of the 40-year generations. That is, in our population formula, assume $c = 4$, $n = 10$, and $x = 5$. The world population at the time of Abraham (neglecting any possible gaps in the genealogies of Genesis 11) is then calculated as 2,800,000, a figure which more than adequately explains the biblical and archaeological population inferences for this period of earth history.

The Tower of Babel seems to have been built about the time of the birth of Peleg (whose name, meaning "division," probably was given by his father Eber in commemoration of that event—Gen. 10:25) 101 years after the Flood. Using the same constants as above, the population at this time would have been only 85 people (using equation [2]). However, it is probable that at least one generation is missing in the genealogy of Peleg as given in Genesis 10:21-25 and 11:10-16. In the corresponding record in Luke 3:35, 36, the name of Cainan is inserted between those of Arphaxad and Salah.

If we assume that, in the course of transcribing the lists in the Old Testament, Cainan's name somehow was omitted from the received text, but that his name was preserved in the Septuagint version from which Luke obtained his data, would mean one or more generations in the interim from the Flood to Babel. On this basis, the population would be 340.

This is probably still too small, but the assumed family size of eight may very well be too small for the early centuries after the Flood. Assuming an average family of ten children gives a population at Babel of over 700. An average of twelve children gives 1,250. Both these figures assume 40-year generations, with, therefore, 3.5 generations from the Flood to Babel.

Since there are 70 nations mention in Genesis 10 as resulting from the "division" at Babel, it is reasonable to infer that there were 70 families at Babel, representing probably the generation of Noah's grandsons and great grandsons. Seventy families containing 800 or 1,000 individuals altogether seem to fit the situation described at Babel very adequately.

We conclude, therefore, that the biblical chronologies are all eminently reasonable in the light of population statistics, and that any significant departures from these chronologies, as required to meet evolutionary speculations, are highly unreasonable and improbable.

XVIII

EVOLUTION AND THE PROBLEM OF MAN

George F. Howe

The Humanity of Fossils

"Man" shall be defined presently as a creature that possesses the combined traits of emotion, will, reflection, moral knowledge, and intellect, coupled with the abilities of communicating by verbal symbols and making or using tools. With this definition, or some similar one, it is easy to distinguish between a man and a gorilla.

Man has some concept of "good" and "evil." Man likewise reflects about yesterday's rainstorm, or is perhaps worried about the threat of impending death from disease. But the gorilla gives no indication of such reflective activity. Furthermore, a fossil is found without either flesh or hair, and the fossil certainly affords no basis for behavioral analysis.

Yet anthropologists and paleontologists try to assess the spiritual nature of fossil materials from direct studies on the bones or artifacts found near them in the strata. Is it possible to erect a developmental series and to assign each man-like fossil to some category such as "non-human," "ancestral," "primitive," "sub-human," or "human" by analysis of existing evidences? The reader will perhaps be prepared to answer this question for himself after considering the criteria and problems involved.

Morphology.—Morphology is the study of gross form and structure of organisms. Differences in form of living men do not necessarily indicate differences in intelligence or humanity, as Klotz[1] has demontrated in discussion of Maurice Tillet, "The Angel." This famous wrestler possessed the grossly distorted body and facial features which result from an imbalanced thyroid condition known as acromelagy. Despite his bizarre appearance, Tillet was neither intellectually inferior nor "sub-human."

In evolutionary documents dealing with man's origin, the word "primitive" is attached to skulls that differ morphologically from those of modern man. From a broad perspective, however, at least two other possibilities exist in the evaluation of such a "primitive" skull: (1) the skull may differ only in form and may have otherwise pertained to a truly human individual (as with Tillet), or (2) the so-called "primitive" fossil may represent an extinct and entirely non-human group, biologically unrelated to man.

Pursuing the former possibility in a well-documented paper, Custance has shown that bone morphology can be affected by environment and development as well as by genetics.[2] Custance has provided evidence, for example, that such factors as sex, physiology, and diet may bring significant change in bony structure of modern humans. This same knowledge applies to studies of fossil man; and one cannot be sure that morphologically "different" skulls are necessarily sub-human or ancestral.

Parenthetically, the concept of a supposedly primitive morphology has led certain well-respected investigators to ignore or otherwise disregard primary geological evidence of depth as Custance demonstrated by quoting the famous anthropologist, Franz Weidenreich:

> In determining the character of a given fossil form and its special place in the line of human evolution, only its morphological features should be made the basis of decision: neither the location of the site where it was recovered, nor the geological nature of the layer in which it was imbedded is important.[3]

The unguarded statement of Boule and Vallois[4] also manifests how morphological considerations have insidiously hindered open evaluation of hominid fossils from North America: ". . . in some cases it is the deposit which is questioned, *sometimes the bones themselves are obviously modern*: often the evidence is unsatisfactory in every respect." The italics are my own and show how the geological position of some deeply buried skulls has been brought to question, because they happen to look like modern man, who should not appear in deep strata, if evolutionary theory and uniformitarian geology are believed to be valid.

Allied to morphology is the matter of various "linking" fossils. A fairly complete set of morphological links relating man to some anthropoid ancestors would be necessary (but not entirely sufficient) evidence in support of evolutionism. The great paucity of fossil intermediates between man and animal, however, is so well known that it needs little further attention here. De Wit presented diagrams of the actual fossil material fitted into a supposed evolutionary "tree" for man (after Johannes Huertzler). De Wit made this comment about the vacant spaces in the "family tree":

> From the diagram it appears that the group representing the human family is strikingly small in comparison with the long and empty branch of descent which, as the transformist hypothesis demands, goes back to the Oligocene and in which, up to the present, no fossil documentation whatsoever with respect to the assumed animal ancestors of man, has been found.[5]

Taxonomy.—Taxonomy is the attempt to name and classify organisms. Some taxonomists are nicknamed "lumpers" because they habitually establish large groups, while others, the so-called "splitters," tend to create smaller groups by instituting many separate species.

It is difficult enough to build meaningful and coherent species groups among the living plants or animals, but erecting a taxonomy of fossils is a far more vexing problem. The paleontologist studying man-like remains is frequently so preoccupied with only a very small segment of the biological world that he is tempted to magnify slight differences between separate fossils and to give each minor variant a new species and genus name.

Ernst Mayr believed that unbridled "splitting" has been practiced in fossil taxonomy to such an extent that the classifications have become unrealistic and certainly out of phase with the rest of biology:

> This difference in standards becomes very apparent if we, for example, compare the classification of the hominids with that of the *Drosophila* flies. There are now about 600 species of *Drosophila* known, all included in a single genus. If individuals of these species were enlarged to the size of man or of a gorilla, it would be apparent even to a lay person that they are probably more different from each other than are the various primates and certainly more than the species of the suborder Anthropoidea. What in the case of *Drosophila* is a genus has almost the rank of an order or, at least, suborder in the primates. This discrepancy is equally great at lower categories. . . .[6]

Mayr referred with regret to the fact that various hominid skulls such as the so-called China Man, Java Man, and South Africa Ape Man have been partitioned by taxonomists into distinct genus groups: *Sinanthropus, Pithecanthropus,* and *Australopithecus,* respectively. To the contrary, Mayre suggested using only the common names of the fossils and refraining from an absolute taxonomy because:

> The formal application of generic and specific names simulates a precision that often does not exist. To give the impression of an

unjustified precision is as much of a methodological error as to make calculations to the fifth decimal when the accuracy of the original data extends only to the first decimal.[7]

These uncertainties and others indicate that one cannot turn to fossil taxonomy for evidence in support of man's proposed evolution. A taxonomy of bones is too indefinite to produce the absolute linking groups and transition stages that would be required by such a theory of development. Although Mayr[8] embraces the evolution theory of man's ancestry, he believes that all the man-like fossils are really quite similar and that they should be lumped together into only one genus: "It is proposed to classify fossil and recent hominids tentatively into a single genus (*Homo*) with three species (*transvaalensis, erectus, sapiens*)."

Reconstructions.—From the standpoint of appearance, much of the difference between man and ape rests upon the attitude and expression of the face. Key evidence for development of men from beasts should therefore include a series of changes in which the animal face is gradually converted into the expressive countenance of a man.

Those who foster the evolutionary view have produced elaborate reconstructions of the fossil hominids.[9] A reconstruction is an attempt by artist and scientist to demonstrate how the extinct organism *might* have looked while living. Unfortunately, skulls and bones do not give an adequate basis upon which to rebuild the physiognomy, as Howells has indicated:

> The one kind of reconstruction which anthropologists are universally suspicious is that which tries to show a fossil man in the flesh, desirable though this is, especially to the public. The reason is that there is no possible way of judging what the soft parts were like, while at the same time these soft parts determine the whole impression which the thing creates. On the same skull two different and equally possible coverings of flesh can make the individual look brutal and apish or human and refined. Suppose only that your own face were tinted and bewhiskered like Gargantua's, and you will see the force of this, to say nothing of substituting his lips and ears for yours.[10]

The philosophical and religious views of the workers who create a reconstruction will insidiously influence its quality. In three splendid series of illustrations, Custance[11] has shown that a particular fossil head such as that of China Man, or Neanderthal Man, might have had an expression of greater intelligence and humanity than the brutal visage conferred upon them by evolutionary artists.

The Neanderthal skull looks quite "modern" when given appropriate brush-work or ink sketching of flesh and hair. The China skull indeed demonstrates a striking resemblance to the Russian delegate at the 1958 Cairo Conference. A reconstruction by Neave Parker (Leakey's artist) gave the puzzling *Zinjanthropus* skull a truly soulful expression.

While of possible interest as an exercise in art or creative imagination, a reconstruction can hardly furnish acceptable scientific evidence for or against the humanity of any particular hominid fossil.

Tools.—Since manufacture and use of tools is one human trait, perhaps the tools associated with a fossil hominoid will shed light upon its status. Following this assumption, some workers have concluded that tools indicate the presence of human beings. With tools, as with other criteria, however, several problems arise.

Animals other than man use simple natural tools. The whiteneck crow drops rocks on ostrich eggs in dive-bombing action.[12] Weaver ants will grip and use their thread-forming larvae as living spindles for sewing leaves together, as Goetsch reported:

> The use of these ants as a tool not provided by their own bodies sets them off as a rarity in the animal kingdom. Tools were long thought to be an exclusive characteristic of man. Although this is untrue (the apes, for example, use stones for cracking nuts), the use of tools is most uncommon even among the higher vertebrates. Its "implement" enables the weaver ant to live in trees and to build solid nests, without—like related varieties—digging passageways in the wood, a labor for which it is not equipped.[13]

In at least one instance, a male chimpanzee has been seen by Köhler to make tools from bamboo tubes and pieces of wood for the purpose of reaching bananas. In such cases, however, Oakley[14] noted that "Köhler could obtain no clear indication that apes are ever capable of conceiving the usefulness of shaping an object for use in an imaginary future eventuality."

Despite the use of natural or even wooden tools by some insects, birds, or apes, a shaped stone tool is often considered the hallmark of human industry. If this is so, then the presence of shaped tools in fossil strata might help establish the intelligence of hominids nearby. Tools linked to a fossil are certainly better evidence of personality than are reconstructions, taxonomy, or morphology.

Discounting an obvious evolutionary bias, Oakley's book is a helpful analysis of fossil tools.[15] He has presented many detailed illustrations of various tool types found near particular skulls. Impressive beauty and skill are seen in the Acheulian hand-axes supposedly formed by Swanscombe Man—a fossil believed to antedate the Neanderthal cave types. On the other hand, tools attributed by Oakley to the Africa Ape-man resemble the naturally chipped rocks, "eolith," so closely that one wonders if they are really tools or simply freaks of nature.

Attributing one certain tool to a specific fossil is not always feasible. How can one be sure that the creature buried near the tool actually formed it? An arrowhead found in the skull of a wild pig probably was used by a hunter to kill the pig. But the question becomes more hazy and yet more acute in the case of a tool associated with an ape-like creature. Did the creature make the tool, or was the tool simply buried near the creature, having been formed by another organism existing contemporaneously? This built-in problem has led to endless controversy about the famous South Africa Ape-men. Some workers, like Robinson, consistently believed they were able to use, but not to make tools:

> I submit therefore, that there is no good evidence in support of the thesis that australopithecines were stone toolmakers but that there is very pertinent evidence against it, favouring the idea that this group consisted essentially of tool-users.[16]

On the contrary, Leakey originally believed that the East Africa Man group of Australopithecines were the builders of tools found in the Oldowan deposits, as this quotation and picture caption indicate:

> Such a being, who set about shaping the raw materials of nature in a regular pattern to suit his needs, was the one worthy to be considered the earliest human. And at last we have found him.
>
> I call him *Zinjanthropus*, or "East African Man."
>
> Sharpened pebbles enabled *Zinjanthropus* to skin animals. He made the tools by chipping jagged cutting edges.[17]

In the mid-1960's, however, Leakey discovered remains that were more human in character at *deeper levels* than the bones of his East Africa Man. These new finds caused him to change his mind, attributing the tools to the new skull (which he has named *Homo habilis* meaning "Handy Man"), and he has finally assumed that *Zinjanthropus* was one of the non-tool-making Australopithecines:

The subsequent discovery of remains of *Homo habilis* in association with the Oldowan culture at three other sites has considerably altered the position. While it is possible that *Zinjanthropus* and *Homo habilis* both made stone tools, it is probable that the latter was the more advanced toolmaker and that the *Zinjanthropus* skull represents an intruder (or a victim) on a *Homo habilis* living site.[18]

Aside from the fact that a reappraisal such as this is highly commendable in the face of new evidence, it demonstrates that gross misunderstandings of culture can arise even when tools and bones are buried together in the same sedimentary deposit. It is obviously impossible as yet to assess the character of either fossil—East Africa Man or Handy Man. The tools of that layer might have been fashioned by East Africa Man, by Handy Man, by both, or by neither.

Exploring the last option, perhaps Oldowan fossil types represent extinct non-humans, and the associated implements were accordingly made by a true man whose skull has not as yet been discovered. Such confusion, in this particular instance, shows that tool culture, good evidence as it is, cannot give unequivocal support for the intelligence or humanity of a particular skull.

Brain Size.—Although it is tempting to assume that brain size in a fossil creature (as calculated from the cranial volume) would be an obvious index of its intelligence, such is not the case. Absolute, and even relative, fossil cranial volume may have little correlation with mental ability, as Mayr has asserted:

> Attempts have been made to measure the attainment of this *Homo* level in terms of brain size. This method is fraught with difficulty. First of all, brain size is to some extent correlated with body size. If, for instance, a large gorilla should have a brain of 650 cc. this is not at all necessarily equivalent to the brain of a fossil hominid of 650 cc., if that hominid were much smaller than a gorilla. If the brain of the gorilla averages one-fourth larger than that of the chimpanzee, it does not mean that he is on the average 25 per cent more intelligent. The correlation between brain size and intelligence is very loose. There is good evidence that the brain size of late Pleistocene man may have averaged larger than that of modern man. If true, this does not mean necessarily that there has been a deterioration of man's intelligence since the Pleistocene for intelligence is determined not only by brain size. It is, of course, still unknown what neurological structures affect intelligence but the folding of the cortex and all sorts of specializations within the cortex appear

to be as important as size. It is therefore dangerous, in fact outright misleading, to use size as an absolute criterion and to say that the *Homo* state was reached when brain size reached a level of 700 or 750 cc.[19]

Adult human beings may possess the largest brains among the primates, but they are surpassed in "relative brain size" by others. For various primates, Shultz[20] has divided the cranial capacity in cubic centimeters (cc) by the total body weight in grams (g) to yield percentage figures of relative brain size: cranial capacity (cc)/body weight (g) × 100 = relative brain size.

Shultz showed accordingly that man has a high relative brain size (2.02) which is larger than that of the gibbon (1.94). But even such a parameter cannot be used as an absolute indicator of humanity, because the squirrel monkey, *Saimiri orstedii*, has a relative brain value of 2.97—even higher than that of Man!

Brain size and intellect among living peoples have been thoroughly explored by Clark,[21] who reported that skulls from men of normal intelligence vary in cranial capactiy all the way from 900 to 2,300 cc. He cited the report of one apparently normal human being whose brain was only 720 cc, a surprising figure since the cranial capacity of a gorilla has been recorded as high as 685 cc.

Coon[22] presented a photograph of a living aboriginal woman (cranial capacity estimated at less than 1,000 cc) on the same page with that of a Chinese sage of cranial volume nearly 2,000 cc—yet both individuals are obviously human and contemporary.

Weidenreich[23] showed that there was great disparity between the calculated brain volumes of famous and talented authors—Anatole France at about 1,100 cc and Jonathan Swift at about 2,000 cc. It may be safely inferred from such data that brain volume cannot be used to estimate intelligence even among living men, as Clark has aptly summarized:

> . . . so far as it has been possible to apply appropriate tests, there is within such limits no marked correlation between the brain size and intelligence. . . . To the palaeo-anthropologist this lack of correlation is particularly disconcerting, for it means that he has no sure method of assessing the mental capacity of extinct types of hominid simply by reference to cranial capacity.[24]

Speech and Language.—The facility to mimic sounds or words, present in such birds as the parrot and the parakeet, does not show original linguistic ability. Amazing transfer of information through the dance is reported from the bee hive, but here too, no suggestion of reflection or abstract conversation among the bees exists. If speculations about possible vocal contact among porpoises are presently ignored, it can be safely asserted that man is unique in his capacity to communicate ideas by verbal symbols.

Unfortunately, no known technique of fossil analysis can reveal the probability of speech. Some workers attempt to judge this quality by estimating the musculature of the mouth and throat in reconstruction—but such studies are at best only speculative.

Evolutionary stages between the simple communication in animal societies and the complex speech patterns of man have not been discovered. Some authorities believe there is a qualitative difference between human communication and that of animals—something akin to a quantum jump, as expressed by the British neurologist, Macdonald Critchley:

> It was implicit in this particular hypothesis as to evolution that differences between human and animal structure and function are matters of degree. Were this principle to be firmly established, then it would be difficult to avoid the idea that animal communication leads by insensible gradations to the faculty of speech in man. There are numerous linguistic objections to this view however. It is important to realize, too, that language does not stand alone in this matter and that there are other weighty considerations which lead to the well-nigh inescapable conclusion that some potent qualitative change occurs at a point somewhere between the anthropoid and *Homo sapiens*. . . . No "missing link" between animal and human communication has yet been identified.[25]

Similar opinions are presented by Lord Brain, former president of the British Association for the Advancement of Science:

> It is important to remember that man is different from other animals and that scientists should not think of animal behavior in human terms. At present, at any rate, we cannot imagine what an animal perceives but we can avoid thinking that this is like our own ideas or experiences. Man's relationship to his fellows and to the universe is uniquely different from that of any other animal. He faces different problems and solves them in different ways. Man's superiority is due to his intelligence, and his ability to manipulate the objects in the universe around him. These manipulations help him to increase his perception—by use of a microscope, for instance—an increased perception in turn aids his manipulations. Most important of the manipu-

lations is the use of verbal and printed symbols which we call language. Of all known life forms, only man is self-conscious. Only man is aware of himself as a part of the greater world, and only man has ideas of right and wrong and theories concerning his feelings.[26]

The Absolute Depth Sequence of Certain Hominid Remains

Despite the symphony of problems under the previous topics, some anthropologists have continued to apply the labels of "primitive" or "advanced" to fossil man-like types, and have thereby attempted to illustrate the supposed history of human evolution. Dates have been applied to specimens in keeping with the usual stratigraphic assumptions.

Problems of uniformitarian geology versus catastrophism, and dating assumptions versus the young earth concept have been discussed adequately by Morris and Whitcomb[27] and elsewhere.[28] It is sufficient here to state that not all qualified scientists agree to the uniformitarian dating assumptions, or agree to the concept of gradual fossilization over vast epochs of time.

Such words, however, as "Pleistocene," "Oligocene," or "Second Interglacial" are bantered about in the semi-popular and scientific writings of anthropologists as if the designated time periods were scientific verities. The particular term "Second Interglacial," for example, will be applied to a layer containing a fossil, but the reader is given little or no exact information about the absolute depth (below surface) at which the fossil was found or the physical condition of the confining strata.

Uniformitarian time-philosophy has thus become so completely ingrained that many authors gloss over the whole topic of fossil depth. Some authors will list a few animal bones found with the supposed man, and then give the reader the uniformitarian name for the layer—e.g., "Mid Pleistocene." Such information is less than adequate for any serious student of paleontology, and it certainly does not satisfy the catastrophist's desire for empirical data.

The field of anthropology is in dire need of an objective survey in which factual data along the following lines will be presented for each fossil hominid:

1) depth of finds,
2) condition of strata,
3) number of kinds of bones discovered,

4) tools or other artifacts related to the layer,
5) results of appropriate dating analyses, etc.

Tabulated information of this sort is sorely needed before a scientific approach to fossil man can be initiated. Cousins[29] has taken a pioneer step in this direction with publication of his work *Fossil Man*. In this small treatise, one finds a useful atlas of skulls with numerous photographs, drawings, excerpts from original literature, and descriptions of the bones.

When a worker does wish to establish the depth position of a fossil, he must be certain that it was deposited when the original stratum formed. Some human remains are obviously "intruders" to a particular layer—having been buried by their peers long after the stratum was deposited. The paleontologist tries to find evidence of ceremonial burial, or tries to determine if the specimen was actually engulfed in the original sediments.

Certain structural features may aid in answering the question. The absolute depth may be of significant help in itself. A fossil discovered beneath 65 feet of gravel, for instance, can hardly be attributed to artificial human burial. A fossil cemented conformably in a firm matrix of limestone or breccia also bespeaks natural deposition.

Chemical analysis of the fossil may provide additional, valuable information. Fluorine occurs in most ground waters as the fluoride ion which is gradually absorbed and fixed ". . . in the phosphatic material of bones and teeth buried in permeable formations." [30] Oakley, the originator of this dating technique, has clearly foreseen its problems and limitations:

> The fluorine method is most suitable for the relative dating of bones in gravelly or sandy alluvial deposits in temperate regions. It is applicable to some extent where the containing deposit is alluvial clay, but it is of little or no use in cave-earth or other cave deposits where calcite seams have prevented the percolation of fluorides. The method is not reliable in tropical or volcanic soils. . . . The fluorine content of fossil bones increases with their geological antiquity, but at a rate which varies from site to site, being dependent on the hydrological conditions, climate, type of matrix, and amount of fluorine in circulation. . . . It cannot be emphasized too often that fluorine analysis is not a means of estimating the absolute ages of bones beyond the limits of carbon-14 (as one might have falsely gathered from some popular expositions).[31]

Evolution and the Problem of Man

In this same reference, Oakley described other, relative, chemical dating methods based on uranium deposition and on the disappearance of nitrogen from buried bones with time.

The fluorine method is good only for relative dating, and then only at one particular site.[31] The method finds its greatest value, however, in this very manner. If a given fossil contains the same amount of fluorine as other bones near it in the stratum, it was probably buried naturally and its position is probably valid. If a particular skull gives very low percentages of fluoride, while nearby bones have a significantly higher fluorine content, one might logically infer that the skull was buried some time after the fossil layer itself had formed.

Based on these considerations, several pairs of fossil hominids will presently be studied. In each case, both fossils of the pair were found in approximately the same site or region. One member of each pair is believed (in terms of evolutionary theories) to be "primitive" or possibly "pre-human," while the other is more like modern man. It will be instructive to ascertain the depth position of each, and to relate these data finally to the problem of man's origin.

Zinjanthropus and Homo habilis.—*Zinjanthropus* (East Africa Man) was discovered in 1959 by Mary Leakey, wife of anthropologist Louis S. B. Leakey. The skull was found embedded in the strata of a canyon, the Olduvai Gorge, which ". . . slices through 300 feet of sediment covering the bed of a prehistoric lake"[32] in the present country of Tanzania.

In his 1960 article, Leakey mentioned the "Bed I" stratum in which East Africa Man was found in the bottommost layer, with note made of so-called "Bed II" deposits starting from about 40 to 100 feet above Bed I, above which are still higher formations.[33] Bed I evidently is of considerable depth, because Leakey's technical report[34] gave the position of the skull as approximately 22 feet below the upper limit of Bed I, as follows:

> An extensive and rich living floor of approximately 1-2 in. in thickness has been uncovered. It rests on a bentonitic deep-water clay and is immediately overlain by a consolidated deposit of water laid volcanic sand. This living floor lies some 20 feet below the uppermost surface of Bed I.[35]

The skull was found lodged in the soft rock in the process of being eroded from the cliff, ". . . contraction of the rock had cracked the fossil into more than 400 fragments."[36] After assembling the pieces, it became apparent that the skull shared some bony resemblances to man and yet some "primitive" traits.

Like man, the skull had large, flat-crowned molar teeth together with small incisors and canines. The forehead region, however, was flatter than that in modern man, ". . . the flat forehead is primitive, even apelike."[37] And again, "Our man also had a sagittal crest, a bony ridge crowning the skull, that is seen in certain of the lower primates and some near-men."[38] The cranial capacity of East Africa Man is estimated at 530 cc.[39]

But *Homo habilis* (who shall here be called "Handy Man" to avoid taxonomic commitment) was discovered at a *deeper* layer. As Leakey reported, "In addition to the excavations at this main site, a second site has been located, not far away, at what appears to be a slightly lower level of Bed I."[40] In this second and deeper fossil site were found a hominid mandible, parts of two other hominid mandibles, skull fragments, teeth, two clavicles, a part of the left foot, six finger bones, and two ribs.[41] Leakey gave attention to one object:

> Perhaps the most remarkable object from his second site (F.L.K.N.N. 1) is a genuine bone tool. . . . This would appear to be some sort of a "lissoir" for working leather. It postulates a more evolved way of life for the makers of the Oldowan culture than most of us would have expected.[42]

The teeth of Handy Man are described and they are *not* like those of South Africa Ape-man, but are more like the teeth of modern man, "The first molar is well worn and has a general cusp pattern reminiscent of what can be seen in some recent Australian aborigines, but it is of course larger."[43]

A portion of the original report of these deeper fossils is of particular interest:

> The two parietals are especially remarkable because, although they apparently belong to a young individual only twelve years old (or less), they are larger than those of *Zinjanthropus*. They are remarkably thin, and exhibit no sign of a sagittal crest or of any marked temporal line. The lack of both these may, perhaps, be due in part to the youthful age. Nevertheless, these parietals suggest that we are dealing with a hominid with a larger brain capacity, as well as somewhat less specialized, than *Zinjanthropus*.[44]

Tobias calculated the possible range for the cranial capacity of Handy Man to be from 642.7 cc. to 723.6 cc., with an average value

Evolution and the Problem of Man 219

of 680.8 cc. This is, of course, significantly greater than the 530 cc. of East Africa Man. Tobias commented,

> All these values lie in the area between the largest known australopithecine (530 c.c.-600 c.c. as the estimate for an adult corresponding to the Taung child, Tobias 3) and the smallest known *Homo erectus* capacity (775 c.c.).[45]

While the intellectual-spiritual status of neither creature can be determined with certainty, it is interesting that the Handy Man fossils, considered more "modern" on several counts by evolutionists, lie *deeper* in the strata of Olduvai Gorge than the skull of the supposedly more "primitive" East Africa Man.

Neanderthal and Swanscombe Man.—There are many cave sites in Europe, Africa, Gibraltar, Palestine, and elsewhere that have yielded skulls and many other bones of so-called Neanderthal Man. From such plentiful fossil material, specialists have reconstructed entire skeletons, and completed detailed studies on body structure.[46] The anatomy of Neanderthal Man has been summarized as follows:

> Body of short stature but very massive. Head very large, with facial region much developed in comparison with cerebral region. . . . Skull much flattened; orbital arches enormous, forming a continuous ridge; forehead very receding; . . .
>
> Face long and projecting with flat and receding malar bones. . . . Orbits very large and round. Nose very large. . . . Lower jaw strong and chinless. . . . Dentition massive, structure of back molars retaining certain primitive characters. Vertebral column and limb bones showing numerous simian characters and indicating a less perfect bipedal or upright carriage than in modern Man. Legs very short.
>
> Brain capacity averaging about 1,450 cubic centimeters. Brain formation presenting numerous primitive characters, especially in the relatively great reduction of the frontal lobes and the general pattern of the convolution.[47]

This description by the noted fossil students Boule and Vallois contains both fact and philosophy. It is apparent, nonetheless, that evolutionists believe Neanderthal man was "primitive" in structure, if not also in behavior. Both of these points are debatable, since it is not permissible on strictly scientific grounds to call a bone "primitive" just because it varies in shape from that of modern man.

As has been noted, a "primitive" creature may have been completely non-related to man and hence not a primitive ancestor at all. Or else the supposedly "primitive" individual may have differed only in form, but not in intellect or the other spiritual qualities which mark mankind. In either case, it is more accurate to say that Neanderthal simply differs from modern man in these particular ways and others.

The Neanderthal man had a cranial capacity as large or larger on the average than that of modern man, although this also is an inadequate criterion of judgment.

Concerning behavior, Oakley[48] presented plates of the so-called "Mousterian" tool industry that is believed to be the product of Neanderthal man. These tools are admittedly well shaped and, if made by the Neanderthals, are evidence of noticeable skill and craftsmanship. In one particular cave that contained Neanderthal remains, bear skulls were found systematically stacked—an occurrence that Howells[49] suggested might indicate some form of worship as with the Menominee Indians of today.

The mental status of Neanderthal man in relation to modern man cannot be determined, although it can be stated that his bones are plentiful and are somewhat different than corresponding bones of modern man. Furthermore, it is clear from writings of evolutionists that this creature has been judged as "primitive" in terms of developmental theory. The association of Neanderthal fossils with particular animal remains (certain extinct elephant, hippopotamus, and rhinoceros types)[50] has caused historical geologists to place the creature in the supposed "Mid Pleistocene" and "Upper Pleistocene" periods of uniformitarian geology theory.[51]

A knowledge of the facts and theories surrounding Neanderthal Man is a prelude to the study of Swanscombe Man. In 1935, Marston (an English dentist and amateur archeologist) found, as Lasker stated:

> ... several pieces of a skull deep in a stratified deposit of the 100-foot terrace of the Thames River. The circumstances of the find were investigated and confirmed by a committee of the Royal Anthropological Institute.[52]

These bones were buried to a depth of 24-26 feet in the gravel of the Thames River at Swanscombe, Kent.[53]

Three bones of the skull were found at different times—the occipital and both parietals.[54] Although the skull is not complete, cranial capacity has been estimated at 1,325 cc.[55]

Evolution and the Problem of Man

The character of these deeply buried bones is remarkable, as evidenced in the following excerpts quoted from various anthropologists:

> There is nothing in these bones to distinguish them from those of *Homo sapiens*, except, perhaps, their thickness (Broderick).[56]

> The two bones, in excellent condition, appeared at first sight very similar to those of modern man and very different from those of Neanderthal Man. In particular, two very typical characteristics of the latter—the elongation of the occipital into a "chignon" and the presence on this bone of a relatively marked torus—are totally lacking in the Swanscombe skull (Boule and Vallois).[57]

> As far as these go, little except unusual thickness would appear to distinguish the remains from the corresponding parts of modern man (Lasker).[58]

> If these women were not sapiens, neither are any of the living female Australian aborigines and New Caledonians, whose skulls Steinheim and Swanscombe resemble in grade, but not in line (Coon, speaking of both Swanscombe and Steinheim skulls).[59]

Fossils discovered near Swanscombe bones in the Thames terrace included the extinct elephant and rhinoceros[60] that are related to the supposed "second interglacial" time period.[61]

Tools found near the Swanscombe specimens included over 600 artifacts of the Acheulian type.[62] The well-formed Acheulian hand axes reputed to have been made by Swanscombe are pictured by Oakley.[63]

On the basis of fluoride and nitrogen percentages, it can be reasonably inferred that the Swanscombe bones were a valid part of the original gravel deposits and probably do not represent a later burial.

(FROM A TABLE BY OAKLEY)[64]

Specimen	% Fluoride	% Nitrogen
Modern Bone	0.01	4.0
Neolithic Skull	0.3	1.0
Swanscombe Skull	1.7	traces
Bones of fossil mammals from Swanscombe gravels	1.5	traces

It can be seen here that percentages of fluorine and nitrogen for both Swanscombe and nearby animal fossils are similar, whereas the amount of these two chemicals in Swanscombe and its associated animals differs greatly from corresponding percentages in modern bones or even more "recent" fossils such as the Neolithic Skull. After considering these chemical and stratigraphic evidences, Clark concluded:

> Taking all the evidence into account, it may be affirmed that in no other example of Paleolithic man is the dating more completely attested than it is in the case of the Swanscombe bones.[65]

Lasker also asserted:

> Furthermore, fluorine analysis of the human bones indicates a degree of fossilization comparable to that of the Middle Pleistocene animal bones from the same 100-foot terrace. Here we have well-attested evidences of an antiquity greater than that of any of the Neanderthalian or Neanderthaloid specimens known.[66]

Considering their truly "human," or "modern" character (from the standpoint of evolutionism), the position of the Swanscombe bones is significant—deep in the fossil strata, *deeper* than nearly all Neanderthal materials. As in the case of East Africa Man and Handy Man, there is with Swanscombe another instance in which a specimen of supposedly more "modern" character is found deeper than its reputed "ancestors."

Neanderthal and Fontéchevade Man.—In 1947 Mlle. G. Henri-Martin undertook excavation of a deposit at Fontéchevade in southern France. This cave and its entrance had been previously studied. The superficial strata had yielded stone tools of Mousterian (Neanderthal) type. In the upper part of the cave deposits, as Coon related, Mlle. Henri-Martin had:

> . . . found Mousterian artifacts of a kind characteristically made by Neanderthal men, but no human remains. Below this level lay a limy crust, which not only effectively sealed off what lay below but also indicated a considerable time gap between the two layers.[67]

Lasker stated:

> It is believed that the cave roof extended over this part at the time these men lived, because the layer was completely sealed off by an overlying layer of stalagmite from the former ceiling of the cave. Above the stalagmite were strata containing stone tools of Mousterian type (the culture of Neanderthal man) and later Paleolithic types.[68]

The thick, limy layer seemed to be the floor of the cave mouth. Actually, it was a layer of stalagmite which had formed when the cave mouth was enclosed. Mlle. Henri-Martin penetrated the stalagmite layer and under it found seven meters of deposits[69] in which, at a depth of 2.60 meters, she discovered many animal fossils, stone tools, and two apparently human skull bones.

The one skull fragment was a patch from the brows (the frontal or forehead bone) about the size of a silver dollar[70] while most of the top of the skull of the second skull-crown was present.[71] A calculation of cranial capacity gave the value of 1,450 cc. or greater.[72]

Not all the frontal bone was present, but from what exists, Fontéchevade man did not appear to possess the supraorbital ridges typical of Neanderthal:

> The forehead of Fontéchevade Man was therefore shaped like that of Modern Man and quite differently from that of Neanderthal Man.[73]

Lasker concluded that:

> The brow ridges are of feeble development, such as occur in European women today. . . . The one distinctive feature, it seems to me, is that the frontal region, especially of the first specimen, is apparently of modern type.[74]

Animal fossils found in the deep deposit included mammalian bones and other "warm temperate fauna."[75] Coon[76] listed the following faunal members in the deposit: the extinct Merck's rhinoceros, fallow deer, bear, tortoise, and *Cyon*, a wild dog now found mostly in southern Asia. On this basis, uniformitarian theorists put these layers in the "last interglacial" period:

> The animal fossils are of forms associated with a warm to temperate climate, hence consistent with a date of the last interglacial period.[77]

Tools were also present in the deposits, sealed beneath the stalagmite floor:

> The stone flakes found at the level of the skulls are of a coarse type called "Tayacian" and ascribed to the Lower Paleolithic.[78]

Plates of representative Tayacian tools have been provided by Oakley.[79]

Fluoride tests have been applied to the Fontéchevade skull remains:

> Oakley was asked to test the remarkable fossils found in a deeper level in a cave of Fontéchevade, France. Their fluorine content and that of animals from the same level averaged 0.4 and 0.5. Fossils from the upper part of the cave had a fluorine content of 0.1 per cent.[80]

> Their content of fluorine is of the order of the animal bones in the lower layers where they were found, and greater than that of bones from above the stalagmite floor which sealed them over.[81]

> Finally, the fluorine test showed the skull bones to contain 0.4-0.5 per cent fluorine, as compared with a range of 0.5-0.9 per cent for mammalian bones of Tayacian date and 0.1 per cent or less for human and mammalian bones from the superimposed Aurignacian level. As in the case of the Swanscombe skull bones, therefore, the evidence for the antiquity of the Fontéchevade skulls seems to be well assured.[82]

Again the striking anomaly of a "modern" man buried *deeper* than the different or "primitive" forms is seen. The position of the Fontéchevade man in the strata is unimpeachable. Custance has seen the importance of such data for the entire theory of man's origin and has summarized by saying that:

> What this really boils down to, is that instead of a nice orderly series of fossil specimens, passing from very primitive to quite modern types, we in fact find the record supports no such pattern. Some of the lowest levels present us with fossil remains that are to all intents and purposes completely modern in appearance, while some of the latest levels throw up specimens which nicely fit the preconceived picture of what the earliest representatives of man are supposed to have looked like. Naturally there had been some tendency to disregard these misfits by questioning whether the levels at which they were found had been correctly reported—until Fontéchevade.[83]

Conclusions

It is impossible to construct an evolutionary tree of man's origin for the simple reason that the intelligence and humanity of man-like fossils cannot be evaluated with certainty. Furthermore, fossils that closely resemble modern man are often buried *deeper* than those which are supposed to be his ancestors according to evolution theory.

Following a creation origins model, these data have better fit, and problems vanish. Bible creationism proposes that all men, modern or fossil, have descended from two ancestors who were formed quickly and miraculously from the dust of the ground (Gen. 2:7). Then this pair, presumably rich in genetic endowment, may have given rise to variant morphological races through the mechanisms of mutation and selection. Before, during, and after the great flood (Gen. 6-8), many of these truly "human" types may have undergone burial and fossilization in sedimentary, cave, or volcanic deposits.

Furthermore, there may have been anthropoid (ape-like) "kinds" that were separate creations and of no biological relation to man. Some of these may have resembled man quite closely. Such non-human kinds may have also experienced extinction and fossilization. In this creation view, then, there is no difficulty if relatively "modern" fossil bones are found beneath the "primitive" skulls.

Creationist students of anthropology can presently contribute to the discipline, if they will ignore the "ages" concept of the rock layers, and begin to correlate the absolute depth of fossils in the strata to their morphological patterns. A compendium of such information is greatly needed.

In either view, creationism or evolutionism, however, one key problem remains unanswered: What was the character, intellect, linguistic ability, and general spiritual capacity of each particular hominid or anthropoid fossil? In most cases as yet, this important question can be given no proper answer.

NOTES AND REFERENCES

1. John W. Klotz, *Genes, Genesis, and Evolution* (St. Louis, Mo.: Concordia Publishing House, 1955), p. 198.
2. Arthur C. Custance, *The Influence of Environmental Pressures on the Human Skull*, Doorway Papers, No. 9 (Ottawa, Canada, 1957).
3. *Ibid.*, p. 9.
4. Marcellin Boule and Henri Vallois, *Fossil Man* (New York: The Dryden Press, 1957), p. 475.
5. J. J. Duyvéne De Wit, *A New Critique of the Transformist Principle in Evolutionary Biology*, J. H. Kok, N. V. (The Netherlands: Kampen, 1965), pp. 24-25.
6. Ernst Mayr, "Taxonomic Categories in Fossil Hominids," *Cold Spring Harbor Symposium on Quantitative Biology* (1951), Vol. 15. Reprinted in C. Howells, *Ideas on Human Evolution* (Cambridge: Harvard University Press, 1962), p. 243.
7. *Ibid.*, p. 253.

8. *Ibid.*, p. 256.
9. Clark Howell and Editors of *Life, Early Man* (Sacramento, Calif.: California State Department of Education, 1967), pp. 42-45, 57-69, 73-74, 155-157, 132-135.
10. William Howells, *Mankind So Far* (Garden City, N.Y.: Doubleday and Co., Inc., 1952), p. 128.
11. Arthur C. Custance, *The Fallacy of Reconstructions*, Doorway Papers No. 33 (Ottawa, Canada: 1966).
12. Annie Martin, *Home Life on an Ostrich Farm* (Liverpool: George Philip and Son, 1892).
13. Wilhelm Goetsch, *The Ants* (Ann Arbor, Mich.: University of Michigan Press, 1957), pp. 56-58.
14. Kenneth P. Oakley, *Man the Toolmaker* (Chicago: University of Chicago Press, 1959), pp. 3-4.
15. *Ibid.*, entire volume.
16. J. T. Robinson, "The Genera and Species of the Australopithecinae, *American Journal of Physical Anthropology* (n.s.) (1954), Vol. 120. Reprinted in Howells, *Ideas on Human Evolution*.
17. Louis S. B. Leakey and Des Bartlett, "Finding the World's Earliest Man," *National Geographic Magazine* (1960), 118(3):422, 425.
18. Louis S. B. Leakey, P. V. Tobias, and J. R. Napier, "A New Species of the genus *Homo* from Olduvai Gorge, *Nature* (1964), 202(4927):9.
19. Ernst Mayr, *op. cit.*, p. 254.
20. Adolph H. Schultz, "The Physical Distinctions of Man," *Proceedings of the American Philosophical Society* (1950), Vol. 94, reprinted in Howells, *Ideas on Human Evolution*, p. 60ff.
21. Wilfred LeGros Clark, "Bones of Contention," *Journal of the Royal Anthropological Institute* (1958, Vol. 88, Part II, reprinted in Howells, *Ideas on Human Evolution*, pp. 357-360.
22. Carleton S. Coon, *The Origin of Races* (New York: Knopf, 1966), p. 371, Plate XXXII.
23. Franz Weidenreich, "The Human Brain in the Light of Its Phylogenetic Development," *Scientific Monthly* (August 1948), pp. 103-106.
24. W. L. Clark, *op. cit.*, p. 357.
25. Macdonald Critchley, as quoted by John C. Greene, *Darwin and the Modern World View* (New York: Mentor Books, 1963), p. 114.
26. Lord Brain, "Human Behavior Unique," *Science News Letter* (Sept. 5, 1964), 86:151.
27. Henry M. Morris and John C. Whitcomb, Jr., *The Genesis Flood* (Philadelphia: Presbyterian and Reformed Publishing Co., 1961).
28. *Creation Research Society Quarterlies* and *Annuals*, Walter E. Lammerts, editor. Each volume and number listed has an article about uniformitarianism, catastrophism, or time concepts on the pages given: 2(2): 19-28; 2(4):28-31; 3(1):16-37, 51-52; 3(2):12-16; 3(4):23; 4(1):5-12.
29. Frank W. Cousins, *Fossil Man*. Evolution Protest Movement, Santhia, Stoke, Hayling Island, Hants, England (1966).
30. Kenneth P. Oakley, "Fluorine, Uranium, and Nitrogen Dating of Bone,"

The Scientist and Archeologist, ed. Edward Plyddoke (New York: Roy Publishers, 1963), p. 112.
31. *Ibid.* Cf. also Wilfred LeGros Clark, *The Fossil Evidence for Human Evolution*, 2nd ed. (Chicago: University of Chicago Press, 1964), p. 57; and Ruth Moore, *Man, Time, and Fossils*, 2nd ed. (New York: Alfred A. Knopf, 1961), pp. 360-377).
32. Leakey and Bartlett, *op. cit.*, p. 422.
33. *Ibid.*, p. 429.
34. L. S. B. Leakey, "A New Fossil Skull from Olduvai, *Nature* (1959), 184(4685):491-493.
35. L. S. B. Leakey, "Recent Discoveries at Olduvai Gorge, *Nature* (1960), 188(4755):1050.
36. Leakey and Bartlett, *op. cit.*, p. 433.
37. *Ibid.*
38. *Ibid.*, p. 434.
39. P. W. Tobias, "The Olduvai Bed I Hominine with Special Reference to Its Cranial Capacity, *Nature* (1964), 202(4927):3.
40. Leakey, *loc. cit.*, "Recent Discoveries . . . ," p. 1051.
41. *Ibid.*
42. *Ibid.*
43. L. S. B. Leakey, "New Finds at Olduvai Gorge, *Nature* (1960), 188 (4765):649.
44. *Ibid.*
45. Tobias, *op. cit.*, p. 4.
46. Boule and Vallois, *op. cit.*, pp. 214-252.
47. *Ibid.*, pp. 251-252.
48. Oakley, *op. cit.*, p. 88.
49. Howells, *op. cit.*, p. 164.
50. Boule and Vallois, *op. cit.*, p. 51.
51. *Ibid.*, pp. 50, 51, 193; cf. Howells, *op. cit.*, p. 119.
52. Gabriel Ward Lasker, *The Evolution of Man* (New York: Holt, Rinehart and Winston, 1961), p. 117.
53. Boule and Vallois, *op. cit.*, p. 186; cf. Clark, *op. cit.*, p. 68.
54. Coon, *op. cit.*, pp. 495-496; cf. Boule and Vallois, *op. cit.*, p. 186.
55. Boule and Vallois, *op. cit.*, p. 186; cf. Alan Houghton Broderick, *Man and His Ancestry* (London: Hutchinson and Co., Ltd., 1960), p. 204.
56. Broderick, *op. cit.* note 55.
57. Boule and Vallois, *op. cit.*, p. 186.
58. Lasker, *op. cit.*, p. 118.
59. Coon, *op. cit.*, p. 497.
60. Broderick, *op. cit.*, p. 204.
61. Lasker, *op. cit.*, p. 117.
62. Broderick, *op. cit.*, p. 204; cf. Boule and Vallois, *op. cit.*, p. 186.
63. Oakley, 1959, *op. cit.*, pp. 59, 83, 116.
64. Oakley, 1963, *op. cit.*, p. 117.
65. Clark, *op. cit.*, p. 68.
66. Lasker, *op. cit.*, pp. 117-118.

67. Coon, *op. cit.*, pp. 498-499.
68. Lasker, *op. cit.*, p. 118.
69. William Howells, *Mankind in the Making* (Garden City, N.Y.: Doubleday and Co., Inc., 1959), p. 221.
70. *Ibid.*
71. Lasker, *op. cit.*
72. Howells, *op. cit.*
73. Boule and Vallois, *op. cit.*, p. 190.
74. Lasker, *op. cit.*, p. 119.
75. Clark, *op. cit.*, p. 70.
76. Coon, *op. cit.*
77. Lasker, *op. cit.*, p. 118.
78. *Ibid.*
79. Oakley, 1959, *op. cit.*, p. 83.
80. Moore, *op. cit.*, note 31, *supra.*
81. Howells, *op. cit.*, p. 222.
82. Clark, *op. cit.*
83. Custance, *op. cit.*, p. 3.

XIX

IMMORALITY IN NATURAL SELECTION

William J. Tinkle

Many church people consider natural selection merely as an academic principle. Since they are not trained in science, they are content to let such matters be decided by the scientists. Such an attitude, however, entails drifting with majority opinion, which never should be done in an important matter. The results of such doctrines as natural selection affect society in general.

The term *selection* is used in agriculture in a somewhat restricted and technical sense. A good farmer does not plant just any seed from his crop, but chooses seed from the plants which please him most. He does not keep animals indiscriminately to become parents of the next generation, but chooses those which have the best characteristics. If the next generation of plants or animals is better, because of such restricted parentage, we say that the selection was effective; but, if the progeny are no different from those from unrestricted breeding, the selection is ineffective.

This choice of parents by man is called artificial selection. If the forces of nature accomplish a similar result we call it natural selection.

For instance, if a mixture of corn, *Zea mays*, is planted in central Canada, only a part of the crop will produce viable seed, the rest being killed by the early cold weather of autumn. It is as if nature had selected the early-ripening plants to become the parents of the next generation. If viable corn seed is planted in the same Canadian climate for several seasons, an early maturing strain will be sorted out.

Albino seedlings (plants without green coloring) sometimes come up in a corn field, and of course soon die. Animals born in a crippled condition soon die if they are wild animals, and thus do not reproduce their type. In this way natural selection maintains a standard, a type of lower limit, in the kinds of plants and animals.

Differences of Opinion

To this extent the effectiveness of natural selection is recognized by all observant persons. But differences of opinion become evident when it is claimed that living things reached their present structure by natural selection. Evolutionists insist that natural selection not only maintains a lower limit and sorts out types for new habitats, but also improves the kinds, making plants and animals which are larger and better organized than anything which preceded them. Thus new and improved families, orders, and phyla are said to have been formed.

It was this doctrine which convinced a large portion of scientists that evolution is correct. Ever since ancient times, a few writers claimed that living things arose from very simple beginnings, but these writers were not believed. Then Charles Darwin presented his theory of natural selection in great detail and "sold" the idea of evolution.

Furthermore, the doctrine of natural selection is still depended upon as the basis of evolution. "*Homo sapiens*, like all other organisms, has evolved from prior, extremely different species, by natural means and under the directive influence of natural selection." [1]

A thoughtful person can readily see that the theory of evolution by natural selection encourages selfish aggression and violence. It not only condones selfishness; it is founded upon it. The animal which asserts itself and overcomes its fellows is supposed to do so because it has superior genes. It therefore leaves more descendants than the average; and, thus, in time a superior strain is built up, and later, an improved species. But if a human being follows this example—asserting himself and disregarding the rights of others—we say that he is immoral.

Indeed, there is no question but that those from whom Darwin received his examples were immoral. The struggle for existence was going on among *people* in nineteenth century England. Factory owners, in the absence of regulatory laws, were making fortunes and elevating their social standing. This was done by forcing women and children to work for twelve hours a day in miserable surroundings. Factory owners liked Darwin's writings because he gave them the idea that the struggle in industry was natural, as being among all living things, and in this way some industrialists justified their dealings.

Struggle Based on Logical Deduction

Now it is true that, if the truth of this principle of forming improved kinds by struggle were well established, we would simply have to make the most of it. But it is not supported by modern findings.

There is serious dearth of observation of the results of the process. "It must be admitted that even today our belief in the efficiency of selection depends on logical deduction rather than experiment." [2]

Experiments actually give results which show that selection is not very effective. After a few generations of selection a certain strain of organisms has genes which are alike for a given character; then it is clear that it does not matter which seed is selected to plant, the progeny will be the same.

The example of Johannsen's beans is well known. By selecting beans of different size, Johannsen established strains which he kept growing in separate plots. As was expected, a large bean usually produced beans which were large on the average. He called these strains pure lines. Yet, when Johannsen selected large beans from a pure line, and also small beans from the *same pure line*, he found that they bore beans of the same size on the average. Selection within an isolated strain or pure line was ineffective.

The reason for this limitation of selection is that the genes for seed size were the same throughout the pure line. Within the line there was some difference in size, but this was due to environment rather than heredity. It is well known that changes caused by environment are not inherited.

Similar results have been observed in other species, but in those which are normally cross-pollinated it takes longer to reach the limit of effective selection than in beans, which are self-pollinated. In France, beets were selected for sugar, and from 1800 to 1878 the sugar content rose from 6 percent to 17 percent. From 1878 to 1924, however, the percentage remained 17, even though the same selection methods were used.[3] (Figure 1)

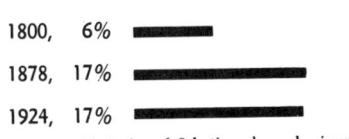

1800, 6% ▬▬▬
1878, 17% ▬▬▬▬▬▬▬
1924, 17% ▬▬▬▬▬▬▬

Figure 1. Limitation of Selection, shown by improvement of sugar beets. The best beets at the beginning of the project had 6 per cent of sugar. 78 years of selecting the sweetest ones for seed increased the sugar content to 17 per cent. But at that time, all the best genes had been sorted out and there was no further increase. Likewise, selection in nature can not make changes beyond certain limits. Selection does not give evidence that simple types of plants and animals changed into complex types.
Redrawn from *Heredity: a Study in Science and the Bible*. By W. J. Tinkle, St. Thomas Press, Houston, Texas, 1967.

The science of genetics has established the truth that genes remain the same indefinitely unless they mutate. Such changes take place only rarely; and few, if any, have been observed which are beneficial to the particular plant or animal. In the above examples either there were no mutations, or none that made larger beans or sweeter beets.

Of course, natural selection

affects mutant plants and animals with the result that a large proportion die without leaving offspring, because mutants have less vigor than normal organisms. Selection never forms new or improved genes, but only chooses among the ones which appear naturally. *Scientists never have observed the appearance of a new character which would aid in changing an order into a higher order;* for instance, a lizard with a milk gland or a feather.

Influence on Human Behavior

But let us return to the influence which the doctrine exerts upon human behavior. If man evolved from animals, it is easy to feel that he still is an animal at heart with a veneer of civilization. And, if this evolution was accomplished by selfish initiative at the expense of other living things, it is easy to justify the same conduct now.

In all fairness we must admit, however, that there are proponents of evolution who advocate moral behavior.[4] But the ethical obligations of the scientists of which they write have been realized in spite of the doctrine of natural selection rather than because of it. The antisocial effects of the doctrine may be seen among persons whose moral characters are undeveloped, such as young people or persons who have never become morally mature. Our crime waves, which tend to become worse each year, are examples of the effect of selfish assertion.

There are many church people who are loath to disagree with scientists, and, therefore, they admit that evolution may be true, but add that God guided the process. These people do not achieve agreement after all, for in the doctrine of natural selection there is no provision for interference from the outside. It is just a free-for-all struggle.

Such church people do not know that it is unnecessary to accept such a doctrine in order to agree with scientists. There is a sizeable group of scientists who accept the doctrine of divine creation.

If we feel that man is an animal, we are in danger of losing our sense of responsibility, for animals do not and cannot have this trait. Leading evolutionsts do claim that man is an animal. G. G. Simpson states:

> Man is not *merely* an animal, that is, his essence is not simply in his shared animality. Nevertheless he *is* an animal and the nature of man includes and has arisen from the nature of all animals (italics are his).[5]

It is true that man has much in common with animals in a physical sense, but to claim that his mental and spiritual endowments have come from animals is not only inadequate—it is dangerous!

Conscience, Responsibility Important

Consider that little spark of divinity in the human heart which is called conscience. It makes one aware of doing right or wrong. If one has been taught rightly, and has not seared his conscience by repeated disobedience, it prompts him to do the best that he knows. Can you imagine an animal with such a mentor in its heart? It is most contented when its stomach is full, regardless of the method of filling that organ. It may learn to shun punishment, but it never feels remorse.

Of equal importance is man's sense of responsibility, which an animal does not and cannot have. It is not alone in the Bible that responsibility is taught; every nation assumes it when it formulates laws. Animals are not responsible, laws are not made for them, but they are fenced in. This is exactly what will befall people, if they insist on adhering to the idea that they are animals, and therefore not responsible for their conduct. They will be fenced in by autocratic governments.

It cannot be denied that the doctrine of evolution by natural selection gives aid and comfort to dictators. Adolph Hitler and Benito Mussolini were logical, if you grant the validity of their belief. They overlooked the truth that man's inmost nature has come down from God above.

It is not only unproved, it is even dangerous to believe that man is the product of struggle among selfish, irresponsible lower organisms.

NOTES AND REFERENCES

1. G. G. Simpson, *Science* (1966), 152:472.
2. S. S. Carter, *A Hundred Years of Evolution* (New York: Macmillan, 1957).
3. D. F. Jones, *Genetics in Plant and Animal Improvement* (New York: Wiley, 1924), p. 414.
4. Bently Glass, "The Ethical Basis of Science," *Science* (1965), 150:1254-1261.
5. Simpson, *op. cit.*, p. 472.

XX

LAND-DWELLING VERTEBRATES AND THE ORIGIN OF THE TETRAPOD LIMB

P. W. DAVIS, JR.

Most students become acquainted with many of the current concepts in biology whilst still in school at an age when most people are, on the whole, uncritical. Then when they come to study the subject in more detail, they have in their minds several half truths and misconceptions which tend to prevent them from coming to a fresh appraisal of the situation. In addition, with a uniform pattern of education most students tend to have the same sort of educational background and so in conversation and discussion they accept common fallacies and agree on matters based on these fallacies.

The answer (to the quest for the origin of higher categories of organisms) will be found by future experimental work and not by dogmatic assertions that the general theory of evolution must be correct because there is nothing else that will satisfactorily take its place.[1]

Terrestrial and amphibious tetrapods generally locomote with the aid of distinctive paired appendages which we refer to as "limbs," "arms," or "legs." Since the structures of the arm and the leg are basically similar, this discussion will treat them as if they were equivalent.

Fish, on the other hand, employ a fundamentally different form of locomotion. (This is true even when they are locomoting on land, as in the case of the nocturnal excursions of eels, or the normal life of the mudskipper, *Periopthalmus*, or the African *Clarius lazera*, which actually steals millet out of gardens.) The locomotion of the fish is accomplished by serial contractions of the segmentally arranged *myotomal* musculature, producing a resultant force which tends to propel the fish forward by reaction when in water, or by contact when on land. Some fish are able to utilize their limbs, or projections from the opercula of the gills, or other devices, to secure a hold on the substrate when not actually swimming. However, such appendages never contain the intrinsic musculature which would enable true walking to be accomplished. Generally they serve as stabilizers or as a point of contact to minimize lateral slippage while wriggling.

In contrast to this, most tetrapods rely little upon the segmental musculature in locomotion. Instead, in order to drag their bodies over obstacles in the terrestrial habitat, they utilize the muscles in the *limbs themselves* or in direct association with them (*par ex*: the *gluteus maximus* of man). The basic source of power in these animals is not the *trunk* but the *appendicular musculature*. Obvious exceptions to this rule are salamanders, which seem to combine the two modes of locomotion, and snakes, which are confirmed wrigglers. In both of these forms and in similar forms the limbs are reduced or entirely absent.

Additionally, the tetrapod limb functions to support the body at a distance from the ground. We may compare the typical land vertebrate to a bridge supported by two pairs of trusses. If the trusses are near to the center of the main axis of the bridge, they will support it much more effectively than if they are arranged at either side. Similarly, tetrapods which have their limbs joined directly below the body axis do not need to employ great effort to stand up; their construction is essentially stable. On the other hand, those tetrapods whose legs are placed more laterally than ventrally must employ much effort and considerable musculature on the distal surface of the limbs just to lift their bellies off the ground. Most, but not all, of the latter are extinct at the present time.*

As a generalization, the tetrapod limb is divided into three segments, the *stylopodium,* the *zeugopodium,* and the *autopodium.* Their composition is as follows:

Segment	Anterior limb	Posterior limb
Stylopodium	Humerus (upper arm)	Femur (thigh)
Zeugopodium	Radius Ulna (forearm)	Tibia Fibula (shank)
Autopodium	Carpus (wrist)	Tarsus (ankle)
	Metacarpus (hand)	Metatarsus (foot)
	Phalanges (fingers)	Phalanges (toes)

---

* The reader is advised at this time to refresh his memory on anatomical terminology, which has necessarily been employed in the following section. Any standard textbook of comparative anatomy may be consulted.

Please note that this division is not based upon evolutionary presuppositions. It is purely functional. If these functional divisions are the basis for one's thought regarding the comparative anatomy of the limb, it is especially difficult to derive the limb of the tetrapod from the limb of the presumed fish ancestors of the tetrapods. Such divisions are never found in fish fins, ancient or modern, so far as is known. Thus, if one is committed to the thesis that land dwelling tetrapods are derived from a fishlike ancestry, one is faced with the problem of stating the *way* in which the transition from an aquatic to a terrestrial animal was accomplished. The ancient rhipidistian crossopterygian, or lobe-finned fish, appeals to the evolutionist as the most likely ancestor for the terrestrial vertebrates.

These fish had a number of characteristics which might have suited them for the role. Some of them had nostrils communicating with the mouth cavity (which is not the case among sharks and teleosts), and some had ventral air bladders which might have been serviceable as lungs. Most important, perhaps, is the fact that with sufficient imagination one can present a reasonably plausible scheme for the derivation of the tetrapod limb from their fins. The structure of the fins of all other fish is so remote from that of the tetrapod limb no one has yet appeared with a sufficiently good imagination to make it look plausible.

There is a fundamental difference between the walking and the stabilization functions of the fins. Either the fin is held like a rudder and serves that purpose, or else (rarely) the fin is used as an oar or as a support. The pattern of tetrapod locomotion differs from this, involving an overhand motion with flexion at the wrist and elbow. In order to accomplish such a motion, the crossopterygian would have to bend its fin in a most peculiar and unnatural fashion for a fish. However, such a position would be necessitated, since an attempt to preserve the "rowing" motion on land would bring the delicate edge of the fin into contact with the ground, and would probably damage it or wear it away. The natural consequences of this are that the tip of the fin would have to be directed anteriorly, but in such a way that the "flat" of the fin was flat upon the ground. This situation would result in a double flexion of the limb corresponding to the joints of the wrist and elbow, with a corresponding change in the orientation of the bones. Specifically, the elements of the fin which were previously *anterior* (that is, preaxial) now tend to become medial and those previously *posterior* (postaxial) now tend to become distal.

It is characteristic of the crossopterygian fin that the radial rods of the fin are present only on the anterior side. Hence, these preaxial radii would become medial.

By the above hypothesis, one ray would elongate to form the radius of the limb. Such an intermediate stage is purely hypothetical. No such fossil has ever been found. Other elements are also supposed to elongate and/or change. A point to be emphasized and re-emphasized is that no form intermediate between a rhipidistian crossopterygian and a labyrinthodont, primitive amphibian has ever been found. The closest known example[2] is not very close.[3]

There is another point to be made in this connection, and that involves fossilized amphibian trackways. Only a very few of these are known, and it might well be argued that tracks left by limbs of an intermediate form might well have remained undiscovered, as have the limbs themselves. However, even the tracks of fairly advanced labyrinthodonts could be expected to show certain characteristics if they were originally derived from fish. As a matter of fact, the labyrinthodont tracks which *have* been discovered cast considerable doubt upon the above evolutionary theory of tetrapod limb derivation.

In the earlier stages of limb development the leg musculature could not have been very well developed. It is reasonable to suppose if the above hypothesis were correct, that the animal possessing a moderately well-developed limb would still be relying heavily on the segmented muscles of the trunk for its locomotion. In support of this contention it may be argued as follows: If the evolutionists are correct in their supposition that modern amphibians are derived from labyrinthodont ancestors such as the ones under discussion, then salamanders must be considerably closer to the ancestral form than, for example, the more highly modified frog. The salamander has for the most part well-developed leg musculature, although the legs themselves are diminutive. Hence, the salamander is a *more* advanced tetrapod than any really early labyrinthodont is likely to have been, and it *still* relies on trunk-wriggling for the bulk of its locomotion. Therefore, it is reasonable to suppose that its ancestors relied on the trunk at least as much as the salamander of today.

When one leg of such a wriggling animal is off the ground, the others form a most unstable tripod until the one off the ground has been advanced by the wriggling motion of the body. The other feet (especially the foot contralateral to the one that is off the ground) will tend to rotate, and on a slippery surface would tend to slip rotationally, forming a track in which soft earth or mud would be pushed up in a ridge at the *lateral* edge of the foot.

Now this, or something even more exaggerated, is the kind of track that the labyrinthodont amphibians could be expected to make if they are indeed derived from crossopterygian ancestors in the way which has been discussed. In actual trackways of such labyrinthodonts, however, there is no evidence whatever for rotational slippage. Slippage exists, but it is antero-posterior; that is, it is simply the result of trying to run across a slippery substrate and would appear today under similar circumstances. The posterior position of the mud ridge indicates that these animals relied completely upon the musculature of their limbs for locomotion. In summary, there is no fossil evidence for the existence of forms intermediate between crossopterygians and amphibians. Not only this, but what little pertinent fossil evidence exists is inconsistent with such intermediate forms. In view of these facts, the very existence, not to say credence, of such an inherently improbable idea is puzzling.

There is certainly no unanimity regarding the evolutionary "motivation" behind this change. The investigator is confronted with a cloud-cuckoo land of fantasy when he begins his inquiry into this area of thought. The writer was impressed forcefully at that time by the fact that this kind of thinking requires great faith—that is, faith that the evolutionary process actually took place. The frame of mind seems to be: "Evolution took place. That is our postulate. Therefore, intermediate forms *must* have existed whether they are known or not, and there must have been a reason to produce these intermediate forms." This is an example of blind faith raised to the second power of fantasy. That such forms existed is in the first place a fideistic statement. A discussion of the conditions which may have produced such speculative forms seems to be at the same level of significance as the more futile scholastic debates of the Middle Ages.

Limitations of space prohibit a full discussion of this controversy, so a brief summation must suffice. The controversy began, for the purposes of our discussion, with Romer, the noted paleontologist. He argued that at the time the transition from aquatic to terrestrial life was taking place, intermittent droughts made it necessary for crossopterygians to leave drying fresh water pools, stopping along the way perhaps to snack upon a cockroach or other insect. The availability of such food supply eventually gave the fish which spent the most time out of water an adaptive advantage, so that the best walkers among them would come to predominate in the population, and so on. Doubt was cast upon the Romer hypothesis by the seeming discovery that the era in question was not necessarily drought-ridden, but that the geological formations characteristic of it were more likely to have been laid down in a rain forest.

In the following summary I have presented the name of the author, his main arguments, and my comments.

Author—Orton,[4] 1954
Thesis—Land locomotion does not require limbs. A drought is a hostile environment. You could not expect a fish to expose itself to desiccation by overland journeying. Modern lungfish *burrow* in drought. The tetrapod limb was originally a burrowing device.
Comment—Modern lungfish burrow *without* legs. This theory would in any case account for the front legs. The early amphibians and crossopterygians were also probably too large for effective burrowing.

Author—Ewer,[5] 1955
Thesis—Why should a structure be evolved for burrowing and then be changed so as to be suitable for walking? What caused this *further* change? (Ockham's razor). Even amphibians at present, which burrow, migrate in response to *population pressure.*
Comment—By itself, this tells us nothing about what might have brought the limbs about in the first place.

Author—Gunter,[6] 1956
Thesis—In order for limbs to be effective at all in migration, they have to be strong *before* migration becomes necessary. He thinks the fin became a sort of leg to support the fish halfway out of the water in order to exploit the food value of the shallows and to escape large predators.
Comment—Crossopterygians were large, very carnivorous fish with little to fear from predators. They were obviously moderately deep-water fish, and the insects, etc., of the margin would not be enough to support them. Limbs would be a handicap in a generalized ecological niche in competition with fish.

Author—Goin & Goin,[7] 1956
Thesis—Population pressure was the stimulus for migration. Rainfall and humid conditions occasionally permitted it. Fish could begin to exploit the land environment *once the legs were developed.*
Comment—Why did the legs develop? They are simply not needed for migration under humid conditions (e.g., eels)!

Author—Inger,[8] 1957
Thesis—Modern air-breathing fish do not migrate to avoid drought or stagnation. They breathe air so as to be able to *stay* in stagnant water. They migrate to find food and uncrowded habitats. A continuously humid climate would favor invasion of the land.
Comment—Again, how can a limb be of aid in migration unless it has already come into existence from some other cause?

Author—Romer,[9] 1958
Thesis—Limbs were developed prior to terrestrialism. Few insects were originally found on land, but some must have inhabited shallow water. Limbs enabled fish to exploit this environment as in Gunter's 1956 theory. In subsequent geological time, drought conditions forced migration with development of insectivorous habits. (Insects were by now abundant.)
Comment—See criticism of Gunter's 1956 theory. It is controversial that subsequent (Devonian) time *was* arid. Inger's 1957 argument still refutes Romer's major thesis.

Author—Warburton & Denman,[10] 1961
If the crossopterygian *larvae* could exist in the shallows, predators could not get to them. When the pools began to dry up, the larvae might be isolated in mud puddles. In that case, limbs would enable them to walk back to the main body of the pool. These limbs would also enable adults to seek out mud puddles in the first place, which were initially isolated and free from the competition of other fish larvae.
Comment—What could the larvae eat in the puddles? Would not limbs initially *handicap* the adults while they were still competing with fish? Since returning larvae would have to be big enough to compete with adults, the puddle they just left would have to be sizeable indeed!

In summary, we may tabulate these theories as follows:

Larva		Warburton & Denman		
Adult	Romer	Goin & Goin Ewer Inger	Gunter Romer	Orton
Ecological motivation	Migration - drought	Migration - Population pressure.	Exploitation of margin	Burrowing

Obviously there are a number of as yet unused combinations, combinations of combinations, or even new ideas. For instance, by combining the two concepts of exploitation of the margin and larval adaptation we have a most attractive theory which states that the larva exploited the marginal food supply and also thereby avoided the larger predators. Legs would give it an advantage over the ordinary minnow, and the loss of these legs as an adult would remove the handicap of their presence. The larvae might take to spending more and more time on or near land, and eventually get to the point where they become capable of reproduction while retaining their larval form (Paedogenesis). Perhaps one might even propose a *burrowing* larva. It is an entertaining game, and any number, it seems, can play.

In the opinion of this writer, an attempt to press evolutionary thought to its logical conclusion is in reality a *reductio ad absurdum* and cannot result in anything other than paradoxes, riddles, and enigmas. When we survey the wonderful and variegated patterns of living creation, we behold an almost unlimited display of great virtuosity expressed in a great number of variations on a limited number of basic themes. This view of the living universe is more consistent with the facts than the views of the evolutionist.

Appendix

The Westoll Hypothesis

The basic argument of Westoll is as follows: Inasmuch as Rhipidistia primitively possess only pre-axial radii (later, postaxial radii are thought to be neomorphic), and the pre-axial aspect of the fin is directed ventrally in them, an inward turning of the entire limb towards the body axis would cause several of these radii to roughly parallel the median elements. Westoll feels that:

A. The most proximal radius became the radius of tetrapods.

B. In its consequent enlargement it interfered with, and suppressed in a manner of speaking, the second radial element.

To shorten an otherwise involved discussion, Westoll believes that he can homologize the structures of the labyrinthodont forelimb with the above-considered rhipidistian structures as presented below in the following table:

Rhipidistian fin
1. Median elements
2. "Postaxial process" of median elements
3. Radial elements
4. No equivalent

Labyrinthodont limb
1. Ulna, intermedium, distal, and proximal axial centralia
2. Ulecranon, postocentralia
3. Radius, precentrale, radiale
4. Supposedly neomorphic phalangeal structures (formed as heterotopic bones in the fin membrane?)

NOTES AND REFERENCES

1. G. A. Kerkut, *Implications of Evolution* (Pergamon Press, 1960).
2. T. H. Eaton and Peggy L. Stewart, "A New Order of Fishlike Amphibia from the Pennsylvanian of Kansas," Univ. of Kansas Publs. (1960), 12: 217-240.
3. The hypothesis here advanced was first presented by T. S. Westoll, and is discussed in somewhat more detail in the appendix to this paper. The interested reader is referred to Westoll's original paper, "The Origin of the Primitive Tetrapod Limb," *Proc. Roy. Soc. Lond.* B (1943), 131:373-393.
4. G. L. Orton, "Original Adaptive Significance of the Tetrapod Limb," *Science* (1954), 120:1042-1043.
5. D. W. Ewer, "Tetrapod Limb," *Science* (1955), 122:467-468.
6. Gordon Gunter, "Origin of the Tetrapod Limb," *Science* (1956), 123: 495-496.
7. C. J. Goin and O. B. Goin, "Further Comments on the Origin of the Tetrapods," *Evolution* (1956), 10:440-441.
8. R. F. Inger, "Ecological Aspects of the Origin of the Tetrapods," *Evolution* (1957), 11:373-376.
9. A. S. Romer, "Tetrapod Limbs and Early Tetrapod Life," *Evolution* (1958), 12:365-369.
10. F. E. Warburton and N. S. Denman, "Larval Competition and the Origin of Tetrapods," *Evolution* (1961), 15:566.

XXI

HOMOLOGY, ANALOGY, AND CREATIVE COMPONENTS IN PLANTS

GEORGE F. HOWE

Evolutionary theory assumes that biological likeness necessarily implies kinship. Yet brothers sometimes differ more from each other than from unrelated men. Some particular cases of similarity do indeed indicate relatedness such as the blue-eyed children found in a human family from blue-eyed parents. These limited illustrations, however, give us no reason to assume that similarities between the kinds of plants and animals must point toward organic descent. Although likeness *may* derive from kinship, it can likewise stem from the activity of a common originator or creator. Various models of automobiles produced by the same firm resemble each other. Similarity here indicates a common creator rather than a common ancestry. Likewise, parallelism between models of Chrysler, General Motors, and Ford indicates that all three manufacturers respond to customer needs by use of the same designs and materials.

Evolutionary biologists have decided that some similarities are meaningful and indicate close relationship (homology), while others do not (analogy). For example, the underlying bony similarities between man's fingers and a bat's wing bones are thought to demonstrate a very close relationship. But the superficial similarity between an insect wing and a bat wing is assumed to illustrate evolutionary convergence (analogy) between widely different groups. Such an arbitrary choice between the "true" similarities and "apparent" ones is open to question since it rests partially on the subjective bias of the investigator. If evolutionists are so certain that analogy is a "false teacher" when it comes to demostrating phylogeny, perhaps much of what is called homology is really analogical. Some of the so-called analogous similarities are just as striking and close as others that are classed as homologies.

Biblical creation of distinct and non-related "kinds" is a scientific model in which the artificial distinction between homology and analogy disappear. All homologous and analogous resemblances are accordingly attributable to what could be called "creative interchange of components." In the field of automobile manufacturing such widespread interchangeability is clear evidence for design. Distribution of similar tissues, organs, and organ systems throughout widely diverse plant forms likewise speaks for the creation of distinct kinds. There is no need, then, to postulate great evolutionary divergences followed by incredible convergences. Only one postulate is essential to the creation system—the originating God. He worked by obvious outline (homology) but integrated various patterns in the distinct kinds as He chose (analogy). A catalog of analogous similarities in plants will demonstrate the great faith required to attribute all such parallelism to chance evolutionary convergence.

Parallelisms in Bacteria

Bacteria of the order of Myxobacterales have a life cycle that is plainly similar to that of the slime molds (Myxomycophyta—members of an entirely different botanical division). In both groups there is a swarming amoeboid stage followed by formation of a fruiting body which produces spore-like reproductive cells.

Other bacteria (such as Streptomycetaceae and the Actinoplanaceae) have a tubular shape (hypha) that resembles the hyphal strands of true molds. Likewise the reproductive spores and spore cases (sporangia) formed by these bacteria are similar to those of the fungi.

The "trichome" or thread-like colony of the Caryophanales bacteria clearly parallels the pattern of the blue-green algae (e.g., *Oscillatoria* sp.). The Beggiatoals (a sulfur metabolizing bacterial group) closely resemble the blue-green algae in their colony structure also.

Parallelisms in Fungi

The common bread mold reproduces across a tube that unites two parent strands. This process emulates the conjugation between cells of *Spirogyra* (green alga) although exact nuclear details vary.

The large egg enclosed in the oögonium (egg sac) and the male nuclei enclosed in a smaller tubular antheridium (sperm sac) in the Peronosporales order of the Phycomycetes fungi closely approximates the reproduction by oögonium and antheridium in the golden-brown alga *Vaucheria* sp.

Some fungi (mycorrhizae) invade the roots of other plants and thereby enhance their nutrient absorption and growth. At the same time the fungus supposedly receives food and shelter from the root. Many distant groups show such a mutualistic union between fungus and green plant. It occurs in the gametophytes of certain lycopods, the root of the fern *Ophioglossum*, and in the roots of many woody seed plants. In fact, mycorrhizae are coming to be recognized as very important and extensive in the plant world.

Parallelisms in Algae

It has been assumed that phloem sieve tubes (food conducting elements) are the evolutionary hallmark of vascular plants. It is interesting to discover that there is a phloem-like tissue in the stipes of brown algae and in certain mosses.[2] Since most evolutionists regard brown algae, mosses, and vascular plants as distant branches of the evolutionary tree, it must be assumed that phloem tubes arose independently at least three times. To attribute such an amazing amount of parallel structure to evolutionary convergence demands a stretching of the scientific imagination.

Algae of the diatom group and unicellular Radiolarian animal types independently show complex silicon wall formation. Certain separate groups of multicellular vascular plants also incorporate silicon into walls of the outer cells—*Equisetum*, ferns, grasses, Cyperaceae, palms, and some dicot flowering plants. Has the ability to build glass cell walls been the product of chance evolution in more than three different instances?

Parallel Life Cycle Patterns

Some plants have two distinct generations that alternate with each other. One generation (gametophyte) has haploid cells and bears gametes that unite forming a diploid zygote. The other generation which results from the growth of the zygote (sporophyte) is diploid and eventually produces reproductive spores. It is sometimes argued that an alternation of two equal generations in one life cycle is a "primitive" evolutionary characteristic in plants. It is also argued that the dominance of the spore-bearing generation over the gametophyte is a more "advanced" status. This assumption is made because the sporophyte generally is larger in "higher plants." There is likewise a decreasing size of the gametophyte generations in ascending representatives of the supposed evolutionary series (algae, mosses, ferns, pines, etc.). Within the same group (green algae), however, there is a full spectrum of typical life cycles with no indication of which type is most "primitive." Some have a gamete-forming generation only—*Spirogyra* sp. Other green algae have only one generation, but it is the diploid sporophyte—*Cladophora* sp. Still others exist with a complete alternation of independent sporophyte and gametophyte generations—*Cladophora* sp.[4] In the brown alga *Fucus* the gametophytic generation is greatly reduced. Haploid spores are retained in the parent sporophyte and directly produce gametes. Such reduction and retention of the gametophyte generation clearly resembles the life cycle of the flowering seed plants. Such a scramble of supposedly primitive and advanced life cycle patterns within the algae themselves is further evidence in support of creation with interchangeable systems.

Evolutionary Problems with Bryophytes (Mosses, Liverworts, Hornworts)

It is frequently assumed that the delicate leafy-liverworts arose from a leafless flat thalloid liverwort like *Marchantia*. But it is also assumed that the most advanced sporophyte among bryophytes is the type found in the hornworts. This complex cylindrical stalk has growing tissue which continually produces new spores from below. In the hornworts the most advanced sporophyte grows out of a typically primitive thalloid gametophyte—this of course presents a great problem to any theory of evolution.

Parallelism in Vascular Plants

All plants which have water conducting tissues (xylem) and food conducting tissues (phloem) can be classed as "vascular plants." Some authorities, however, believe that the category is artificial and that there are several distinct groups of vascular plants that have arisen independently from the algae by parallel evolution. Within paragraphs that follow, convergences and parallelisms between the different kinds of vessel-bearing plants will be considered.

Most vascular plants grow in length as the rapidly dividing regions at the tips of stems and roots form new cells. Some vascular plants can grow wider as cambial growth layers produce whole new sheets of cells around the entire girth of the stem. Such growth in width is called "secondary growth." The following lists demonstrate the widespread distribution of secondary growth in a few groups that are otherwise quite distinct:

(a) *Groups Showing Secondary or Woody Stem Tissues:*
1. Anomalous fossil Pentoxylaceae[5]
2. Fossil Lycophyta (Lepidodendrales and Sigillaricaceae[6]
3. Some living Lycophyta (Isaetaceae—quillworts)
4. Some fossil Sphenophyta (Calamites)[7]
5. Some fossil ferns (Zygopteridaceae)[8]
6. Some fossil Gymnospermae (Cordaitales, Voltziacea)[9]
7. Living Gymnospermae (Coniferales)
8. Living Angiospermae (Dicotyledonae)

(b) *Groups Showing Secondary Bark:*
1. Fossil Lycophyta (Lepidodendrales, Pleuromeiaceae of Isoetales)[10]
2. Fossil Sphenophyta (Sphenophyllales and Calamites)[11]
3. Fossil Gymnospermae (Cordaitales)[12]
4. Living Gymnospermae (Coniferales generally)
5. Living Angiospermae (Dicotyledonae generally)

The term "stele" is applied to the total mass of xylem and phloem tissue in a plant stem. The pattern and arrangement of xylem in relation to phloem varies and several stele patterns exist. In a "protostele" a central solid mass of xylem tissue is surrounded in some fashion by the phloem regions (see Diagram 1). If, however, the center of the stem is composed of soft-walled non-xylem cells (pith) with the xylem and phloem arranged around this central region, the stele is classed as a "siphonostele." Various subcategories of siphonosteles exist. If the xylem and phloem tissue are arranged in discrete parallel bundles in a peripheral ring (with the phloem cells outside the xylem) or in a cylinder with phloem outside, the stem is called an "ectophloic siphonostele." If the phloem of each vascular bundle lines both the inside and the outside of the xylem regions of the bundle or cylinder, the stele is classed as an "amphiphloic siphonostele." If there is more than one ring of vascular bundles (many sets of bundle rings or cylinders) the stem is a polycyclic siphonostele. Since protosteles are frequently encountered in the simpler fossil vascular plants, and since various siphonostelic types are common in gymnosperms and dicot angiosperm flowering plant stems, it is generally postulated that steles with a pith probably evolved from the solid protostelic stem type. This theory leads to the preposterous conclusion that carrot stems (which are siphonostelic) may be more "advanced" than carrot roots (which are protostelic). It also makes the improbable assertion that various siphonosteles evolved from protosteles not once, but several times in different parallel plant lines.

Some plant groups previously judged to be "primitive" in the light of evolution theory show wide and diverse stele arrangements. In the Selaginella family (little club mosses), for example, several stele patterns are known: protosteles, siphonosteles, and polycyclic siphonosteles. The polycyclic siphonosteles of the Selaginellaceae are quite complex. There may be as many as 16 different stele cylinders in one particular cross sectional region of the stem.[13]

A study of different vascular plant groups shows that the various stele types are present throughout most of the categories with no indication of which arrangement is actually "ancestral." The following documented lists will illustrate the wide distribution of stele types regardless of supposed "phylogenetic" or evolutionary family trees.

(a) *Groups with Prostelic Members:*
1. Fossil Psilophyta (*Rhynia*)[14]
2. Living Psilophyta (*Psilotum*)[15]
3. Living Lycophyta (*Lycopodium phlegmaria* "ground pine" in which the stele resembles that of flowering plant root)[16]
4. Fossil tree-like Lycophyta (Bothrodendraceae—smaller stems protostelic, larger siphonostelic)[17]
5. Fossil Sphenophyta (Calamites—roots protostelic, but stem siphonostelic)[18]
6. Living Sphenophyta (*Equisetum*—roots protostelic, stem siphonostelic)[19]
7. Fossil Filicinae (ferns) (Protopteridales and Coenopteridales)[20]
8. Living Filicinae (many fern groups—Marattiales, Osmundaceae, Matoniaceae, Dipteridaceae, Cyatheaceae, and *Ophioglossum* roots and lower stem—upper stem siphonostelic)[21]
9. Fossil Gymnospermae (Cordaitales—roots protostelic, stem siphonostelic)[22]
10. Living Gymnospermae (roots generally, while stems are siphonostelic)
11. Fossil and living Angiospermae (Dicotyledonae) (roots, while stems are generally siphonosteles)

Likewise, the wide distribution of siphonosteles in nearly all the vascular plant categories means that there is no basis for the statement that siphonosteles are necessarily more "advanced."

Homology, Analogy, and Creative Components in Plants 249

(b) *Groups with Siphonostelic Members:*
1. Living Psilophyta (*Tmesipteris tannensis*)[23]
2. Fossil Lycophyta (Bothrodendraceae—larger stems siphonostelic, smaller ones protostelic)[24]
3. Fossil Sphenophyta (Calamites—stems siphonostelic, roots protostelic—Calamophyton)[25]
4. Living Sphenophyta (*Equisetum* or horsetail)—stems siphonostelic, roots protostelic)[26]
5. Living Filicinae (ferns—stems frequently siphonostelic, roots or lower stems protostelic—*Ophioglossum*, Marattiales, Osmundaceae, Cycatheaceae, Polypodiaceae, etc.)[27]
6. Fossil Gymnospermae (Cordaitales, Voltziaceae)[28]
7. Living Gymnospermae (stems generally)
8. Living Angiospermae (Dicotyledonae—stems generally)

(c) *Groups with Ectophloic Siphonostelic Members:*
1. Living Filicinae (such ferns as *Schizaeae molocceana* and *Ophioglossum* sp.) [29]
2. Living Gymnospermae (stems generally)
3. Living Angiospermae (Dicotyledonae—stems generally)

(d) *Groups with Amphiphloic Siphonostelic Members:*
1. Living Filicinae (ferns—species of *Marsilea, Matonia, Dipteria, Cibotium, Pteris, Lindsaya, Polypodium, Gleichenia, Jamesonia,* and *Loxsonia*)[30]
2. Living Angiospermae (Dicotyledonae—Curcurbitaceae or Cucumber family)

(e) *Groups with Polycyclic Siphonostelic Members:*
1. Living Lycophyta (Selaginellaceae)[31]
2. Fossil Pteridospermales (seed ferns—Medullosaceae)[32]
3. Anomalous fossil group Pentoxylales[33]
4. Fossil Filicinae (Cladoxylaceae)[34]
5. Living Filicinae (ferns—Matoniaceae and Polypodiaceae)[35]

Within ferns, lycopods, sphenophytes, gymnosperms, and angiosperms are protosteles and all sorts of siphonosteles. How much convergence will be permitted before neo-Darwinianism is considered inadequate as a working model in origin studies? Far from being guides to evolutionary family trees, the stele types appear to be components which the Creator used in various scattered segments of His creative outline.

Origin of Vascular Elements

Much evolutionary discussion has centered upon the supposed origin of the various water conducting elements in the xylem. Briefly, there are two distinct water conducting units in the xylem—the tracheid, and the vessel member. Tracheids are cells that elongate and become spindle shaped. During their differentiation, tracheid cell walls are thickened excepting in small patches (pits) which do not become covered with cellulose and lignin (the thickening chemicals). Usually a number of such pits connect one tracheid to each neighboring tracheid. When the cell matures, it usually dies, and thus a hollow water-containing element results. Sometimes tracheids have a scalariform (ladder-shaped), spiral, or ringed pattern of wall thickening rather than the pitted pattern. Vessel members, on the other hand, elongate but eventually lose the top and bottom end walls. This means that a vertical column of vessel member cells will eventually lose the end walls that separate them (or else the end walls become extensively perforated) and a hollow, water-conducting vessel many cells in length results because the protoplast of each cell dies. Such multi-cellular vessels may have cell walls thickened in a pitted, scalariform, spiral, or ringed pattern. Katherine Esau[36] and others express the belief that the tracheid is the most primitive xylem element and that xylem vessels have evolved from tracheids of ancestors. Such a decision, however, is not necessarily confirmed by comparative plant anatomy. Vessels occur independently in five separate plant groups as Katherine Esau points out: (1) gymnosperm Gnetales (*Ephedra*), (2) most dicot angiosperm, (3) monocot angiosperm, (4) in certain ferns (*Pteridium aquilinum*, and roots of *Nephrodium felix-mas*)[37] and (5) in the genus *Selaginella* of the Lycophyta. She interprets these results as follows: "Vessels arose independently, through parallel evolution, in the five groups of plants named above. . . ."[38] It would tax the idea of natural selection to produce vessels from tracheids in just one evolutionary line during the supposed ages. To suggest that vessels arose five times by chance is not a scientific deduction from data but an evolutionary afterthought. Evidently God used whichever types of steles or xylem were most likely to fill the needs of the particular plant He was creating.

Frost, Bailey, Cheadle, and others have performed extensive statis-

Homology, Analogy, and Creative Components in Plants

tical examinations of the xylem in various stems.[39] They believe that the anatomical correlations of wood overwhelmingly support the evolution hypothesis. A compelling alternative view would suggest that the formation of various xylem and phloem elements is controlled by physiological laws within genetic limits originally established by the Creator.

Parallelism in Guard Cells

Certain paired cylindrical cells in the epidermis of various plants (guard cells) change shape by swelling and thus create a pore (stomate) between them. Gases can readily diffuse through this open portal. Since guard cell pairs are found in such divergent groups as moss sporophytes, hornwort sporophytes, fossil Psilophytes, *Psilotum, Tmesipteris, Lycopodium, Selaginella, Equisetum,* ferns, gymnosperms, and flowering plants, evolutionists must again plead that such mechanisms arose by chance several times.

The upper surface of a *Marchantia* (flat or "thalloid" liverwort) thallus is composed of polygonal air chambers whose walls and ceiling are composed of green cells. In the top of each chamber there is a pore surrounded by several cells in concentric rings.[40] The pore bears a striking superficial resemblance to the guard cell complex found in other plants. In some liverwort genera the pore has been found to open and close due to imbibitional changes in walls of nearby cells.[41] Such parallelism fits the biblical creation view.

Two different kinds of guard cells have a scattered distribution in vascular plants. In some plants a single mother cell divides, yielding two guard cells. Certain nearby epidermal cells then become the subsidiary cells. (Subsidiary cells are oriented epidermal cells surrounding the guard cell apparatus.) Such a stomatal type is called "haplocheilic." Haplocheilic stomates occur in these groups: Nilssoniales (Cycads), Cycadales, Pteridospermales, Coniferales, *Ginkgo, Ephedra,* and some angiosperms. In other plants, however, one mother cell divides twice yielding three cells. The middle cell then divides, forming two guard cells and the other cells then form the subsidiary cells—the whole unit having come from just one mother cell. Such stomates are called "syndetocheilic" and are found in the Bennettitales, Pentoxylales, Cycadeoidales, *Gnetum, Welwitschia,* and some angiosperms.[42] It appears that the stomatal apparatus is likewise a widely distributed creation component. Stomates in *Lycopodium phlegmaria* "have been shown to be identical in structure with those of certain angiosperms."[43]

The Problem of Pentoxylales

If there ever existed a vascular plant group that strained the theory of evolutionary convergence, it is the Pentoxylales. Delevoryas states that their stems are like coniferous gymnosperms, yet they are polystelic like the seed ferns. They have leaves like cycads, but their stems resemble those of *Ginkgo*. Their microspore structures are unlike any others.[44]

Other Anatomical Parallelisms

Endodermis.—Since an endodermis is characteristically present in many of the simpler vascular plants and in angiosperm roots, but not in angiosperm stems generally, some investigators have suggested that the presence of an endodermis is a "primitive" condition. However, some Psilophyta such as *Rhynia*[45] and *Tmesipteris tannensis* (which evolutionists call "primitive") must then be classed as "advanced" because they lack an endodermis in their aerial branches. Some herbaceous dicotyledonous angiosperms have an endodermis in the stem (*Trophaeolum majus*—nasturtium) and are thus "primitive" despite their complex and otherwise advanced floral anatomy.

Latex vessels.—Another fascinating situation that challenges evolutionary theories is the distribution of latex vessels (lactifers) in various flowering plants. Latex tubes form in two or three distinct and different modes. Sometimes longitudinal chains of cells lose their end walls, yielding so-called "lactiferous vessels." In other plant forms single cells grow and develop into much branched tubes. The single cell thus keeps pace with the growing seedling and the latex tube thus formed is actually a "lactiferous cell." These and other latex vessel types occur scattered in widely different plant families.[46]

Stem succulence.—Some plants manifest greatly thickened stems which contain much water. It would be difficult to suggest the steps by which just one plant family might evolve succulent members. Then when it is seen that several different families such as the Cactaceae, Euphorbiaceae, and the Asclepiadaceae have parallel or convergent types with succulent stems, one is tempted to postulate that there has been definite planning and proportioning. There is just such a direct convergence between the cactus *Astrophytum asteras* and the euphorbiaceous plant *Euphorbia obeasa* (both having a ribbed, balloon-shaped succulent stem). An outside observer would be tempted to entertain the idea that God decided to create such succulent types along entirely different family lines. Accordingly He created various plants according to their kinds and formed succulent members in various segments of the creation outline.

Parallelisms in External Shape or Function

"Leaves."—Some plants that have no leaves as such have either petioles (*Acacia melanoxylon*) or whole side shoots (cladophylls of *Ruscus* spp.) that are flat and act as "leaves." Thus leaflike structures are produced in several distinct anatomical patterns.

"Cones."—An apparent parallelism exists between the flower clusters (catkins) of betulaceous trees (birch, alder) and the cones of Redwood trees. They are members of entirely different classes—Angiospermae and Gymnospermae respectively—yet they both bear their seeds in woody "cones." In *Sequoia* the seeds are borne nakedly on scales of a woody cone (Figure 1). In *Alnus* (alder), pistils are borne on a separate female stalk. Because the female flowers lack both sepals and true petals and because the catkins bear the nutlets between persistent woody scales,[47] the female catkin bears a resemblance to the female cone of *Sequoia* (Figure 1). There are certain differences of course—the seeds of alder cones are housed in a pistil or ovary whereas those of *Sequoia* rest nakedly on the cone scales. But the apparent similarity that exists is striking and not easily explained by neo-Darwinianism.

"Fruit."—The *Ginkgo* tree bears a reproductive organ which outwardly resembles the true drupe fruits of the cherry tree, but which is not really a fruit but simply a seed with one fleshy seed wall. The cherry fruit (Angiospermae) is an entire ripened ovary with the seed deeply encased in an outer fleshy fruit wall and an inner bony "pit." This is another example of two distinct groups with unbelievably similar organs.

Parallelism of Nuclear Disintegration in Female Gamete and/or Spore Formation

In mammals three out of four sets of meiotic female chromosomes are shunted into various polar bodies, and only one functional egg is generally formed. In *Ascaris* worms, a similar production of an egg and polar bodies occurs. In flowering plants three out of four sets of meiotic chromosomes disintegrate in the reduction division of the megaspore mother cell and only one functional megaspore eventually arises. By repeated nuclear division this functional spore gives rise to the egg inside an embryo sac. In the megasporangium (female spore case) of *Selaginella* (Lycophyta) many megaspore mother cells begin to develop, but all except one of these disintegrate. The one functional megaspore mother cell is nourished in part by the fluid resulting from the degeneration of the others.[48] In the Coniferales (e.g., pine) one megaspore mother cell forms in the young seed or ovule. This cell undergoes meiosis, yielding four megaspores. Here, too, three out of the four chromosomal sets eventually disintegrate. Such amazing parallelism in the development of female gametes, spores, or spore mother cells suggests that there has been the creative repetition of a common feature throughout extremely different forms.

Parallelism Between Beefwood and Horsetail Plants

A final and arresting morphological similarity concerns the genus of beefwood trees (*Casuarina*). By virtue of its reproductive structures, *Casuarina* is a dicotyledonous flowering plant genus. Female flowers are borne on short dense heads that eventually have the appearance of "cones." Male flowers are borne in slender spikes. *Casuarina stricta* Dry. is therefore a flowering tree of some 10-30 feet in height with drooping branches. Figures 2 and 3 further demonstrate that the branching pattern and the detailed external appearance of the young *Casuarina* stem bears an amazing resemblance to stems of *Equisetum telematei* Ehrh. var *braunii* (Milde) Milde-giant horsetail. The stems of the species *Casuarina equisetifolia* bear an even closer resemblance to *Equisetum* stems in certain aspects.[49] (See Figure 4.) Figures 5a and 5b show photomicrographs demonstrating that the two stems are not entirely similar internally. They both have sclerenchyma patches at the margin, but the placement of vascular tissues and the chlorenchyma (darker-colored patches of green cells) is somewhat different. They also differ in that *Casuarina* alone is perennial and later forms layers of secondary wood. The main stems of *Equisetum* are hollow, while those of *C. stricta* are solid. The side branches or "verticils" of *E. talmateia* var. *braunii* are solid when very young, like the branches of *C. stricta*, however.

Despite the internal differences, one would hardly expect a greater degree of *external* morphological similarity between two plants within the same genus. It is a staggering thought then, to realize that these two plants must be placed on different phyla or plant divisions on the

Homology, Analogy, and Creative Components in Plants 255

Figure 1. Right, *Alnus rhombifolia* Nutt. female catkin. Left, *Sequoia sempervirens* Endl. female cone. Note similarities.

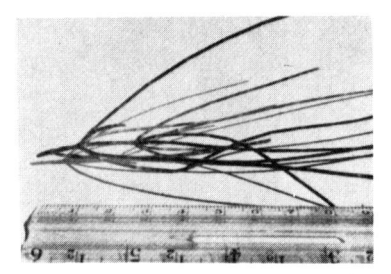

Figure 2. *Casuarina stricta* Dry. young stem. Compare with Figure 3.

Figure 3. *Equisetum telmateia* Ehrh. var braunii (Milde). Milde. young shoot. Compare with Figure 2.

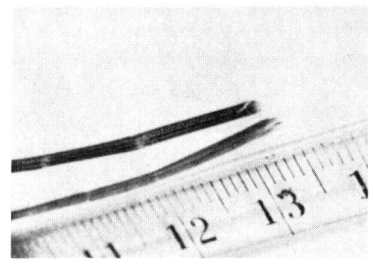

Figure 4. Bottom, *Equisetum telmateia* Ehrh. var braunii (milde) Milde. Closeup of young side shoot (verticil). Top, *Casuarina stricta* Dry. closeup of young stem. Note striking similarities.

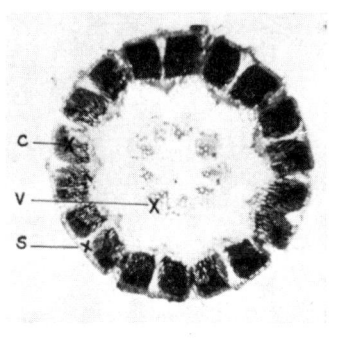

Figure 5a. Photomicrograph (about 80X) fresh cross section of *Casuarina stricta* Dry. young stem. "C"—chlorenchyma patch, "S"—sclerenchyma (thick walled) patch, "V"—vascular bundle.

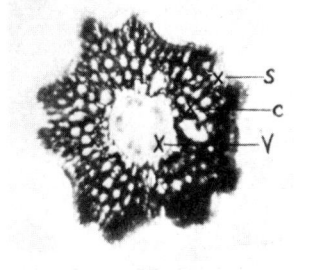

Figure 5b. Photomicrograph (about 80X) fresh cross section of *Equisetum telmateia* Ehrh. var braunii (milde) Milde young verticil. Note continuous chlorenchyma region "C," other symbols as in Figure 5.

basis of reproduction—*Equisetum* sp. in the Spenophyta (no seeds, only one kind of spore), *Casuarina* sp. in the dicotyledonous Angiospermae of the Pterophyta. Regarding *Casuarina*, Eames says that it *must* be classified as a dicot despite its affinities to *Ephedra* and the stems of *Equisetum*.[50] Such a similitude in appearance and structure of two obviously diverse plants fits very nicely with the idea of creative use of various patterns in different basic plant forms.

There are many unbelievable parallelisms in the botanical world. A study of the work of Berg[51] and of Short[52] will reveal numerous other examples of "convergence" in the animal world. It is presently postulated that the principle of creative interchange of components is a more adequate model in the explanation of these numerous parallelisms than is convergent evolution by neo-Darwinian mechanisms of chance mutation and natural selection.

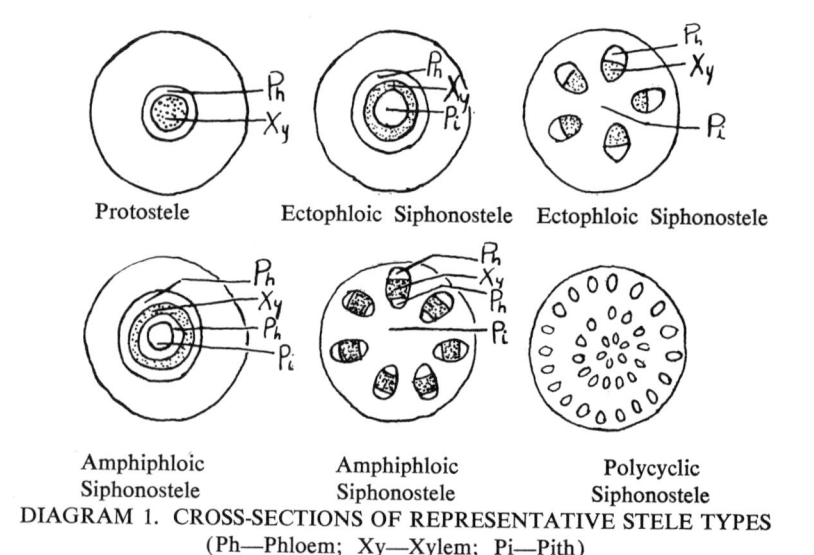

DIAGRAM 1. CROSS-SECTIONS OF REPRESENTATIVE STELE TYPES
(Ph—Phloem; Xy—Xylem; Pi—Pith)

Protostele / Ectophloic Siphonostele / Ectophloic Siphonostele / Amphiphloic Siphonostele / Amphiphloic Siphonostele / Polycyclic Siphonostele

NOTES AND REFERENCES

1. Paul A. Zimmerman (editor), chapter by John W. Klotz, *Darwin, Evolution and Creation* (St. Louis, Mo.: Concordia Publishing House, 1959), p. 109.
2. William C. Steere, editor, chapter by Vernon I. Cheadle, *Fifty Years of Botany* (Golden Jubilee volume of the Botanical Society of America [New York: McGraw-Hill Book Co., Inc., 1958]), p. 96.
3. Katherine Esau, *Plant Anatomy* (New York: John Wiley & Sons, Inc., 1953), p. 31; cf. R. D. Preston, editor, chapter by C. R. Metcalfe, *Advances in Botanical Research*, Vol. I (London and New York: Academic Press, 1963).
4. Theodore Delevoryas, *Morphology and Evolution of Fossil Plants* (New York: Holt, Rinehart and Winston, 1962), p. 363.
5. R. D. Preston, editor, chapter by Alan Wesley, *Advances in Botanical*

Homology, Analogy, and Creative Components in Plants   257

      Research, Vol. I (London and New York: Academic Press, 1963) p. 50.
6. Gilbert M. Smith, *Cryptogamic Botany*, Vol. II (New York: McGraw-Hill Book Co., Inc., 1955), pp. 187, 220.
7. *Ibid.*, p. 248.
8. *Ibid.*, p. 275.
9. Delevoryas, *op. cit.*, p. 151.
10. Smith, *op. cit.*, pp. 213, 222.
11. *Ibid.*, pp. 243, 249.
12. Delevoryas, *op. cit.*
13. Smith, *op. cit.*, p. 197.
14. *Ibid.*, p. 161.
15. *Ibid.*, p. 170.
16. *Ibid.*, p. 187.
17. *Ibid.*, p. 218.
18. *Ibid.*, p. 249.
19. *Ibid.*, p. 256.
20. *Ibid.*, pp. 272, 275.
21. *Ibid.*, p. 285ff.
22. Delevoryas, *op. cit.*, p. 152.
23. Smith, *op. cit.*, p. 170.
24. *Ibid.*, p. 218.
25. *Ibid.*, pp. 241, 248.
26. *Ibid.*, pp. 254, 255.
27. *Ibid.*, p. 285ff.
28. Delevoryas, *op. cit.*, p. 152.
29. Smith, *op. cit*, pp. 282-285, 314.
30. *Ibid.*, pp. 302, 328-329, 345; cf. A. C. Seward, *Fossil Plants*, Vol. II (New York and London: Hafner Publishing Co., 1963, reprint date), p. 312.
31. Smith, *op. cit.*, p. 197.
32. Preston, *op. cit.*, p. 32.
33. Delevoryas, *op. cit.*, p. 33.
34. Smith, *op. cit.*, p. 273.
35. *Ibid.*
36. Esau, *op. cit.*, p. 232.
37. Smith, *op. cit.*, p. 141; cf. Anna M. MacLeod and L. S. Cobley, editors, chapter by C. W. Wardlaw, *Contemporary Botanical Thought* (Chicago: Quadrangle Books, 1961).
38. Esau, *op. cit.*
39. Steere, *op. cit.*, p. 106.
40. Smith, *op. cit.*, pp. 47-78.
41. *Ibid.*
42. Delevoryas, *op. cit.*, 136.
43. Smith, *op. cit.*, p. 186.
44. Delevoryas, *op. cit.*, p. 145.
45. Smith, *op. cit.*, p. 161.
46. Esau, *op. cit.*, p. 307.
47. Howard E. McMinn and Evelyn Maino, *An Illustrated Manual of Pacific Coast Trees* (Berkeley, Calif.: University of California Press, 1935), p. 159.
48. Wilfred W. Robbins, T. Elliot Weier, and C. Ralph Stocking, *Botany*, Second Edition (New York: John Wiley & Sons, Inc., 1957), p.469.
49. McMinn, *et al., op. cit.*, p. 141.
50. Steere, *op. cit.*, chapter by Arthur J. Eames, pp. 610-611.
51. Leo S. Berg, *Nomogenesis or Evolution Determined by Law* (London: Constable & Co., Ltd., 1926).
52. A. Rendle Short, *Modern Discovery and the Bible* (London: The Inter-Varsity Fellowship of Evangelical Unions, 1943).

XXII

REMARKABLE ADAPTATIONS

E. V. SHUTE

Plants and animals display a superb series of tight adaptations, so remarkably integrated that a multitude of creatures can fill every environmental and ecological niche in sea, on land, or in the air and endure, more or less happily, generation after generation. The evolutionist says this process is the result of mutation and natural selection. The creationist does not discount these natural though negative forces but believes that the directing hand of God plays more than a permissive role in the glorious pageant of fitness to live. If He made living forms at all, presumably He would make them "good."

Are there any examples of adaptation so remarkable that they should snap the elastic credulity of those who believe that natural laws free of any interjection of a purposeful Providence are responsible for all life as we know it? Let me try to provide some samples of this sort for everyone's consideration. All are taken from recent scientific journals and therefore some may not yet have come to the attention of other readers. My preoccupation with this theme has found previous expression in a chapter in my book on evolution.[1]

Respiration

Burton[2] remarks that some fresh water turtles can submerge for as long as 15 hours because they have accessory breathing organs—in some a vascular lining of the throat, in others an adaptation of the rear end of the gut, these acting as "gills"!

Diving animals are highly adapted.[3] As soon as the nose of a seal submerges its heart beat falls to a tenth of the normal rate. Bradycardia develops in every diving creature, and in fishes removed from water! But the central blood pressure of the seal remains the same, as the pressure in the peripheral flipper drops to near zero. Muscle circulation is shut off as long as the seal is submerged, even in the mesenteric and renal arteries. Similarly, the metabolism of the body is damped down. The heart of the mudskipper in the mudhole in northern Australia is also very slow. Hibernating animals also show the same kind of metabolic deterioration and peripheral vasoconstriction with bradycardia.

Senses

The Australia Mallee fowl keeps its eggs at constant temperature by burying them under soil and debris. Its thermometer is its sensitive tongue. When it pecks the sand it can decide by this means whether to add or remove soil from its nest.[4]

Pacific salmon return to their own stream, even the same tributary, to spawn. How do they orient themselves at sea and recognize it without landmarks? It is due to odor imprinting.[5] An eel can detect as little as two or three molecules of a soluble chemical such as beta-phenylethyl alcohol! A minnow can differentiate between the smell of water from Georges Bank and samples from the Sargasso Sea! Holzman[6] points out that many fish have electro-receptors to detect obstacles. Each of these species emits waves of a characteristic frequency of 50 to 1600 cycles per second. Such a fish can thus detect the movement of a rubbed comb in front of an aquarium or respond to a magnet there—a sensitivity which will pick up even a change in field in the water of .0003 microvolt per millimeter, a fantastically small change. The rattlesnake has temperature receptors sensitive to a change of 10 to 11 calories (small) in 0.1 seconds, equalling a change in tissue temperature of 0.001 degrees Centigrade. Insects have amazingly accurate smell—and mechano-receptors. Thus the praying mantis integrates all its information about a fly and captures it within 50 milliseconds.

Thorpe and Griffin[7] found that owls were not only silent but ultrasonically quiet—unless they were very large. However, the Asiatic fishing owl, which feeds on fish and crustaceans, does not need such silence and is not so adapted. The wings of silent owls have a downy upper surface and fringes of feathers on the lead and trailing edges to act as silencers.

Plants

The red flowers of the lousewart, *Pedicularis densiflora,* have purple shades in coastal California, where they are pollinated by Anna hummingbirds with gorgets of the same shade. But in the Sierra Nevada, where pollination depends on rufus hummingbirds with orange-red gorgets, the flower is orange-red.[8] The flowers of some tropical trees visited by bats smell like bats. Male hymenoptera visiting the orchid *Ophrys* in the Mediterranean region find the flower is insect-like and are aroused to copulatory activity by the stimulus of its hairs, this activity leading to transfer of pollen. Tropical epiphytic orchids have the most intricate pollination systems, operable only by particular insects. Unfortunately for evolutionists, there is no high degree of correlation of floral "evolution" with the differentiation in these insect visitors. The orchid, *Coryanthes speciora*, attracts male bees by its fragrance. As the bee lands on its mesochile it fans its wings vigorously, eventually striking a drop of fluid hanging over its head (which had been secreted by glands at the base of the column). The drop dislodges the bee into the liquid-filled bucket formed by the epichile. The bee struggles but can escape only by pushing up past an anther with two pollinia attached to it. The flower has now lost its fragrance and the bee flies off—till next day the flower becomes fragrant again and bees return to cross-fertilize it. Yet this same bee species is involved in the cross-pollination of an entirely different orchid, *Gongora maculata*, with a very different mechanism—no change appears in the bee designed to fit the two different mechanisms! How could such a change have developed gradually? The females of these bees have other tastes, and waste no time on flowers because they lack chemoreceptive hairs on their tarsi.

The fossil record of the bats does not go back beyond the Palaeocene, and the flower- and fruit-visiting bats seem to have appeared too late to enter the New World tropics. Here, when the new flowers appeared, nectar-lapping bats were called for immediately from quite a different stock, the insectivorous micro-chiroptera. The tree, *Parkia,* is pantropical and is pollinated by bats everywhere with the same specialized adaptations everywhere—a real evolutionary problem since the plants were ready for the bats before the bats appeared! A similar problem is presented by the flowering Kapok tree, *Ceiba pentandra,* pollinated by bats in Africa and South America![9] The evolutionist here has to fall back on "lucky pre-adaptations" by either the flowers or the pollinating agents!

How does sap rise in tall trees,[10] where perhaps at the tip the sap pressure can run at −20 atmospheres? It seems incredible that water can flow upward in this way. It is done by combining capillarity with check-valved compartmentalization. The latter prevents a cut twig from letting air penetrate beyond the wounded area. What happens to northern trees in winter? Are they frozen or supercooled? It appears that nearly all free water in the xylem does freeze at about —6 to —10 C. There is a real puzzle here.

Ocean Fish

Some fish have been caught at 15,000 foot depths where the gas in their swim bladders must have exerted a pressure of more than 7,000 pounds per square inch to withstand sea pressure.[11] This gas is largely oxygen, unlike that found in the shallow swimmers. In some mid-ocean fishes, fat replaces gas in and about the swim-bladder, and thus constant volume is maintained under varying pressures by a material close to the density of water. Other fishes meet the pressure situation in the deep-sea by having lighter body parts. The cuttlefish has a large bone that serves for buoyancy. It is built up of thin lamellae and pillars forming chambers. This constitutes about 9.3 percent of the total volume of the fish and its density is only 0.6 that of water. The bone chambers hold varying amounts of gas and water. The fish uses this bone as a submarine uses buoyancy tanks, filling up with water or blowing water out with gas. A yellowish membrane over the rear of the cuttlebone by a complex arrangement sucks fluid from the bone into the bloodstream and so changes its osmotic pressure at various depths in the sea. The bone can withstand severe compression by the sea by altering the salinity of its fluid. The squid maintains its buoyancy by holding in its coelomic cavity a great deal of low density fluid containing an astonishing concentration of ammoia (9 gms. per liter). Unlike mammals, the squid excretes its nitrogen as ammonia rather than urea, and this is diffused into and trapped in the coelomic cavity. The squid can be almost independent of external water pressure and can dive more deeply than the cuttlefish, but its fluid sac is very bulky (200 percent of the rest of the cranchid squid). It is really a kind of bathyscaph.

The rhizopod protozoan *Arcella* (about 1 mm. in diameter), which is found in shallow freshwater, produces gas bubbles of oxygen (?) in its cytoplasm to control its buoyancy. A coastal foraminiferan, *Tretomphalus bulloides* (size 0.02 mm.), lives on the bottom until ready to release its flagellated gametes. Then it produces a large terminal gas chamber by means of which it floats on the top of the sea. A special gas gland secretes oxygen in the swim-bladders of deep sea fish, involving a *rete mirabile* with the longest capillaries known in nature, perhaps 50 times longer than the long capillaries of muscles! Some fish have a valved duct leading to the esophagus through which gas enters the swim-bladder. Others have a structure called the oval, which is surrounded by a ring of muscle and this controls the filling of the swim-bladder with gas.

Food

The jaws of the ant lion have deep grooves which act as syringes to inject digestive juice into its prey. As soon as its victim's body inside its chitinous covering is dissolved the juices are sucked up by the ant lion. The latter never needs to expel faecal material during its one to two years of life because no undigested material enters its bowel—which has no posterior outlet!

The bees' dance[12] is now regarded as a classic of adaptation. The honeybee talks to its mates in the hive with a round dance for near sources of nectar, but with a tail-wagging dance for sources 275 feet or more distant. It tells them the direction and distance more accurately than could any communication system but human speech. When the other bees seek the original source they go to it directly, ignoring other directions or nearby decoys. By means of a built-in chronometer they allow something for the movement of the sun through the sky in the interim. The language is genuinely innate and not learned, as von Frisch has proven. However, the Italian honeybee talks a little differently from the Austrian honeybee and confuses the latter with its instructions. Yet they are of the same species and interbreed. Their offspring are even more confused! The Indian honeybee talks the language of the European bees. The dwarf bee can dance only on a horizontal platform, however, and cannot transpose from sight to gravity. The dung beetle and many others can transpose from sight to gravity, although only the bees use this ability to speak to their fellows.

Symbiosis

The symbiosis of fungi and insects is often remarkable, as von Frisch points out.[13] The biscuit weevil, *Sitodrepa,* excretes its symbiotic yeast cells while laying, thus infecting its eggs as they exit from the rectum. The emerging larvae bite their shells and thus ingest some of this yeast. One kind of a leaf bug, *Coptosoma,* has bacterial symbionts which live in a mycetome communicating with the gut. When this insect lays its eggs batches of encapsulated bacteria are also expelled one at a time in between the eggs. As soon as the embryo opens its egg it pierces a capsule with its proboscis and sucks in the bacteria it needs! If it does not get them it usually dies before undergoing metamorphosis because of a lack of vitamin B_1. Similarly, other insects lacking vitamins live in symbiosis to get them. Or insects may lack nitrogen for the synthesis of what proteins they need, and require nitrogen-fixing micro-organisms for this, just as the roots of legumes do. Many insects contain three or more different symbionts in their mycetomes. Each passes out on the egg and is then allotted its special area in the mycetome of the young insect.

A typical frog egg[14] lies encased in gelatin that prevents jostling or overcrowding and is both unpalatable and slippery to predators. It acts like a tiny greenhouse to concentrate the sun's rays. Chinks between the spheres of jelly are taken up by unicellular plants and rotifers which are oxygen-liberating and so help the tadpoles to emerge in four to 15 days.

Small fish cleaning the mouths of big or predator fish present a rare problem.[15] In the Bahamas the Pederson shrimp (*Periclimenes pedersoni*) waits till passing fish call on it, stop nearby, and present any injured or troublesome part to the shrimp. The shrimp crawls aboard, inspects the client, even makes minor incisions which the client tolerates as it remains motionless. The fish even opens its gill covers seriatim to let the shrimp in to inspect them. Similarly it inspects the mouth (Figure 1). As was said, fish will line up for such inspection, even waiting for it when the shrimp has retired from work! The known cleaners include 26 species of fish, six shrimp, and Beebe's crab. The little senorita (*Oxyjulis californica*) cleans black sea bass, ocean sunfish, even the bat ray—both bony and cartilaginous fishes! Even distantly related species of cleaners may have analogous specialized cleaning structures—convergent evolution? Senoritas seem never to be eaten, although they enter the mouths of the kelp bass, which eats similar-sized fish. Some fish mimic them in color and conformation, even doing so to become predators! Shrimps clean the mouth of the moray eel—but do get eaten occasionally. All this suggests that nature exhibits much cooperation, rather than merely a bloody tooth-and-claw struggle for existence!

Immature pelagic octopods or devilfish (*Tremoctopus violaceus*) have suckers adapted to holding fragments of tentacles of the coelenterate *Physalia,* the Portuguese man-of-war, using their nematocysts[16] or stinging cells having a trigger-like mechanism discharging barbs and a fluid which paralyzes action of animals penetrated by the barb! These can render fish defensless with the sting. It is not known if the adult octopod retains this habit. This is a unique use of only parts of a coelenterate as weapons, and may imply the octopod's ability to know when these weapons need to be replaced! Just how the devilfish is able to activate or fire the stinging cells of such an unrelated creature as the Portuguese man-of-war is not too clear, especially since only a part of its tentacle is involved. And how by natural selection was this trick incorporated into the DNA system of the devilfish? The pickpocket type of dexterity required to steal enough tentacle fragments to cover eight rows of suckers would make even a "big-time" operator envious.

Reproduction

Nestless birds such as the murres lay pear-shaped eggs which cannot roll off the ledges and cliffs where they are laid. Other birds, like some of the sandpipers and killdeer, lay eggs on the ground, which hatch into youngsters which can run to safety as soon as they hatch and dry.

The female Indochina swift[17] at nesting time has glands under her tongue which begin to swell. She flies to a cave, presses her beak against the rock wall, thus expresses a crystal-clear fluid which she weaves back and forth on the rock wall. When it hardens it provides a glass-like nest for her eggs—and the source of bird's nest soup!

A malarial mosquito in Panama can lay its eggs through the tiniest holes in bamboo internodes by hovering outside the holes and shooting its eggs in with great force and accuracy.[18] A species in Ceylon that faces the same problem meets it by laying its eggs on one of its legs, then inserting the tiny leg into the tiny hole. The larvae of these mosquitoes must escape through these tiny holes, of course. It turns out that they are very persistent and can wriggle through almost any tiny aperture, unlike the larvae of other mosquitoes, being able even to penetrate absorbent cotton.

Locomotion

For the first few days after hatching the moorhen chick[19] cannot stand on its legs but gets about by using its legs and a long claw on each thumb—here is a feature shared with the hoatzin chick. It is a remarkable adaptation for a peculiar defect of locomotion and one shared with one very dissimilar bird which uses such a claw for climbing trees!

Attack and Defense

The giant electric ray[20] (*Torpedo nobiliania*) puts out pulses of 50 amperes at 50 to 60 volts, able to electrocute a large fish. The African catfish (*Malapterurus*) puts out up to 350 volts. The electric eel (*Electrophorus*) puts out more than 500 volts. The evolutionist is puzzled by such a "convergence" in unrelated families, among the "ancient" cartilagenous fish as well as more recent bony fish. Moreover, the electric organs are very differently arranged in the various fish possessing them. They may be longitudinal and constitute 40 percent of the fish's bulk—or be vertical columns mainly in the wings (as in the ray), or be a mantle under the skin of the whole body. Curiously, to the evolutionist, studies on the giant ray, the skate, a Southern Atlantic ray, and the bony fish *Astroscopus* found that the electroplaques in all are electrically inexcitable! Moreover, even the weakly electric fishes use their powers for guidance. Indeed, the African *Gymnarchus* can detect a potential gradient of about .03 microvolt per mm. It was once thought that stalked electroplaques were to be found only in the African fresh water families, but lately they were found in one of the American knife fishes! The firing mechanism in the brain differs in all types of fishes! In the rays and *Astroscopus* the skin near the trigger area has much lower electrical resistance than the rest of the skin. In the eel, where the organ can be a meter long, the synapse resistance is so arranged in a gradient that all the electroplaques are fired at the same time. The knife fishes discharge repetitively and have a pace-maker which excites the spinal motoneurones at a rate as high as 1500 pulses per second. Even warm-blooded animals show no such rate of continuous nerve activity. The electric skates remain a puzzle to evolutionists for their electric organs are in their long tails, are weak, and seem to have no obvious adaptive value. Elsewhere the picture is one of strange "convergence."

The mormyrid African fish *Gymnarchus niloticus*[21] has a *weak* electric organ in its tail which emits a continuous stream of discharges. Two other fish do this, too—another mormyrid and a small South American fresh water relative of the electric eel—far removed from the mormyrids. It uses these impulses to dodge objects in the water as small as 2 mm. in diameter, even when swimming backward! Skates, which are cartilaginous and not teleosts like the mormyrids and gymnotids, also have a weak electric organ in the tail. All swim rigidly in order not to upset their electrical field unduly. The skin of the mormyrid is made up of many layers of remarkably hexagonal platelike cells. Pores in the skin contain tubes leading to the electric sense organs. These tubes contain a jelly-like substance and widen at their central end into a capsule containing a group of specialized cells. In half these fishes the electric organ emits constant frequency pulses. In the other half of these species the rate varies with the fish's state of excitation. It is interesting to find both types of sensory systems in the two different families, one in South America and one in Africa!

The polydesmid millipede[22] (*Apheloria corrugata,* Wood) has paired glands in most body segments. Each of these has two compartments. In one is an undissociated cyanogenic compound and in the other a chemical factor able to trigger hydrogen cyanide production when needed—not before. At the instant of discharge, for example against ants, the contents of the two compartments mix, and cyanide is generated. Among millipedes this two-compartmented gland may be exclusive to the order *Polydesmida.* Other millipedes may use quinones and phenols similarly. These do not require chemical activation when discharged.

The Mexican bean beetle (*Apilachna verivestis* Mulsant) displays reflex bleeding when molested or handled,[23] always bleeding from the tibio-femoral leg joints, considerable loss of blood being tolerated. This blood drop is larger than the volume of the whole leg! The larvae of this species are densely spined on the top and sides; the spines are hollow and brittle, and bleed when broken. They too can tolerate much blood loss in this way. If ants get entangled in this blood they are immobilized for a few minutes. The adaptation is an eminently useful defense against ants.

Burton[24] calls attention to the purple emperor butterfly of England, which at every stage of its life closely resembles something else, either a gall, a slug, a young or an old leaf. He adds that this suggests intelligent design and makes the biologist think of many adaptations toward survival. But Burton adds that this species and many another showing such remarkable adaptations are often not successful in the world!

General Comment

It is possible to contend that all special adaptations have arisen in response to need and have developed gradually by natural selection. But there are certain adaptations which are so intricate and complex that it is impossible to imagine a single mutation having achieved so much and no half-way measure would have helped toward the end desired. We have given many examples of these. Then there are the even more wonderful synchronized and complex adaptations of flower and insect, or of two different families or orders, of which examples have also been given. The world of the parasite is one long instance of this. How could adaptations of such complex inter-action be achieved in one single step or in a series of steps? The snapdragon does not explain this, although we know that in the snapdragon genus, *Antirrhinum,* the usually two-lipped flower can become radially symmetrical by the mutation of a single gene. Whether the reverse occurs is unknown.[25]

Creation is a much more plausible explanation—the only one, indeed. These are all instances of lock and key or hand and glove adaptations. It is not enough to use any key, but only the right one. Then imagine the simultaneous development of a hand inside a glove inside a suit inside a submarine—which is approximately analogous to what we have in many of the more complex adaptations in nature!

Why the *remarkable perfection* of the dolphin's or bat's sonar or the rattlesnake's perception of heat or the moth's perception of odor? Less would have done quite well.

Figure. 1. Grouper fish (Epinephelide) and small fish cleaning off parasites.

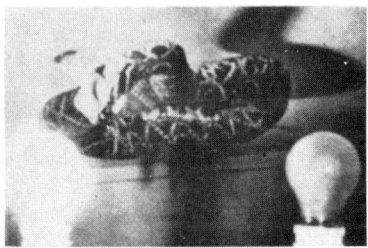

Figure 2. Blindfolded rattlesnack hits light bulb. Courtesy Life Magazine (April 28, 1958).

NOTES AND REFERENCES

1. E. V. Shute, *Flaws in the Theory of Evolution* (London, Canada: Temside Press, 1962).
2. M. Burton, *Illustrated London News,* March 19, 1960, p. 576.
3. P. F. Scholander, *Scientific American* (December 1963), p. 92.
4. *Illustrated London News,* January 31, 1959, p. 170.
5. A. D. Hasler, *Science* (1960), 132:785.
6. B. G. Holzman, *Science* (1960), 132:793.

7. W. W. Thorpe and D. R. Griffin, *Scientific American* (April 1962), p. 78.
8. H. G. Baker, *Science* (1963), 139:877.
9. *Ibid*.
10. P. F. Scholander, E. Hemmingsen, and W. Garey, *Science* (1961), 134:329.
11. E. J. Denton, *Endeavour* (1963), 22:3.
12. K. von Frische, *Scientific American* (November 1963), p. 110.
13. K. von Frische, *Triangle* (1960), 4:206.
14. *M.D. of Canada* (May 1960), p. 101.
15. C. Lembaugh, *Scientific American* (August 1961), p. 42.
16. E. C. Jones, *Science* (1963), 139:764.
17. J. George, *Audubon* Magazine (March, April 1961).
18. M. Burton, *Illustrated London News*, May 16, 1964, p. 786.
19. M. Burton, *Illustrated London News*, September 17, 1960, p. 484.
20. H. Grundfest, *Scientific American* (October 1960), p. 115.
21. H. W. Lissman, *Scientific American* (March 1963), p. 50.
22. T. Eisner, H. E. Eisner, J. J. Hurst, F. G. Kafatos, and J. Meinwald, *Science* (1963), 139:1218.
23. G. M. Happ and T. Eisner, *Science* (1961), 134:329.
24. M. Burton, *Illustrated London News*, December 1, 1962, p. 892.
25. Baker, *op. cit.*

XXIII

PLANNED INDUCTION OF COMMERCIALLY DESIRABLE VARIATION OF ROSES BY NEUTRON RADIATION

Walter E. Lammerts

Introduction

In March, 1961, the successful induction of a wide range of variations in rose plants grown from high energy neutron irradiated Queen Elizabeth rose buds was reported.[1] Among the variants, increase in petal number, elimination of the dominant and undesirable M or magenta factor, and dwarf types, were sufficiently frequent to make this technique seem worthwhile commercially. Frequently as a result of carefully planned cross-pollination hybrids are obtained which are desirable in every way except that they have only 15 to 20 petals and accordingly are not useful either as garden or as hot house varieties. When breeding for the very desirable currant red color, varieties having all the qualifications for commercial introduction are obtained but, unfortunately, are magenta red. The following experiments were made in hopes of demonstrating that when semi-double hybrids having the right variability potential are irradiated, commercially desirable varieties having increased petal number and good form may be obtained. Also, the possibility of eliminating the dominant magenta or M factor from otherwise desirable hybrids was investigated.

Material and Methods

Buds of H55059/16, a rose red hybrid of Queen Elizabeth x Red Delight having 14-18 very large petals, H56024/39, a hybrid of Queen Elizabeth x Red Delight having 15-20 medium large petals, H56022/9, a hybrid of Queen Elizabeth x Cavalier, a large fully double high centered magenta red, heterozygous for the very desirable currant red color, Pink Sensation, a double salmon pink hot house variety, the well-known floribunda Garnette and Queen Elizabeth for a comparison with the results of 1961 were used in the experiments. Fifty buds of each variety were cut from budsticks and placed in petri dishes on moist filter paper. Two petri dishes or 100 buds of

H56024/39 were used in the experiment, placing one on top of the other. This "piggyback" experiment was included to see if the same unusual decrease in radiation effect occurred in the upper dish furthest from target. The buds in these petri dishes were exposed to 14 MeV neutrons from a Cockcroft-Walton accelerator, August 9, 1961. These neutrons resulted from deuterons accelerated to 500 kev bombarding a tritium target. The petri dishes were placed two to four inches from the target in a basket type of holder. The total dosage in rads of the various petri dishes varied from 1870 rads on one side to 2710 rads on the opposite side of dish No. 1 down to 1020-1460 rads on dish No. 7, the top dish of the "piggyback" pair. Other dishes ranged from 1440-1890, 1720-1840, 2010-2200, 2080-2440, and 2180-2520 rads. The exposure lasted for about six hours, following which the buds were immediately budded into Rosa *multiflora* understock, August 9, 1961.

Acknowledgment

The author wishes to acknowledge the advice and help of Dr. Howard Tewes of the Lawrence Radiation Laboratory, Livermore, California, who irradiated the rose buds and calculated the dosage rates of each petri dish exposed to the neutron radiation.

Results

With the exception of the buds from the upper dish of the "piggyback" experiment, all the neutron irradiated buds were retarded and slow in starting. Only 8 of the 50 Garnette buds grew into plants. Other buds started growth but were not able to form shoots and soon died. This variety evidently is more sensitive than others to radiation. As the buds of all varieties began growth, they were very deformed in foliage shape and leaf appearance. As in the 1961 experiment, many became more normal by growth of axillary buds from the very deformed primary shoots. However, even these shoots were abnormal, having thick "strap" like sections of leaf tissue and leaves. Segments of heavily pigmented tissue and abnormally light green tissue were characteristic of these first shoots and leaves. By midsummer of 1962, however, most of the plants were superficially fairly normal in appearance. They exhibited as much variability in height and shape of plant, vigor, petal number, and color of flower as most populations of seedlings resulting from cross-pollination. The variation was not transgressive, however.

As in 1961, the buds from the petri dish above the one next to the target grew into plants which were typical of the hybrid H56024/39, except for one plant which had only 6 to 8 petals. Also, the buds were only retarded slightly as compared to those of the petri dish beneath. This differential result in the "piggyback" experiments continues to be puzzling since the total number of rads recorded for the upper dish were 1020-1460 as compared to 1870-2710 for the lower dish next to the target and 1440-1890 for one of the other dishes.

In the fall of 1962, the most vigorous plants were harvested, planted in 2 gallon rose-tainers, and placed in the hot house for closer observation and study. The results may best be summarized by variety.

H55059/6. Queen Elizabeth x Red Delight. This population of 20 plants selected from the 47 surviving plants showed more plant and flower variability than any other one. Leaves varied in shape from thin "straplike" ones (Figure 1) to very much thickened rugose ones (Figure 2). As shown in Figure 3, the leaf variability was great, affecting size of leaflets and stipules, thickness of midrib, size of marginal serrations, and color, some leaflets being very dark green and others much lighter green with greater development of anthocyanin pigment.

The variability in plant vigor and habit is shown in Figure 4. Selection 13, having a large dark green leaf and stem much greater in diameter (1½x) was studied with special interest since at first it seemed to be an exception to the general rule that all plants from the neutron irradiated buds showing observable variations from the normal were either less vigorous or partially sterile. Careful comparison under hot house conditions indicated that it also was significantly less vigorous. At first, after caning up, it grew fully as rapidly as H55059/6. However, it did not "break" as rapidly following flower production and so in a few months was about 2½ feet lower in height than H55059/6 which was then over 8 feet high. Also, it was almost completely sterile. Examination of the pollen indicated that only about two percent was viable. All of the other selections shown in Figure 4 were definitely weaker than normal, though the slender type 2 and 8 grew as rapidly at first. Several plants in this group had from 25 to 40 petals but were too weak to be worth testing.

Among the 20 plants, several were indistinguishable from normal and one was particularly intriguing from the commercial viewpoint.

It had 29-36 large petals instead of the usual 14-18 of T55059/6. The buds were long pointed and had a lovely regularly imbricate high centered form when one-quarter to one-half open. Comparison of the typical H55059/6 flower and this neutron radiation induced "high double" sport is shown in Figure 5.

Hot house testing shows that it buds true and also breaks fully as rapidly as the normal type. H55059/6 is more vigorous than the average hot house rose, so the slight reduction in vigor of this sport is not a handicap. Whether it will meet all of the other exacting requirements for a good hot house rose remains to be seen.

The significant fact is that we have demonstrated that a semi-double variety can be converted into a commercially desirable one as regards petal number and bud form. Incidentally, the color is very similar to H55059/6.

H56024/39. Queen Elizabeth x Red Delight. The plants from buds in the upper dish of the "piggyback" pair were not transplanted since they showed no variability. Twenty of the 44 plants from the lower dish showed great variability in habit of growth, leaf form, vigor, and petal number. Several plants had only 8-12 petals. All except one plant had flowers typical in color, and it was a light rose red. One plant had flowers only 2½ inches in diameter, with 50-60 small petals instead of the usual 4-4½ inch flower with 15-20 petals. Another had 36 petals and a vivid currant red color. The flower was smaller than H56024/39. As may be seen by reference to Figure 6, the same range of variation in leaf characteristics was found as in H55059/6. Though not clearly evident from the figures, one would never mistake a variant plant of H56024/39 for one of H55059/6.

H56022/9. Queen Elizabeth x Cavalier. Tyrian Purple-MMMm. Only a few of the plants observed in the field as having a bright currant red color instead of the usual magenta one were transplanted to rose-tainers in the fall of 1962. Considerable variation in color range was observed. Only one selection was sufficiently free of magenta to bud and observe more closely. In the winter of 1963-64, plants of this selection were again dug up and benched in the test hot house. It continued to be much more currant red in color and relatively free of magenta. However, when fully open, especially on the second day and thereafter, it still showed too much magenta to be worthwhile commercially.

Though complete success was not attained, enough improvement in color was effected to justify belief that a large scale neutron irradiation of varieties or selections having the magenta or M factor would result in complete inactivation of this undesirable dominant factor. The color resulting would, of course, depend on the recessive factors carried by the variety irradiated.

Pink Sensation. Sport of Pink Delight having more petals and a somewhat deeper pink color but showing magenta on outer surface of petals when bud opens.

Many of the surviving plants were so much weaker than normal as to be of no commercial value. At least six reversions to a red color identical to Red Delight occurred. Pink Sensation is a sport of Pink Delight, a salmon pink variety which frequently sports to Red Delight. Some of the variations showed less magenta coloration on the outer surface of the petals and so may be an improvement over Pink Sensation, which has too much of a magenta tone when in the one-quarter to one-half open bud stage. However, it is questionable if any of these selections are vigorous enough to be worth introducing. Some idea of the range in bud form of the variations obtained may be seen by reference to Figure 7. As with H55059/6 and H56024/39, a great range in leaf form and size occurred.

Garnette. A very popular, long-lasting floribunda hot house variety. Though unfortunately only 8 plants survived, each was very distinct from normal and one was a very interesting dwarf having flowers similar to Garnette but only about one inch in diameter. It was hoped that variations to pink scarlet or even white would have resulted, since these occur naturally and make up a large "family" of Garnette sports. However, all of the 8 plants were variations of the typical Garnette color, some showing less magenta than others. Five of the variations are shown in Figure 8.

Queen Elizabeth. The same range of variation was found in the 47 surviving plants from neutron irradiation as in Experiment I of the 1961 series of experiments. One interesting variation of a scarlet color may be worth introducing. Several almost white variations are being tested. But the leaves are also lighter green in color than Queen Elizabeth. Accordingly, it is doubtful if they would be popular, as the public usually associates pale green color with weak growth. Even though these variations are almost as vigorous as Queen Elizabeth, they would suffer from this usually well-grounded prejudice.

Discussion

As in 1961, these experiments have again demonstrated that neutron irradiation of buds cut from bud sticks and placed in petri dishes produce a remarkable range of variation. In discussing the 1961 results the observation was made that "success of a radiation experiment depends not only on dosage rate, but the variability potential of the hybrid or variety used." This relationship has been clearly demonstrated in the above series of experiments. Thus H55059/6 is a hybrid of Queen Elizabeth with Red Delight, and the 14-18 petals are very large ones. As indicated by previous experiments,[2] doubleness is dominant, but also quantitative in its inheritance. Red Delight is a sport of Pink Delight and has 25-30 large petals. Several neutron-induced variations had from 25-40 petals. One of these, as reported, was almost identical in every way to H55059/6 except that it had 29-36 petals and was only slightly less vigorous. It had a very lovely long bud, and opened to a high centered regularly imbricate flower. Evidently neutron radiation effected the desired result because H55059/6 was capable of variation to *both* increase in petal number and expression of this in large-sized *extra* petals.

By contrast, H56024/39, which has a flower only about one-half inch to one inch smaller in diameter than H55059/6, did not have the variability potential for increased number of large-sized petals. Although also a hybrid of Queen Elizabeth x Red Delight, it evidently did not carry factors for large petal size. Accordingly, the vivid currant red mutation with 36 petals was commercially undesirable because most of the extra petals were small.

It would seem, then, that in order to be successful in converting a semi-double hybrid into a commercially desirable one, at least one of the parents should be a fully double variety in which the extra petals, those from 10 on to the total of 35, are *large* size. Also, the semi-double hybrid selected for irradiation should have large petals and relatively few small petaloids which usually indicate that the extra petals which may result from mutation will be small also.

Though the experiment to eliminate the magenta or M factors was only partially successful, the great improvement in color indicates that the dominant M factor is rather easily inactivated. In the case of H56022/9, three M factors were involved, since genetically the hybrid was MMMm as regards this locus.[3] Obviously, rose red hybrids carrying only one M factor or solferino purples with two M factors would be more easily converted to currant red.

From the viewpoint of origin of varieties in the sense of truly unique and great ones such as Peace, Charlotte Armstrong, Herbert Hoover, Queen Elizabeth, and Fashion, mutations have little value. There are, of course, whole "families" of varieties such as the Garnette series of sports. Some of these such as the lovely light pink Carol Amling have sold in fairly large quantities, and the new currant red Mohican sport gives promise of much popularity. Also, as indicated previously, Pink Delight, a hybrid of Senator x Florex, sported to Red Delight, Aristocrat and Pink Sensation. Many other examples of such "families" of sports could be given. Better Times, a sport of Briarcliff, which sported from Columbia a hybrid of Ophelia x Mrs. George Sawyer, is the most successful hot house rose so far discovered. It sells in greater quantity than the combined total of all other varieties. However, the varieties in each of these "families" of sports are in general very similar to one another. Thus any variety which is a sport of Garnette can easily be recognized by anyone familiar with the parent variety.

This is definitely not the case, however, with varieties which are the result of hybridization. Thus, no one looking at Queen Elizabeth could ever guess it was a hybrid of Charlotte Armstrong x Floradora. This unique genotype is the result of a combination of genetic factors tracing back to at least five and probably six different original species. The "gene pool" of variation resulting from inter-specific hybridization of these original species is continually re-shuffled, so to speak, by each generation of rose breeders, and occasionally truly distinctive varieties are originated. Once this new varietal pattern of development is set up, mutations can only modify its expression, but can never really change it basically. By this I mean that mutated strains of Garnette or Queen Elizabeth are always distinctly recognizable as such. The mutations are not transgressive in the sense that they transform Garnette into a variety indistinguishable from, for example, a sport of Pink Bountiful, another rather successful hot house floribunda. Similarly, mutations of Queen Elizabeth do not transform it into a variety similar to Charlotte Armstrong or Floradora.

In terms of the pre-patterning theory, it would seem that mutations can only alter various phases of its expression, but the *pattern itself cannot be changed*. In terms of this theory, Queen Elizabeth is the expression of a definite pre-pattern. The expression of this pattern depends on the interaction of the environment and the DNA genetic code. Changes in the environment or mutations in the code can alter the expression of the Queen Elizabeth pattern but cannot basically change it.

It is understood that this concept reduces the role of mutations to a relatively minor one. The variability with which rose breeders, or indeed, any plant or animal breeder, works is traceable to an original diversity of either species or varieties existing naturally within a species. This diversity is the result of numerous patterns which depend for their physical expression on the environment and the genetic code.

Mutations generally are harmful because the complex genetic code was created to perfectly express the pre-pattern in a hospitable environment. Any derangement in either the environment or the code will result in an imperfectly formed expression of the pattern. As indicated in the discussion of the results of both this and the 1961 experiment, by far the greater majority of all mutations resulting from neutron irradiation are defective. Most of them are weaker, "break" less frequently, or are partially sterile. This is, of course, exactly what one would expect from consideration of the remarkably complex code system created to express the various patterns existing in the mind of God—patterns we recognize as species, varieties, and individuals.

Evolutionists recognize that most mutations are harmful. Thus Fraenkel-Conrat,[4] in discussing the genetic code of a virus, reports on 200 chemically induced mutants of the tobacco mosaic virus. One of them made the protein coat of the virus much more susceptible to digestion by an enzyme that removes amino acids from the carboxyl (COOH) end of a protein chain. This enzyme was able to digest or chop off the amino acid threonine at the end of a protein chain. The very first mutant studied by Fraenkel-Conrat and his group made the virus protein much more susceptible to digestion by the enzyme. As a result the enzyme was now able to clip three amino acids off the virus, thus rendering it distinctly less viable. Other RNA mutations render the RNA incapable of even forming the protein coat. Fraenkel-Conrat comments, "One can assume that the protein coat of the common strain of the virus as it evolved by natural selection is highly efficient, and that any mutation is likely to reduce the virus' ability."

This sort of reasoning inverts the logical deduction from the overwhelming burden of evidence that mutations tend to be harmful, hence cannot be useful in explaining the evolution *assumed*. Actually, our evolution-minded colleagues are now saying, "Yes, of course, most or possibly all mutations are harmful since natural selection has eliminated all except those most effectively integrated into the DNA code." Hence, *all* plants and animals *now* have the most perfect combinations of mutations, and it would be unreasonable to expect to find mutations increasing the viability or conferring any other advantage to the organism studied. This is actually saying that the course of evolution they postulate is now completed. One might well ask just when in the past was it incomplete? Presumably, according to orthodox paleobotanical theory, very disinctive flowering plants originated in the Miocene time. At least 11 are described as new by MacGinitie in his very excellent report on the Kilgore Flora.[5] Whether they originated somewhat earlier in the Eocene or late Cretaceous is not the question. Rather one might well ask "if geneticists had been living at that time, would they have concluded that evolution was complete since almost all mutations studied are harmful?" One could thus go back to the Devonian time and argue that because mutations of the then existing simple plants such as Psilophyton (actually probably Psilotum *nudum*) were harmful, natural selection had eliminated all except those most effectively integrated into the DNA code. In fact, Axelrod does essentially this when he tries to explain the survival of Psilotum as being due to slow evolving rates and calls them bradytelic types.[6]

Actually, this whole argument of our evolution-minded colleagues is very amusing. In essence they first say that all existing lines of evidence clearly prove that evolution has occurred and that all existing plant and animal species trace back to one, or at most, a few "primitive" forms. Then, in searching for a possible mechanism by which this presumed evolution has occurred, they find a source of variation in mutations. Natural selection is then assumed (since actually no one has demonstrated even the origin of a variety by it) as the effective mechanism for selecting the best of these mutations and assembling them into a new or distinct plant or animal. Once these assumptions are granted, they then say, "Well, of course we cannot demonstrate evolution as occurring since it has all been completed."

In essence, then, evolution is reduced to the same status as creation with DNA, mutation, and natural selection taking the place of God in presenting us with a *completed* product!

A little reflection should show that *if* evolution occurred by natural selection of mutations, it *should* be a continuing process. Surely this is not the most perfect of worlds, and plants and animals should be changing in their basic patterns of expression to meet the challenges of new environments. The fact that they change only within the limits of their variability potential and that most mutations are harmful should make evolution-minded scientists reconsider their basic assumptions. Do the various lines of evidence from an impartial study of nature conclusively point to evolution as the mechanism by which the remarkable diversity we see around us originated? As we have endeavored to show in various articles, many of us, competent in various fields of sciences, do not think so. Rather we see clear evidence for creative design, a past environment much better suited for the ideal expression of the various patterns of life, and a series of catastrophes[7] which have marred a world originally created perfect in every way.

Summary

1. Data are given which indicate that semi-double rose hybrids having only 14-18 petals may be converted into fully double ones having commercially desirable high centered regularly imbricate flowers by neutron irradiation of the buds cut from bud sticks and placed on wet filter paper in petri-dishes.

2. Elimination of the dominant M or magenta factor may easily be accomplished by neutron irradiation, thus allowing the desirable crimson or currant red factor to be expressed.

3. The importance of selecting hybrids having the right variability potential for effecting these changes is discussed.

4. Biologically, all of the mutations were defective variations from the pattern of development characteristic of the variety irradiated.

5. The interrelation of environment, pre-pattern, and mutation is discussed, and the observation made, that mutations obtained are not transgressive.

6. Mutations can alter only the various phases of the basic varietal pattern expression; the pattern itself is not changed. Truly unique and outstanding varieties such as Peach, Charlotte Armstrong, or Queen Elizabeth would never result from the accumulation of mutations.

7. The evolutionary concept that mutations are harmful because natural selection has accumulated the most efficient combination of

mutations is examined in terms of its implication that the assumed process is complete. The conclusion is reached that environments are not always ideal for plants now. Therefore, if the present variation we see is due to natural selection adapting species and varieties to their environment, the process should be continuing and experimentally demonstrable.

8. The overwhelming lines of evidence indicating that under the usual normal environmental conditions, mutations are for the most part harmful, indicates a need to re-examine the presumed evidence for evolution.

9. It is our belief that the evidence clearly indicates creative design, a past environment much better suited for the ideal expression of the manifold patterns of life, and a series of catastrophes which have marred a world originally created perfect in every way.

Figure 1 — H55059/6 normal compared to No. 2 strap leaf.

Figure 2 — H55059/6 normal compared to No. 13 rugose thick leaf.

Figure 3 — H55059/6 normal leaf on left compared to four-leaf variations on right.

Figure 4 — H55059/6 (Top left) No. 20—Dwarf. (Top Right) No. 9—Dark red large double flower. (Bottom left) No. 2—Slender elongate. (Bottom right) No. 13—Thick dark green leaf and stem.

Figure 5 — Mutation with 24-36 petals on left compared to normal H55059/6 having 14-18 petals on right.

Figure 6 — H56024/39 normal leaf at left compared to four-leaf variations on right.

Figure 7 — Flower bud of Pink Sensation at left compared to induced mutations on right.

Figure 8—Variations in flower form induced by neutron irradiation of Garnette. Typical Garnette at left.

NOTES AND REFERENCES

1. Walter E. Lammerts, "Neutron Induced Variation of Roses, *American Scientific Affiliation Journal* (March, 1961).
2. Walter E. Lammerts, "The Scientific Basis of Rose Breeding, *American Rose Annual* (1945), pp. 71-79.
3. Walter E. Lammerts, "Inheritance of Magenta Red Color in Roses," *American Rose Annual* (1960), pp. 119-125.
4. Heinz Fraenkel-Conrat, "The Genetic Code of a Virus," *Scientific American* (October, 1964).
5. H. D. MacGinitie, *The Kilgore Flora* (University of California Publications in Geological Sciences), Vol. 35, No. 2, pp. 67-158; 16 plates, 2 figures in test.
6. D. Axelrod, "Evolution of the Psilophyton Paleoflora, *Evolution* (June, 1959), Vol. XII, No. 2, pp. 264-275.
7. John C. Whitcomb and Henry M. Morris, *The Genesis Flood* (Philadelphia: Presbyterian and Reformed Publishing Co., 1961).

XXIV

SEED GERMINATION, SEA WATER, AND PLANT SURVIVAL IN THE GREAT FLOOD

George F. Howe

Introduction

The topics of seed dormancy, germination, and growth have challenged the minds of botanists for many years. Several thorough articles and monographs on these topics provide information about the longevity,[1] preservation,[2] and metabolism[3] of seeds. Some of these references and certainly the paper by Ungar[4] provide information about the effect of salts in the soil water at time of germination. Boyko has investigated the use of salt water as a source for irrigation.[5]

None of the above studies has dealt specifically with the effect of soaking during storage on the survival of seeds. Since this topic is of interest from the standpoint of experimental plant physiology and also from the vantage of seed germination after the flood recorded in Genesis, the present investigation was undertaken to determine some of the effects of previous soaking upon germination of the seeds. Charles Darwin studied this problem of soaking and floating seeds in order to determine how plants might have traveled across large stretches of ocean water.[6]

Materials and Methods

Fresh fruits containing seeds of the five following different plants (from five different families) used in these studies were collected in weedy fields surrounding Westmont College, Santa Barbara, California, in late June, 1967: *Raphanus sativus* L. (Brassicaceae or mustard family), *Rumex crispus* L. (Polygonaceae or buckwheat family), *Cirsium edule* Nutt. (Asteraceae or sunflower family), *Medicago hispida* Gaertn. (Fabaceae or legume family), and *Malva parviflora* L. (Malvaceae or hollyhock family).

All the specimens collected were dry and apparently ripe fruits from the current growing season (December through March, 1967). Fruit types involved were indehiscent silique (*Raphanus*), achenes (*Rumex* and *Cirsium*), legume (*Medicago*) and shizocarp (*Malva*).

Taxonomic verification was conducted by the author, using Jepson[7] for genus and species and Porter[8] for family.

On June 24, 1967, fruits of each species were divided into four groups and treated as follows: (1) control fruits stored dry in paper sacks, (2) fruits soaked in sea water, (3) fruits soaked in sea water mixed with tap water, and (4) fruits soaked in tap water. Soaking baths were changed every fourth day to prevent stagnation, microbial bloom, or gross changes in saline content.

Sea water for soaking was collected fresh from the Pacific Ocean about every 4 days in a 20 liter bottle, along the beaches of Santa Barbara. The city water of Montecito, California, was used to supply the tap water treatment. Approximately 10 liters of fresh sea water were mixed every fourth day with 10 liters of the tap water to provide a "mixed" soaking bath for each species tested.

Fruits were floated in shallow plastic containers holding about 2 liters in the case of *Rumex*, 1 liter for *Malva* and *Medicago*, and about 4 liters for *Raphanus* and *Cirsium*. Floating and soaking of these fruits in the liquids mentioned were performed in a glasshouse. No temperature control was provided during either the soaking or germination phases of this work.

At the beginning of the experiment, fruits of all the species floated for several days, as reported also by Darwin.[9] By the end of the second week, however, nearly all fruits except those of *Cirsium* had sunk to the bottom of the liquids in the shallow storage pans, where they remained submerged throughout the rest of the soaking period. The *Cirsium* fruiting heads floated throughout the entire period of soaking.

Soaking began on June 24 and continued until November 11, 1967, a period of exactly 20 weeks or 140 days, which corresponded roughly to the 150 day period in which water prevailed upon the earth during the Great Flood (see Gen. chapters 7 and 8).

At intervals of 4, 8, 12, 16, and 20 weeks after June 24, seed samples of the various plant species were removed from the several treatments and placed under conditions favorable for germination. Seeds selected for a germination study were removed from the fruit and counted before planting. Most germination tests were performed in 4-inch clay pots containing a soil mixture of sand, local clay soil, and peat moss blended in proportion of 1:2:1 respectively.

Ten seeds selected for a particular germination analysis were sown in a pattern as shown in Figure 1, to a depth of one-half inch for *Cirsium* and about one-quarter inch for all other species. Soil pots were subsequently watered with tap water during the germination tests.

Since the soil was not sterilized, there remained the possibility of volunteer seed growth within the experimental pots, since the species studied are all common weedy plants of Southern California. The geometry of sowing noted in Figure 1 allowed for easy distinction between the experimental seeds and "volunteer" seedlings of the same or other species. Actually, only two of the test species had volunteers in the other treatments: *Malva parviflora* and *Rumex crispus*.

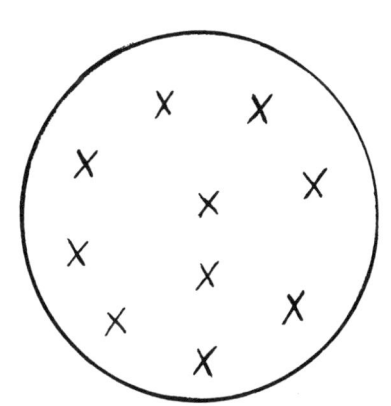

Figure 1. Surface view of a pot as used in germination trials. Each "X" indicates the position in which one seed was planted. This planting pattern enabled one to distinguish clearly between experimental seeds that had been planted and any volunteers present accidentally in the soil.

In the case of the *Rumex* germination studies, most tests were carried out in tap water contained in 50 ml beakers rather than in the soil pots mentioned. The seeds of *Rumex* germinated well this way and were completely visible, so that all possibility of volunteers affecting the *Rumex* count was removed. In the trials of the 16th and 20th weeks, separate observations were made on the germination of *Malva* and *Rumex* seeds in beakers of tap water and in soil-pots. The results of these parallel studies are included in Tables IV and V.

Since the two sets of data concur quite closely, it is evident that the problem of volunteer seedlings was minimal even among those two species which had some volunteer germination from the natural soil. On the basis of the position analysis of planted seeds and on parallel germination trials within beakers or pots, it can be inferred safely that these data represent actual germination of the experimental seeds.

Observations on each germination trial were made for several weeks after planting. Seeds in the soil were scored as "germinated" if the cotyledons emerged and expanded. Although a few of the *Medicago* seedlings later showed signs of "damping off" in one experiment, they were still scored as "germinated." Some of the *Rumex* seedlings, however, that were germinated by soaking in water, grew a root but did not unfurl the cotyledons or cast off the fruit wall, and such seedlings were not considered as "germinated," despite their root growth.

Early germination trials indicated that controls of *Medicago, Malva,* and *Cirsium* showed little or no germination. It was obvious that some dormancy mechanism prevailed in these three types.

It was discovered that these same three species would germinate readily if the seed coats were first cut tangentially with a razor blade before the germination trials were begun. Cutting was performed on the back of the seed to avoid injury to the radical or the epicotyl. It will be noted accordingly in the tables that seed coats of various lots were routinely scarified by cutting to break the seed-coat dormancy.

Furthermore, control seeds of *Medicago* and *Cirsium* germinated if they were soaked for about 10 minutes in concentrated sulfuric acid prior to planting. No cutting or acid scarification was attempted on seeds of *Rumex* or *Raphanus* because control seeds of these two species germinated readily. The whole fascinating topic of seed-coat dormancy has been reviewed adequately in various plant physiology textbooks.

Results

Data on the germination of various seed aliquots after 4, 8, 12, 16, and 20 weeks of soaking are presented in Tables I-V. Each table indicates time after soaking period began, the exact starting date for the germination study, and the number of days during which germination data were recorded after planting the seeds or placing them in beakers.

Listed opposite each species is the soaking storage treatment, the scarification procedure (if any), and the number of seeds germinating out of 10. Tables IV and V also provide the results of both soil-pot and beaker germination trials in fresh water, as indicated earlier.

Throughout these tables the phrase "grew in soaking bath" appears opposite those *Rumex* fruits stored in tap water. This indicates that seeds of *Rumex crispus* germinated while they were soaking in the fresh water storage bowl, and continued to grow well until about the 16th week, at which time they became heavily covered with algae.

It can be concluded the *Rumex* seeds in fresh water will germinate and grow for long periods of time. After resting upon moist soil, it is conceivable that these seedlings would survive and become established. This germination of *Rumex* seeds even while they are soaking

TABLE I—Week 4 (28 days of soaking)

PLANTING DATE: JULY 22
DATA RECORDED FOR: 44 DAYS

Seeds	Storage	Scarification	No. Seeds Germinating out of 10 Soil-pot Results
Raphanus sativus	Control	—	3
,,	Sea Water	—	5
,,	Mixed Water	—	8
,,	Tap Water	—	6
Rumex crispus	Control	—	6
,,	Sea Water	—	8
,,	Mixed Water	—	9
,,	Tap Water	—	Grew in soaking bath
Cirsium edule	Control	cut	4
,,	Sea Water	cut	2
,,	Mixed Water	cut	0
,,	Tap Water	cut	1
,,	Control	—	0
Medicago hispida	Control	cut	10
,,	Sea Water	cut	10
,,	Mixed Water	cut	9
,,	Tap Water	cut	8
,,	Control	—	0
Malva parviflora	Control	cut	8
,,	Sea Water	cut	1
,,	Mixed Water	cut	1
,,	Tap Water	cut	2
,,	Control	—	0

TABLE II—Week 8 (56 days of soaking)

PLANTING DATE: AUGUST 19   DATA RECORDED FOR: 29 DAYS

Seeds	Storage	Scarification	No. Seeds Germinating out of 10 Soil-pot Results
Raphanus sativus	Control	—	8
,,	Sea Water	—	1
,,	Mixed Water	—	5
,,	Tap Water	—	6
Rumex crispus	Control	—	7
,,	Sea Water	—	3
,,	Mixed Water	—	4
,,	Tap Water	—	Grew in soaking bath
Cirsium edule	Control	cut	10
,,	Sea Water	cut	0
,,	Mixed Water	cut	0
,,	Tap Water	cut	0
Medicago hispida	Control	cut	10
,,	Sea Water	cut	8
,,	Mixed Water	cut	10
,,	Tap Water	cut	6
Malva parviflora	Control	cut	4
,,	Sea Water	cut	7
,,	Mixed Water	cut	9
,,	Tap Water	cut	2

TABLE III—Week 12 (84 days of soaking)

PLANTING DATE: SEPTEMBER 16 DATA RECORDED FOR: 31 DAYS

Seeds	Storage	Scarification	No. Seeds Germinating out of 10 Soil-pot Results
Raphanus sativus	Control	—	10
,,	Sea Water	—	0
,,	Mixed Water	—	3
,,	Tap Water	—	2
Rumex crispus	Control	—	9
,,	Sea Water	—	3
,,	Mixed Water	—	8
,,	Tap Water	—	Grew in soaking bath
Cirsium edule	Control	cut	9
,,	Sea Water	cut	0
,,	Mixed Water	cut	0
,,	Tap Water	cut	0
Medicago hispida	Control	cut	8
,,	Sea Water	cut	8
,,	Mixed Water	cut	7
,,	Tap Water	cut	10
Malva parviflora	Control	cut	6
,,	Sea Water	cut	4
,,	Mixed Water	cut	8
,,	Tap Water	cut	4

TABLE IV—Week 16 (112 days of soaking)

PLANTING DATE: OCTOBER 14   DATA RECORDED FOR: 24 DAYS

| | | | No. of Seeds Germinating out of 10 ||
Seeds	Storage	Scarification	Soil-pot Results	Beaker Results
Raphanus sativus	Control	—	9	—
,,	Sea Water	—	0	—
,,	Mixed Water	—	0	—
,,	Tap Water	—	5	—
Rumex crispus	Control	—	7	10
,,	Sea Water	—	4	10
,,	Mixed Water	—	2	6
,,	Tap Water	—	Grew in the soaking bath	
Cirsium edule	Control	cut	8	—
,,	Sea Water	cut	0	—
,,	Mixed Water	cut	0	—
,,	Tap Water	cut	0	—
Medicago hispida	Control	cut	8	10
,,	Sea Water	cut	10	10
,,	Mixed Water	cut	10	10
,,	Tap Water	cut	10	10
Malva parviflora	Control	cut	3	4
,,	Sea Water	cut	3	9
,,	Mixed Water	cut	5	9
,,	Tap Water	cut	6	5

TABLE V—Week 20 (140 days of soaking)

PLANTING DATE: NOVEMBER 11
DATA RECORDED FOR: 22 DAYS

No. of Seeds Germinating out of 10

Seeds	Storage	Scarification	Soil-pot Results	Beaker Results
Raphanus sativus	Control	—	9	—
,,	Sea Water	—	0	—
,,	Mixed Water	—	0	—
,,	Tap Water	—	3	—
Rumex crispus	Control	—	6	2
,,	Sea Water	—	7	2
,,	Mixed Water	—	2	7
,,	Tap Water	—	Grew in the soaking bath	
Cirsium edule	Control	cut	10	—
,,	Sea Water	cut	0	—
,,	Mixed Water	cut	0	—
,,	Tap Water	cut	0	—
Medicago hispida	Control	cut	10	—
,,	Sea Water	cut	10	—
,,	Mixed Water	cut	10	—
,,	Tap Water	cut	10	—
Malva parviflora	Control	cut	5	6
,,	Sea Water	cut	7	10
,,	Mixed Water	cut	6	9
,,	Tap Water	cut	9	4 (fungus present)

in water may contribute to the growth and survival of the species in swampy or otherwise moist situations.

After 4 weeks of soaking in sea, tap, or mixed water, seeds of all species tested showed at least some germination (with the one exception of *Cirsium* in the mixed soaking bath).

After 8 weeks it was apparent that *Rumex crispus, Raphanus sativus, Medicago hispida,* and *Malva parviflora* seeds from all soaking treatments germinated. Seeds from *Cirsium edule* taken from the sea, tap, or mixed water storage did not germinate.

After 12 weeks of soaking, germination results were similar to the 8 week data, excepting that the seeds of *Raphanus sativus* stored in sea water did not germinate.

After 16 weeks of soaking in sea water, tap water, or mixed water treatments, seeds of *Rumex crispus, Medicago hispida,* and *Malva parviflora* germinated well. It is seen finally in Table V that after 140 days of soaking in the three storage treatments, seeds of *Rumex crispus, Medicago hispida,* and *Malva parviflora* germinated well in the soil-pot trials (and in the beaker tests where indicated). Thus seeds from three out of five weedy species randomly selected germinated and grew after seven weeks of soaking in sea, tap, or mixed water.

These data indicate that there is widespread resistance to salt or fresh water soaking among the seeds of flowering plants. Such resistance may be at least partially attributable to seed-coat dormancy in the case of *Malva parviflora* or *Medicago hispida,* but is also evident in *Rumex crispus,* where no such dormancy exists.

Discussion

Cells of many plants require a high concentration of oxygen to maintain their metabolism.[10] Many land plants die when a region is subjected to prolonged flooding. Dead trees are often visible in the waters of man-made lakes, where the roots have died from suffocation before the whole tree or shrub perished. Death in such instances is apparently caused by oxygen deficiency, and can also be noted in "water-logged" soils or overly watered potted plants.

The high oxygen requirement of many land plants presents an apparent problem to the concept of total flood during the days of Noah. Possible survival mechanisms for various kinds of plants will be examined presently in the light of the Bible narrative.

Much destruction of plant life would have been expected in a global flood. Extinction of many species would be a predictive consequence. Reference to any standard text in paleobotany will demonstrate that numerous kinds of plants found in fossil beds are not known on earth today.

Whole groups such as the Calamites, Cordaitales, Cycadofilicales, Bennettitales, and the Caytoniales—just to mention a few—have vanished. It is of course impossible to know with absolute scientific certainty if some of these plants became extinct before the flood or if they were all destroyed by it.

Evidence does suggest, however, a much richer flora in time past and great extinctions among the fossil plants. Extinction of many species is exactly what one would predict if there had been a great flood. The first suggestion in answer to the problem of plant survival during the world-wide flood is that many plants did not survive!

The record of the flood (Gen. 6-9) contains much detail concerning provisions for animal survival. Although no mention is made of similar activity for preservation of plants, it is entirely probable that Noah and his family stored seeds or other propagules of important crop plants on the ark. If this conjecture is probable, then an interesting suggestion arises about crop plants and centers of ancient civilization.

Edgar Anderson and numerous other workers report that crop plants originated historically at ancient centers of human culture. Thus oranges, tea, and rice came from China; maize from the American Indians; and various cereal grains and fruit crops from the Indo-European area. It is at least possible that valuable plants stored on the ark were preserved by the children of Noah. If certain economic plants were cherished by the different races, one would expect to find important crop plants coming from the several centers of post-flood civilization. Although this idea is admittedly speculative, it does inject an interesting answer to the unsolved problem of crop plant origin.

The ark itself no doubt served to preserve the seeds of some species of plants either on the fur of animals or as various foods provided for them.

Sir Charles Darwin reported that trees floating in the ocean can contain seeds that will germinate:

> I find that when irregularly shaped stones are embedded in the roots of trees, small parcels of earth are frequently enclosed in their interstices and behind them,—so perfectly that not a par-

ticle could be washed away during the longest transport: out of one small portion of earth thus completely enclosed by the roots of an oak about 50 years old, three dicotyledonous plants germinated: I am certain of the accuracy of this observation.[11]

This mechanism in itself may have provided for survival of seeds from many plants during the flood.

Darwin stressed the role of icebergs in transporting plant propagules, a phenomenon which also may have contributed to endurance of seeds or other plant parts in the flood:

> As icebergs are known to be sometimes loaded with earth and stones, and have even carried brushwood, bones, and the nest of a land-bird, it can hardly be doubted that they must occasionally, as suggested by Lyell, have transported seeds from one part to another of the arctic and antarctic regions; and during the Glacial period from one part of the now temperate regions to another.[12]

Darwin discovered that seeds contained in dead bodies would readily germinate and grow after the carcases had been floated in salt water:

> Again, I can show that the carcases of birds, when floating on the sea, sometimes escape being immediately devoured: and many kinds of seeds in the crops of floating birds long retain their vitality: peas and vetches, for instance, are killed by even a few days' immersion in sea-water; but some taken out of the crop of a pigeon, which had floated on artificial sea-water for 30 days, to my surprise nearly all germinated.[13]

Carcases of animals strewn upon the surface after the Flood may have contained seeds which eventually germinated.

Finally, the results of this present study indicate that seeds of certain plants will grow after soaking for as long as 140 days in various water baths. It may be argued that the Flood waters were almost as salty as our ocean waters of today, or it may be possible that they had a far lower saline content. In either case, the data of my study demonstrate that three out of five species tested germinated after long soaking periods in sea, mixed or tap water.

Darwin also experimented with survival of flowering plant seeds after floating the fruits upon a salt-water solution:

> Until I tried, with Mr. Berkeley's aid, a few experiments, it was not even known how far seeds could resist the injurious action of sea-water. To my surprise I found that out of 87 kinds, 64 ger-

minated after an immersion of 28 days, and a few survived an immersion of 137 days.[14]

Altogether, out of the 94 dried plants, 18 floated for above 28 days; and some of the 18 floated for a very much longer period. So that as 64/87 kinds of seeds germinated after an immersion of 28 days; and as 18/94 distinct species with ripe fruit (but not all the same species as in the foregoing experiment) floated, after being dried, for above 28 days, we may conclude, as far as anything can be inferred from these scanty facts, that the seeds of 14/100 kinds of plants of any country might be floated by sea-currents during 28 days, and would retain their power of germination.[15]

Oddly enough, Darwin concluded that legume family members survived the effects of salt water badly and would not germinate after soaking:

It deserves notice that certain orders were far more injured than others: nine Leguminosae were tried, and with one exception, they resisted the salt-water badly; . . .[56]

This negative result may be explained by the fact that many legume type plants require scarification (cutting or acid treatment) to break their seed-coat dormancy. Perhaps Darwin would have noted better germination of soaked legume members had he understood this scarification requirement. In my experiments, it is evident that the legume (*Medicago hispida*) germinated quite well with scarification after 140 days of soaking in any of the water solutions.

Since plant species are so often limited to relatively small geographic areas, as for example, many California species of *Ceanothus*, it would seem that mostly plants survived the Flood by resistance of either the seed or plant parts to salt water. Extensive experimentation as regards survival of *Ceanothus* seeds, cuttings, and even parts of the plant with roots attached, would no doubt give us much insight on this survival problem.

From these data and from Darwin's it may be concluded that seeds of many flowering plants could have resisted the direct contact of flood waters and germinated vigorously after the Flood. Thus seed plant survival during the Flood may have occurred by many means—both inside and outside the ark.

Several questions remain as yet unanswered. More studies are needed to find how widespread this resistance to prolonged soaking may be among seeds of flowering plants. It would be of interest to investigate factors which prevent germination and growth of *Raphanus sativus* and *Cirsium edule* seeds after soaking.

The Bible indicated that a dove released by Noah returned with an olive leaf in its mouth. How much soaking in salt or other water solutions would an olive plant be able to resist and still propagate afterwards?

These and other projects might provide data which would be of value in experimental plant physiology and in the understanding of Bible history.

NOTES AND REFERENCES

1. H. T. Darlington, "The Seventy-year Period for Dr. Beal's Seed Viability Experiment," *American Journal of Botany* (1951), 38:379-381.
2. Lela V. Barton, *Seed Preservation and Longevity* (New York: Interscience Publishers, 1961).
3. W. Crocker and Lela V. Barton, *Physiology of Seeds* (Waltham, Mass.: Chronica Botanica Co., 1952).
4. Irwin A. Ungar, "Influences of Salinity and Temperature on Seed Germination," *The Ohio Journal of Science* (1967), 67(2):120-123.
5. Hugo Boyko, *Salinity and Aridity* (The Hague, The Netherlands: Dr. W. Junk Publishers, 1966); cf. by the same author, "Salt-water Agriculture," *Scientific American* (1967), 216(3):89-96.
6. Charles Darwin, *The Origin of Species* (1859). See Chapter XII, "Geographical Distribution," subsection "Means of Dispersal," for Darwin's salt-water studies. Mentor Book Edition, pp. 346-352.
7. W. L. Jepson, *A Manual of the Flowering Plants of California* (Berkeley, Calif.: 1923-1925).
8. C. L. Porter, *Taxonomy of Flowering Plants* (San Francisco: W. H. Freeman Co., 1959).
9. Darwin, *op. cit.*, p. 347ff.
10. Bernard S. Meyer and Donald B. Anderson, *Plant Physiology* (New York: D. Van Nostrand Company, Inc., 1952).
11. Darwin, *op. cit.*, p. 349.
12. *Ibid.*, p. 351.
13. *Ibid.*, p. 349.
14. *Ibid.*, p. 347.
15. *Ibid.*, p. 348.
16. *Ibid.*, p. 347.

XXV

WILD FLOWERS: A PROBLEM FOR EVOLUTION

William J. Tinkle

When the chill winds of spring vie with warm, sunny days, we look in corners and nooks of the woods for the bright faces of wild flowers. While they cannot assure us that snow will not return, we feel certain that warm skies and green grass are on their way. Using food stored in roots or bulbs, these tiny plants push up leaves and flower very promptly, while the trees still have no leaves to intercept sunshine from them.

Let us enquire how these tiny organisms attained their present attractive state. According to the inclusive explanation of evolution by natural selection they developed by chance variation. Quoting Darwin:

> Nothing at first can appear more difficult to believe than that the more complex organs and instincts have been perfected, not by means superior to, though analogous with, human reason, but by accumulation of innumerable slight variations, each good for the individual possessor. Nevertheless, this difficulty, though appearing to imagination insuperably great, cannot be considered real if we admit the following propositions, namely, that all parts of the organization offer, at least, individual differences—that there is a struggle for existence leading to the preservation of profitable deviations of structure or instinct—and, lastly, that gradations in the state of perfection of each organ may have existed each good of its kind. The truth of these propositions cannot, I think, be disputed.[1]

Utilitarian Changes vs. Stable Genes

Such utilitarian changes, accumulated over thousands of years, were thought to account for the present structures of plants. But in the middle of the nineteenth century only one man, Gregor Mendel, knew much about the action of genes, and Charles Darwin knew nothing of his works.

We now know that genes are stable and the rare changes which do occur in them do not add anything which would build higher species.

Most genes are exceedingly stable. This applies both to normal "wild-type" genes and to genes which have arisin by mutation. The natural mutation rate is very low. Many species have remained much the same for long geologic ages. The brachiopods among animals and the seaweeds and others among plants are examples of organisms in which almost no changes are observed in present-day species as compared with fossils.[2]

Returning to the nineteenth century theory, a plant with a simple, green body (a thallus) happened to develop stems with branches, which happened to become flattened into leaves. Thus, it could catch more sunlight and have an advantage in the struggle for existence. It is postulated:

(1) that at the tip of a branch, spores were formed and some chanced to be enlarged by storing food, thus becoming seeds;

(2) that leaves on this branch were changed into carpels, stamens, petals, and sepals respectively;

(3) that petals which happened to enlarge and develop color attract insects which carry pollen from one plant to another;

(4) and that flowers which happen to have sweet juice (nectar) also attract insects, which cross one variety with another (the basis of hybrid vigor).

Useless variation also occurred, but such plants were lost in the struggle for existence.

A Certain Species Considered

Now let us ask how well this glittering generality applies in concrete species. The Dutchman's Breeches, *Dicentra cucullaria*, is a perennial herb which thrives in deep humus (see Figure 1). The compound leaves grow up directly from bulbs. The flower stalks are scapes, that is, they grow up from the bulbs without leaves, and the flower cluster is a raceme.

Now look at the flower itself. The sepals are very small. There are four petals, two of which are slender but the other two look like the legs of fancy breeches and thus give the name to the flower. This species seems to be self-pollinated, since the stamens and pistil are near each other. There is no nectar, and bees seldom visit the flower.

It would require a lively imagination to visualize a leafy branch developing, by chance, utilitarian changes into such a flower, especially in this plant *where there are no leafy branches*. Another difficulty in this explanation is that we find *no intervening forms* of plants either in the woods or in the rock strata.

The principal utilitarian value of flower color, odor, and nectar seems to be cross-pollination. Some flowers are formed so as to favor receiving pollen from another plant rather than from their own stamens. For instance, the pistil may be longer than the stamens, such that the visiting insect touches it first and places pollen upon it from another flower. Or some stamens and pistils mature at different times, making self-pollination impossible.

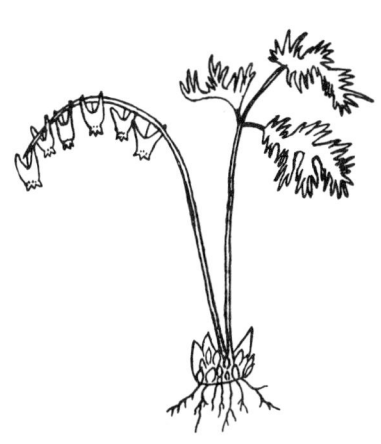

Figure 1. Dutchman's Breeches *Dicentra cucullaria*

But these are only special cases, for in many plants—wheat, beans, and peas, for instance—pollen from the stamens regularly fertilizes the ovules of the same flower. It is hard to see how any utilitarian process such as natural selection built up the flowers of beans and peas. (And if this is not enough difficulty, consider the dandelion, in which many seeds develop by parthenogenesis, having had no union with pollen.)

Evolution vs. Purpose

The theory of evolution by natural selection may look reasonable as a whole, but we learn in mathematics that the whole is made up of its parts. If the parts of a theory do not contribute to the general idea, then the whole theory is defective and untenable. In a freshman course, the theory of evolution often is more attractive than in an advanced course because fewer exceptions are encountered.

Most evolutionists rule out purpose on the part of the Creator; not because of their observations, however, but because of a philosophy which they prefer. It suits their bent of mind to believe in materialism and utilitarianism. But having espoused such a philosophy it is hard to account for beauty, and even harder to account for altruism.

We say that bees are attracted by the beauty of flowers, but why not say that grazing animals also are attracted, making natural selection work against beauty? Neither statement can be substantiated.

There is reality in the beautiful purple color of a raspberry cane just as much as in the thorns which are supposed to protect it, but natural selection does not account for this color. Again, what utilitarian theory can account for the striking colors of autumn leaves? The yellow is explained by the loss of chlorophyll leaving xanthophyll; but what is the utility of the bold, red anthocyanin, except to beautify the landscape?

When faced with altruism in nature, the evolutionist is in difficulty, for his theory is based upon self-interest. He may reply that some altruism is only apparent, for fruits pay animals for delivering seeds to favorable planting places. This is true in many cases, but it is hard to see such value in a squash and impossible to see it in cotton. The fibers do not transport cotton seeds, but rather hold them. In many other species the fruits and seeds are more lavish than needed to perpetuate the kind.

In another respect, the oxygen which plants give off in their food-making process does not help them but is of great value to animals. Conversely, plants use the carbon dioxide which animals breathe out. Bacteria of decay perform a valuable service to nature by changing dead plants into soil; indeed, the very best of soil. These organisms do not consciously try to help somebody, but the world is so planned that this aid goes on naturally. Evolution by natural selection, based as it is upon selfish struggle, stands silent before these important natural processes.

Let us recognize that God made plants beautiful, and formed them in such a way that they serve other living things in addition to themselves. He made an interesting wealth of variety, just as we should expect a personal Creator to do.

NOTES AND REFERENCES

1. Charles Darwin, *The Origin of Species* (New York: Colliers, Library of Universal Literature, Part I. Vol. 2), p. 276.
2. L. H. Snyder and P. R. David, *The Principles of Heredity* (New York: Heath, 1957), p. 349.

XXVI

"THE PLANTS WILL TEACH YOU" *

Harold W. Clark

In the deserts of the Southwest grows an interesting plant, the yucca, or Spanish bayonet. The name is derived from a dense rosette of long, dagger-like leaves that rise a foot or two above the ground. In the spring a flower stalk grows upward from the center of this rosette, reaching a height of from four to six feet. It is crowned at the upper foot or two with scores of cream-colored lily-like blossoms, each about two inches long and drooping from the end of a short branch.

The remarkable feature of these beautiful flowers is their manner of pollination. The stigma, that sensitive area on the end of the style, which must receive the pollen from the stamens in order to stimulate the growth of the seeds, is not like most stigmas. On the contrary, it is hollow, and the sensitive area is inside the hollow. Hanging down as it does, no pollen can drop into it. Ordinary methods of pollination are impossible. Neither wind nor passing insects are of any use in the pollination of the yucca.

Here is where the female pronuba moth enters the picture, just as if she had been given a special role to play in the economy of the desert. Entering a flower, she brings in her mouth a wad of pollen which she has gathered from other flowers. Having taken enough to suit her instincts, she now goes about her business. Searching about in the flower, she crawls upward until she comes to the bulbous ovary, the case in which the seeds will be developed. Here she deposits her eggs.

As soon as she has done this, she performs a most surprising act. Crawling back down the long, hanging style, she finds the tubular stigma at the lower end and proceeds to pack it full of pollen she has

---

*Reprinted by kind permission of Richard H. Utt of the Pacific Press Publishing Association, Mountain View, California, from *Wonders of Creation*. The beautifully illustrated book has 13 chapters, all showing the wonderful design in nature.

been carrying in her mouth. Her mission has now been accomplished. Provision has been made for her offspring and at the same time for the reproduction of the yucca.

The yucca ovary contains about 200 ovules, each of which, fertilized by the pollen packed into the stigma, is capable of developing into a seed. About twenty seeds are all that will be needed by the growing pronuba larvae, so an abundance of seeds will mature.

How, by any stretch of the imagination, can we account for this remarkable feat performed yearly by thousands of pronuba moths? How did the process originate? In the first place, a yucca plant could not produce seed without the aid of the moth. But how does the moth know enough to pack the stigma full of pollen? Instinct, you say? Yes, but instinct is merely an inherited action pattern. Before the pattern can be inherited, it must be formed. But how could yucca plants mature seeds while waiting for the moths to learn the process and set the pattern?

The whole procedure points so strongly to intelligent design that it is difficult to escape the conclusion that the hand of a wise and beneficent Creator has been involved.

But the yucca is not the only case where miraculous events occur in the plant world. In fact, the growth of every seed is a miracle.

In many flowers, such as the apple blossom, tiny nectar pits are placed at the base of the petals. The odor of the flowers, and probably the color also, attracts the honeybees. Seeking the nectar, from which they manufacture honey, the bees brush against the stamens and become covered with the sticky yellow pollen. Not only do they seek nectar, but they also deliberately gather pollen and pack it into pollen sacs provided on one pair of legs. In the course of gathering the pollen, they brush against the end of the style in the center of the flower. Some of the pollen is left sticking to the soft syrupy surface of the stigma. In this way the honeybees not only benefit from the nectar and pollen, but they return the favor by pollinating the flowers.

Again we may well ask how such an arrangement could have come about by accident, or how either the flowers or the bees could have survived alone. Intelligent design is again evident.

Sometimes it is better for a flower if it can receive pollen from another plant rather than to be pollinated by its own. Elaborate mechanisms ensure this cross-pollination. In some flowers the stigma and stamens mature at different times. This makes self-pollination impossible. Some flowers have two kinds of styles and stamens—

long and short. A bee will enter a flower with a short style and long stamens, and will receive pollen on the rear portion of its body. Then when it enters a flower with a long style, it will rub off some of the pollen on the stigma. At the same time it will obtain pollen on the front of its body from the short stamens, and this in turn will be rubbed off on the next short style the bee encounters. Remarkable, isn't it? A miracle? Surely no ordinary growth processes could account for such marvelous adaptive relationships. Such precise adaptations require something more than trial and error. They require intelligent planning.

You will notice that so far we have spoken only of sticky pollen. Some flowers have dry pollen that would not stick to the body of a bee, or even be held by the thick hairs that cover its body. These flowers put out no brilliantly colored flowers or sweet scents to attract the bees, but they have another way of carrying on their necessary functions.

Take the grasses for instance. Their large stamens are dangled out on long filaments, which sway with every passing breeze and release their pollen to the wind. The pollen is so light and dry that it flies everywhere (ask any hay-fever victim), and the grasses are freely pollinated.

This kind of pollen distribution may be observed in many trees. In the dense pine forests, for instance, living conditions are not favorable for honeybees, and if the pine trees were to depend on them to carry pollen, the process would be poorly done. But the pines hang out thousands of tiny cone-like structures, each one with many pollen-bearing stamens. Every movement of the branches in the wind shakes loose a mass of minute powdery golden grains. I have seen a strong wind sweeping over a pine forest, picking up a cloud of yellow dust and sending it filtering through the trees. So dense was the cloud of pollen that it could be followed with the eye for miles. The wind-blown pollen is so abundant that it colors the surface of mountain lakes and collects in golden masses along the shores. Here is ample provision, and to spare, for the development of new pine seeds, and the bees are not needed.

After all, the process of pollination itself is a miracle. A tiny pollen grain lighting on the sticky surface of the stigma, begins to sprout, using the sugary secretion as food. The sprout becomes a tube, which burrows its way down through the tissues of the stigma and style until it reaches the ovary, or egg case. Here it does not wander about aim-

POLLINATION OF YUCCA FLOWER BY PRONUBA MOTH
A. General view of Yucca in bloom
B. Single flower (Note stigma protruding on left side)
C. Moth placing ball of pollen inside open end of stigma, which is a hollow tube
D. Seed capsule showing opening where moth emerged
E. The pronuba moth
F. Longitudinal section of stigma showing hollow into which pollen must be placed —Drawings by H. W. Clark

lessly, but leaves the walls of the ovary and enters the cavity inside. Here are located the ovules, each one destined to become a seed. Each is attached to the ovary by a short stalk, and at the base of the ovule, near to its attachment to the stalk, is a tiny opening, the micropyle. Into this micropyle the pollen tube enters. Once inside the ovule, it discharges its sperm cells, which immediately unite with egg cells to produce a new seed.

What causes the pollen tube to grow downward along the style? Some botanists suspect there is some kind of chemical attraction. But if this is true, how did it get that way to begin with? Even though we may find some cause for the directional growth, we are puzzled to know why it is that way. The whole process is so purposeful that it cannot be explained as mere coincidence.

These principles have been so well expressed by another that I would like to close this discussion with a short quotation:

"A mysterious life pervades all nature—a life that sustains the unnumbered worlds throughout immensity, that lives in the insect atom which floats in the summer breeze, that wings the flight of the swallow and feeds the young ravens which cry, that brings the bud to blossom and the flower to fruit." —Ellen G. White, *Education,* page 99.

In this age of scientific skepticism, we need to realize the hand of God in nature, and to recognize His power at work in all the things He has created.

XXVII

DNA: ITS HISTORY AND POTENTIAL

Duane T. Gish

First isolation of nucleic acid from the nuclei of cells, now known as deoxyribonucleic acid (DNA), was accomplished by a medically trained Swiss physiological chemist, Friedrich Miescher, in 1869.[1] This work was performed in the laboratory of Hoppe-Seyler at Tübingen. Hoppe-Seyler was one of the outstanding chemists of that era, and Miescher's accomplishment was so significant that Hoppe-Seyler held up publication of results for two years until Miescher's work could be fully confirmed.

Because of their availability, Miescher used pus cells from discarded bandages as his source of cells. He first isolated the cell nuclei, and from these he extracted a grey-white powder which he later called "nuclein."

Miescher next turned to the sperm of Rhine salmon as a source of nuclein. He isolated what he recognized as a salt-like compound formed by the combination of a nitrogen-rich base and a phosphorus-rich acid, his nuclein. The base he called "protamin," and he developed a method for isolating it. The purified nuclein had a phosphorus content of 9.6 percent, and after acid hydrolysis, all of the phosphorus was recovered in the form of phosphoric acid.

Miescher also investigated sperm of frogs, carp, and bulls. He detected nuclein in all of them. He pointed out the nuclein seemed to be the genetically active chemical which had been postulated as being present in spermatozoa.

From about 1875, other workers became active in this field, and by 1900 all of the major bases which occur in nucleic acid had been isolated. Later it became apparent that there were two types of nucleic acid, differing in origin and composition. The nucleic acid from yeast or from wheat embryo was hydrolyzed to yield four bases, adenine, guanine, cytosine and uracil, phosphoric acid and a sugar identified in 1909 by Levene as the pentose, ribose.

From thymus was isolated the other type of nucleic acid, from which was obtained the four bases, adenine, guanine, cytosine, and thymine, phosphoric acid and a pentose sugar identified by Levene in 1930 as deoxyribose. Today the type of nucleic acid containing the base, uracil, and the sugar, ribose, is known as ribonucleic acid (RNA), and the other type containing thymine and deoxyribose is known as deoxyribonucleic acid (DNA).

During the decade 1940-1950, results indicated that DNA is almost always found in the cell nucleus as part of the chromosomes, while RNA is mainly found in cytoplasm. It is now known that cell nuclei, as well as the cytoplasm, contain both DNA and RNA. It was found that nucleic acid is a polymer consisting of thousands of sub-units. These sub-units are called nucleotides. The nucleotides are composed of a base, either a purine or a pyrimidine, linked to a sugar, either ribose or deoxyribose, depending upon the type of nucleic acid, and the sugar in turn is linked to phosphoric acid. One such nucleotide, adenylic acid, is shown in Figure 1.

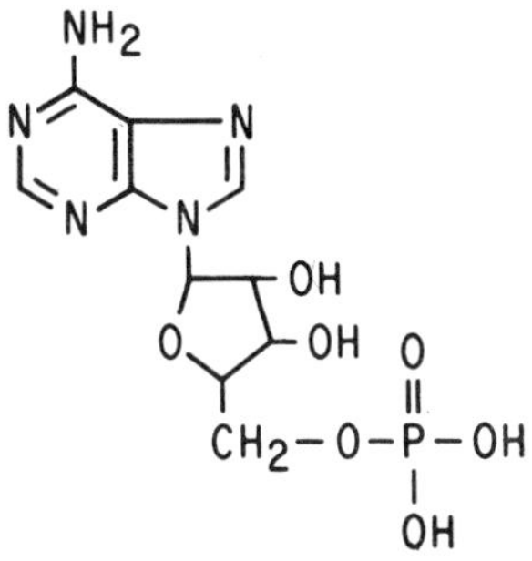

Figure 1. Adenylic acid, a nucleotide.

The sub-units, or nucleotides, of nucleic acid are joined through phospho di-ester bonds, the phosphate being combined with the 3'-hydroxyl of one sugar and the 5'-hydroxyl of the sugar of the adjacent unit. This "backbone" structure is shown schematically in Figure 2.

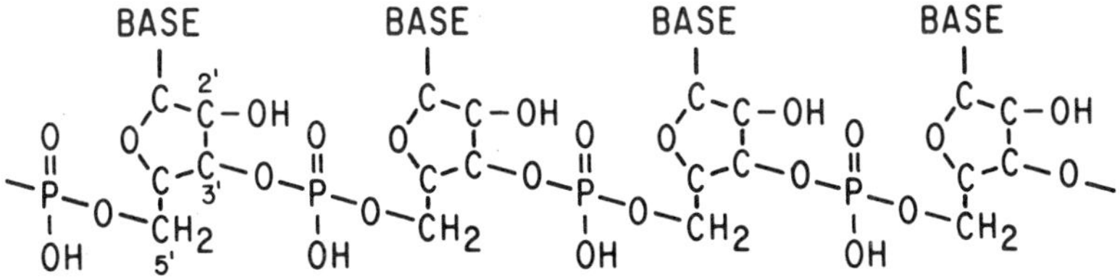

Figure 2. Schematic representation of nucleotide arrangement in nucleic acid.

Molecular weight values range up to 2,000,000 or more for RNA (tobacco mosaic virus RNA contains about 6600 nucleotides and has a molecular weight of 2,000,000) to 10,000,000 and higher for DNA.

The almost forgotten suggestion by Miescher that nucleic acid might play a central role in inheritance was confirmed by Avery and co-workers in 1944.[2] They extracted DNA from "smooth" or encapsulated pneumococcus bacteria and added it to the culture of "rough" or unencapsulated pneumococci. A new generation of "smooth" bacteria was produced which continued to produce the "smooth" type. The DNA from the "smooth" type had been incorporated into the genetic material of the "rough" type, converting it permanently to the "smooth" type. This established that genes are composed of DNA. This event gave great impetus to research into all aspects of DNA.

In 1950, Chargaff[3] recorded the fact that among the bases of DNA the amount of adenine was always equal to thymine, and guanine was always equal to cytosine (in molar quantities). This observation provided one of the keys to the structure proposed for DNA in 1953 by Watson and Crick. In that year Watson and Crick,[4] combining the data of Chargaff and X-ray crystallographic data, proposed for DNA the structure that is now widely accepted.

Watson-Crick Model

According to the proposal of Watson and Crick, DNA exists in the form of a double-stranded helix, the two helical chains being coiled about a common axis. They proposed that one chain of the double helix is the complement of the other, with adenine in each chain pairing with thymine of the other, and guanine in each chain pairing with cytosine of the other. The two chains of the double helix are held together by hydrogen bonds between the purine bases (adenine and guanine) and the pyrimidine bases (cytosine and thymine).

A purine is always paired with a pyrimidine, because two purines would occupy too much space to allow a regular helix, and two pyrimidines would occupy too little. Because of stereo-chemical relationships, adenine always pairs with thymine and guanine with cytosine. The base pairing of a section of two complementary DNA strands is shown in Figure 3.

$$A-C-G-A-T-T-G-A-C-A-G-T$$
$$T-G-C-T-A-A-C-T-G-T-C-A$$

Figure 3. Base pairing in DNA (A=adenine, G=guanine, T=thymine, C=cytosine).

From the structure proposed for DNA implications could be drawn concerning its replication by the cell. These implications were published by Watson and Crick[5] a few months after their paper on the structure of DNA.

They proposed that prior to replication, the hydrogen bonds holding the double-stranded helix of DNA together are broken, and the two chains unwind and separate. Each chain then acts as a template for the formation onto itself of a new complementary chain, so that eventually two pairs of chains are formed where only one existed before.

After the two original strands have separated, along each of these intact chains are assembled free nucleotides (these nucleotides at this stage are in the form of triphosphates). This assemblage takes place according to the base pairing pattern described above. That is, every place in the intact chain where adenine occurs, a nucleotide containing thymine will become loosely attached by hydrogen bonds; where guanine occurs in the intact chain, the nucleotide containing cytosine will become attached by hydrogen bonds, etc.

When the nucleotides have been assembled in place along the intact chain, the enzyme DNA polymerase joins the free nucleotides together by forming regular chemical bonds between them to form the new DNA strand. The result is a double-stranded DNA helix, one strand having been derived intact from the previously existing DNA and the second having been formed from the nucleotide sub-units.

DNA Replicated by Cell

It should be pointed out here that DNA does *not* replicate itself. *It is replicated by the cell.* DNA does furnish important information for its replication in the form of the sequence of its individual nucleotides, but the complex apparatus in the cell is required to synthesize the sub-units or nucleotides that are polymerized to form DNA.

The cell, through the complex apparatus designed for this purpose, supplies the energy required for the synthesis to take place. A certain concentration of magnesium is required and, of course, the presence of the enzyme DNA polymerase, in the absence of which no synthesis would take place, is an absolute necessity.

Here evolutionists are faced with a dilemma. The presence of a protein, the enzyme DNA polymerase, is indispensable for the synthesis of DNA. On the other hand, the information required for the synthesis of all proteins is contained in DNA. In an evolutionary scheme, which could have come first? Protein is required for DNA synthesis, and DNA is required for protein synthesis. Which preceded the other? The best answer seems to be that neither arose before the other, but both have existed together from the very beginning.

It is now believed that most genetic information resides in DNA. This information is contained in the form of a "genetic code" built into the DNA molecule. This genetic code is fashioned from the sequence of the bases in DNA. What this code is, and how this information is transmitted so that a protein with a fixed and specific structure is synthesized, I will not attempt to explain here. Nevertheless, there is a message built into each DNA molecule, and this message is used to dictate the structure of every other molecule in the cell.

Complexity of Apparatus

I must emphasize the extreme complexity of the apparatus required to transfer the message or code in a structural gene into a specific protein molecule:

> The code in the gene (which is DNA, of course) is used to construct a messenger RNA molecule in which is encoded the message necessary to determine the specific amino acid sequence of the protein.
>
> The cell must synthesize the sub-units (nucleotides) for the RNA (after first synthesizing the sub-units for each nucleotide, which include the individual bases and the ribose). The cell must synthesize the sub-units, or amino acids, which are eventually polymerized to form the protein. Each amino acid must be activated by an enzyme specific for that amino acid. Each amino acid is then combined with another type of RNA, known as soluble RNA or s-RNA.
>
> There is a specific s-RNA for each individual amino acid. There is yet another type of RNA known as ribosomal RNA. Under the influence of the messenger RNA, the ribosomes are assembled into units known as polyribosomes. Under the direction of the message contained in the messenger RNA while it is in contact with polyribosomes, the amino acid-s-RNA complexes are used to form the protein. Other enzymes and key molecules are required for this.
>
> During all of this, the complex energy producing apparatus of the cell is used to furnish the energy required for the many syntheses.

A brief description as the one above may leave one more confused than enlightened, yet it does emphasize the tremendously complex apparatus that is required to synthesize a protein molecule in the living cell. Four types of nucleic acid are involved—DNA, messenger RNA, soluble RNA, and ribosomal RNA. In the synthesis proper, about 30 different enzymes are involved, and if we include the synthesis of the sub-units and of the energy producing apparatus, hundreds of different enzymes are required.

The specificity of the synthesis is amazing. The sequence of the sub-units, or amino acids, in each protein molecule is very definite and precise. Along the complex pathway from DNA to protein molecule, which involves the interaction of many different molecules and includes passage from the nucleus to the cytoplasm, where polyribosomes are found, the code contained in the DNA is perfectly transcribed into the structure of the protein molecule.

The DNA serves two purposes in the cell. In DNA is encoded the information which, on demand of the cell, is converted by the cell into the message necessary for the production of other complex molecules and structures of the cell. The DNA also serves as the genetic unit of the cell, its replication serving as the means of transferring to the daughter cell all of the information encoded in the parent DNA.

DNA: Master or Servant?

What of DNA? Is it the "master chemical," the "secret of life"? Is it true, as claimed by Jukes,[6] that "the purpose of life is the perpetuation of a base sequence"? It seems inescapable to me that DNA, rather than being the master of the cell, is the servant of the cell. DNA is kept under strict regulation by the cell. Its operation or message is repressed by the cell until needed. Derepression follows, and when the need for the message, or the molecule produced by this message, is no longer needed, the gene is once more repressed.

When the cell replicates, and before cell division takes place, it reproduces a second set of DNA molecules and from this constructs a second set of chromosomes. The parent cell utilizes its replication of DNA to pass on to the daughter cell the genetic information contained in the parent cell. While DNA occupies a key position in the cell, it is only one of many important features of the cell. Commoner[7] has aptly stated that, rather than DNA being the secret of life, "life is the secret of DNA."

Williams[8] stated in his review of Juke's book, mentioned above, that in this book we have witnessed "the deification of a molecule."

There is a widespread tendency today among scientists and laymen alike to prostrate themselves before an altar upon which is enshrined DNA.

Many believe that the solving of the genetic code will open up a marvelous new future for man whereby he will be able to "control his own evolution." Such a belief rests in ignorance. The solving of the genetic code would eliminate only one of the many problems involved in understanding how the numerous features of life are uniquely determined. Even if we understood all of this, how to alter DNA specifically in order to bring about a desirable change would remain an insuperable difficulty.

The first problem involved in altering our genetic make-up is the fact that the carriers of the genes, the chromosomes, are located in the nuclei of the egg and sperm cells. In order to subject this material to treatment, some means must be devised for removing it from the egg or sperm and replacing it, after treatment, with retention of viability by the egg or sperm.

Today we have some understanding about the relative positions of a few of the many thousands of genes in some microorganisms. By their linkage we can determine whether or not they occupy adjacent positions on the chromosome. We do not have the slightest idea where their actual positions on the chromosome are, however, and have no way at present of determining this. Even if we knew which gene is which, how could one particular gene be separated from among the tens of thousands present?

If, in the future, we could devise a method for removing a particular gene for treatment in order to alter it, several practical impossibilities would yet stand in the way of altering our genetic properties selectively.

In each gene there are thousands of nucleotides, or sub-units. A change in only one of these thousands of sub-units causes profound changes in the genetic properties of the gene. We do not have the slightest idea, however, what effect on an organism will be caused by a specific change at some point in the gene.

In a recent series of newspaper articles, Professor James Bonner of the California Institute of Technology was quoted as saying that in the future man will so control his own genetics that, for instance, if a person wants four arms, he can have four arms. Some of his speculations even went beyond this.

If we alter one of the genes governing the arms, however, what do we get—four arms, short arms, long arms, or no arms at all? The almost certain result would be some crippling effect, for in spite of the claims of evolutionists, *all* mutations are in the nature of injuries. If man ever begins to tinker with his genes, he had better construct many additional institutions to house the monsters that result.

It could also be pointed out that most, if not all, of our characteristics are polygenetic, that is, they are under the control of not one but a number of genes. For instance, eye color in *Drosophila* is under the control of 15 genes. The desirable alteration of a certain characteristic, if that is possible at all, most likely would require changes in more than one particular gene. Precisely coordinated changes in several genes would probably be required.

Great Difficulty Remains

If all the above problems were solved, which seems incredible, one insuperable difficulty would yet remain. In each gene there are thousands of nucleotides, but only four different kinds of bases. In a gene of 10,000 nucleotides, there would be, on the average, 2,500 of each of the four different kinds of bases.

Let us say we knew that to bring about a specific desirable change, we had to change the adenine, at position 5,263 of the chain, to a guanine. If a chemical or irradiation or some other kind of treatment were used, how could the effect of that treatment be limited to position 5,263 without affecting one of the other 2,499 adenines in this DNA? It could not.

Chemical action, irradiation, or other mutagenic treatments are completely random in effect. We cannot "tell" a nitrite ion which base to attack. Since these treatments are by their very nature random in effect, it is obvious that they can never be utilized to bring about a specific change in the genetic material.

Other possible means of altering genetic properties could be discussed with much the same results. In spite of the bold claims of Dr. Bonner and others, man will have to get along with the two arms he has, as well as with the other features with which he is endowed. Man is "fearfully and wonderfully made" (Ps. 139:14), the product of the Master Planner. If we can learn to preserve that creation in reasonably good health for three score and ten, we will do well.

As we learn more and more about DNA and how it functions in the cell, we should view this great master plan with awesome wonder. Its complexities and intricacies are beyond our comprehension;

the results of the plan, marvelous. Who is it that conceived and brought this into being? Unbelieving man, willingly ignorant, prefers to believe it was inherent in the properties of the neutron. It seems to me immeasurably more reasonable to accept the clear proclamation of Scripture, "In the beginning God created. . . ." The purpose of life is not, as Jukes claims, to perpetuate a base sequence, but the purpose of DNA is to perpetuate life.

NOTES AND REFERENCES

1. For historical reviews of the chemistry of DNA see D. Cohen, *The Biological Role of the Nucleic Acids* (New York: American Elsevier Publishing Co., Inc., 1965), and V. R. Potter, *Nucleic Acid Outlines*, Vol. I (Minneapolis: Burgess Publishing Co., 1960).
2. O. T. Avery, C. M. MacLeod, and M. McCarty, *J. Exp. Med.* (1944), 79:137.
3. E. Chargaff, *Experientia* (1950), 6:201.
4. J. D. Watson and F. H. C. Crick, *Nature* (1953), 171:737.
5. *Ibid.*, p. 964.
6. T. H. Jukes, *Molecules and Evolution* (New York: Columbia University Press, 1966).
7. B. Commoner, *Nature* (1964), 202:960.
8. C. A. Williams, *Science* (1967), 155:308.

XXVIII

THE SPONTANEOUS GENERATION OF LIFE

PAUL A. ZIMMERMAN

Man has an insatiable curiosity concerning his origin. This urge to know more about his beginning has provided a powerful stimulus for scientific investigation concerning the origin of "life" from non-living material. In late years advances in biochemistry, microbiology, and allied sciences have provided powerful new tools for such inquiry.

In an age dominated by materialistic philosophy one finds infrequent reference to the possibility of life having been initially created by God. It is usually asserted that "chance," operating over a long period of time, provides all the creative force that is needed. Gaffron states, "It is the general climate of thought which has created an unshakable belief among biochemists that evolution of life from the inanimate is a matter of course." [1]

It is true, of course, that evolutionary theory, to be successful, needs to account for the origin of life. Darwin himself, prior to 1871, in one of his letters spoke of the spontaneous generation of life. He speculated concerning the chance formation of a protein compound in "some warm little pond with all sorts of ammonia and phosphoric acid salts, light, heat, and electricity." [2]

The search for the answer to the origin of life proceeds along several lines. One is the attempt to synthesize living material today. A second approach is to use modern scientific knowledge to reconstruct how life might have evolved from inorganic chemicals. Another is to attempt to find evidence of life forms in extra-terrestrial sources.

Newspapers and popular magazines often carry misleading headlines. It is not uncommon to read "Life Created in Test Tube," and then go on to discover that the accomplishment has been considerably less significant. So much depends on the definition of life.

What is living material? Actually, it is difficult, if not impossible, to offer a definition satisfactory to all. Certainly life involves far more than the mere ability to reduplicate one molecule from the pattern of another. Inorganic crystals have this ability in a suitable medium. Life as an organized process calls for much more. Mora recently listed four characteristics of living material which provide a more comprehensive approach to a definition. (1) A living organism must be autonomous, similar to others of its kind, but not an exact duplicate. (2) It must be self-maintaining, i.e., able to repair itself and to duplicate itself. (3) A living organism must be able to adjust to changing environmental conditions to survive. (4) Finally, it must have what Mora calls an "urge" or drive toward "self-fulfillment." [3] Certainly it is not too much to say that any theory seeking to account for the origin of life must start with the obviously inorganic and go at least as far as a functioning cell. Viruses, often regarded as a primordial type of life, do not meet the requirements of this definition. Essentially, they consist of a shell of protein enclosing a core of nucleic acid. They multiply themselves only by invading cells of another organism and using its chemistry to produce virus particles. They thus depend entirely on other life and may be regarded as parasitic.

The theory must first reasonably account for the origin of the macro-chemicals which play such vital roles in the machinery of the cell. Most vital are the highly complex giant molecules called proteins. They are found in every form of life and are involved in every basic function of living organisms. Closely allied in the complex are the various deoxyribonucleic acids (DNA) and ribonucleic acids (RNA). These remarkable molecules represent the genetic material of living organisms and are the materials which direct protein synthesis. They almost infallibly pass down to succeeding generations the pattern of each and every living organism. Life without these complex molecules is unimaginable.

Virtually all scientists agree that spontaneous generation is impossible today under existing conditions. The environmental conditions obtaining in our world render organic molecules of the required complexity much too unstable. Oxygen in the air and existing organisms would quickly kill any such new product of spontaneous generation before it had taken its first toddling step. It is universally agreed that such complex molecules as make up living material need the indispensable protection of living systems. They cannot live outside this protective environment.

Thus man is led to attempt a simulation of conditions which he theorizes might have obtained in the early days on the earth. It must be recognized at the outset that this type of scientific activity amounts to speculation. It may rest upon biochemical laws and be judged

The Spontaneous Generation of Life 319

with reference to them. But it cannot be said to reproduce actual conditions. The Dutch geologist, Rutten, states, "The time elapsed is so enormous that it is difficult to prove anything at all, because the record is not only incomplete in the extreme, but is also often changed beyond recognition by younger events." [4]

Mora agrees. He writes, "This question is not within the scientific domain, at least if we consider probability as an essential part of a scientific statement." [5] Fuller and Tippo give as their judgment, "The evidence of those who would explain life's origin on the basis of the accidental combination of suitable chemical elements is no more tangible than that of those people who place their faith in Divine Creation as the explanation of the development of life. Obviously the latter have as much justification for their belief as do the former." [6]

The difficulty of accounting for the evolution of life by spontaneous generation (sometimes called "biopoesis") is of the highest order. It amounts to cloaking "chance" with all the attributes of deity. In this writer's opinion it requires a greater act of faith to embrace spontaneous generation than it does to believe in a divine creative act.

The difficulty of explaining the evolution of life from the non-living lies in the amazing complexity of the chemistry of the living cell. Even in 1964 biochemists and microbiologists do not profess to understand the intricacies of cell chemistry. Nor do they yet claim confidence in the ability to duplicate its wizardry. To then postulate that the cell, with its rich panoply of chemicals, developed from a few simple inorganic compounds, is to face odds which stagger a statistician and would scare off any gambler. Moreover, such an assumption runs contrary to the consistent experience of the chemist who knows the careful controls he must impose when he synthesizes far less complex molecules in his laboratory.

Despite the strong evolutionary dogma against teleology, design is evident in living organisms. Twenty amino acids are commonly found in proteins. The total number, including those discovered by chromatographic techniques, is considerably larger. Only four organic bases occur in the nucleic acids. Yet these few components are linked and coded in such a marvelous way as to spell out the chemistry of life in all its glorious variety. The amino acids in proteins are built chain-like into an architecture of molecules with weights ranging from 12,700 to 760,000. DNA and RNA molecules range as high as two million molecular weight units. These molecules are so structured as to provide coded information for the cell that enables the cell to develop, to maintain itself, to preserve its identity, and to produce offspring with the characteristics of the living organism. The development of the various systems of the organism as well as the metabolic processes by which they function are governed by this coding. All structure and all activity of living organisms is made possible by the complicated symphonic action and reaction of miraculous molecules in a vast number of cell systems. All are coded and directed by the master chemicals!

Synge has calculated that for one typical protein with a molecular weight of 34,000, containing 288 units selected from 12 amino acids, it is possible to obtain 10^{300} isomers of distinctly different protein structures.[7] If only one molecule of each of these possible proteins existed, the weight of the earth from organic material alone would be 10^{280} grams. Contrast this with the actual weight of 10^{27} grams. How, then, were the correct codes selected for living material in view of the vast possible number of "nonsense" codes that the continuous rolling of the dice of biochemical chance would produce?

But far more is necessary than merely to be assured of the production of the right molecules. They must be organized in the right systems. Furthermore, they must be protected against degradation so that they might multiply. Living systems are extremely sensitive. Almost all soluble proteins denature upon heating. They are extremely unstable in this regard. Most of the enzymes that catalyze reactions in the cell are damaged irreversibly if exposed to temperatures as high as 40-50 degrees centigrade. Only a few are able to survive above 60 degrees.

Furthermore, peptides decompose readily by hydrolysis to revert to amino acids. The thermodynamic equilibrium for this reaction strongly favors the decomposition. Thus the reaction causes peptides, the precoursers of proteins, to degrade to amino acids, rather than to build more complex protein molecules. The amino acids must be activated by the complex ATP (Adenosine triphosphate) before it can pass the energy barrier and be linked in a peptide chain.

Reactions in the living cell call for an exquisite symphony of cooperation. For instance, the oxidative decarboxylation of amino acids requires the cooperation of no fewer than five complex cofactors, each of which is essential. What are the odds that such exquisite and vital balance, such well-coordinated chemical syntheses, such intricate coding of living material arose by chance? It is beg-

The Spontaneous Generation of Life

ging the question to say that originally life proceeded by simpler and unknown pathways.

Despite the staggering odds against spontaneous generation, many scientists prefer this hypothesis to the creation hypothesis. They have performed experiments with ammonia, hydrogen, water, and other simple chemicals in an effort to simulate a "primordial" atmosphere. Electricity, ultraviolet light, high speed electrons, etc., have been used to induce these simple compounds to combine into more complex molecules. The results have been interesting.

As long as half a century ago Emil Fischer linked amino acids in smaller peptide chains. In more recent years Calvin used radiation from the Berkeley cyclotron to bombard carbon dioxide and hydrogen. He obtained formic acid and formaldehyde. Three years later (1953) Urey and Miller used a mixture of methane, water, hydrogen, and ammonia. This mixture was subjected to discharges of high-voltage electricity. Several amino acids were found in the mixture after bombardment. In 1960 Wilson succeeded in producing larger polymers forming sheet-like solids.

Another, more recent, approach is that of Fox, who heated mixtures of amino acids in molten glutamic acid. He felt this simulated conditions which might have existed alongside some primordial volcano. This process produced polypeptides resembling proteins in many respects. Molecular weights ranged from 3,000-9,000.[8] More recently adenine, one of the organic bases occurring in the structure of DNA was produced by the bombardment of a "primitive earth environment" with beams from a 4.5 million electron volt linear accelerator.[9]

From these and similar experiments it has been concluded that bombardment by cosmic rays, ultraviolet, radioactive materials, and lightning can produce fairly complex molecules. It is then postulated that beginning with these molecules, more and more complicated interrelationships developed until finally "life" had arrived. Indeed, a strong spirit of optimism usually accompanies reports of research in this area. Is this optimism justified? One may begin a critical appraisal by noting that these experiments have been characterized by some scientists as exercises in chemistry and nothing more. Consider the formation of amino acids in Miller's experiment. The results might well have been predicted from the thermodynamic properties of these compounds. They are quite stable, possessing an inner salt structure (zwitterionic). Those who seek to explain the origin of life must start with an explanation of why these compounds have these characteristics? Why do atoms form bonds as they do? For that matter, how do we account for the origin of matter? One may push back the ultimate question; but it cannot be eliminated.

Bombardment of chemical compounds by high energy particles also very understandably tears atoms apart, opens active linkages, and gives rise to more complex chemicals. But far more than that is required. Useful chemicals, formed along with a host of useless compounds in the reaction mass, would have to be able to function and fight off degradation back to more simple chemicals. They would have to organize themselves into a highly structured system capable of producing the catalysis necessary to pass difficult energy barriers and ultimately to accomplish their own reduplication.

In evaluation of this point Mora judges, "These polymerizations are only exercises in synthetic organic chemistry. They use similar monomers, but they do not really resemble a self-perpetuating, coordinated process, and they do not lead to the synthesis of a living unit with the characteristic urge. They do not even produce functional polymers with a specific structure." [10] In effect, it is as though a number of meaningful words have been produced by chance rolling of children's alphabet blocks. But what is required is that of the meaningful wisdom and complexity of the Encyclopedia Americana. What are the odds against this having been produced by the rolling of wooden alphabet blocks?

A survey of the literature easily reveals a long list of special environmental conditions which must be provided for life to have been formed of its own accord by spontaneous generation. Unless these special conditions are assumed the theories fall flat. The problems faced by the hypothesis of spontaneous generation are truly challenging.

Most scientists agree that the original environment must have been free of oxygen. Oxygen in the atmosphere would effectively oxidize any early organic molecules and prevent the development of life. It would also, by the formation of ozone, effectively shield the earth's surface from the high energy ultraviolet radiation required by the theories. On the other hand, ultraviolet light has a lethal effect on living organisms. If it were not filtered out by the atmosphere, no life could exist on earth today. It thus seems a most unlikely source upon which to depend for starting life. The problem is for the theory to account for a manner in which plants would form oxygen quickly

The Spontaneous Generation of Life 323

enough to prevent ultraviolet rays from sterilizing any living matter that had developed. Since our present supply of green plants would require 5,000 years to double our present oxygen supply, it is most doubtful that the necessary oxygen could have been provided quickly enough by primordial life forms.[11]

Even the transition from an oxygen-free atmosphere to an oxygen-containing environment would be most traumatic for anaerobic organisms. Ehrensvard is of the opinion that the increasing oxygen concentration would have represented a "catastrophe, a brutal intervention in their metabolism." [12] He believes there must have been "wholesale eradication" of organic life with only a few survivors. We regard the survival of any organisms under the stipulated conditions most unlikely and question the "escape clause" that some must have quickly and resourcefully developed specialized enzyme systems.

Moreover, the possibility of the synthesis of macro-molecules having been carried out by ultraviolet rays has been challenged. Calvin has pointed out that ultraviolet is most abundant in the wave length range from 2,000 to 2,500 Angstroms. However, these wave lengths are not absorbed by methane, hydrogen, or water. Hence he feels this source of energy may not have played the major role assigned to it by some theories. He turns instead to radiation from Potassium-40.[13]

This, however, seems an unlikely prospect in view of the comparatively weak radiation provided by this isotope, unless we postulate a rate of radioactivity far higher than that which we observe today.

A realistic view of any chemical process will consider the concentration of reactants. Most theorists seem to assume a convenient meeting of chemicals in just the right concentrations. This, however, is a most unlikely assumption. Ehrensvard calculates that the concentration of non-carbonate carbon in the forms of organic compounds in the seas could not have amounted to more than 0.00001 percent.[14] It is not plausible to assume that increasingly complicated reactions would take place in such a thin primeval soup. This objection is usually met by assuming concentration processes in inland lagoons. This weakness of this reply is implicit in the additional assumption required, namely, that the prerequisite concentrations were held more or less constant over vast periods of time.

An additional restriction is imposed by the solubility of phosphorus compounds. Phosphorus is essential for life processes. Today available phosphorus is quite limited because it is present in the oxidized form. Calcium ions tend to precipitate calcium phosphate and thus reduce the amount in solution. It is thus unlikely that sufficient phosphorus would have been available in the primordial seas to make it possible to form the requisite compounds. Gulick seeks to overcome this objection by suggesting that originally phosphorus was present in the more soluble hypophosphite form. However, this form tends to oxidize extremely easily to the insoluble phosphate. This means that no oxygen can be tolerated in the early atmosphere. Here again, very special conditions and delicate balance and transition are called for to such a degree as to strain the limits of credulity.[15]

Spontaneous generation must also account for the origin of the enzymes which speed up life processes, many of which otherwise proceed with great slowness. Indeed, any satisfactory theory must account for the development of the cell which governs life processes and makes them possible today. It is not enough for Oparin to postulate the concentration of chemicals in little droplets (coacervates). The cell is vastly more than a little sac. The old idea of the protoplasm as a colloidal system has been replaced by the knowledge that the cell is a chemical factory with many different compartments. Under the electron microscope the cell is seen to consist of a three dimensional network of tubules and globules with a diameter of 100-150 millimicrons. Inside this network proceed all chemical processes. They operate under the control of the cell for the service of the living unit. Not only have investigators thus far failed to account for the chance development of such a highly specialized organization, they freely admit we still have much to learn of what goes on in this area of biochemistry.

It is often overlooked that the concept of a delicately balanced, ordered functioning organism developing from simple inorganic molecules runs counter to the second law of thermodynamics. Disorder comes naturally in nature. Or, to be more exact, an increase in entropy is to be expected. Only in the living cell do we find today entropy decreasing. This is true of the growing state. However, at death the chemicals immediately revert to an increase in entropy, that is, to decay and degradation. No one has shown how material originally dead could have reversed this universal principle of nature.

Calvin has observed that the same forces which tore apart the primitive inorganic molecules would start tearing apart the more complex ones formed from the simple.[16] He and others call upon "natural selection" to promote the cause of the more complex compounds by giving them somehow more survival value. However, selection at the molecular level is a far different thing than selection among living plants and animals. Experience with the latter cannot be appealed to in support of the former. Selection at the molecular level is selection only in the passive, physicochemical sense. Under such conditions our knowledge of chemistry indicates we should expect indiscriminate mixing of the chemicals with dispersion and degradation. To say it is not so is to beg the question. Certainly the least that can be expected in support of the theory would be well-worked-out models, taking into full account the questions of mixing and degradation.

Invariably probability is invoked as proof that selection would be successful at the molecular level. It is argued that given enough time and opportunity it is certain the very complex arrangements of the right compounds would come into the proper relationship. Some of these "right" compounds and systems would somehow escape destruction and be given an opportunity to take the next step up the organizational ladder. They would function in such a way that finally a pattern, a pathway, would be established and preserved. "Given enough time the improbable becomes the inevitable." This is the creed.

This line of reasoning must be recognized as wishful thinking. The very fact that very long times are invariably involved for these developments in itself is an admission of the improbability of such development. Mora says of this line of thought: "Using such logic we can prove anything. . . . When in statistical processes the probability is so low that for practical purposes indefinite time must elapse for the occurrence of an event statistical explanation is not helpful." [17]

What we know of chemical processes indicates that such items as the stability of certain configurations of molecules, e.g., the helix, are limited processes. They resemble crystallization, stopping at the next level without any tendency in the non-living state to go on and on to higher organizational levels. To invoke probability and infinite time to overcome this observed difficulty is to operate on the level of faith.

Living forms have certain peculiarities which any theory of spontaneous generation must take into account. One of these is the optical activity of amino acids. Peptide chains are formed universally of natural amino acids of the levo-configuration. This is most unexpected, since ordinary chemical processes produce racemic mixtures of D and L isomers. Living cells, however, have special mechanisms to hinder racemization and insure the production of the levo-isomers. Gause, Russian expert on optical activity, indicates this as proof that all life on this planet arose from a single source.[18] It should be noted, however, that dextroseries amino acids occur in nature to a very small extent, e.g., in the proteins of certain bacteria.

It is simple to account for optical activity if life was created. However, if it evolved, then the question arises, how did this peculiarity of living material arise? It is most strange, since it does not exist in the inorganic world. Several explanations have been offered. One is that the first synthesis took place on an optically active quartz crystal. However, in nature there are as many dextro surfaces of quartz grains as levo surfaces. It is also pointed out by some that sunlight, having passed through the atmosphere, has a slight right circular polarization which might have selectively destroyed dextro forms of early organic compounds. But this presumes a selective destruction not justified by the amount of rotation. It is more likely that all such early unprotected organisms would have been destroyed. Thus optical activity remains as one more indication of created life, as opposed to spontaneous generation.

Finally, it is important to note two trends. One is a seeming lessening of interest in the theory that life came from another planet. Some feel that life forms have been found in meteorites, but this has not yet been demonstrated beyond question. It has been pointed out that explaining that life drifted in from another planet only transfers the locale of the problem. Moreover, there is little chance that the spore of any living organism would survive years of drifting through space and enduring fierce radiation. Then, too, the hope of life on Venus has been exploded since it was learned that its surface temperature is about that of molten lead. Mars remains a possible, though unlikely, candidate as a source of life. Certainly it is far less hospitable than the planet earth. The next star system is many light years away. Thus accounting for life seems to be a local problem.

The other trend is a growing recognition that there is something to the idea that life has a design and what inescapably seems to be a purpose. Waddington recently pointed out that it is inadequate to think of basic processes as being "non-finalistic." He stated, "The non-finalistic mechanisms interact with each other in such a way that they form a mechanism which has some quasi-finalistic properties, akin to those of a target-following gunsight." [19]

Mora suggests that science remove its mental block on teleology and consider the "purpose" shown by living things.[20]

It may well be concluded that modern biochemical research has served to unravel much of the mystery of the chemistry of life. But in the unravelling of the vast complex of cell chemistry it has exposed still more the satistical improbability of spontaneous generation. It is an improbability so large as to be equated with "impossible." The facts point to the hand of God the Creator, who brought matter into being, who fashioned the solar system, who placed life on this planet by the word of His mouth. "For every house is builded by some one, but He that built all things is God" (Heb. 3:4).

NOTES AND REFERENCES

1. Sol Tax, editor, *Evolution after Darwin*, Vol. I, *The Evolution of Life*, Hans Gaffron, "The Origin of Life" (Chicago: (University of Chicago Press, 1960), p. 46.
2. Melvin Calvin, *Chemical Evolution* (Eugene, Ore.: Condon Lectures, Oregon State System of Higher Education, 1961), p. 2.
3. Peter T. Mora, "Urge and Molecular Biology," *Nature* (July 20, 1963), 199:212.
4. Martin G. Rutten, *The Geological Aspects of the Origin of Life on Earth* (Amsterdam-New York: Elsevier Pub. Co., 1962), p. 4.
5. Mora, *op. cit.*, p. 214.
6. Harry J. Fuller and Oswald Tippo, *College Botany* (New York: Holt, Rinehart & Winston, 1961), p. 25.
7. A. I. Oparin, A. G. Pasynskii, A. E. Braunstein, T. E. Pavlovskaya, editors, *The Origin of Life on the Earth* (Pergamon Press, 1959), p. 281.
8. Sidney W. Fox, "The Thermal Copolymerization of Amino Acids Common to Protein," *JACS* (1960), 82:3745.
9. *Sci. N. L.* (May 25, 1963), p. 323.
10. Mora, *op. cit.*, p. 214.
11. Gosta Ehrensvard, *LIFE Origin and Development* (Chicago: University of Chicago Press, 1960), p. 135.
12. *Ibid.*
13. Calvin, *op. cit.*, p. 24.
14. Ehrensvard, *op. cit.*, p. 102.
15. Ross F. Nigrelli, "Modern Ideas on Spontaneous Generation," *Annals of the New York Academy of Science* (Aug. 30, 1957), 69:281.
16. Calvin, *op. cit.*, p. 9.
17. Mora, *op. cit.*, p. 215.
18. Oparin, *et al., op. cit.*, p. 292.
19. Conrad H. Waddington, *The Nature of Life* (London: Ruskin House, 1961), p. 98.
20. Mora, *op. cit.*, p. 218.

XXIX

THE POSSIBILITY OF THE ARTIFICIAL CREATION OF LIFE

Harold L. Armstrong

There has been talk lately about the "artificial creation of life" in the laboratory. Christians have been concerned about the matters; may I suggest some thoughts which might be helpful?

The proposal is that a living being (let us say that, for it is a being, a something, a substance in Aristotle's sense, of which we are talking, not the attribute "life"; just as a carpenter could build a white house, but not "whiteness"), might be produced in the laboratory, in some way other than from a previously existing living being.

First of all: if this were done, it would not make God any the less, any more than my reproducing a line of Hamlet would decrease Shakespeare's genius. Or consider it another way: suppose (as could have happened, although it did not) that when our Lord fed the multitudes, bread had never been made and so was seen for the first time, but that subsequently men had learned the art of baking. Would that have made the miracle any the less? Obviously not!

Secondly: until two hundred or so years ago, men believed that living beings, certain worms and insects, for instance, were produced without the intervention of living beings, by what was called "spontaneous generation." And this belief made no trouble for their Christianity; Sir Thomas Brown, for instance, a devout man certainly, believed in spontaneous generation, and mentioned it in passing in his "Religio Medici." The suggested "creation of life" would, in fact, be just spontaneous generation under special conditions. And if this notion did not bother our forefathers, why should it bother us?

In the third place: can we be sure that living things have never been created artificially before? We are told in Exodus 8:7 that the magicians of Egypt produced frogs. And Revelation 13:15 might mean that something like that will happen again.

Incidentally, the fact that the magicians succeeded in their attempts—up to a point—does not, of course, show that God had lost control. He was longsuffering, then as always (II Peter 3:9), but, when He judged that things had gone far enough, that was the end. The magicians, even with Satan's help, were not able to do any more (Ex. 8:18). It is true that the extent of Satan's help should not be underestimated; he who was likely present when the sons of God shouted for joy at the creation (Job 38:7) would be in a good position to know something about how life was created. But for all that, just as in Egypt, his power was puny in comparison with God's power working through Moses, even so it is and shall be. So if, in the future, we should see something presented as "creation of life artificially," we could expect to see it go just as far as God in His long-suffering is willing to allow—thus far and no further.

Finally: even though the artificial production of a living being (should it come about) need be no threat to our faith, yet the attempt to do such a thing may be something in which no Christian (or Jew, or, for that matter Moslem) should be engaged. The building of the tower of Babel, so far as we know, threatened no one's faith, but for all that it was presumption. Incidentally, if it be said that the magicians of Egypt had help from dark powers, can we be sure (I say this in all seriousness) that the same might not be true of similar attempts today? The devil can think of many ways of working with man to man's harm, nor is he limited to appearing complete with horns and tail and stirring the cauldron with his pitchfork.

Finally: if we look around, we will likely find that some of those who are most interested in "creating life" are some of those shouting loudest that we must do something about the "population explosion." Is it not strange that men should with one breath cry that we have too much "life," and with the next urge that we strive mightily to make more?

XXX

A SCIENTIFIC ALTERNATIVE TO EVOLUTION

Thomas G. Barnes

Introduction

One of my colleagues, a Ph.D. in philosophy, who has been reluctant to speak out publicly against evolution, privately expressed his concern. He said, "Evolution is a *dogma* and not a science." This is a very serious charge because there are a great many disciples of Darwin in the scientific community. I believe, however, that a critical analysis of the literature on evolution justifies his statement.

A scientific fallacy in evolution may be seen by noting that its whole superstructure is built upon *extralogical* considerations. Extralogical considerations are the *extensions* of a propostion beyond the scope of true logic. *In evolution, an extralogical error occurs when phenomena with observable limits are cited as evidence in support of an unbounded proposition.*

A recent speaker on our campus defined evolution as "change." He then said, "Change is fact; therefore evolution is fact." It soon became evident that the evolution he adheres to is far more than an observable change. He committed the extralogical error of defining evolution as an observable and employing it as an unlimited process. Fabrications upon that kind of premise are nothing more than figments of imagination.

The failure to give adequate definition of evolution is a common failing among evolutionists; definitions implying observables are employed to frame speculative propositions. It is not uncommon, however, to find these same adherents to evolution charging that the remaining scientific community ignores the observable evidence.

No scientist questions the validity of *variety, change, and development within groups of living things.* The works of Luther Burbank, Walter Lammerts, and others in California have made it obvious that it is possible to breed new forms differing from parent forms. But it is also observable that this type of breeding is limited and invariably shows bounds beyond which it cannot go. One would say in mathematics that the curve of these real processes has asymptotes which never cross finite boundaries. Evolutionists ignore those asymptotes.

After more than a hundred years of research in biology, evolution remains without a solid foundation. Dr. G. A. Kerkut states it this way, "The evidence that supports it [general evolution] is not sufficiently strong to allow us to consider it anything more than a working hypothesis." [1]

It is amazing that after all these decades of toil by scientists in numerous disciplines that evolution is still a mere hypothesis and not a law!

By now it should be clear that the evolutionary hypothesis is neither necessary nor sufficient. There are scientific laws which are much more successful in specifying the processes of nature. These laws can be checked by experiment and may profitably be employed as guides to invention and progress.

I therefore invite your attention to a *scientific alternative to evolution,* an alternative that has present processes which follow the basic laws of science.

Three Basic Laws

Let us consider three of the great laws of science *which are included in the present processes of the alternative to evolution.* These laws are: the *First Law of Thermodynamics,* the *Law of Biogenesis,* and the *Second Law of Thermodynamics.*

The First Law of Thermodynamics is also known as the Law of Conservation of Mass-Energy. It states that energy may have different forms (including mass); that it is possible to change from one form to another, but the total energy remains constant.

The Law of Biogenesis states that *life comes from life.* Every living organism came from some other living organism.

The Second Law of Thermodynamics states that there is an irreversible tendency for processes in a self-contained system to go toward lower order. This means an increase in randomness, disorder, and decay if the whole system is taken into account. That is to say, systems run down hill, not up hill; they don't wind themselves up; they tend to run down. Biologist Harold Blum says, "One way of stating this law is to say that all real processes tend to go toward a condition of greater probability." [2]

Please remember his statement of this law (that real processes tend to go toward a condition of greater probability), because he is an evolutionist, and we shall see later he points out the improbability of major evolutionary events.

Validity of the Three Basic Laws

No laws of science are more firmly established than these three laws. They hold priority over all other laws of science. There are no known violations of these laws.

There was a 300-year debate on the Law of Biogenesis. During this period, maggots were claimed to be products of *spontaneous generation* of life and that was disproved. Then, after the invention of the microscope, micro-organisms were claimed to be evidence of spontaneous generation of life. In a series of masterful experiments, Louis Pasteur showed that there was no such thing as spontaneous generation of life.

Pasteur's sealed vessels, which contain a yeast infusion and pure air from the top of the Alps, can be seen even now in the Pasteur Institute Archives in Paris as a testimonial to that conclusion. After more than a century no life has appeared out of the inanimate. The Law of Biogenesis is accepted today by all reputable scientists.

Again I quote the aforementioned Dr. Blum in regard to the validity of the Second Law of Thermodynamics. He states, ". . . for the Second Law is in a sense an empirical and pragmatic law which owes its acceptance to the fact that it has worked whenever it has been put to the test."[3] Dr. Blum is one of the most scholarly evolutionists and as you see he agrees that there are no known violations of this law.

How Do Evolutionsts Handle These Three Laws

1. They are a real problem to an evolutionist.
2. Most evolutionists evade the critical issues exposed by these laws.
3. Some admit that evolution violates some phase of these laws.
4. Others make rhetorical claims of consistency.

The following admission by Professor George Wald illustrates the evasive rhetoric of evolutionists:

> As for spontaneous generation, it continued to find acceptance until finally disposed of by the work of Louis Pasteur—it is a curious thing that until quite recently professors of biology habitually told this story as part of their introduction of students to biology. They would finish this account glowing with the conviction that they had given a telling demonstration of the over-

A Scientific Alternative to Evolution 333

throw of mystical notion by clean, scientific experimentation. Their students were usually so bemused as to forget to ask the professor how he accounted for the origin of life. This would have been an embarrassing question, because there are *only two possibilities: Either life arose by spontaneous generation, which the professor had just refuted: or it arose by supernatural creation, which he probably regarded as anti-scientific.*

For my part, I think the only tenable scientific view is that life originally *did* arise by spontaneous generation. What the history we have just reviewed demonstrated is that spontaneous generation no longer occurs. (emphasis added).[4]

So you see he only uses rhetoric. He has no scientific evidence to support his opinion. The Law of Biogenesis stands in his way.

Dr. Blum attempts to show that evolution is consistent with this law, but when he gets down to cases such as the origin of life he sees real trouble. I shall quote two of his statements to illustrate:

I do not see, for example, how proteins could have leapt suddenly into being. Yet both Heterotrophic and Autotrophic Metabolism are, in modern organisms, strictly dependent upon the existence of proteins in the form of catalysts. The riddle seems to be: *How, when no life existed, did substances come into being which today are absolutely essential to living systems yet which can only be formed by those systems?* It seems begging the question to suggest that first protein molecules were formed by some more primitive "nonprotein living system," for it still remains to define and account for the origin of that system.[5]

After mentioning an extension of Oparin's hypothesis by Horowitz, he further states:

. . . I must point out that Horowitz's hypothesis still leaves a seemingly unbridged gap in the story of the origin of life. For does not the invoking of natural selection postulate the prior existence of that for which the origin is sought? Natural selection itself seems only possible in systems having a complexity corresponding to at least that of the proteins. Who would venture much more than to suggest that time's arrow played an important role?[6]

By "time's arrow" he means the Second Law of Thermodynamics, which can point in only one way—and, as we previously noted, Blum himself specifies that direction as the direction of greater probability.

But it should be obvious that evolutionists will gain nothing by invoking the second law, because it actually points down hill, not up hill; toward the probable, not toward the improbable.

I maintain that Blum is attempting to reverse the direction of time's arrow. Blum is a scholar and I do not mean to imply dishonesty. He continually admits his perplexing difficulty. For example, he states in an addendum to Chapter X of his book: "The more we study living systems the more we marvel at their beautifully ordered complexity; and we may estimate that the forming of such system (or even much simpler ones) by a single chance act would have an improbability of the order of a miracle, that could have happened only once in our universe." [7]

Let me summarize this point. Dr. Harold Blum has failed to account for evolutionary processes, including the origin of life, by means of the Second Law of Thermodynamics. A careful reading of his book will reveal that he really admits that he hasn't proved the case. He stated that second law processes go irreversibly in the direction of the greater probability. Then he identified some of the major evolutionary events as extremely improbable. As a further example, he states that the probability of evolution of the human brain is so small that it "occurred" only once.[8] But if it is that improbable, surely the Second Law of Thermodynamics shows that it could not happen while that law is valid.

Constraints Imposed by the Three Laws

It is well to enumerate the constraints which are imposed by these laws. They are as follows:
1. *Matter and Energy cannot be created, while* the First Law of Thermodynamics is valid.
2. *Life cannot be created out of the inanimate, while* the Law of Biogenesis is valid.
3. *An increase in ordered-complexity cannot happen* (in a self-acting system), *while* the Second Law of Thermodynamics is valid.

These constraints are not mysterious. They are observable and common sense tells us to expect them. They remind us that you cannot get something for nothing. Extralogical considerations cannot override the cold facts of nature. Nature's basic laws spell out these specific constraints.

Mankind has always had its would-be inventors of perpetual motion machines, but each one of them has had to eventually face fact: The observable constraint of the First Law of Thermodynamics.

A Scientific Alternative to Evolution

Mankind has always had its advocates of spontaneous generation, and today there are those who make bold claims that scientists will fabricate life itself within the next ten years. May I recommend that you not buy any stock in their proposed life factory. They must face fact: the observable constraint of the Law of Biogenesis.

The validity of these three laws is observable beyond any doubt today. One might ask, then, how did anything get started if these constraints prevent such beginnings. That leads us to inquire about the time sequence of the origin of these laws.

Logical Time Sequence of the Laws

A logical time sequence of the origin of these laws is self-evident. It is as follows:
1. *The First Law of Thermodynamics began after the origin of mass and energy.*
2. *The Law of Biogenesis began after the origin of life.*
3. *The Second Law of Thermodynamics began after the existence of a fully wound-up system with living maturity.*

It is foolish for one to claim that our present laws can be employed to explain the beginnings of the physical universe, or living matter, or man himself. These laws specify their own limitations and make it obvious that their origins are indeterminant by science *per se*.

It is difficult for me to see how one can question the logic of the above-mentioned time sequence of the beginnings of these laws. That sequence must hold for the laws to be self-consistent.

Evolutionists make the mistake of trying to invoke present natural phenomena to "explain" the winding up processes and the beginning of life and even man himself.

There is another interesting inconsistency in evolutionary logic. Evolutionists try to date a hypothetical winding-up process by a running down radioactive clock. Time's arrow cannot point in *both* directions.

The question then arises, Is there a scientific alternative to evolution that is consistent with the time sequence of the origin of these laws?

Special Creation Makes the Time Sequence
of These Three Laws Consistent

It is clear that the processes involved in any of these origins lies outside the realm of science. Indeterminancy principles are commonplace in science; true scientists always acknowledge the limitations of science. Postulates at any beginning stage are of necessity arbitrary ones. There is nothing unscientific, then, about postulating special creation for the beginnings. The scientific virtue lies in the consistency which can be shown to follow after we get into the time frame represented by present laws.

The postulates of special creation make the time sequence of the three laws consistent. That time sequence runs as follows:
1. The creation of the physical universe preceded the First Law of Thermodynamics.
2. The creation of life preceded the Law of Biogenesis.
3. A fully wound-up biophysical world preceded the Second Law of Thermodynamics.

All of the present observable processes are consistent with that type of beginning. This makes a strong scientific base. Everything runs toward the probable.

Perspective of This Alternative to Evolution

The perspective of this alternative to evolution is as follows:
1. *The domain in which science is indeterminant is satisfied by special creation.* To be sure, that is miraculous, but any other beginning must lie in the realm of metaphysics. There is certainly no more logic in beginning with the metaphysical hypothesis of a "materialist" than to begin with the postulate of a God of creation. This is particularly true when one realizes that present scientific processes are more consistent with a system that begins with special creation.
2. *Present processes obey the established laws of science.* These processes behave as if a full-blown system was initiated, a system such as provided by special creation. No new matter and energy are being created, nor are they needed. Life does come from life. There is a need for conservation because of the tendency for processes to go toward disorder and decay.

The Fruits of This Alternative to Evolution

This alternative to evolution leads to *progress with confidence* because it deals with present processes that are founded on the *Laws of Science*. There is no danger of being hoodwinked by artifacts, whereas evolution is based on extralogical considerations that can only be supported by unreliable evidence. For example, the Piltdown Man was exhibited in the British Museum as basic evidence of evolution. But the famous Piltdown Man was really the fabrication of a clever trickster who had fitted an ape's jaw to a chemically aged human cranium. Yet it took 41 years to expose this fraud.

The *realistic Laws of Genetics* can be credited to this alternative. They give no comfort to total evolution. Dr. Walter Lammerts states that evolutionists are misled in plant breeding because they are accustomed to thinking that immense time may get results, whereas the process can be accomplished in a limited number of generations or not at all.[9]

Finally, preventive medicine developed out of the alternative to evolution. In reality, Louis Pasteur laid the foundation of preventive medicine when he established the Law of Biogenesis by empirical means. He demonstrated that bacteria come from other bacteria and that bacteria pass from one individual to another. His effort to arrest this inexorable downgrading process in living systems can be attributed in part to the importance he placed on the *tendency toward disorder*, that is to say, the principle embodied in the Second Law of Thermodynamics.

This alternative to evolution has always been sound and it will continue to produce fruit because it is based upon a foundation that will not fail.

NOTES AND REFERENCES

1. G. A. Kerkut, *Implications of Evolution* (Pergamon Press, 1960), p. 157.
2. Harold Blum, *Time's Arrow and Evolution*, Torchbook Edition (New York: Harper and Brothers, 1962), p. 5.
3. *Ibid.*, p. 6.
4. George Wald, *Frontiers of Modern Biology* in *Theories of Origin of Life* (Houghton Mifflin Co., 1962), p. 187.
5. Blum, *op. cit.*, pp. 170, 171.
6. *Ibid.*
7. *Ibid.*, p. 178A.
8. *Ibid.*, p. 212A.
9. W. E. Lammerts, "Newton-Induced Variation of Roses," *Journal of the American Scientific Affiliation* (March, 1961).

XXXI

SOCIAL DARWINISM

Bolton Davidheiser

Application of the principle of "survival of the fittest" to human affairs came to be known as Social Darwinism in the nineteenth century. It is generally believed that Darwin did not condone the extrapolation of his natural selection theory into social relationships, but the fact is that he himself taught that human evolution proceeded through warfare and struggle between isolated clans.[1]

Robert E. D. Clark says, "Darwin often said quite plainly that it was wrong to ameliorate the conditions of the poor, since to do so would hinder the evolutionary struggle for existence." [2]

In a letter to H. Thiel in 1869, Darwin wrote:

> You will really believe how much interested I am in observing that you apply to moral and social questions analogous views to those which I have used in regard to the modification of species. It did not occur to me formerly that my views could be extended to such widely different and most important subjects.[3]

Wallbank and Taylor in their textbook *Civilization Past and Present* say that Darwin's theory of the survival of the fittest "became a vogue that swept western thought in the late nineteenth century. It also became a convenient doctrine for justifying various economic and political theories." [4]

Unscrupulous Men Misused Theory

Unscrupulous industrialists took advantage of Darwin's theory to condone their unethical practices. When they put others out of business, they declared that it was just another case of survival of the fittest.

The railroad magnate, James J. Hill, manipulating to get more railways under his control, said that "the fortunes of railroad companies are determined by the law of the survival of the fittest." [5]

In his autobiography, Andrew Carnegie, who made his fortune

in steel, describes his conversion to evolution on reading Darwin and Spencer as follows:

> I remember that light came as in a flood and all was clear. Not only had I got rid of theology and the supernatural, but I had found the truth of evolution. "All is well since all grows better," became my motto, my true source of comfort. Man was not created with an instinct for his own degradation, but from the lower he had risen to the higher forms. Nor is there any conceivable end to his march to perfection. His face is turned to the light; he stands in the sun and looks upward.[6]

John D. Rockefeller declared to a Sunday school class: "The growth of a large business is merely a survival of the fittest.... This is not an evil tendency in business. It is merely the working-out of a law of nature and a law of God." [7]

Robert E. D. Clark comments, "Evolution, in short, gave the doer of evil a respite from his conscience. The most unscrupulous behavior towards a competitor could now be rationalized; evil could be called good." [8]

Darwinism Influenced Social, Racial Ills

Evolution soothed the consciences of not only the big industrialists in their dealings with competitors, it also aided those who took advantage of the poor. Efforts to improve the living and working conditions of the poor and of women and children were opposed by the ruling class on the grounds that this would be contrary to the principle of evolution, for the prosperity of the wealthy and the miserable condition of the destitute was just the working out of the principle of the survival of the fittest.

Darwinism also offered a basis for acts which have resulted in racial strife. Wallbank and Taylor say:

> The pseudo-scientific application of a biological theory to politics . . . constituted possibly the most perverted form of social Darwinism. . . . It led to racism and antisemitism and was used to show that only "superior" nationalities and races were fit to survive. Thus, among the English-speaking peoples were to be found the champions of the "white man's burden," an imperial mission carried out by Anglo-Saxons. . . . Similarly, the Russians preached the doctrine of pan-Slavism and the Germans that of pan-Germanism.[9]

Darwin postulated, in the sixth chapter of his *Descent of Man,* that the time would come when the white peoples would have destroyed the black. He also thought that the anthropoid apes would become extinct. He believed that when these two eventualities had occurred the evidence of evolution among living creatures would not be as strong as previously.

Militarists Used Darwinian Theory

The Darwinian theory of evolution has also been used by militarists to glorify war. They said that the outcome of a war is determined by the principle of the survival of the fittest.

The Prussian militarist, Heinrich von Treitsche, said, "The grandeur of war lies in the utter annihilation of puny man in the great conception of the State, and it brings out the full significance of the sacrifice of fellow-countrymen for one another. In war the chaff is winnowed from the wheat." [10]

The German philosopher Frederich Nietzche, who held Christianity in contempt, said, "You say, 'A good cause sanctifies war,' but I say, 'A good war sanctifies every cause!' " [11] Wallbank and Taylor comment,

> Likewise, he ridiculed democracy and socialism for protecting the worthless and weak and hindering the strong. Social Darwinism and the antidemocratic cult of naked power, as preached by advocates like Nietzche, were laying the foundations of fascism, which would one day plunge the world into the most terrible convulsion in its history.[12]

Frederich von Bernhardi was a German soldier, who retired in 1909, and wrote an inflammatory book, *Germany and the Next War,* which extolled militarism. Of this book anthropologist M. F. Ashley-Montagu says,

> "War," declared Bernhardi, "is a biological necessity"; it "is as necessary as the struggle of the elements of nature"; it "gives a biologically just decision, since its decisions rest on the very nature of things." "The whole idea of arbitration represents a presumptuous encroachment on the natural laws of development," for "what is right is decided by the arbitration of war." In proof thereof such notions of Darwin's as "The Struggle for Existence," "Natural Selection," and the "Survival of the Fittest" are invoked with sententiousness quite military both in logic and in sense. According to Bernhardi, it is plainly evident to anyone who makes a study of plant and animal life that "war is a universal law of nature." This declaration and fortifica-

tion of Germany's will to war—for it had the highest official sanction and approval—was published in 1911. Three years later the greatest holocaust the world had ever known was launched. . . .[13]

Benito Mussolini, who brought fascism to Italy, was strengthened in his belief that violence is basic to social transformation by the philosophy of Nietzche.[14] R. E. D. Clark says, "Mussolini's attitude was completely dominated by evolution. In public utterances he repeatedly used the Darwinian catchwords while he mocked at perpetual peace, lest it should hinder the evolutionary process." [15]

Likewise, Adolph Hitler in Germany based his fascism on evolutionary theory. This is evident from his speeches and his book *Mein Kampf*. R. E. D. Clark has pointed out that in the large number of books which have appeared describing every phase of the Hitler regime, there is hardly a mention of the evolution of Charles Darwin. He interprets this to mean that the authors refrain from mentioning evolution in this context because they fear they might be considered to be anti-evolutionary.[16]

Communists, Like Fascists, Used Darwinism

Friederich Engels, one of the founders of Communism, wrote to Karl Marx, December 12, 1859, "Darwin, whom I am just now reading, is splendid." [17] Karl Marx wrote to Friederich Engels, December 19, 1860, "Although it is developed in the crude English style, this is the book which contains the basis in natural history for our views." [18]

Again Marx wrote to Engels, January 16, 1861, "Darwin's book is very important and serves me as a basis in natural selection for the class struggle in history . . . not only is a death blow dealt here for the first time to 'teleology' in the natural sciences but their rational meaning is emphatically explained." [19]

Marx wished to dedicate to Darwin his book *Das Kapital,* but Darwin declined the offer.

E. Yaroslavsky, a friend of Joseph Stalin, wrote a book on the life of Stalin. This book was published in Moscow by the Communists while Stalin was in power. The author says, "At a very early age, while still a pupil in the ecclesiastical school, Comrade Stalin developed a critical mind and revolutionary sentiments. He began to read Darwin and became an atheist." [20]

Yaroslavsky quotes another boyhood friend of Stalin, who relates the following:

> I began to speak of God. Joseph heard me out, and after a moment's silence said: "You know, they are fooling us, there is no God. . . ."
>
> I was astonished at these words. I had never heard anything like it before. "How can you say such things, Soso [a name for Stalin]?" I exclaimed.
>
> "I'll lend you a book to read; it will show you that the world and all living things are quite different from what you imagine, and all this talk about God is sheer nonsense," Joseph said.
>
> "What book is that?" I inquired. "Darwin. You must read it," Joseph impressed on me.[21]

But the Marxists were never completely sold on Darwinism. Conway Zirkle, Professor of Botany at the University of Pennsylvania, says that the Marxists do not accept or reject biological theories in accordance with objective evidence, but by how well they fit Communist doctrine. Darwinism does not altogether fit.

T. D. Lysenko, whose ideas supplanted the science of genetics in Russia until recently, said in 1948, "Darwin was unable to free himself from the theoretical mistakes which he committed. These errors were discovered and pointed out by the Marxist classicists." [22] Evolution by natural selection is at present not acceptable under Communism, but evolution by a Lamarckian type of environmental influence. (In his old age Darwin himself came closer and closer to this view.)

Some Evolutionists Embarrassed

There are a few evolutionists who have been embarrassed by the social implications of evolution and who have stressed cooperation (instead of struggle) as a factor in evolution. Kropotkin and Allee may be cited here.[23] Others have said that the theory of evolution is improperly applied when it is used to defend militarism and social abuses.

Of course, the application of Darwinian survival of the fittest to human affairs by unscrupulous men has no direct bearing on the question of whether human beings and other creatures evolved from simple forms of life. But these abuses have been sanctioned and abetted with evolution as an excuse; and, if evolution is not true, it seems all the more tragic.

NOTES AND REFERENCES

1. There is evidence of this in various places; for example, the disagreement between Darwin and Wallace on the evolution of the human brain. See also R. E. D. Clark, *Darwin: Before and After* and Arthur Kieth, *Essays on Evolution.*
2. Robert E. D. Clark, *Darwin: Before and After* (London: Paternoster Press, 1958), p. 120.
3. Francis Darwin, editor, *The Life and Letters of Charles Darwin* (New York: D. Appleton and Co., 1896), Vol. 2, p. 294.
4. T. Walter Wallbank and Alastair M. Taylor, *Civilization Past and Present,* Fourth Edition (New York: Scott, Foresman and Co., 1961), Vol. 2, p. 361.
5. Richard Hofstadter, *Social Darwinism and American Thought,* Revised Edition (Boston, Mass.: Beacon Press, 1955), p. 45.
6. *Ibid.*
7. *Ibid.*
8. Clark, *op. cit.,* p. 106.
9. Wallbank and Taylor, *op. cit.,* p. 362.
10. *Ibid.* (This is quoted from H. G. von Trietsche, *Politics,* translated by B. Dugdale and T. de Bille [London: Constable and Co.], Vol. 1, pp. 66, 67.)
11. *Ibid.*
12. *Ibid.,* p. 363.
13. M. F. Ashley-Montagu, *Man in Process* (New York: World Pub. Co., 1961), pp. 76, 77.
14. *The Encyclopedia Britannica* (1962), Vol. 16, p. 27.
15. Clark, *op. cit.,* p. 115.
16. *Ibid.,* p. 117.
17. Conway Zirkle, *Evolution, Marxian Biology, and the Social Scene* (Philadelphia: University of Pennsylvania Press, 1959), p. 85.
18. *Ibid.*
19. *Ibid.,* p. 86.
20. E. Yaroslavsky, *Landmarks in the Life of Stalin* (Moscow: Foreign Languages Publishing House, 1940), p. 8.
21. *Ibid.,* pp. 8, 9.
22. Zirkle, *op. cit.,* p. 24.
23. Peter Kropotkin, *Mutual Aid* (New York: W. Heinemann, 1902); cf. W. C. Allee, *Cooperation Among the Animals with Human Implications,* Revised Edition (New York: Henry Schuman, 1951).